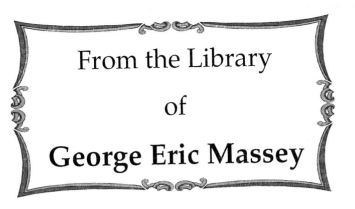

The Nature of Things

The Nature of Things

by
Anthony Quinton

Routledge & Kegan Paul
London and Boston

First published 1973
by Routledge & Kegan Paul Ltd
Broadway House, 68–74 Carter Lane,
London EC4V 5EL and
9 Park Street,
Boston, Mass. 02108, U.S.A.
Printed in Great Britain
by Unwin Brothers Limited
The Gresham Press, Old Woking, Surrey, England
A member of the Staples Printing Group
ISBN 0 7100 7453 0

Contents

To Marcelle

Preface and Acknowledgments

The writing of this book was begun in 1965 during a period of sabbatical leave for which I am grateful to the Warden and Fellows of New College, Oxford. It was largely completed during my tenure of a Radcliffe fellowship in the academic years 1968-9 and 1969-70. I am most grateful to the trustees of the Radcliffe Foundation for the very generous and welcome award of one of their first fellowships. The substantial reduction it brought about in my teaching duties made the completion of this large book possible.

Some of the material in this book has been published before, for the most part in a considerably different form. The publications in question, together with the corresponding passages in the present text, are as follows:

'Matter and Space', in *Mind*, vol. 73, 1964 (ch. 4, pp. 46–53).

'The Soul', in *Journal of Philosophy*, vol. 59, 1962 (ch. 4, pp. 88–97).

'Mind and Matter', in *Brain and Mind*, ed. J. R. Smythies, Routledge & Kegan Paul, London, 1965, pp. 201–33 (ch. 4, pp. 97–102 and ch. 11).

'Two Conceptions of Personality', in *Revue Internationale de Philosophie*, 22nd year, 1968, pp. 387–402 (ch. 4, pp. 103–5).

'The Foundations of Knowledge', in *British Analytical Philosophy*, ed. B. Williams and A. Montefiore, Routledge & Kegan Paul, London, 1966, pp. 55–86 (Part II, Introduction, chs 5, 6 and 8).

'The Problem of Perception', in *Mind*, vol. 69, 1955, pp. 28–51 (ch. 7).

'Properties and Classes', in *Proceedings of the Aristotelian Society*, vol. 53, 1957–8, pp. 33–58 (ch. 9, pp. 257–65).

'The *A Priori* and the Analytic', in *Proceedings of the Aristotelian Society*, vol. 59, 1963–4, pp. 31–54 (ch. 9, pp. 265–81).

'Ethics and the Theory of Evolution', in *Biology and Personality*, ed. I. T. Ramsey, Blackwell, Oxford, 1965, pp. 107–30 (ch. 12, pp. 351–66).

'The Bounds of Morality', in *Ethics and Social Justice*, ed. H. E. Kiefer and M. K. Munitz, S.U.N.Y. Press, Albany, 1970, pp. 122–41 (ch. 12, pp. 374–80).

I am grateful to the editors and publishers of the periodicals and books in which this material first appeared for permission to use it here.

New College, Oxford

Part I
Substance

Introduction

The four problems of substance

Substance is the oldest topic of philosophical inquiry and it is also one of the most entangled. The Ionian philosophers are generally recognised to have inaugurated western philosophy by asking the question: what is the ultimate stuff or raw material of the world? Substance is the central theme of the first and most influential of philosophical text-books, Aristotle's *Metaphysics*. From that time to this every major philosopher has occupied himself with the problem of which of the many kinds of thing the world appears to contain really or fundamentally exists. In the course of this development a number of disparate issues have been brought together under one head. I shall argue that there are four quite distinct, even if not wholly independent, problems of substance whose solution has been obstructed by persistent failure to recognise the distinctions between them. This confusion has been assisted by the fact that three of the problems of substance, at any rate, are of much the same general form. In each case the idea of substance is invoked to explain how things in general or some large and important class of things, admitted to be complexes of elements of some kind, are unified as wholes. Positive theories of substance explain the unification of these complexes by their connection with a special additional unifying element. The negative theories that reject substance hold that there is no more to the complexes in question than the collection of elements of which they are composed.

(1) *Individuation* The first of these problems concerns things in general. It arises about every possible object of reference, about everything whose existence can be significantly affirmed. It starts from the fact that every individual or object of reference has a number of qualities and relations which may be truly predicated of it and it asks whether there is any more to an individual thing than the collection of qualities and relations that it possesses. The distinction in language between subject and predicate suggests that

3

the individual is related to its properties as an owner is to his possessions. The correctness of this suggestion is confirmed by the apparent incapacity of a thing's properties, which are general and may apply to many things, to individuate it, to pick it out as the unique individual it is. The positive theory in this field holds that a concrete thing is composed of an individuating substance as well as its qualities and relations. The negative theory identifies the thing with the bundle or collection of its properties.

Aristotle's view that every concrete individual is a compound of shareable form and individuating matter is the first clear formulation of the positive theory of individuating substance. It has persisted in subsequent philosophy in the form of the principle of inherence which asserts that qualities can exist only as qualities of a substance. On the opposite side is the view of Hume, Russell and the empiricist tradition generally that an individual thing is just a bundle of qualities. Russell's theory of descriptions expresses the negative view in the logical or linguistic idiom congenial to philosophers of the present century. It provides a technique for the elimination of singular terms, expressions referring to unique individuals, which are replaced by variables and purely predicative general terms. Quine, Goodman and Ayer have all affirmed that, in the last analysis, language is, or need only be, predicative and that the proper names of individuals can be dispensed with.

(2) *Identity* The second problem is that of identity through time. Since it arises about only those things that endure or persist it has a smaller scope than the first. It is clear that most of the things we speak about are temporally extended. It can also be shown that if we are to have a single, unitary world to think and speak about there must be persisting things. But only exceptionally do we observe a thing throughout the whole of its temporal career. What, then, confers identity as states or phases of a persisting thing on the temporally disconnected and more or less short-lived things we actually do observe? The positive theory here is that only an unchanging substance can confer identity through time on a series of changing states. The atomic theory of Democritus, drawn on by Locke to account for the identity through time of inorganic bodies, is one example of this position, the pure ego theory of personal identity is another. On the opposite side is the serial or relational account of identity through time, upheld by Locke for persons and by Hume for all temporally extended things. A special form of the positive theory maintains that there must be not merely enduring but eternal things if the fact of change is to be accounted for. I shall call such ingenerable and incorruptible entities *atoms*, in honour of their first defenders. Merely enduring things I shall call *continuants*, following a familiar usage.

(3) *Objectivity* The third problem arises from the supposed fact that the direct or immediate objects of perception are private impressions or appearances. We take ourselves to perceive public or objective things but, it is alleged, we really perceive only the private appearances they present to us. This problem is smaller in scope than the first, since it concerns only public individuals and not individuals in general, and it is distinct in scope from the second, since there would seem to be public things that do not persist, objective events as well as objective continuants (though it has been held that every event is part of the history of some enduring thing). The problem is: what confers unity as an objective thing on the set of impressions which we take to be appearances of that thing? The positive theory is that only an objective substance or *substratum* can confer objectivity on a system of appearances, which must be understood as being caused by and representative of it. Locke's substratum, Kant's thing-in-itself and Price's physical occupant are all versions of objective substance. Opposed to this kind of representationist theory is the phenomenalism that derives our conception of objects with continued and distinct existence from the constancy and coherence of our impressions. This project of Hume's is continued in Mill's permanent possibilities of sensation, Russell's classes of appearances and Ayer's logical constructions out of sense-data, which are conceptions of objects wholly in terms of the impressions we have or could have of them.

(4) *The foundations of knowledge* The fourth and final problem concerns the foundation of knowledge. Has empirical knowledge foundations and if so of what kind? This problem is of a different form from others. Where they ask how various kinds of element—qualities, phases and appearances—are unified in various kinds of complex wholes—individuals, continuants and objects—it asks whether there is one elementary kind of individual out of which all other kinds of individual are constructed. This problem about the existence and nature of an elementary or basic type of individual has, therefore, a less proprietary claim to the term *substance* than the others. But Descartes' definition of substance as that which requires nothing but itself in order to exist shows that it has a claim nevertheless. Descartes was concerned to pick out substance in the sense in which it is opposed to qualities, as that on which, by the principle of inherence, qualities are dependent but which is not itself dependent on anything else. Hume gave a different turn to this notion of substance as the logically independent by saying that if anything is substance it is simple impressions. Everything we can conceive presupposes impressions but impressions presuppose nothing. From this view of Hume's that impressions are the terminal objects of belief or knowledge has developed the conception of knowledge as

5

a hierarchy whose components are arranged on a scale of comparative epistemological priority. Xs are epistemologically prior to Ys, for example impressions to material objects or human beings to social groups, if the existence of Ys entails the existence of Xs but not vice versa. There can be sense-impressions which are not appearances of any material object, namely dreams and hallucinations, and there can be men who are not associated with other men. But there cannot, it is argued, be objects that could not appear or social groups without members. If Xs are epistemologically prior to Ys it is because the only access we have to Ys is through Xs and it follows that Ys must be defined or analysed or interpreted in terms of Xs. The terminus of a system which arranges things in accordance with such asymmetrical relations of priority and dependence will constitute the indispensable foundations of knowledge. Those things, which, being dependent on nothing, are prior to everything else, are the true epistemological substances.

It has been questioned whether any such division of the objects of knowledge into basis and superstructure can be carried out. This puts the fourth problem of substance on a different footing from the others. No one can intelligibly deny that there are any individuals at all, even though the existence of individuals is contingent. No one can seriously deny that there are any continuants or any objects, though there may be disagreement about how these kinds of individuals are to be interpreted. But two kinds of philosopher have denied that knowledge has foundations without obvious insincerity or muddle. There are, first, the coherence theorists of knowledge, who regard all beliefs as inferential and as resting for their justification on other beliefs, and, secondly, there are those like Anderson, Goodman and Austin who deny that there are any intrinsically prior starting-points for inquiry on the ground that any belief whatever may occur either as evidence or as hypothesis. The most thorough and influential defence of the opposed view that there must be basic individuals is contained in Wittgenstein's *Tractatus*.

For those who believe that the objects of knowledge can be distinguished into the basic or absolutely prior on the one hand and the inferred or constructed on the other there is the problem of determining which the basic objects are. The traditional opinion of supporters of the theory of foundations from Hume to Russell and Ayer has been that impressions are the basic individuals. Carnap, Reichenbach and Popper have defended the competing claims of objective physical things. More recently the issue of priority has been considered from a different point of view by Strawson. Instead of asking what kind of things must we take to exist if we are to have reason to believe that anything else exists, he asks what must we be able to refer to and identify if we are to be able to refer identifyingly

6

to anything else. His answer is that material bodies and
conceived as embodied, are the basic individuals.

Failure to recognise the distinctness of the four pro
substance has given rise to a number of confusions which
a large and destructive influence. The result has been that a
and considerations relevant to substance in one of its se:
been misapplied to attack or defend it in another. More
the idea of substance has become the focus of earnest
emotions. Philosophers of rationalist sympathies give it
endorsement; empiricists repudiate it with scorn or dist:
of its forms. I shall describe four of these confusions.

(a) The most important of them runs the problems
duation and objectivity together by assuming that appe:
impressions are qualities. This has conflicting results. Ph
of a Lockean tendency are led by their conviction that the
to a thing than the set of its qualities to suppose that the
to a thing than its actual and possible appearances. Acc
individuator they are compelled to swallow the substratu:
empiricists, on the other hand, turn the inference roun
they are convinced that there can be no substratum they
a thing must be a bundle of qualities. Both, I shall argu
false conclusion from a true premise because of their co
mistaken assumption that appearances and qualities are c
same. But appearances are not qualities, not even sensib
They are individuals, things *with* qualities. The red p:
perceive in the middle of my visual field, the standard ex:
object of immediate experience, is not just the quality
It is a particular instance of redness, a unique individua
at a particular moment of time, in a particular place in v
in the history of a particular perceptual consciousness.]
datum theory of perception is correct, as the problem o
presupposes, the direct objects of perception are priva
sense-impressions and not material objects. But both se
sions and material objects are individual things. We do
qualities on their own but only as qualities of things, wh
or private. We perceive redness only to the extent that
red things.

This confusion derives directly from the identificatio
Locke, explicit in Berkeley, of qualities and ideas. For L
of sensation is the representation of the quality that cau
terminology a quality is a public, objective characteri
the private replica of such a characteristic. Berkeley
dualism of public and private characteristics but i
fortified the error embodied in it. For him *idea* an
synonymous terms. More remotely the confusion wa

by Aristotle. He combined with his view that every individual thing is composed of individuating matter and shareable form the proposition that only the form of things, in other words their properties, can be apprehended by the knowing mind. For different reasons he and later empiricists have agreed that form alone is knowable: he because form alone can be grasped by the intellect, they because appearances alone can be grasped by the senses. Both parties consistently go on to admit that individuating matter is unknowable. But here their attitudes diverge. What for Aristotle was an important mystery becomes an 'unknown somewhat' for Locke and an empty metaphysical invention for Berkeley and later empiricists.

(b) A second confusion of some importance mistakenly assimilates the problems of individuation and identity. At a time when their thoughts were running closely together Russell and Whitehead both took the position, against what they called Aristotelian substance, that a continuant, anything identifiable as the same thing at different times, is simply a lawful sequence of events. But the fact, if it is a fact, that there is no more to a continuant than the lawful sequence of its phases has no relevance whatever to the question of whether there is more to a thing than the set of its qualities. Once again the events or phases that compose a continuant are themselves individuals, even if momentary ones. The question of whether there is more to them than their properties arises just as much as for the continuants to which they belong. This assimilation of properties and events is assisted, though it is not justified or even excused, by the Aristotelian account of what it is for a thing to persist through change. By this account a thing changes if its properties come and go. This is true enough if it is not understood to mean that what exists of the thing at any one moment is no more than the properties the thing has at that moment. What changes in a thing are its properties. But this does not mean that a changing thing simply is its changing properties.

(c) A third confusion runs together the ideas of an unchanging substance or identifier as the indispensable basis of identity through change and of the real or objective nature of things as a substratum distinct from any of the appearances the thing presents. This atomistic doctrine explains change as a matter of the rearrangement of eternal and unchanging things. Now everything we perceive is liable to change and decay. So the Parmenidean conclusion is drawn that all that really exists are unchanging substrata that are quite distinct from the appearances that are our objects of perception. Descartes' account of the piece of wax, all of whose qualities change and whose substance must therefore be a transempirical entity accessible only to the intellect, is an instance of this line of argument. It is reasonable enough, as I shall argue later, to infer that if there were an

8

identifier it would be unobservable. But this does not justify the conclusion that atomism is inevitably a metaphysical doctrine. It is only a contingent fact, if it is a fact at all, that everything we perceive changes. It is possible that we should discover empirically that the ultimate constituents of matter are Democritean atoms, eternally persisting material things which undergo no changes in quality though they would have to undergo changes in spatial position. Furthermore the Parmenidean identification of phases and appearances is mistaken. From the fact that something is momentary, does not endure through a lapse of time, let alone all time, it does not follow that it is in any way private or subjective, though it can well be argued that all private things are momentary.

Considering these three confusions together we may say that properties, phases and appearances are different from one another. Phases and appearances are not properties but individuals. Momentary individuals may be public or private, material objects or appearances. There is a sense in which only momentary things are observed and thus that every perception of a thing as a continuant embodies an inference or assumption. So to that extent only the phases of continuants and neither the continuants themselves, nor, a fortiori, their identifiers, 'appear'. And on the other hand, no private individuals, no appearances or impressions, are continuants. Coloured patches in one's visual field can be identified through time, if at all, only by way of their relation to identifiable expanses of objective colour. So observables are phases or events and all appearances are events. But this does not add up to the identity of phases and appearances.

In the philosophy of Russell all three of these notions are brought together under the concept of the event. For Russell everything is an event or a collection of events, these being conceived as momentary awarenesses of properties. Thus an individual is a bundle of qualities, a continuant a series of phases and an object a system of appearances. In his mouth the principle that the only direct objects of knowledge are events can be taken to mean three distinct things: that only properties *or* phases *or* appearances can be known, and therefore significantly said, to exist. In his work the three confusions so far considered are superimposed.

The final confusion runs together the notions of an individuating substance and of that which has independent existence. The principle that properties must inhere in a substance retained the authority of Aristotle long after it had come to be understood in a different sense from his. As he intended it it meant that form, with one exception, could occur only in concrete individual things along with individuating matter. There could be no separation of the forms. He did not hold that properties were dependent on individuators in a way that individuators were not dependent on properties, but that properties *and* individuators were both dependent on the concrete wholes that were composed of them. But later philosophers, taking substance in a non-Aristotelian sense to be the individuating element in an individual (Aristotle's matter) rather than the individual itself, have concluded that the individuating element is prior to, more basic and independent than, the properties with which it is conjoined. In an embryonic form this error is to be found in Descartes' theory of substance. But Descartes does not wholly deprive substance of qualities. Matter and mind are each accorded an essential attribute. For matter this is extension, which, I shall argue, is only the ghost of a property by itself and has the effect of identifying matter with empty space. For mind it is thought and Descartes preserves the concreteness of mental substance only by implausibly insisting that the mind is always active.

In the theory of a pure ego or mental substance there is, indeed, as in Russell's doctrine of the event, an assimilation of three of the four problems of substance. The pure ego or subject is seen as standing in a threefold relation to its experiences or states: that of individuator to properties, that of identifier to phases and that of independent basis to dependent superstructure. Experiences are individuated by their belonging to a particular subject, of which they are seen as the qualities, and they are identified by belonging to a continuing identical bearer. Subjects do not have experiences at all times in their histories but experiences cannot occur except to a subject so there is a one-way dependence of experiences on the subjects who have them. Even the remaining sense of substance is brought into play for the pure ego is conceived as the substratum of its experiences which alone are accessible to introspection.

In part I of this book I shall examine the problems of individuation and identity, accepting a somewhat chastened version of individuating substance but rejecting the identifier. I shall argue that continuants are necessary, even though their identity through time is relational and not substantial, but that atoms are contingent. In part II I shall examine the problems of objectivity and the foundations of knowledge. I shall argue that since private impressions are not the only direct objects of perception the problem of objectivity does not arise and I shall defend a somewhat qualified version of the theory that knowledge has foundations and that they are material objects. In part III I shall consider four dualistic doctrines of major historical importance that have asserted the independent existence of four kinds of 'ideas': the essences of Platonic dualism, the experiences of Cartesian dualism, the theoretical substrata of Lockean dualism, and the values of Kantian dualism. My object here is to support the metaphysical doctrine of reism which holds that the fundamental constituents of the world are material bodies in space and time (cf. Kotarbinski, pp. 420–37) by showing that essences can be interpreted in terms of language and behaviour, experiences as states of the brain, the theoretical entities of science as material bodies or as constructions out of them, and values in terms of the responses of sensitive organisms.

1
Individuation

Substance and qualities

Why should it be supposed that there is more to a thing than the sum of its properties? To many contemporary philosophers it has seemed that there is no better reason for this supposition than the linguistic fact that when we ascribe a property to a thing we use one term for the property and another to refer to the thing itself. If this were all that was to be said for individuating substance there would be little reason to believe in it. We have different terms for wholes and for the parts of which they are composed. We can talk of houses and of the roofs, walls and floors of which they are made. We say that a house has a roof, two floors and four walls. But it does not follow that there is anything more to the house than the things of which it is composed. The house is strictly identical with the appropriately arranged totality of its parts. But the relation between a house and its properties, its shape, size and colour, is not that of a whole to its parts. The roof of a house is just as much a concrete individual as the house itself but the shape of a house is not. A house can be built by literally putting together the antecedently existing roof, floors and walls. But it cannot be constructed by physically assembling its properties. What is the significance of this difference between properties and parts? Does it entail that there is a difference in reality between an individual and the properties that it possesses corresponding to the difference between their names?

The fundamental reason for thinking that there is more to a thing than its properties is that by their nature properties are general. They can apply to many, to an indefinitely large number, of individual instances, whether or not they do in fact. To ascribe a property to a thing is to classify it, compare it with other similar things. We learn to use many predicative terms by being shown numerous instances of their application and we could not understand any predicative terms unless some were introduced in this way.

So some such terms *must* have a plurality of instances, most of them *do*, and all of them *may*. Now this multiple applicability of properties may be reduced, in a way, by conjoining them in groups. There are many red things and many round things but there are fewer red and round things than there are of either. It is necessarily true that there cannot be more red and round things than there are red things. It is not necessarily true that there are less but it is quite certain that there are. The set of F and G things will be identical in size with the set of F things only if all F are G. And this is not true of most pairs of predicative terms. It might seem, then, that you could in the end pin down an individual by progressively specifying its properties. We do just this when we have to make clear to someone which particular thing we want them to get for us. We go on enumerating the properties of the thing in question until there is no danger of another, qualitatively similar thing, being fastened on instead of it. But however long we go on with such a specification it never follows that we have arrived at a set of properties which has one and only one instance, the individual thing in question. So it is always a contingent fact that the complete set of a thing's properties will be sufficient to individuate it, to pick it out from everything else as the unique individual that it is. For although there are fewer red and round things than there are red things, and fewer red, round and hard things than there are red and round things, there are still indefinitely many. The complete set of a thing's properties is, of course, very large. But this does not affect the point of principle. It ensures only that it will be very difficult and perhaps impossible to establish that a specification of a thing's properties is in fact complete. Even if, as a matter of fact, the set of a thing's properties is peculiar to it, it will be very hard to be sure that this is so. We can be reasonably sure that the properties of a given thing are not shared, as a group, by any other thing in its immediate spatial and temporal neighbourhood. We may have reason to suppose that the properties of a given thing are not at all likely to be shared by anything else, where its being the way it is can be traced to a highly fortuitous conjunction of circumstances. But we can have no conclusive assurance that any group of properties, however large, has one and only one instance, let alone that every group of properties which is the set of all the properties of some individual thing has that thing as its unique instance.

It has been said by Lewis that the set of a thing's properties is infinitely large, as a consequence of the law of excluded middle (cf. Lewis (3), p. 439). By this law every individual must either possess or lack every property that there is. The conclusion would follow only if there were an infinity of properties. That there is such an infinity of properties is not ruled out by the fact that in any language there is only a finite number of general terms. Language is capable of indefinite improvement. A property is the possibility of a predicative term, it is not brought into existence by the acquisition of meaning by the terms that express it. All the same this is rather a tenuous consideration. It might be argued that any language containing the real numbers contains an infinity of predicates, for example 'being 1 inch long', 'being 1·2 inches long', 'being 1·23 inches long' and so on. But apart from the fact that there will be no empirical difference between the more minutely specific of these predicates, it should also be noticed that the properties they express are not all that distinct from each other. If a thing is just 1 inch long an infinity of negative predications of length are true of it: it is not 4 or 5 or 6 ... *ad infinitum* inches long. But this does not make its length an infinitely complex matter. It still has just one length. A more substantial consideration is that the properties of a thing must be understood to include its relations to other things. Now if the number of things occupying a space is infinitely large it follows that each of those things has a doubly infinite stock of relations. In the first place there is the infinite set of its spatial relations to other things and, secondly, there is the infinite set of its comparative relations of size to other things. But while it cannot be proved that there is not an infinite number of concrete individuals, it equally cannot be proved that there is. In these circumstances it might be more prudent and economical to make the less extensive assumption (cf. Barker, pp. 74–5). We would certainly have factual reasons for thinking that the number of concrete individuals is finite, if, for example, we had reason to think that space or its materially occupied part, at any rate, was finite and if we had reason to think that the occupants of space were in fact only finitely divisible. Space itself, of course, is of necessity infinitely divisible. For any interval of space that we can describe, however small, there are describable smaller intervals. But this does not prove that matter can be divided without limit. At a certain point in the process of division it might either be annihilated or just resist all attempts to divide it. We could always *conceive* things smaller than these *minima divisibilia*, but there might not be any.

None of these three arguments from the improvability of language, from the real number predicates and from the infinity of spatial and comparative relations clearly establishes that the complete set of a thing's properties is infinite. But even if the properties of a thing were infinitely numerous it would not affect the earlier argument that the set of all a thing's properties does not necessarily individuate it. It would show only that it must be impossible to make quite sure that two things have exactly the same properties. However qualitatively alike two things might be it would always be

14

possible that there was some as yet undiscovered distinguishing feature marking one of them off from the other. But the impossibility of *making sure* that two things have exactly the same properties is not the same as the impossibility of two things' *having* exactly the same properties. If the set of a thing's properties is infinite it necessarily follows that any assertion of the qualitative identity of two things is inductive or conjectural. As such it may turn out to be false, but it does not follow that any such assertion is or must be false.

So far, then, it appears that since a thing's properties are not demonstrably sufficient to individuate it there can be pairs or larger groups of things which though qualitatively identical are numerically distinct. The unique individuality of a thing is something over and above its properties and an explanation must be found for it.

Ordinal properties

But is it true, as I have so far been taking for granted, that there are no necessarily individuating properties, that all predicative terms are multiply applicable? The first exception that comes to mind is the ordinal properties such as *being the tallest man* or *being the fourth largest fresh-water lake*, which are clearly unique in their application. Everything we can think of must, it would seem, have many properties of this kind. If we take any characteristic of a thing which varies in degree we can form the ordinal property of that thing in respect of that characteristic and it will give the unique place of the thing in the series of all the things which have the characteristic in any degree whatever. From this it follows that a thing must have as many individuating ordinal properties as it has characteristics that can vary in degree. It seems reasonable to infer that everything has a large, perhaps very large, number of properties that are proprietary to it and possessed by nothing else.

There are two objections to this theory of the individuating power of ordinal properties. The first arises in a more or less practical form but it has a theoretical implication. The practical difficulty is that we can never know what the ordinal property of a thing in a given respect is unless we are acquainted with all the other possessors of the same variable characteristic. This is an important consideration since ordinarily the number of things possessing such a variable characteristic will be very large. It is easy to tell who has the ordinal property of being the tallest man in this room because the number of men in this room is small. It is, no doubt, possible to determine who is the tallest man on earth provided that we restrict our inquiry to an interval of time not reaching too far from the present. But it is impossible to find out for sure who is the tallest man anywhere and at any time. The difficulty is compounded if we are searching for the ten thousandth tallest man. Very tall men readily secure attention, their prodigies of altitude are remembered and recorded. But ordinal mediocrity is much more elusive.

The theoretical difficulty is that the things possessing some variable characteristic can be intelligibly ordered as first, second, third, only if they are finite in number. If they are not there is neither a maximum nor a minimum to the degrees in which the characteristic is possessed, just as there is no largest rational number less than one and no smallest rational number greater than one. We can, then, only ascribe ordinal properties to things in theory if they are finite in number and in practice if their number is manageably small. But I have already argued that it cannot be proved that there is an infinite number of concrete individual things and the objection of practice is irrelevant. Even if we cannot tell what the individuating ordinal property of a thing is, it will still individuate it, though not for us.

The second and more powerful objection is that two distinct things may occupy exactly the same place in the ordinal array of the possessors of a variable characteristic. Even with a finite set of men it is not necessarily true that one of them is the tallest. There may be two men who are taller than everyone else in the set but of the same height as each other. In that case *being the tallest man in the set* has no instance. Ordinal properties will individuate only if there is no sharing of ordinal positions. If an ordinal property applies to anything it applies to only one thing but it may apply to nothing. It is clear that the assumption that ordinal positions are not shared is simply the assumption that there are properties which have only one instance, the properties, namely, which determine the ordinal position. And this assumption is not a necessary truth. Because there are as a matter of fact *some* unshared properties ordinal arrangement of the strongest kind is possible. Even then it is ordinarily possible only under some spatio-temporal limitation. When we list the largest lakes we list the largest lakes on the surface of the earth at the present time. The significance of this limitation will emerge shortly.

I said earlier that the ordinal property of a thing might still individuate it even if, being undiscoverable by us, it did not individuate it for us. Since we are here considering what *makes* things the individuals that they are and not how we *find out* which they are the qualification is not directly relevant. Nevertheless we are able to individuate many things and it is because we have this knowledge of the uniqueness of things that the nature of individuality is a serious problem. The two issues are not separable. If the determinant of individuality were something we could not know it would have to be explained how it is that we can carry out the individuations that we do.

Positional properties

Another kind of necessarily individuating property is position in space and time. If we are confronted by two distinct things between which we can find no strictly qualitative difference of length or weight or colour we can always distinguish them by reference to their respective positions. What proves this is the familiar but highly important metaphysical truth that no two things can be at the same place at the same time. Take any place at any time. It is not a necessary truth that there should be anything there at all. But, if there is anything there, there can be only one thing. Individuals are, to use an old word, *impenetrable*, which does not mean that they are never soft or porous. The only apparent exception to this rule is not an exception in principle. A whole is at every place and time that its parts are. Wholes and parts share positions. But they share only some of their positions. If A has B as a part they are not indistinguishable in position. For although all of B's positions are also A's, not all of A's positions are B's as well.

Considered on their own, position in space and in time are properties in the most straightforward sense. They are predicable of individuals in the same way that shape or size are and they are, furthermore, predicable of indefinitely many individuals. There is no limit to the number of things that can be present at a particular map-reference, provided that they occur there at different times. Equally there is no limit to the number of things that can be in existence at a particular moment of time, provided that they are to be found at different places. But this boundless promiscuity of positions in space and time considered separately is replaced by the most rigorous propriety when they are conjoined. A complete, that is to say spatial *and* temporal, position is either monogamous or virginal, ontologically speaking. So to state the position of a thing is to predicate a conjunction of properties of it and is necessarily to individuate it.

It would seem, then, that if the only obstacle to the bundle theory is the requirement of individuation it can easily be overcome. In any complete listing of a thing's properties its positional characteristics must occur and these of necessity distinguish it from everything else, however similar to it they may be in all other respects.

There is, however, a peculiarity of positional predications which significantly differentiates positions from other properties. This is that to ascribe a position to an individual in space or time involves an essential and ineliminable reference to another individual or position. If I state the location of something as being exactly seven miles south of St Giles's Cathedral in Edinburgh the determinacy or definiteness of my remark is due to the reference to that particular building. Being exactly seven miles south of a building of just the shape, size and so forth of St Giles's Cathedral would indeed be a spatial characteristic but it would be one which many things could share at one moment of time. Position individuates parasitically. To put the point in linguistic fashion, a language can individuate only if it contains singular terms. That I cannot state the position in space and time of a particular thing without stating its spatial and temporal relation to some other particular thing is obviously true of the positional locutions of ordinary speech: 'east of Suez', 'under the clock at Waterloo', 'pre-Columbian', 'medieval'. The situation is not altered, though it is to some extent concealed, when positions are assigned to things in terms of a co-ordinate system. But here, too, a further individual is involved, or more properly a further position, namely the point of origin of the co-ordinate system. In the most common case this is that point in the sea off the West Coast of Africa where the Greenwich meridian cuts the Equator at the first moment of the year A.D. 1.

Individuals cannot be decomposed into sets of properties that are sufficient to individuate them unless positional properties are included in the set. But if positional properties are included the decomposition into properties is incomplete. Further individuals remain to be decomposed, inviting us into an infinite regress. We can identify one individual with the set of its properties, but only if a reference to at least one further individual or position is made in the specification. If the point of origin of a system of positional reference is described in purely qualitative terms and without reference to any other individual or position it is always possible that the set of qualities in question has more than one instance. In that case positional references made in terms of it would be ambiguous. Things that were in fact spatio-temporally distinct could be occupants of the same 'position' in the system in just the way that distinct individuals can have the very same shape or colour. In short, a complete decomposition of individuals into properties, which mentions no further individuals, does not individuate and an individuating decomposition is necessarily incompletable.

How, then, do we understand full positional predications of the sort which do not just state the *kind* of things to which individuals we are concerned with are spatially and temporally related but which specify their unique position in time and space? In the first instance we make use of a familiar stock of positional reference-

18

points, geographical and historical landmarks, which are either well known and prominently noticeable things or else conventionally selected positions such as the equator or the presumed but not actual birth of Christ. To pick these out as the unique individuals or positions that they are we have to be able to relate them to ourselves or to the here-and-now. We do not have to be able to state the precise spatial and temporal relation of these standard points of reference to the here-and-now on every occasion on which we have recourse to them. The fact that we have been able in the past to determine our relation to them is sufficient ground for assuming that we could do so now if we were called upon to do so.

A system of positional reference is much like a map. Before we can use a map we must know where we are on it and before we can use a scheme of standard positions to characterise the location and date of other things we must correlate those positions with the place and time at which we are. But we do not have to be precisely aware of our position on the map whenever we are attending to it. I can plan a trip while in the middle of a railway journey at a time when I have only the most general idea of where the train is. But I am confident that at the end of the trip I shall soon be able to orient myself with regard to some of the places on the map. Similarly I am confident of my ability to orient myself with regard to the standard points of positional reference when the need arises.

Now this confidence might be misplaced. I might go out to find that in whichever direction I moved I did not come across familiar things standing in familiar spatial relations to one another. But in that case the standard scheme would just have ceased to apply altogether and I should have to fabricate another. On the other hand I might find familiar-looking things standing in unusual spatial relations. In that case I should have to amend the scheme, perhaps by dropping from it its more vagrant elements. Maps too often prove useless or unreliable. The map of a piece of country is no use at all in a totally different place and may be of little use after a large earthquake or comparable natural catastrophe.

We tend to ignore the dependence of our ordinary scheme of standard positions on the here-and-now not only because we generally can establish the relation of its elements to our current position without difficulty but also because the spatio-temporal region we occupy is a great deal smaller than the region we speak about. In other words our actual position at most times, provided we are not aviators or astronauts, is very stable in relation to the standard positions, which have themselves been chosen for their stability in relation to one another. In consequence our actual position comes to be treated as something fixed and determinate enough in the standard scheme to be neglected altogether.

The position where I am at the present moment is, then, the absolute point of origin of all my positional characterisations of things. It is the one position I do not have to pick out by its relation to something else and by their relation to which in the end everything else is individuated. The linguistic correlate of this absolute point of origin or absolute position is the demonstrative part of language, such terms as 'here', 'now', 'this' and 'I', which require for their understanding in any particular employment a knowledge of the context in which they are uttered. There is a demonstrative aspect to the understanding of every singular term that purports to refer to a unique individual. It may be practically sufficient to explain a singular term to someone by enumerating the properties of its bearer but misidentification can be ruled out conclusively only by bringing in the position of the thing in question. But any reference to position that is sufficient to individuate must connect it to the here-and-now.

The elimination of singular terms

Since Russell propounded his theory of descriptions there has been a number of attempts to use it for a purpose Russell himself did not endorse: the total elimination of singular terms. Quine has proposed a regimentation of language in which the elliptical and contextually dependent sentences of ordinary speech are replaced by eternal sentences using definite descriptions that contain only general, predicative terms to pick out the subjects of discourse (cf. Quine (4), p. 191). Goodman has treated the concrete individuals of the phenomenal realm in a similar way (cf. Goodman (1), p. 160). Interpreting sense-impressions as colour-spot-moments, wholes composed of a colour, a place in the visual field and a moment of time, he has held that all three kinds of component are strictly qualitative in nature. Ayer has suggested that there could be a purely predicative language purged of all demonstratives and proper names (cf. Ayer (3), p. 16).

Quine's eternal sentences and Ayer's predicative language both fail to provide any guarantee of individuation. At one point Quine suggested that for every named individual a a property A could be found which was possessed by a alone. Instead of saying 'a is F' we could say 'there is something which is A with which everything that is A is identical and everything that is A is F'. To these *ad hoc* predicates Ayer has objected that they are either unique and not predicates at all or else they are really conjunctions of ordinary, general predicates which cannot be counted on to individuate. What is really wrong with them is that they can only individuate their possessors if they contain a mention of their

20

position and thus a demonstrative element. Similarly eternal sentences, as Quine agrees, must contain a mention of date to eliminate the demonstrative feature of tense to be found in the verbs of ordinary speech. But if the demonstrative is removed here it must creep back behind the standard temporal references if they are to be understood as referring to a unique date.

Goodman's solution to the problem of concretion for phenomenal things admits that place and time are essential individuators or 'concretors'. But Goodman maintains that position in the visual field and in the time-sequence are qualitative. This is certainly defensible for the former. *Being at the top left hand corner of the visual field* is a genuinely qualitative property of colour-patches to the extent that it can be possessed, successively, by many different patches. It also appears, at first sight, to involve no reference to a further individual or position. The space of one's momentary visual field seems absolute rather than relative. But there are difficulties in this view. In the first place the ideas of left and right, up and down, seem to involve a reference to the asymmetries of the human body, to the rather vestigial asymmetry of the ordinary position of the heart in one case, to the gross asymmetry of head and feet in the other. A disembodied or wholly symmetrical observer would be able to distinguish two-colour patches at different places in his visual field at one moment but how would he be able to identify the position of either with the position of a patch occurring later in his visual history? It has sometimes been held that the visual field is not unbounded, most memorably in the diagram of an eyebrow-, eyelash- and moustache-fringed late-nineteenth-century scene of boots and fireplace contrived by Mach (cf. Pearson, p. 59). Here the visual field is eye-shaped and offers sufficient asymmetries, which do not demand a physical interpretation, to make possible the introduction of qualitative spatial terms. The trouble here is factual. The visual field is very seldom Machian. If judgment remains uncertain on this point there can be less doubt about Goodman's account of moments of time as qualitative. A moment of time has no intrinsic features which could serve to distinguish it from all other moments. It would have to be distinguished by its content and the content of its predecessors. But if a phenomenal sequence were cyclic in content and infinitely long it would contain distinct moments that were wholly indiscriminable in respect of their own and their temporal neighbours' content. Only those like Plato and McTaggart who accept pre-existence would admit phenomenal sequences without a beginning. So any actual sequence could in fact have its momentary elements picked out by their relation to the moment without a predecessor. (The fact that intervals of sleep entail that many elements will have no immediate predecessor does not undermine the uniqueness of the absolutely first element, always supposing that a purely phenomenal consciousness could form the idea of temporal gaps in its history.) However, it is only a contingency that a phenomenal sequence has a backward end. Individuation in terms of the hitherto accepted starting-point would be always at the mercy of a sudden recovery of earlier memories. The quality of being unpreceded is not one that a phenomenal consciousness could ever confidently ascribe to a moment of time. This, together with the practical consideration of rapidly fading phenomenal memory, ensures that the individuation of phenomenal times would have to be based on the only demonstratively expressible present. It should be noticed that whether or not Goodman's account of concretion is correct of such private or phenomenal individuals as the elements of sense-impressions, it certainly does not apply to the concrete individuals of the physical world.

Russell did not propose to apply the theory of descriptions to all singular terms. By his analysis statements with singular subject-terms were interpreted as existential, as being of the form 'there is something which . . .' and, in his view, such existential statements are generalisations. Generally speaking statements of the form '(Ex)Fx' require the support of statements of the form 'Fa', where 'a' is the logically proper name of an individual. Quine and Ayer have been prepared to drop this requirement and to allow statements of the form '(Ex)Fx' to be basic. In effect Quine dismisses the category of logically proper names by his assumption that a unique predicate can be found or constructed *ad hoc* for each singular term. Ayer considers the most plausible candidates for the status of logically proper name directly: 'I', 'here' and 'now', as well as Russell's favourite 'this'. He concludes that these can be replaced by definite descriptions though he admits that such a replacement is not a translation. It is at best a paraphrase. But although it is not identical in meaning with the statement it paraphrases, it can convey the same information, carry out the same communicative or descriptive task.

He concludes that singular terms in general and demonstratives in particular could be dispensed with without any impoverishment of our powers of description. They are merely devices of economy and an exclusively predicative language is possible. In such a language instead of saying 'that banana is tasteless' one might say 'the yellow, slightly-curved, six-inch-long thing is tasteless', or even 'yellow, slightly-curved, six-inch-long together with tasteless'. In the strictly predicative rendering only predicates occur: two sets of descriptive predicates separated by the logical predicate 'together with'. The predicates before 'together with' would have a referential, those coming after it a descriptive, *function* but there would be no purely referential terms. He admits that in such a language there would be no guarantee of uniqueness of reference. But, he argues, such a guarantee is not needed, since we can in practice remove any ambiguity of reference that may occur, and would not seem to be possible anyway, since we have no such guarantee in the language we actually use.

If the reference of a purely predicative statement is misunderstood all we have to do is to add further predicates to the referential part of the statement until the hearer's attention is redirected correctly. What Ayer clearly has in mind here is a situation in which the communicating parties are in approximately the same position or at least know where each other is. In such circumstances if I refer to 'the ABC thing' and my hearer picks out the wrong ABC thing he is not going to go wildly wrong for he is naturally going to start his search for what I am talking about in the spatio-temporal neighbourhood of our joint position or, in a more detached kind of colloquy, in the neighbourhood of the region we have succeeded in picking out for consideration in the earlier part of our discussion. In other words, he will interpret 'the ABC thing' as 'the *nearest* ABC thing' (either to our position or the established locus of the conversation). But 'nearest' is a demonstrative word. The nearest X is the X at the smallest distance in space and time from here-and-now. In other words, his explanation of the practical adequacy for reference to individuals of a purely predicative language is one which renders its predicativeness impure. If this cryptic insertion of the demonstrative is excluded ambiguity of reference may be ineliminable by linguistic means. Ayer does not believe that the identity of indiscernibles can be shown to be a necessary truth. It follows that it is always possible for two distinct things to share all their properties.

His other point is that there is no guarantee of uniqueness of reference in the language we actually use. We have to rely on various describable landmarks to individuate the things we talk about, including ourselves. Certainly if we were in radio communication with some intelligent being about whose position we knew nothing whatever, we should have to rely on something like Ayer's purely predicative language. We might have reason to suppose that our interlocutor had picked out the wrong thing. All we could do here would be to add further specifying predicates in Ayer's manner and this might not succeed. On the other hand, there might really be a difference between what he and we have picked out without either party recognising the fact.

But this type of communication is highly exceptional. The standard case is one in which, because the communicating parties are in much the same position, they can make use of demonstratives to pick out individuals. Ayer's proposal is really a self-denying ordinance by which we restrict ourselves to linguistic devices that only those in an extreme and unusual situation are confined to by their circumstances. Finally, even if it were true that we could in practice remove any ambiguity of reference by purely predicative means it would not follow that a thing is a bundle of properties. What we could manage to get on with for the purposes of communication in practice is not the decisive matter. We are asking whether there is anything more to an individual than the properties ascribable to it in purely general terms and not whether we could not get on quite well without mentioning anything but these properties. And in fact, as we have seen, it is not at all clear that we could get on very well in practice limiting ourselves to these alone.

The identity of indiscernibles

The belief that there is no more to a thing than its properties owes a good deal of its hold to the authority of the principle of the identity of indiscernibles. If everything that has all and only the properties of a given thing is identical with that thing it follows that the total set of a thing's properties is proprietary to it. Anything that had all and just those properties would be that very thing. Two things can be different only if there is a point of difference between them and this point of difference must be a property that can be predicated of one of them but not of the other. As long as the reference to properties in the principle is understood to include positional as well as qualitative properties it is clearly a necessary truth. For it follows from the necessary truth that no two things can have all their positional properties in common. The extension of the principle to cover strictly qualitative properties as well is really a pleonasm. Position alone is sufficient to individuate. From this point of view qualities proper are superfluous; there is nothing left for them to do.

But, if the reference to properties is understood more narrowly, to include only the qualitative properties that are applicable to many things, there is, as we have seen, no reason to suppose that the principle is necessarily true. By conjoining multiply applicable properties we may reduce, but we do not necessarily reduce to one, the extent of their application. Why should not two pins, for example, be as alike as two pins? It is entirely conceivable that two pins, waiting in a factory to be packed, should reveal no point of qualitative difference whatever to the most minute and elaborate scrutiny, carried out with the aid of every imaginable technical refinement, apart from the fact that one is two inches and the other three inches to the left of the packer's ashtray.

The principle, then, has two forms, in the wider of which it is necessarily, if also to some extent pleonastically, true but in the narrower of which it is, if true at all, only contingently so. Leibniz was compelled to take the principle in its narrow, qualitative sense since by denying that space and time were fully real he was committed to the view that positional properties were the more or less misleading appearances presented by underlying qualities. A symptom of this is the fact that he attempted to derive the principle from the law of sufficient reason, which he took to rule out the possibility that there could be two qualitatively indistinguishable things in distinct places. God, he said, could have no sufficient reason for putting one instance of a set of qualities at one place and another instance of precisely the same set at another place rather than the other way round. His manner of posing this problem shows that he conceived the things involved as mere sums of qualities and did not regard the places at which they were as any part of their constitution as individuals. God, of course, is faced by no such problem. The individuals do not pre-exist their being placed *somewhere*. The charming scene of a gentleman hurrying round a princess's garden in the unsuccessful search for two qualitatively identical leaves is also beside the real point. Any pair of leaves he is preparing to investigate is already discriminated into two distinct individuals by the different positions they occupy in his hand or have occupied in the garden before he sets about examining their shape and markings (cf. Leibniz, p. 228).

The distinction between the two forms of the principle corresponds to that between numerical and qualitative difference. If the narrower form is true all distinct things differ qualitatively. If the wider form alone is true there are numerically, which is to say positionally, distinct things that are qualitatively identical.

Why should it have been supposed that qualitatively indiscernible things are identical? Partly, no doubt, for the empirical reason that most distinct things that at first appear to have the same qualities prove to differ qualitatively on closer inspection. This supports the inductive assumption that a qualitative difference will eventually emerge from closer examination of any two things seemingly identical in qualities. This is, like the principle that every event has a cause, an open-ended hypothesis which no amount of confirmatory ill-success can refute. And it is irrefutable for the same reason. The possible qualities of a thing, like its possible causes, are so numerous that we can never be sure that we have examined them all.

A more fundamental reason, however, is the assumption that qualities are in some pre-eminent way the objects of observation. It is true enough that we observe nothing but the properties of things, provided that properties are taken to include position as well as qualities. Everything that we can observe of a thing can in principle

25

be stated. But this does not entail that it can be stated in general, strictly qualitative terms. We observe and can say where and when things are in relation to ourselves and to other things as well as what they are like. What we observe, indeed, are individuals which have qualities and positions; we do not observe either qualities or positions alone. Certainly we do not see the thing itself as something distinct from its qualities. But nor do we observe the qualities as distinct from the thing that has them. There was an idealist principle to the effect that individuals alone are concrete and that particulars and universals are both abstract. This is substantially correct. What we observe is something red at a particular position. We do not observe redness on its own and we do not observe position on its own. We never come across either sort of entity except in conjunction with the other. We can, of course, refer to unoccupied positions and we can refer to uninstanced qualities. In each case the reference is dependent on and in relation to actual individuals. What there is, then, and what we can observe are concrete individuals. These are in a sense wholly made up of properties, provided that the set of their properties is understood to contain their position as well as their qualities. But they are not to be identified with their qualities alone.

A similar objection can be brought against the argument that if the properties of a thing are removed nothing is left. In one sense this is correct. If we imagine that everything we can predicate of a thing is denied of it, the thing is annihilated. But if we merely eliminate in mind all the qualities of a thing there remains at the end of this logical strip-tease the position in space and time at which these qualities are manifested. It is instructive to reverse the argument. Suppose the position of a thing is imagined away and in a comparable fashion: position is eliminated altogether and not simply replaced just as the qualities were wholly removed and not merely altered. At the end of this somewhat questionable operation there is no individual thing left but there is something left all the same, the collection of that thing's qualities which, since they may be manifested together at an indefinitely large number of times and places, are the possibility of an indefinitely large number of things though now, by hypothesis, the actuality of none. There is, then, no better reason for saying that a thing is nothing but its qualities than there is for saying that it is nothing but its position. It is destroyed if either is removed in the thoroughgoing fashion envisaged. But this is because position and qualities are both essential logical parts of an individual thing and not because either of them is identical with the individual thing itself. In this argument from subtraction a necessary condition of individual existence has been wrongly taken to be a sufficient condition as well.

The two main reasons for supposing that qualities alone can be observed were mentioned in the introductory section to this part. Aristotle justifies the view in a rationalist way. Observation is an exercise of the intellect or understanding and the proper objects of the understanding are general in nature, they are universals or qualities. Certainly there would seem to be no such thing as the awareness of bare particulars. The most elementary cognitive activity of the mind is conceptual, the recognition of something sensibly present as falling under a concept which may have many instances. Observation is always classificatory; to observe something is to observe it as being of a certain kind. But though observation involves intellect it is not an exclusively intellectual matter, it involves sensation as well. If we do not observe bare particulars, we do not observe bare universals either. In so far as the senses are involved in observation they relate it to the here-and-now. The intellect classifies what is present to the senses here and now with individuals at other times and places. The indispensability of both to observation is paralleled by the indispensability of both demonstrative and purely predicative or descriptive terms to discourse about matters of fact.

Empiricists from Locke and Berkeley have concluded that qualities alone are observed, and further, as distinct from Aristotle, that they alone can be significantly said to exist, from the identification of qualities with ideas or appearances. This is a mistake that the word 'idea', the most plastic in the whole philosophical vocabulary, has encouraged. The classical empiricists took it to mean both the meaning of a word, the concept expressed by it, and also the immediate object of perception. Recent empiricists have insisted on the distinction between abstract concepts or qualities and concrete impressions or appearances but with less than complete resolution. 'Those' says Ayer 'who are infected by the primitive superstition that to every name a single real entity must correspond assume that it is necessary to distinguish logically between the thing itself and any, or all, of its sensible properties. But from the fact that we happen to employ a single word to refer to a thing, and make that word the grammatical subject of the sentences in which we refer to the sensible appearances of the thing, it does not by any means follow that the thing itself is a "simple entity" or that it cannot be defined in terms of the totality of its sensible appearances. It is true that in talking of "its" appearances we appear to distinguish the thing from its appearances but that is simply an accident of linguistic usage' (Ayer (1), pp. 32–3). In this argument 'sensible properties' and 'sensible appearances' are taken to be one and the same. It is implied that the shift from one to the other is no more than a stylistic variation. But since appearances are individuals and properties are not it does not at all follow from the premise that a thing is identical with its appearances that it can therefore be identified with its properties. A sense-impression is an individual instance of a sensible property, not just the sensible property itself. It is the manifestation of a sensible property at a particular time and in a particular region of sensible space (cf. Mabbott).

In one way we can observe both particulars or positions, for we can tell by observation where and when things are, and universals or qualities, for we can tell by observation of what kind they are. But in another way we can observe neither, on their own at any rate, for we cannot observe unoccupied positions or uninstanced qualities. What we always observe, whether they are private impressions or public objects, are concrete individuals, complexes of both position and qualities.

In passing it should be noted that there is a tension, perhaps amounting to an incompatibility, between the position of recent empiricists that I have been discussing, which derives the ontological conclusion that things are no more than bundles of qualities from the supposed eliminability of singular terms, and the hostility that they commonly express to the existence of universals. According to the former view, a concrete individual is reducible to, and thus amounts to no more than, a collection of universals. According to the latter, any statement in which apparent reference is made to a universal can and should be replaced by a statement in which the only entities referred to are concrete individuals and in which properties and relations are only predicatively introduced. If both reducibilities are affirmed they cannot both be ontologically interpreted, for if they are, the two parties to the conflict, concrete individuals and abstract universals, will, like Kilkenny cats, devour each other without trace (cf. Pap (3)).

Position as substance

Substance in its first sense, then, as individuator, is position. Position individuates and since it cannot be identified in purely general predicative terms there is more to an individual thing than the sum of its qualities. A concrete individual or Aristotelian substance is a set of qualities manifested at a position and of such things the Aristotelian principle of inherence is correct. Both *form*, that is to say shareable properties, and *matter*, that is to say position in space and time, are essential logical parts of an individual. Position and qualities alone are abstract. We do not encounter them alone in perception, but only in the conjunction with each other that constitutes a concrete individual.

But although they are unobservable on their own, position and qualities are not *radically* unobservable, for they are both essential features of whatever is observed. There is, therefore, a sense in which the bundle theory is correct, for things are not individuated by some radically unobservable substance as critics of the positive theory of individuation have taken it to assert. This criticism of the positive theory is not captious. Aristotle's matter is conceived by him as something closed to the understanding, unutterable and inarticulate. As he conceived it, it is indistinguishable from nothing at all. Furthermore it is objectionable, not merely as radically unempirical, but also as an implicitly regressive notion. For unless it is made clear what it positively is, it is natural to interpret individuating substance as some kind of unobservable individual which inevitably raises the first of an infinite series of further problems of individuation.

If properties are interpreted widely, to include positional as well as qualitative predicates, the bundle theory is true and, indeed necessarily true, as a direct consequence of the wider interpretation of the principle of the identity of indiscernibles. But if properties are restricted to really general, qualitative predicates alone, it is at best contingently true. And, even if it is true as a matter of fact, since there are things between which we know of no strictly qualitative difference, it is not always by their qualitative differences that we individuate things. I have argued that there is good reason to interpret properties as they figure in the bundle theory and the identity of indiscernibles in the narrower, qualitative sense. The qualities of a thing can be stated in strictly general terms; its position can be identified only if some further individual or position is referred to. A fundamental difference of kind is obliterated if position and qualities are run together. Furthermore in its usual formulation the bundle theory invites the narrower interpretation by identifying a thing with the sum of its *qualities*.

So far the view that a concrete individual is a set of qualities at a position has been considered in a fairly abstract fashion. I have not inquired what sort of position an individual occupies. Now it is clear that most individuals at any rate do not occupy the minimum possible position. An individual thing is not a set of qualities at a point in space and at an instant of time. The individuals that we ordinarily observe and discuss are extended in space and enduring in time. It is an empirical fact that however close a thing is to us we shall not perceive it at all unless it is of a certain finite size and unless it persists for a certain finite extent of time. Furthermore we cannot infer the existence of strictly punctual and instantaneous things from what we do observe. It does not follow from the fact that space and time themselves, being extensive magnitudes, are infinitely divisible that their occupants are infinitely divisible as well. In other words, we cannot infer from the fact that there is no limit to the spatial and temporal minuteness of conceivable things that there actually are infinitely minute things. In any case all the things we do observe or speak about have some spatial extent, and thus have shape and size, and also have some temporal extent.

There is a difference between two kinds of temporal extendedness which needs to be mentioned here. It has important consequences and it is not directly paralleled by a comparable distinction between kinds of spatial extendedness. No concrete individual that we perceive or refer to is strictly instantaneous but some do and some do not fall within what may be called the period of observation or what is usually known as the specious present. Events of the former class are temporally extended indeed but their whole temporal extent falls within the scope of a single observation. The latter class of continuants strictly endure or persist in that we can observe parts of their histories that are separated by periods during which we are not observing them at all. About continuants thus defined the problem of identity through time, the second problem of substance, arises. It is important that this distinction is not a precise one. It is no more precise than the idea of a single observation on which it is based. A glimpse at a snowstorm out of a window is a single observation, a series of glimpses interrupted by bouts of attention to what is going on in the room is not. What about a sustained and closely attentive examination for a period of minutes of the activities of a single fish in a single small tank? But the fact that there is no definite sense to the idea of a single observation does not mean that there is no distinction between an event and a continuant. It may mean that individuals are not *absolutely* allocatable to either category and that a thing which is a continuant, namely the object of a series of interrupted observations, to one observer, is not a continuant to another. On this interpretation of the term it remains true that most of the things we talk about are, for us, continuants. Furthermore the lack of absoluteness in the distinction is of little significance from this point of view. However imprecise the notion of a single observation may be, it is quite clear that by the most liberal standard of continued observation a thing can be observed without interruption only for a few hours. (We may be broad-minded enough to forgive blinking but we cannot ignore more or less protracted periods of sleep.) But the very great majority of the things we talk about last for much longer than a few hours. So although it is false to say that what strictly speaking we observe are momentary events or phases of things (the length of the moments involved being determined by the empirically established duration of the specious present), it is a falsehood that can conveniently be used to state the truth that a problem about identity through time arises with regard to most of the individuals to which we refer. A general consideration of this problem of identity through time will occupy the third chapter.

There are two kinds of apparent exception to this principle that all individuals occupy some extent of space and time. The first and more important but less directly relevant of these draws attention to the fact that we do, after all, talk about individuals which are not in space or time at all. This fact is no objection to the view that all *concrete* individuals are in space and time but since that view is a tautology it hardly could be. There are two main varieties of non-concrete individual: mental entities, minds and their states, and abstract entities, univerals, propositions and necessary connections. The well-established tradition of Cartesian dualism distinguishes the mental as that which is in time but not in space from the physical as that which is in both time and space. In part III I shall argue that mental entities are in space and that the mental is, therefore, a department of the physical and not an independently sovereign realm. The even more venerable tradition of Platonic dualism distinguishes the abstract as that which is neither in time nor in space from the inferior sorts of things that are in either or both. In part III I shall argue that reference to abstract entities can be dispensed with and that the two abilities which have been held to require the existence of abstract entities for their explanation— the predicative use of general terms and the apprehension of necessary truths—can both be explained without invoking such things. For the moment, then, the problem of the existence of non-concrete individuals can be ignored.

The second kind of exception draws attention to the fact that we do talk about individuals which are not extended in space and time as ordinary events and objects are, although they are in some sense spatio-temporal. In the first place we do refer to seemingly punctual objects, like the corner of a piece of paper or a table, and to seemingly instantaneous happenings, like the beginning of an earthquake or an explosion. It is significant that the words we actually use in making these references to the punctual and the instantaneous contain a further reference to something spatio-temporally extended: to a material object such as a table or to a process such as an earthquake. Now these references can be understood in two ways. If I say that the corner of the table was dented or that it fell off or that it was covered with spilt gravy I am in fact referring to a spatio-temporally extended part of a spatio-temporally extended whole. The same is true if I say that the beginning of the earthquake halted traffic on a certain road or that it was noticed by no one. I refer here to a temporally extended segment of a temporally extended process.

31

On the other hand I may make merely positional statements about the corner of the table or the beginning of the earthquake, saying of the one that it was exactly four feet from the doorhandle and of the other that it coincided with the blowing of the factory hooter. Now because of the limits of exact spatio-temporal measurement these remarks could be interpreted in the same way as the previous ones, namely as referring to parts of spatio-temporally extended objects or processes. But they could also be understood as referring to the positions alone, to a particular point in space which having no dimensions in space but only position has neither shape nor size, or to a particular instant in time, which has no temporal extent itself but is the limit from which intervals of time may be measured. The fact is that we do make reference to pure positions. We do so most noticeably when we mention a date or the point of intersection of a latitude and a longitude. We do it in a demonstrative way with such words as *here, there, now, then,* and we do it descriptively when we talk of the first moment of the French Revolution or the centre of gravity of the solar system. Now a position is not an individual as I have been using the term, it is, rather, the possibility of an individual. For the moment it is enough to say that there are two apparent varieties of reference to the spatio-temporal: ordinary reference to individuals, to the manifestation of qualities at a particular extended region of space and through a particular interval of time, and also reference to space and time themselves, which may be, although of course it need not be, to spatially unextended points and to temporally unextended instants. In other words, I propose to sustain the principle that individuals must occupy an extent of space and time by defining *individual,* in conformity with the previous discussion, as something narrower than *object of reference in general,* and as involving both position and qualities. Reference to qualities alone has been deferred for later discussion. Reference to positions alone will play a large part in the following chapter.

2

Things

Theories of reference

Singular terms, by which I mean the referring expressions, that are or
contain demonstratives, proper names and descriptions, which serve
as the subjects of sentences, have been a continuing topic of interest
and controversy amongst philosophers in recent times. The function
of those terms in discourse is to denote or refer to individuals. It is
natural to identify this function with their meaning. Yet the sentences
in which they occur are not deprived of meaning if, as sometimes
happens, there is in fact no such individual as that to which they
purport to refer. But it would seem that sentence with a meaningless
constituent must be meaningless itself.

Four main kinds of theory have been proposed to deal with this
difficulty.

(i) What may be called *denotationism*, usually attributed to
Meinong, insists on the connection of meaning with reference and
maintains that the failure of reference of such singular terms as 'the
present king of France' and 'the round square' is only apparent.
Although there is no actual king of France or round square in space
and time for them to refer to, there are such things to be found
somewhere else: in the realm of timeless essences, perhaps, or in the
mind of the referrer. The simplest objection to the theory is that it
seems to entail that, provided that the term 'the X' is meaningful, all
statements of the form 'the X exists' are true and, indeed analytically
true in virtue of their meaning. Further difficulties crowd in if the
attempt is made to meet this objection by recourse to a distinction
between existence and actuality. They all hinge on the theory's
consequence that 'the present king of France' and 'the present king
of Belgium' have quite different kinds of meaning, as do 'the round
square' and 'the brown square'. Thus on this theory it is true that
the present king of France is not a man but necessarily false that the
present king of Belgium is not, for whatever non-actual thing 'the

present king of France' refers to it is not a male human being. In practice the main function of this theory is to serve as a horrible example to be avoided by others.

(ii) Russell's theory was developed over a long period and underwent some variations in detail. It lays down that most singular terms are to be replaced by definite descriptions of the form 'the so-and-so' and sentences containing them are to be analysed in accordance with the theory of descriptions into a compound of universal and existential generalisations in which the only referring elements are quantified variables. Russell has given varying accounts of the composition of this class of eliminable singular terms. In the end (cf. Russell (2), p. 56) it came to embrace all but a very small residue of logically proper names, of which Russell's favourite example was the word 'this', used to refer to an immediate object of perception and not the topic of some previous discourse. Any term but 'this' could fail to refer and any term that could fail to refer was not a logically proper name.

(iii) Quine has proposed that all singular terms should be eliminated in accordance with Russell's technique (Quine (2), p. 220). As against Russell he denies that sentences containing proper names and demonstratives can be *translated* into sentences whose subjects are definite descriptions but he holds that they can be paraphrased in such a way that their linguistic services can be effectively performed by the sentence that replaces them. Russell had retained some residual logically proper names to serve as the evidential support for the generalisations in which his elimination of singular terms terminated but Quine denies that any such backing is required. For him the whole weight of the referential function of language can be carried by quantified variables.

(iv) Strawson, finally, has advanced a view which rejects the whole Russellian approach (Strawson (3)). According to him there are no logically proper names, for any term whatever may fail of reference, and no definite descriptions in Russell's sense. Sentences of the form 'the X is Y' do not entail, as with Russell, that at least and at most one thing is X; rather they presuppose it in the sense that the sentence cannot be used to make a statement, true or false, unless the existence-condition is satisfied. If the sentence 'the X is Y' is seriously affirmed a statement, true or false, is made if there is in fact such a thing as the X. If not, a statement has been attempted but not successfully achieved.

There is a large number of distinct issues in dispute here and they need to be carefully distinguished.

(*a*) *Meaning and reference.* For Meinong they are always one and the same for singular terms; for Russell they are sometimes the same; for Quine and Strawson they are never the same. (*b*) *Elimination of demonstratives.* Quine holds that demonstratives can be eliminated

34

as well as any other singular terms. Russell and Strawson both deny this, but for different reasons. Russell requires demonstratives to provide the total system of singular terms with evidential backing. Strawson requires them partly for the sort of reasons given in the preceding chapter, namely to ensure uniqueness of reference and partly, against Quine, to endow the existential sentences in which Quine's analysis terminates with the kind of meaning they ordinarily have and without which they cannot do what he requires of them. I shall return to examine this point in more detail later. (c) *Translatability*. Against Russell, Quine and Strawson agree that the theory of descriptions does not provide a technique for the translation of the sentences to which it is applied. But where Quine regards this as unimportant since in his view translation is not a goal which philosophical analysis can attain, Strawson regards it as fatal to the theory. (d) *Truth-value gap*. All parties to the dispute except Strawson agree that every meaningful sentence, whether its subject succeeds in referring or not, is either true or false. For Russell it is part of the definition of a proposition, conceived as the meaning expressed by a sentence, that it should be either true or false. In general the majority view rests its case on the law of excluded middle. (Strawson would restrict the law's application to statements: sentences whose subjects succeed in making a reference.) It is also argued that ordinary usage is not, as he claims, unequivocally on Strawson's side in this matter, and that his theory entails that the seemingly equivalent sentences 'the king of France is wise' and 'France has a wise king' are respectively truth-valueless and false.

I shall not be concerned in what follows with either the third or fourth of these issues, with either translatability, about which Quine and Strawson seem to be clearly correct, or the truth-value gap, a problem that seems to have reached the kind of impasse where it can be resolved only by a decision (cf. Ayer (6) and Strawson (6)). My concern will be to explore further the one point about which all parties to the controversy seem to be in agreement. This is that reference to individuals in some way presupposes the existence of the individuals referred to. For the denotationist it follows necessarily from the fact that a reference is meaningful, whether it is, in ordinary terms, successful or not, that the individual mentioned exists. For Russell and Quine every statement whose subject is an eliminable singular term, and for Quine that means every statement whatever whose subject is a singular term, entails as part of its meaning the existence of the thing to which the singular term purports to refer. For Strawson no sentence with a singular term as its subject can make a statement, true or false, unless the corresponding existential statement that asserts that there really is something for the singular term to refer to is true.

On each theory, then, existence is prior to predication. Nothing can be predicated of an individual, on one theory meaningfully, on the second truly and on the third truly or falsely, unless that individual exists. To hold this is, in effect, to hold that existence is not a predicate. For if it were a predicate to assert it of an individual would presuppose, in one of the three ways mentioned, a prior existential statement and so on *ad infinitum*.

Quine forthrightly accepts the clear consequence of this principle of the priority of existence to predication. For him existential statements are the basic or terminal elements of discourse, into which all others are to be analysed, or, as he would put it, paraphrased. But neither Russell nor Strawson is prepared to accept this. Both maintain that there is a sense in which predication is prior to existence. Russell's argument is that existential statements are generalisations and that the only reason we can have for asserting them is the establishment of their singular instances. The ultimate ground for any statement of the form 'something is F' is a statement to the effect that some particular thing is F. The primary kind of backing required by '(Ex)Fx' is 'Fa'. I may, in some cases, infer '(Ex)Fx' from 'Ga' and '(x)Gx→(Ey)Fy'. But there is a reference to an individual in 'Ga' and the generalisation '(x)Gx→(Ey)Fy' must rest on the support of instances of the form 'Ga.Fb'. Thus I can infer that there is a tree from which this orange came from the fact that this is an orange and the law that for every orange there is a tree on which it grew. But to establish the law I must know of a number of particular cases of oranges being associated with trees. Russell deals with the apparent inconsistency of the two principles of priority by restricting the scope of the first of them. Existence is prior to predication only in the case of individuals whose names are eliminable. It does not apply to the ultimate individuals whose names are logically proper. Eliminable reference, then, presupposes existence in a way that reference by a logically proper name such as 'this' does not.

Strawson argues for the priority of reference and predication to existence on different grounds (Strawson (4)). Reference to individuals is required by existential statements, not, as Russell would have it, to justify their assertion, but in order to endow them with the sort of meaning that they actually have. If existential statements are to assert the existence of some thing or things, not otherwise specified than by the predicative terms involved, the idea of reference to individuals must be already understood. If, as in Quine's view, existential statements were basic in discourse they would not mean that something of a certain description existed but that a certain general characteristic was manifested somewhere and somewhen. There is, as Strawson has pointed out, no direct inconsistency here since the sense in which reference is prior to existence is different from that in which existence is prior to reference. Each particular use of a referring singular term presupposes an existential statement appropriate to it. But it is only the general linguistic practice of making existential statements that presupposes an antecedently established practice of using singular terms for reference. But this distinction, while it certainly complicates and possibly mitigates the inconsistency, does not altogether eliminate it. If the development of one speaker's linguistic abilities is considered from his point of view the inconsistency stands out clearly. Before he can master the practice of making existential statements he must have mastered the practice of making references to individuals with singular terms. But every such reference to individuals presupposes the establishment of the corresponding existential statement, if it is to be successful, and at least the understanding of the corresponding existential statement, if it is to be a genuine case of intentional reference.

How are these conflicting demands to be reconciled? I shall argue that something like Russell's class of logically proper names must be allowed to deal with Russell's problem of the grounds of existential statements but my view differs from Russell's theory in not holding the names of any individuals to be logically proper, in particular the demonstrative 'this'. In order to deal with Strawson's problem about the sense of existential statements we shall need to explore the difference between substantival and adjectival concepts. I shall argue that the clue to the solution of Strawson's problem is to be found by following out the implications of his own account of the word 'this'.

Existence and indication

The type of existential statement with which we are concerned here is that which licenses the use of singular terms. If I know that there is such a thing as Mount Everest or the Pope or the Risorgimento I am in a position to make confident references to it. A singular existential statement of this sort is a kind of open licence for the use of the corresponding singular term. How is such a licence acquired? In practice, very often, we rely on the spoken or written words of others. But for this reliance to be possible we must understand the words involved and for it to be reasonable we must have checked the existential claims or assumptions of others for ourselves. In the end our beliefs about the existence of individuals must arise from direct confrontation with them.

I shall call the record or verbal expression of such confrontation an *indication*. The most natural form for such an indication to take is 'this is the so-and-so'. 'So this is the Albert Memorial' we say, finally satisfied that the frequent references we have heard to it really do refer to something. When we say 'this is the Albert Memorial' we assert that the thing in front of us here and now is the Albert Memorial. Thereafter we can say that there is such a thing as the Albert Memorial, meaning that at some unspecified, and perhaps forgotten, place and time the collection of characteristics that make up our notion of the Albert Memorial are manifested. Usually, no doubt, we intend the 'is' in 'there is such a thing as the Albert Memorial' to be understood in its temporal sense. In that case what we are being unspecific about is the object's spatial position. The existential statement is a generalised indication. Where the indication says that there is something of a certain description here, the existential statement says that there is something of that description somewhere.

The trouble with this account of the matter is that 'this' is not, as Russell believed, a logically proper name. It may fail to refer. It is, one might say, existentially presumptuous. Two well-known examples may be mentioned to establish the point. Strawson offers the case of a man walking carefully forward with his hands cupped, uttering the words 'this is a fine, big, red one' and then opening his hands to reveal nothing at all. The man's remark expressed his belief that there was something cupped in his hands and it turned out that there was not (Strawson (3), p. 333). Ayer makes use of the story of the Emperor's clothes (Ayer (6), p. 149). 'These are marvellous clothes the Emperor has on' declare the partially deluded spectators. (They deludedly believe that the Emperor has some clothes on even though they do not, as their words imply, believe that they can see them.) In either case the implied existential presupposition is that there is something here, that the cupped hands are holding something, that the Emperor has something on.

But there is a less presumptuous or existentially committal way of making an indication. Instead of saying 'this is the Albert Memorial' we could just as well have said 'behold: the Albert Memorial' or 'look: the Albert Memorial' or 'here is the Albert Memorial'. Likewise the man with the cupped hands could have said 'here is a fine, big, red one'. In this minimal type of indication only a position is referred to, in the demonstrative way that ensures the uniqueness of the reference.

With these minimal demonstrative indications of position the regress which Russell attempted unsuccessfully to halt with the word 'this' is brought to an end. For demonstrative references to positions are logically proper names. There can be no such thing as the non-existence of the here-and-now. There may be nothing here and now but there must be a here and a now. In fact all pure references to positions, all purely positional singular terms, are logically proper names. The expressions of a co-ordinate system are purely positional terms in this sense. There may be nothing at all at a given map-reference at a particular moment, no qualities whatever may be manifested at the spatio-temporal position it refers to, but there is no meaning to the supposition that the position itself does not exist, provided the origin of the coordinate system is linked to the here-and-now. The only way in which such a purely positional reference can fail is if it is a meaningless one, if it offends against the rules of the coordinate system. There is no such place as 750 degrees N. and 480 degrees W. unless we modify the rules to allow a place to be identified by more than one circuit of the earth. With pure references to positions, then, and in particular with demonstrative references to the here-and-now, we have arrived at a class of singular terms which provide the essential support for the existential statements presupposed by references to individuals without having any existential presuppositions themselves. It is only reference to individuals proper that can fail and which thus presupposes existence.

Ayer has argued that the same kinds of argument that undermine the claims of 'this' to being a logically proper name are also fatal to 'here' and 'now'. He says that these words can be used to refer to imaginary positions just as 'this' can be used to refer to an imaginary imperial garment. It is certainly true that any singular term, whether purporting to refer to a position or an individual, can figure in a piece of imaginative speech or writing. A character in a play or novel can refer or be reported as referring to non-existent individuals. But this is not to the point. Singular terms in imaginative or fictional discourse are simply misunderstood if they are taken to have a normal or 'serious' referring intention behind them. But there is no parallel in the cases of 'here' and 'now' to the failure of reference in normal discourse that can attend the use of the word 'this'. I may have no idea, in public terms, of where I am or what the time is but there is no possible sense to my doubting whether I am really here or that the time is now. I can always significantly wonder whether there is anything here, though I cannot always do so sensibly, but I cannot significantly inquire whether there is any place here for possible things to be at.

Wittgenstein and his followers have often objected to the idea that there is some sort of referential primacy about the act of pointing. This objection would extend to cover the priority accorded in my argument to demonstrative references to position, as is implicitly admitted by calling them indications. Indications are simply verbal acts of pointing. The objection appears to have two sides to it. In the first place it is held that pointing is just as much conventional as any other activity, verbal or otherwise, that has or is intended to have a meaning. It is no doubt conceivable that the pointing gestures we commonly employ might have had a different sense from the one they actually have. It is at any rate a very universal and, so to speak, natural convention. But we are not restricted to literal pointing in our acts of non-verbal indication. We can touch what we are referring to as well as point to it in most circumstances and, provided the object is of reasonable size, we can pick it up and hold it high in front of someone's face as a way of drawing his attention to it. If it is a place we are concerned with we can move our hearer's head and body appropriately. Sticking one's finger out is not the only way of securing somebody's attention to a particular place or thing. This is relevant in so far as it is natural to suppose that such demonstrative indicators as 'look', 'behold', 'here is' are the developed linguistic equivalents and alternatives to non-verbal modes of indication. With a young child we hold an orange up to it and say simply 'orange'. We make the same point to an adult, with a certain economy of bodily endeavour, by saying 'look, an orange' or 'here is an orange'. The child does not have to understand the conventional sense of our holding the orange up in front of it. It just has to be bright enough to have its attention caught. Verbal indication, then, is a conventional activity but it does not presuppose an antecedent understanding of language, in particular indicating terms do not have to be introduced by means of other, non-demonstrative words, though they will of course be introduced in conjunction with such terms.

The other side of the objection is that pointing, and, by implication, the demonstrative indication of position, is ambiguous. When I point in a certain direction the place or thing I have in mind may be at any, presumably visible, distance from my finger, may spread out from the line of my finger to an indefinite extent and may occupy any part whatever of the total region demarcated by these two indeterminacies. The here and now, it could be added, is even less determinate than the pointed-to, at most it limits the region of reference to the part of the currently perceptible universe that is, broadly speaking, in front of me, and it does not always do that. This is true enough. Even though I know well enough what position I am referring to with the word 'here' someone I am talking to may not. This is a difficulty of communicative practice rather than of logical principle and the solution to it is that people are not complete fools and the world they find themselves in does not at all times present a large multiplicity of equally interesting things and events clamouring for their attention. If, in a congested cloak-room, I say to a helpfully-disposed attendant no more than 'here is my hat' I have not advanced matters much until I either point to it or describe its position in relation to some individual that is qualitatively unique in the finite extent of the total common here and now. But just because the total here and now is finite it is reasonable to expect that the narrow, qualitative form of the identity of indiscernibles will be true of it. And if, as is possible, it is not, if the attendant and I are in a perfectly symmetrical cloakroom, with nothing but brand new size 7 bowlers in it, I can move about so that the symmetry of the situation is destroyed or, finally, if I am suddenly stricken with paralysis, I can get her to pick up the bowlers one by one until she hits on mine. In short, verbal, like non-verbal, indication is indeed ambiguous. Ordinarily this does not matter. When it obstructs communication it can easily be eliminated.

The general idea of a thing

In the last section a reconciliation was effected between the principle that all reference to individuals presupposes their existence and Russell's requirement that existential statements, being generalisations, should have some evidential backing. The solution found for this problem was an account of the backing of existential statements by indications, in which the reference is to positions not individuals, and which thus avoids the threatened infinite regress as well as the mistaken view that 'this' is a logically proper name. Strawson's version of the thesis that existence presupposes reference to individuals remains to be considered. So far his argument for it has been sketched in only the most general way.

His point is that the existential statements of ordinary speech do not merely report the manifestation of some quality or qualities at some unspecified location but rather the existence of a thing or things of a certain kind. He draws the conclusion that they can have this sense only if they are derived from an already established practice of reference to individuals. If, as in Quine's theory, the basic elements of discourse were sentences of the form '(Ex)Fx' they would not mean 'there is something which is F' but rather 'F has instances' or 'F-ness exists'.

The point may be made clearer by considering the consequences of the view, argued for in the first chapter, that an individual is a set of qualities manifested at a position in space and time. Consider the four subject-expressions 'that building', 'a building', 'this' and 'something'. 'That building' is explicit about both the qualities and position of the individual referred to. 'A building' is explicit about qualities but not about position, while 'this' is explicit about position but not about qualities. 'Something', finally, is explicit about neither position nor qualities. But despite their variations in explicitness all four of these terms refer to individuals. Consider further what follows from the view that 'this' is not a logically proper name. As making a reference that may fail to an individual it involves a presupposition of existence. The case of the cupped hands that prove empty show what the presupposition is. It is that there is something here or that here is something or a thing.

What seems clear is that the existential statements of ordinary speech—'there is such a thing as the Taj Mahal' or 'there is something green'—embody the idea of a thing in general. Strawson's view is, in effect, that this idea could not be possessed unless the practice of referring to unique individuals were already established, or even that to possess this idea just is to have mastered the practice of referring to unique individuals. And here we appear to have reached a position very much like Russell's. Where Russell said that to have reason to assert '(Ex)Fx' we must be assured of the truth of 'this is F', Strawson says that if we are to mean what we ordinarily do mean by '(Ex)Fx' we must already understand what it means to say 'this (thing) is F'. So, in his view, '(Ex)Fx' presupposes 'this (thing) is F' in one way and 'this (thing) is F' presupposes '(Ex)Fx' ('there is something which is F') in another.

I have suggested, at the end of the first section of this chapter, that the collision between these two principles is not really averted by distinguishing the two kinds of presupposition involved. Once the practice of reference to individuals is mastered no statement making a specific reference of this kind is required by each existential statement in the way that a specific existential statement is required by each reference to an individual. But the acquisition of the technique of reference to individuals remains problematic.

I think, furthermore, that we must admit the substance of Strawson's criticism of Quine. If the initial or basic elements of discourse were of the form '(Ex)Fx' they would mean 'there is some F' rather than 'there is something which is F'. As basic, sentences of this kind would be learnt ostensively. In that case they would have the force of indications, as I have defined them, statements of the form 'here is F', even if there were no verbal mark to distinguish between cases where they were asserted of what was sensibly absent and thus, presumably, spatially or temporally removed from the here-and-now. They would not mean that this thing is F but only that here F is manifested or instanced.

Is there any way in which the idea of a thing in general, as expressed by the words 'this', 'thing' and 'something' and as embodied in ordinary existential statements, could be introduced into discourse otherwise than by introducing the technique of reference to unique individuals? I believe that there is and that it can be found by looking more closely into the heterogeneous collection of predicative notions run anonymously together under the logicians' hospitable predicate-letter 'F'. Strawson himself has drawn an important distinction between three kinds of predicate which can be applied to solve the problem raised by his theory. He distinguishes, though not in these words, between things, stuffs and qualities (Strawson (5), pp. 167–73, 202). Examples of the three kinds are: things—man, horse, tree; stuffs —milk, coal, rain; qualities—hot, round, hard. Thing-predicates are verbally distinguished from the others by always being preceded (only in their predicative use, of course) by the indefinite article 'a'. We say 'the new cook is a man' but not 'the stuff he is drinking is a milk' or 'the room is a hot'. The thing-and stuff-predicates are nouns while quality-predicates are adjectives. Thing-predicates, unlike the others, have plurals. 'These animals are horses', we say, but 'these spots are milk (or round)'. These verbal differences reflect the fact that things alone can be counted while stuffs and qualities can only be measured. Another thing is another thing, but another stuff is another kind of stuff. Generally speaking the parts of a tract of stuff are other smaller tracts of the same stuff but, again generally speaking, the parts of a thing are not other smaller things of the same kind.

I want to suggest that the idea of a thing in general is derived, in the first instance, not from our mastery of the technique of reference to individuals, but from the thing-predicates which are the first predicates we learn. The basic elements of discourse are thing-indications, statements of the form 'here is an F'—'here is an orange', 'here is a cup', 'here is a chair'—even if they are in fact expressed in one-word sentences—'orange', 'cup', 'chair'. What these primary objects of attention have in common is that they are all things, not stuffs or qualities. The general idea of a thing that they enable us to form provides a primary sense for the word 'this', namely 'the thing here', and a primary sense for the word 'something', namely 'a thing (somewhere and at some time)'. Once we are equipped with these notions we can understand existential sentences in the ordinary way.

Where this position differs from Strawson's is in denying that the admitted dependence of reference to individuals on existential statements and of existential statements on the idea of a thing in general requires the antecedent understanding of the technique of reference to individuals. The idea of a thing in general can be acquired from the use and understanding of existential statements provided that the predicative element of these statements is of the thing, rather than the stuff or quality, kind. The language proposed by Quine would not enable the idea of a thing in general to be acquired if all its predicates, its Fs, were quality-predicates. But there is no reason why they should all be of this kind and, as a matter of fact, thing-predicates are the first we learn.

The basic elements of discourse, then, are thing-indications, of the form 'here is an F' (this being the fully explicit transcription of the one-word sentences, 'F', we usually come across at this stage). From these the idea of a thing in general is acquired that permits the introduction of the primary singular term for individuals: 'this'. Proper names and descriptions can be introduced as alternatives to appropriate occurrences of 'this'. They may first appear in a predicative-looking position in the forms 'this is N' and 'this is the D'. What will show that they are not predicates, that the 'is' of these forms is the 'is' of identity not predication, is that they can occupy the usual place of 'this' in a way that quality-predicates cannot. 'This is John' looks just like 'this is a man' and 'John is a man', 'this is tall', 'John is tall'. But 'tall is a man' has no meaning at all and 'a man is tall' has very little, at best it is an odd way of saying that some man is tall. Furthermore the idea of a thing in general renders the existential statements that underlie ordinary singular terms intelligible in the ordinary way and, by permitting the introduction of the word 'this', provides a means for the expression of the evidential grounds on which they rest.

It might be objected that 'thing' is a formal concept and that the idea of a thing in general is an absurdity. The answer to this objection is that the idea of a thing in general that we are concerned with here is not as wide as all that, in particular it is not the widest notion of thing that we have. In its widest sense 'thing' can be applied to any object of reference whatever, to any possible subject of discourse. (The same, of course, is true of 'this' and 'something'.) Numbers, symphonies, economic crises, attitudes, grammatical rules, social classes are all things in the widest sense. The kind of thing we are concerned with here is much more narrowly circumscribed. It is, essentially, an observable, spatio-temporal entity, a concrete object of perception.

The reason why there can be no substantial idea of a thing in the widest possible sense of the term is that nothing is excluded from its field of application; there are, in the nature of the case, no defining characteristics that can serve to mark it off from anything else. To say that something is a thing, in this widest possible sense, is clearly to say nothing at all. That it is a thing, in this sense, is necessarily implied in the fact of referring to it. The situation is quite different in the case of the primary, concrete and perceptible, things we are considering here. They are in the first place, and most essentially, occupants of space. In order to pick out some region of space as occupied by a thing it must be qualitatively demarcated from its spatial environment. This means that there must be a boundary or limit where the thing leaves off and its surroundings begin. A spatially bounded thing, more or less qualitatively distinct from its surroundings and more or less qualitatively homogeneous within the boundary, will have both a shape and a size. And in fact we find that the various kinds of thing have definite and fairly distinctive shapes and also reasonably definite, even if not distinctive sizes. From

44

this point of view, then, a primary thing in general is a collection of qualities, manifested in a particular and definite region of space and thus containing within it a definite shape and size (at any one moment, at least). In practice we fasten on those qualitatively discriminable portions of space whose shape and size persists through time and through change of position relative to other such things.

This characterisation of primary things in general is not very exact but this is because our conception of such things is not very exact either. There is a fair amount of latitude allowed us in the matter of partitioning our spatial environment into distinct things. It happens that there are in our surroundings spatially coinstantiated sets of qualities which are rather persistent in shape and size. What makes it impossible to say just how many things of this primary kind there are in a given region of space is that, generally speaking, what count as things by the criterion have further comparable things as their parts. Our capacity to give a definite answer to a question about the number of things in a given region depends on the fixity or permanence of the wholes within it. If a region can be emptied of its contents by a certain number of ordinary manipulations then that affords us a rough practical criterion for the number of things in the region. I can empty a box with three bunches of grapes in it in three movements. But the grapes can easily be detached from the bunches and the number of things in the box then becomes much greater. It is, then, because things, in our primary sense, are, generally speaking, wholly composed of other, smaller things, that there can be no definite answer to questions about their number in a given region, and not because the concept of a primary thing is formal or vacuous. Primary things are not infinitely divisible. At some point in the process of taking them to pieces they either collapse into elements that are too small to pick out and individuate, though they are still *material* things, or they simply resist further division. But there is no well-determined threshold of primary divisibility here and so we cannot identify a class of minimal primary things for purposes of counting.

Russell drew the conclusion from his view that 'this' is a logically proper name that the sentence 'this exists' is senseless. The verb 'exists' could be attached only to eliminable singular terms, for only about their bearers did a genuine question of existence arise. Although the sentence 'this exists' is hardly a natural form of words, to say the least, a genuine question of existence does arise about the word 'this', the question of whether there is anything here. The idea of an object in general as a determinate, qualitatively demarcated, shaped and sized, occupant of space makes clear the force of this question.

It may be pointed out that the word 'this' can be applied just as well to stuff as to things, conceived as determinate space-occupants. So 'this is white' may just as well mean 'this stuff is white' as 'this thing is white'. But when we *refer* to stuff in this fashion it is always to pieces or bits of stuff, to particular, spatially demarcated tracts of it. These pieces of stuff that we refer to are, in fact, low-grade things, distinguished from ordinary things by the fact that their spatial form is unstable and plays no part in recognising them as being of instances of the kinds of stuff that they are. We derive the idea of a thing in general from indications of things. Indications of stuff and indications of qualities ('it's raining', 'there's greenness here') would not serve for this purpose. But once thing-indications, with thing-terms appearing predicatively in them in conjunction with demonstrative reference to a pure position, equip us with the idea of a thing in general we are able to refer, pre-eminently with the word 'this', to stuff in a thing-like way, that is as individual bits or pieces, as well as to things of the primary spatial, form-retaining kind.

Matter and extension

The absolutely primary objects of reference, I have argued, are positions. Reference to individuals involves the idea of a thing in general. It is acquired by coming to understand elementary ostensive statements in which a demonstrative reference to a position, the spatio-temporal context of utterance, of the form 'here is (now)', is conjoined with a thing-predicate of the form 'a so-and-so', which asserts the manifestation in the region in question of a determinate spatial form.

The determinate occupancy of space is, then, the essential feature of these primary individuals, or things in general. This doctrine is reminiscent of Descartes' principle that extension is the essential attribute of matter and of the view, best-known in its Lockean version, that primary qualities are the essential properties of material objects. We must look more closely into this connection.

In some uses the word 'extension' is a synonym for 'size' but that was not what Descartes meant by the term, which was rather 'occupancy of space'. This, in effect, is voluminousness or geometrical solidity, the occupation of a continuous three-dimensional region in space. Not all possessors of spatial characteristics are occupants of space in this sense. Points have relative position, lines have size, two-dimensional areas have shape. But these are either the limits of material objects, positions or sets of positions defined with respect to geometrically solid material individuals or else, more colloquially, they are space-occupying parts of such individuals. ('What happened to the corner of the table, the top of the chest, the edge of the cupboard door?' 'I put them in the attic.')

Extension understood as the occupancy of space is, therefore, a complex property. It involves shape and size, even if we do not have names for the shapes of all extended things that are not parasitic on the name of the kind of thing in question and even if we do, in common speech, describe many extended things as shapeless, on account of the complexity or irregularity of their shape. It involves position in space, relative to other space-occupying things. When the position of a thing is considered through an interval of time it will either be stable or unchanging in relation to that of the majority of other things, or at any rate in relation to the things that are conventionally picked out as the stable basis of judgment about the movement of everything else. Finally space-occupants are impenetrable or logically solid in that they are the unique occupants of the region of space in which they are at any one time. This is not the same characteristic as tangible solidity or hardness, resistance to touch or pressure, although it is easily confused with it. If a thing is impenetrable nothing else can be where it is, if it is hard other things cannot *get into* the place where it is. Impenetrability rules out cohabitation; hardness rules out replacement. So what occupies space has shape, size, position (and thus, if enduring, rest or motion) and impenetrability. This detailed specification of the Cartesian concept of extension is simply Locke's list of the primary qualities of matter.

These modes of the occupancy of space are all, severally, essential features of a material thing. All those generic qualities of material things which are not forms of the occupancy of space—colour, texture, temperature, smell, taste and so forth—are, individually, dispensable. A wholly invisible material thing, like a curved shop-window of the clearest glass, may have no colour and a wholly intangible material thing, like a cloud of smoke, may have no texture. There is a further comprehensive difference between primary and secondary qualities. The primary qualities, the essential spatial characteristics of material things, are in a way common sensibles, at any rate they are all accessible to both sight and touch. The non-essential secondary qualities are all proprietary to one sense: colour to sight, texture to touch and so forth. We can, of course, infer that a thing seen but not touched is hard or hot but this is only because we have established an empirical association between its visible properties and its tangible or thermal ones.

From the fact that none of the secondary qualities, considered on its own, is essential to a material thing Descartes and Locke concluded not merely that a material thing without any secondary qualities at all is possible but that, in fact, no material thing really has secondary qualities. Both regarded secondary qualities as imaginative embroidery by the observing mind, carried out on the complexes of primary qualities presented to the senses. Locke explained our experience of secondary qualities as the causal outcome of the operation on our senses of the primary qualities of the minute or microscopic parts of the surfaces of material things.

Descartes' reason for holding that primary qualities alone constitute the real character of things is that they alone are objects of clear and distinct knowledge, clarity and distinctness of conception being the mark established by the *cogito* of all that could be known to exist. What appears to have struck him as especially clear and distinct about the primary qualities is that, as spatial properties, they form the subject-matter of the demonstrative science of geometry. This is a doubly inadequate support for his conclusion. In the first place we have necessary knowledge of other than spatial properties. It is as much a necessary truth that red is darker than yellow or that if *a* is harder than *b* and *b* is harder than *c* then *a* is harder than *c* as that the diagonal of a square divides it into two congruent right-angled triangles. No doubt these 'geometries' of the other sensory domains are less impressively systematic than the demonstrative science of extension but there is no difference of principle involved. It is noteworthy that both sides of the comparison are a prime source of examples for defenders of the synthetic *a priori*. Secondly, what is clear and distinct about spatial properties is not their instantiation by things but their logical relations to one another. What we know clearly and distinctly from Descartes' point of view is hypothetical as regards its application to matter. We know for certain that *if* two of the angles of a triangular plot of grass are equal, the sides other than that which joins them are equal in length. But the question at issue is whether we can know that the angles are equal.

Locke stated no very definite grounds for his view that material things have only primary qualities but two considerations would appear to have weighed with him. In the first place the primary qualities formed the subject-matter of classical, Newtonian mechanics. Locke, perhaps excusably, took the precision and system of the physical theory of his day to show that it had an altogether higher degree of truth and its subject-matter a higher degree of reality than the findings and objects of common observation. A second, and not unconnected point, is that the primary qualities are pre-eminently measurable. As against colour and texture they are extensive magnitudes: measurements of size, distance and speed obey the laws of cardinal arithmetic. One thing can be twice as large or be moving half as fast as another, but it cannot be twice as red or half as smooth as another, except in the most figurative and subjective fashion. Neither of these reasons is adequate for his conclusion. If it would be captious to say that Newton's mechanics is less true than the proposition that a particular plot of grass is green it is certainly, in its unamended parts, not more true, though it is a great deal more interesting. As to the second point, even if the secondary qualities are not cardinally measurable they are still measurable, and to a comparable degree of accuracy. Furthermore measurement is not a guarantee against error, even if, because of the stricter conventions that govern it, it is likely to be less, or at any rate less wildly, in error than our judgments about secondary qualities are capable of being. A good reason for this is the fact that we cannot measure primary qualities at all unless we can perceive secondary qualities. To use the pointer of a dial or a foot-rule we have to be able to determine the visible coincidence of marks that are identified by their colour.

Descartes and Locke have not shown, then, that there are any material things with primary qualities alone. They are also mistaken in supposing that there could be any such things, as the last objection to Locke suggests. We can discover what the primary qualities of a thing are, in the ordinary way or by measurement, only if we either see or feel its spatial boundaries. In either case we have to observe a distinction of secondary qualities: a chromatically defined boundary in one case, a change of texture between the thing and its surroundings in the other. This is the point of Berkeley's argument that a material thing as conceived by Locke is an impossibility. Although it does not have to be visible and does not have to be tangible, it must, if it and its primary qualities are to be perceived at all, be one or the other. Most familiar material things, of course, are both. So secondary qualities, although severally dispensable, are not jointly dispensable. A human being does not have to be male and does not have to be non-male, but has to be one or the other.

The purely spatial thing of Descartes and Locke is, in fact, indistinguishable from a chunk of empty space. A geometrically solid region of space has shape, size and relative position, even though there is nothing in it at all. It is, in a rather dubious way, at rest, since it necessarily retains its position with regard to other portions of space through time. Again, in the same dubious way, it is impenetrable, since, of necessity, no other portion of space can be where it is. But unless some other non-spatial characteristics are manifested in that region of space there is nothing there, only the possibility of a thing.

Descartes was aware of this consequence of his conception of matter and forthrightly maintained that matter and space are identical, or, more exactly that there can be no such thing as empty space, backing up this contention with the exemplary sophism, in which the identity of space and matter is assumed in the premises, that a vacuum is impossible since if there were two things with nothing between them they would touch one another. Locke, however, stoutly affirmed that empty space is possible and that matter and space are distinct. This could be attributed to his well-known capacity for failing to discern the logical consequences of his own doctrines, commonly known as his robust common-sense. But an alternative interpretation is possible. It could well be said that the sense of 'solidity' as it occurs in Locke's list of primary qualities, is not, despite what he says, that of impenetrability, but rather mass. There are three grounds for this interpretation. First, the concepts of solidity and density are easily run together; in common speech they mean much the same and there is a fair, although far from complete, correlation between density, strictly understood as mass per unit volume, and sensible hardness. Secondly, mass is an essential element in the vocabulary of classical mechanics. It is, indeed, the hero of the whole Newtonian drama, as is hardly surprising in a theory of gravitation. Finally, mass resembles the spatial qualities and differs from all other secondary qualities in being an extensive magnitude. But it is not a primary quality in the Cartesian sense. It is not a form of the occupancy of space, it is not accessible to both sight and touch and, most important, it is not an essential characteristic of material things. Kant rightly used 'all bodies are extended' as an unquestionable example of an analytic proposition and 'all bodies are heavy' as an unquestionable example of a synthetic one.

I argued earlier that the common characteristic of the primary objects of reference is their possession of a determinate spatial form. The idea of such a form is the idea of a thing in general that is embodied in our use of the word 'this' to refer to directly presented individuals. But possession of a determinate spatial form is much the same as the occupancy of space, accessible to both sight and touch, which, I have argued in this section, is, as Descartes held, the essential attribute of material things. What follows about the relation between primary individuals and material things? Are the two classes identical or is one, at any rate, included in the other?

There are two reasons for denying that all material things are primary individuals. The first is that being material is a property on a different level, so to speak, from being primary, in the sense involved here. Being material is an intrinsic characteristic of things which they possess independently of how any particular person comes to believe in their existence, whether by perception or inference. But things are not intrinsically primary; primacy is an epistemic not an ontological property. For a thing is primary to the extent that someone confronts it directly in perception as a possible object of the demonstrative 'this'. Thus a given material thing may be primary for me at one time, when I directly perceive it, and not at another, when I infer it, perhaps, as the cause of something I do perceive. Again, a thing may be primary for one observer but not for another who, perhaps, comes to accept its existence on the testimony of the first. In so far, then, as primacy is a varying, relative feature of things it cannot be strictly identical with materiality. But even if not all material things are primary they may all be in principle capable of being primary and all primary things may be material. The second reason for holding that not all material things are primary, however, also weighs against the modified claim that at least they are all capable of being primary. This is that there are unobservable material things. (The previous argument was, in effect, that there are unobserved ones.)

There are many different possible interpretations of the statement that a thing is unobservable. The first is the uninteresting one that it cannot be observed by me while I am situated as I am at the moment: I am too far away, there is a wall between us etc. Things unobservable for this reason are, by implication, capable of primacy. The second is, broadly speaking, that it is too small for me to perceive with my unaided senses. There is good reason to hold that there really are material things of this kind since in the case of something we can just see with the naked eye what we thus observe is confirmed and elaborated by what we can perceive of it with the help of a microscope. This analogy justifies our ascription of perceptual characteristics to things that we cannot perceive at all without microscopic help such as the larger molecules that can be 'seen' under the electron microscope. Such things, then, are material all right, but they are not, and could not be, primary. This is true *a fortiori* of things that are unobservable in a third sense, in that they cannot, as far as our present technique of assisted observation, or even any currently conceivable improvement of it, is concerned be observed at all, such as the smaller molecules or their parts. That there really are such things and that they are really material is strongly implied by the fact that we have methods, and sometimes independent, mutually confirming methods, of determining their size and mass. Yet these unobservables, have, it seems, no secondary qualities (and this is also strictly true, it could be argued, of the unobservables of the second class). Does this mean that the Cartesian principle I have been defending is after all false? It certainly needs modification to accommodate these cases. The point is that although, unlike common observables, things of this kind have neither colour nor texture, they do not have primary qualities alone. What distinguishes them from empty space is their causal properties, Locke's tertiary qualities. We can ascribe material existence to them because of their analogy of effect with common material things. Only observable things, then, must have some secondary qualities, must have colour or texture. Of material things in general we can say only that they must have some *non-primary* qualities if any primary qualities, and thus material existence, are to be ascribed to them. There is also a fourth class of unobservables, those whose observation is a logical impossibility in principle, something strictly inconceivable, a supposition without sense, such as gravitational forces. They are not important for our present purpose since there is little temptation to describe them as substantive material things. To them, at any rate, the descriptive or phenomenalist account given of theoretical entities by philosophers of science in the tradition of Mach seems straightforwardly applicable.

So far, then, it is clear that not all material things are either primary or capable of being primary. But material things that are not capable of being primary must rest their claim to existence on their analogy with material things that are. They must either be indirectly observable with observational aids whose reliability is attested by their application to common material things or they must, through their tertiary qualities, display an analogy of effect with common material things. These ordinary material things provide us, in the first instance, with the concept of a material thing in general. Secondly, they are the basis of the analogies on which the ascription of material existence to unobservables rests. Finally, it is from observation of common material things that we derive the evidence on which our inferences to unobservables depend. So, although not all material things are primary, some must be, since every material thing stands in a threefold relation of dependence on the primary, directly observable occupants of space.

We may now turn to the converse proposition that all primary things are material. It might appear that this is unquestionable in the terms of this discussion. For a primary thing has been defined as a directly perceived space-occupant and a material thing as any determinate space-occupant which is rendered perceivable in principle and distinguished from a region of empty space by the possession of secondary or tertiary qualities in addition to its primary, spatial, ones. It might be added that if the discussion hitherto has this consequence it collides with the prevailing philosophical tradition for which the primary things are not public objects, in a unitary, objective space, at all, but rather impressions or appearances. I shall argue for the position that all primary things are material in part II. For the moment it will be enough to point out that the issue has not been closed by the terms of the discussion so far. The vital point is that amongst the primary qualities which constitute the detailed exposition of the essential space-occupancy of matter has been included position which has throughout been understood as position in public, objective, unitary space. The other primary qualities have also been understood in this public, objective sense. Now although it is natural to interpret the possession of a determinate spatial form that constitutes the concept of a primary thing or thing in general in the same objective way it is not strictly necessary to do so. The question of whether the primary individuals are public or private has been left open. Nothing has been said which strictly rules out the possibility that the space in which they are to be found is private and momentary, that their shapes and sizes are apparent or phenomenal and that their position relative to other things is within a momentary perceptual space. I do, indeed, hold that the primary individuals are public material things but the proof of this must wait until part II. The answer to the present question will be given then.

Nouns and adjectives

The doctrine that a thing is a bundle of qualities can be understood as referring not to individual things (the form in which it was criticised in the first chapter) but to *kinds* of thing. This is, in effect, the position of the traditional theory of simple and complex ideas. In linguistic terms it is the view that nouns or substantives (and not singular terms) can be analysed as or reduced to conjunctions of adjectives. An examination of this theory will help to clarify the idea of a thing in general further.

In Locke's version of it simple ideas are conceived as adjectival or strictly qualitative concepts like green, dry and cold, while complex ideas are distinguished into modes, relations and substances. His thesis is that only simple ideas are given, all the varieties of complex ideas are derived from them and must be defined in terms of them. That modes are complex ideas in this sense is unproblematic since a mode simply is a definable adjectival or qualitative concept. The view that relations must be reducible to qualities was classically refuted by Russell who saw it as stemming from the traditional logical principle that every proposition must consist of a subject and a predicate and as responsible for a host of philosophical errors: monism, the rejection of universals, the denial of the reality of space and time. Russell's diagnosis is reasonable. There seems no better reason for Locke's view of relations than the fact that relational statements are referentially complex and, we might say, contain two or more subjects instead of one. But Russell reacted too strongly against the offending subject-predicate doctrine in coming near to neglecting it altogether, except in application to the residual class of statements with logically proper names as their subjects, and, more generally, by ignoring its correct implication that every statement must have a referential and a descriptive aspect. I have argued that this is true even of existential statements, the most favoured exception to the traditional view, maintaining that even in them a reference is made, though of an indeterminate kind and to a position rather than to an individual thing. The irreducibility of relations is most easily demonstrated in the case of asymmetrical relations of the form 'more ϕ than'. If a is more ϕ than b then a will be ϕ to an extent m and b will be ϕ to an extent n. But these are not equivalent assertions, since the first ascribes no specific amount to the extent of ϕ present in a and b. On the other hand 'a is more ϕ than b' cannot be analysed as 'there is some x and some y such as a is ϕ to extent x and b to extent y' unless the further and relational condition is added 'x is greater than y'. It follows that some relational concepts must be indefinable and thus be acquired ostensively.

What of the substantival concepts expressed by nouns? Among these, of course, are to be found the thing-predicates whose occurrence in indications is required for our acquisition of the idea of a thing in general and thus for our understanding of the word 'this' and our mastery of the technique of reference to individuals. It was part of my argument for this position that there is an essential difference of kind between qualitative and substantival concepts. If substantival concepts of kinds of thing are, in Locke's sense, complex ideas and so reducible to conjunctions of adjectival qualities this distinction cannot be maintained.

There are two preliminary considerations that weigh against the traditional theory about the reducibility of nouns. The first is that, as a matter of fact, the first predicates that are learned are substantival and not adjectival. So even if nouns can in principle be learnt by way of their definition in terms of adjectives this is not in practice the way in which they do come to be understood. But does this admission about practice have any theoretical consequences? The second consideration is that the equations between nouns and conjunctions of adjectives that are demanded by the theory do not hold water. Consider some simple substantival concept or natural kind like lemon. Most lemons are yellow, but some are green and rotten ones have even richer hues. Most lemons are sour but over-ripe ones are fairly sweet. Most lemons have a characteristic lemony flavour but some taste of nothing at all. In general lemons will vary quite widely in most of their quality-ranges even if there is a fairly high statistical concentration at some part of each such range.

But a further difficulty about these required translations is of a more fundamentally destructive nature. This is that even if lemons did possess a strictly proprietary set of qualitative characteristics something would still have been left out of the equation, namely 'something'. In these circumstances 'there is a lemon on the table' would mean 'there is *something* yellowy, sour and lemon-flavoured on the table'. This additional element is, of course, the characteristic determinate spatial form of lemons, the shape and size which, within a much smaller range than their other variations of character, lemons have. Now we can call the possession of this spatial form 'being lemon-shaped' for short and thus give it a qualitative appearance. But being lemon-shaped is different from the other qualities of lemons for it enables them to be individuated and counted. Yellowness, sourness and lemon-flavour can be instantiated all over the place, in a spatially wholly indeterminate way. But an instance of being lemon-shaped is clearly demarcated from its spatial surroundings.

There is a parallel between this situation and the position reached in discussing the thesis that an individual thing is a bundle of qualities. In one way that thesis is correct, if, that is, qualities are taken widely enough to include positional properties. But there is a very good reason for distinguishing the positional from the other properties of things and if they are excluded from the set of qualities then the bundle theory, in this interpretation, is false. Similarly here, if having a determinate spatial form is included along with the other characteristic features of a natural kind, then the total set of qualities thus enumerated is sufficient to define the kind. But there is a good reason not to include being of a determinate spatial form, which it should be remembered involves size as well as shape, along with the rest. Symptomatic of it is the fact that the only words we have for such spatial forms in most cases are derived from the substantival words for the natural kinds they define. Being of a determinate spatial form is the same as being a thing in the primary sense of the term. As long as its peculiar importance is recognised, and its consequent radical difference from qualities in the ordinary sense, the theory of substantival concepts as complexes of adjectival ones can be allowed to stand. But it will be standing in borrowed clothing. For an essential member of any set of adjectival concepts adequate to the definition of a natural kind will be the concept of a determinate spatial form which will be adjectival only in form.

To accord this central place to determinate spatial form in substantival concepts of natural kinds is not to say that spatial form (shape and size) is generally, or even ever, sufficient to define that kind. Natural, and, even more, artificial, surrogates abound: life-size statues of politicians, wax fruit, toy revolvers. As Hampshire has pointed out it is commonly an essential part of our concept of a natural kind that its instances should have had a certain sort of origin or, less commonly, should have a certain sort of effect (Hampshire (4), pp. 47–50). A real orange will remain distinct in kind from the most brilliant piece of laboratory fabrication in virtue of its early life on an orange tree. And a real revolver is distinguished from a replica that can be used only for purposes of display by the fact that it can fire bullets. But Hampshire goes too far in taking origin and effects totally to displace appearance, their directly visible properties, from the definition of natural kinds. No doubt some functional kinds like knives and chairs exhibit a wide range of dissimilar spatial forms and other directly perceptible qualities, but most natural kinds have a less qualitatively various membership and even here there is something like a statistically normal spatial form for the kind. These are, after all, artificial rather than natural kinds in the strict sense.

The ultimate error of the traditional theory of simple and complex ideas is that it inverts both the historical and the logical order of things and qualities. It is not just accident or convenience that leads to the prior learning of nouns. We need nouns, first, to sustain the practice of reference to individuals without which adjectival concepts of qualities cannot play their accustomed part in discourse and, secondly, because qualities, as ordinarily understood, are insufficient to introduce them. The use of thing- or natural kind-predicates is, then, presupposed by the use of quality-predicates and cannot be rendered intelligible in terms of the use of quality-predicates. Although substantival concepts of natural kinds are complex in a sense, their complexity is of a sort that can be elicited only by subsequent analysis. In terms of the history of the learning process and of the logical order of dependence which that history reflects they are the simplest of ideas.

3

Identity

Identity and the necessity of continuants

Contemporary discussions of meaning and reference, and general recognition of the need for distinguishing between them, derive from Frege's famous essay on the subject. That essay begins by considering the peculiar nature of statements of identity. If we say that A is identical to B it seems that what we say must be either trivial, if it simply identifies A with itself, or false, if it identifies A with something other than itself. Frege's solution is that a substantial statement of identity must contain two singular terms that differ in meaning but which will, if the statement is true, have exactly the same reference. A further feature of identity statements about concrete individuals that has come to be recognised is that the A and B of an identity-statement must be taken to fall under or be instances of the same substantival concept of a thing or natural kind (cf. Geach (2), p. 39). What makes an identity-statement of this kind true is the reference by the singular terms involved to individuals at the same position. No doubt our *evidence* of identity is often a matter of strictly qualitative identity but what it is evidence *for* is identity of position.

Questions of identity arise wherever an individual is capable of being referred to by singular terms that differ in meaning. In general the main kinds of identity-question can be classified by reference to the distinct modes of access to individuals that lie behind these differences. Many kinds of identity-question arise about contemporaneous individuals whose identity of temporal position is thus assured. Is the person at whose face I am looking at the party the same as the person who is standing on my foot? Is the cheese I can see the same as the cheese I can smell? Is the boy I can see through the window the boy who is making that dreadful noise? These are all cases of identification of the objects of different senses. But questions of identity arise about contemporaneous objects of the

57

same sense. Above the fence I may see a row of blooms, one handsome, the others dejected, and through a gap in the fence I may see an equal number of stalks. To steal my neighbour's best flower I need to know which stalk goes with which bloom, in other words which flower is which. A third type of question concerns interpersonal identity: are you and I looking at and talking about the same car? Again we are called upon to decide on the identity of the perceived and the described, of individuals referred to demonstratively, 'this man', and by description, 'the plumber who promised to arrive at this time'.

But the most philosophically important and interesting problem of identity concerns identity through time. It is clear that by far the greater part of the concrete things we refer to are continuants, in the sense not merely that they occupy some finite extent of time greater than an instant but that they endure for long enough to be the objects of distinct acts of observation which are separated by intervals of time during which the things in question are not being observed at all. The individuals of whose existence we are strictly assured by observation are, in a sense, momentary, although we ordinarily take them to have previous and subsequent histories. It would be more correct to say that we observe individuals as they are at the moment of observation than that we observe phases or temporal slices of continuants or that we observe events, as some philosophers, Russell for example, have maintained. Events, in the ordinary sense of the word, involve things or continuants: a quarrel needs quarrellers, a revolution revolutionaries, a rainstorm sheets of rain. Events, we might say, are tied to verbs. The characteristic way in which we refer to them is with the aid of verbal nouns: her leap, his fall, its disintegration. And verbs need subjects. But like many facts about usage this is worth noticing only to ignore in full consciousness of what one is doing. The point of Russell's, no doubt unwitting, linguistic innovation was to find a convenient word for momentary individuals. Many events, in the colloquial sense of the word, are not momentary individuals at all. Looking from time to time through my neighbours' bedroom window I can see the same quarrel going on. If I am quick about it I can have two temporally distinct glimpses of one and the same dive, most obviously if someone walks in between me and the diver while the dive is going on. Against the view that what we observe and refer to are the momentary parts or phases of enduring things is the fact that while the current phase or slice of the car in front of me is at rest, is empty, did not exist before now and will not exist after now, none of this is true of the car itself which is not always at rest and empty and has a past and a future. What I see and refer to, after all, is strictly identical with something that exists at other times, but a momentary phase is necessarily distinct from anything that exists at any other time than its moment of existence. That we observe continuing things and not their momentary phases is a necessary consequence of the fact that we conceive things as retaining their identity through time. The tendency of philosophers to suppose that we observe only phases can be attributed to the Irish or paradox-producing implication of identity statements that two distinct things are one and the same. But although we assume, and ordinarily assume correctly, that the things we observe endure, have a past and a future lying outside the specious present or period of observation, all that we strictly observe is that there is a thing of a certain description here and now, which may but may also not stretch out temporally in both directions.

It is of the first importance that the things we observe are not momentary and do endure. For on this fact rests the spatio-temporal unity of the world. The field of a single momentary observation constitutes a momentary space in which a number of contemporaneous individuals stand in various spatial relations to one another. A place in such a space must be defined by reference to some individual thing within it. No place in the space of a later observation can be identified with or in any other way related to any place in the earlier unless one of the individual landmarks of the earlier space can be identified with something in the later space. It is also necessary that the enduring landmark should be understood not to have moved during the intervening period. Without continuants to serve as enduring landmarks observation would confront us with a sequence of distinct and wholly unrelated spaces, a series of self-contained and isolated worlds.

The construction of a unitary world with a single space may be conceived in this way. We first identify as many as possible of the constituents of one momentary space with constituents of its closest temporal successor. We then pick out the persisting individuals common to the two spaces whose spatial relations to their contemporaries differ least as between the two momentary spaces. These constitute the stable framework of unmoving things for the period covered by the two moments involved. In this choice we follow a principle of economy, a choice of landmarks which involves the minimum admission of spatial movement. We then repeat the process with pairs of subsequent, temporally neighbouring, momentary spaces. Momentary spaces that are not neighbours thus need not have any common individual constituents and, therefore, need not have any landmarks in common. Space 1 might contain a man sitting on a chair in front of a picture of a mountain and beside him a woman on a bench in front of a picture of a stag. Space 2 could then contain the bench still in front of the stag picture but with the woman now standing beside it while next to her there is a boy on a stool in front of a potted palm. In space 3 the boy is still in front of the potted palm but he now holds the stool in his hands and there is something else next to him. Here the woman is no longer observably present in space 3 and she will be taken to have moved, relative to the bench and the stag, between 1 and 2. If the stag in the picture was looking towards or away from both the man and the boy we shall say the boy and the man were in the same place, even though they were never observed together in one momentary space.

In chapter 1 it was argued that individuals owed their unique individuality to their position in space and time. However, it does not follow from this that nothing can be individuated until the conception of a unitary space has been arrived at. Momentary things and contemporaneous things can be individuated without recourse to the notion of an enduring unitary space. If the momentary things are not contemporaneous they are individuated by the time of their occurrence. Contemporaneous things, whether momentary or not, are individuable by reference to their distinct positions in momentary space. Similarly momentary things and contemporaneous things are identifiable by their identity of position in momentary space. The non-temporal questions of identity listed in the second paragraph of this section all concern contemporaneous things. In the first case I want to know if the person I can see is the person who is treading on my foot. Here I observe contemporaneous bits of persons and I settle the question by tracing the full extent of the two bits and seeing if they coincide spatially. The examples of the highly aromatic cheese and the noisy boy bring out a difficulty that is present but concealed in this example but is absent from the case of the bloom and the stalk. By sight I tell that the foot I see treading on my own is part of the same human body as the face I am now looking at. But how do I tell that the foot I *see* treading on mine is the same as the thing I feel pressing on it? How, in general, do we identify the objects of sight and touch? In the first place, it would seem, by the reliable connection between the visible coincidence of the finger, or some other part of the surface of the body, with a material thing and the awareness of tactual qualities or, broadly speaking, tactual experience. If the only change that accompanies a noticeable change in what is felt is the coming into contact of the finger and an object and if the breaking of the contact is, all else remaining the same, accompanied by a reversal of the change in what is felt, it is natural to identify the visible touching with the feeling, to conclude that the very same thing is touched as is felt. Similar contingent connections underlie the identification of the smelt or heard with the seen. Broadly speaking if a smell or sound is found to vary in intensity with the visible proximity of a thing that thing is identified with the source of the smell or sound.

As far as contemporaneous things are concerned, then, and this includes all identification of momentary things since they can be identical only if they are contemporaneous, identity is simply identity in spatial position. The stalk and the bloom, of course, are not identical in position, only connected in a certain way. But then they are not the same thing, they are distinct parts of the same thing. Seeing a bloom or a bit of stalk I infer that, in the usual way, there is a whole flower there. And there is strict identity of position as between the flower to which the bloom belongs and the flower to which the stalk belongs.

But there are two reasons why identity in spatial position appears inadequate to account for the identity through time of enduring things. The first is, simply enough, that enduring things move. They retain their identity through time despite changes in their positions in space. A thing can be in only one place at one time but it can be in many different places at different times. Secondly, even if a thing was at rest throughout its history its identity would be one of enduring and not momentary position. It would be at the same place in unitary space but, as persisting through time, it would have to be at different momentary places. This raises a serious difficulty since enduring place in unitary space depends on the prior identification of continuants or persisting things. The identification of things through time, it appears, cannot in general be defined in terms of their spatial position since the only relevant kind of spatial position that can be ascribed to them requires the antecedent identification of enduring things.

Enduring, identifiable things retain their identity through time despite change in qualities as well as change in position. So qualitative identity is not a necessary condition of the identity of an enduring thing. It is not a sufficient condition either. Two qualitatively identical things present at different times at the same place may well be distinct. If the dog eats my hat I may buy a replica and leave it for most of the time hanging on the same hook as its predecessor in the hall.

These peculiarities about identity suggest that we should at least give serious consideration to the view that the identity of things through time is due to the presence in them of an identifying component or substance, an identifier, as I shall call it.

Substance as identifier

It has been said that the theory of an identifying substance rests on the argument that because a thing changes it does not change (Anscombe, pp. 3–4). This is a little unkind. Although enduring things change through time in a variety of respects they still remain the same things at the end of the process, if it is one of change and not one of annihilation or complete replacement. We must recognise a difference, in other words, between substantial change, in which things come into and go out of existence, and qualitative change, through which things continue to exist although different predicates come to be true of them. The argument for an identifying substance would seem to be that since it appears that any of the qualities, in the widest sense and including the positional qualities, of a thing may change without loss of identity by the thing itself (an assumption I shall reject later), the only item left to persist unaltered is what has these qualities. The conclusion of the positive theory of individuation is then drawn on to provide an account of the unchanging element. It is not surprising that a certain amount of mystery should attend this conclusion since there is, in a way, nothing left for the identifying substance to be.

If the arguments of chapter 1 are correct this is an illegitimate employment of the notion of individuating substance. For individuating substance is simply position and, as far as the identity of things through time is concerned, position is one of the aspects of things that undergoes change, necessarily in time and possibly in space. Although it is true that there is more to a thing than its qualities, narrowly construed, it does not follow that there is more to a thing than the succession of its temporally distinct phases. For the successive phases of an enduring thing are themselves individuals, qualities manifested at an individuating position.

What could this identifying substance be? It cannot be qualities proper or position alone or in conjunction since both of these may change without interfering with the identity through time of their possessor. It must, then, be some part or component of the thing, an individual element of the whole thing which by its special stability of character confers identity through time on the whole in which it is contained. The classical form of this doctrine is the substance theory of the Ionian cosmologists, reaching its fullest development in the atomism of Democritus, which traces the identity of a thing to the total set of its ultimate parts. According to this doctrine there are one or several kinds of stuff or element out of which everything in the world is made. An ordinary concrete thing is made up of a great deal of this stuff or a great number of these atomic elements. Its changes are to be explained in terms of changes in the condition of the stuff, for example by its rarefaction and condensation in the view of Anaximenes, or by a rearrangement of its constituent atoms. Thales initiated this line of thought with his conception of a single, qualitatively homogeneous world-stuff as the raw material from which the world of differentiated, changing things was made. Anaximander conceived the ultimate stuff to be boundless, transcendent and without qualities in a self-destructive attempt to achieve complete generality. The high metaphysical path begun by his speculations led in the end to the doctrines of Parmenides and Heraclitus, who, instead of solving the problem, eliminated it by denying the reality of one of the colliding terms in need of reconciliation; Parmenides denying the reality of change and Heraclitus the reality of permanence. Anaximenes developed the more realistic side of Thales' hypothesis, offering an explanation of the observed qualitative variety of the world which anticipated atomism by tracing this variety to the spatial distribution of the stuff of which the world was made. Empedocles allowed four and Anaxagoras indefinitely many kinds of ultimate stuff, producing change and variety by their combination and separation. With the atomists the ultimate stuff of the world is finally seen as a set of homogeneous individual things, characterised by unchanging spatial form or primary qualities, arranged in changing configurations in empty space.

Atomism in this sense has a respectable empirical foundation since much observable change is clearly due to the rearrangement of constituent parts that do not change themselves in quality but only in relative position. The assumption of its universal truth has, together with that of the principle of universal causation, governed all fruitful investigation of nature until very recent times. So it is natural that the solution it proposes to the problem of the identity of things through time should have secured support. The solution it proposes is that two complex things existing at different times are in fact one and the same thing if they are composed of exactly the same atoms. This compositional theory of identity received its best-known explicit formulation in Locke's account of the identity through time of inorganic bodies (Locke, p. 442).

It is significant that Locke confined his compositionalism to inorganic bodies, for it testifies to his recognition of the fact that many complex things retain their identity despite replacement of their components. Living creatures may retain their identity for long enough for this replacement to be complete. But this consideration applies to inorganic bodies as well. It is certainly false that any material thing has to retain *all* its original components in order to retain its identity. A building remains the same building even if the entire roof has to be replaced, let alone a single slate. Furthermore a material thing retains its identity if *any* of its components is replaced; things have no specially privileged, identity-bearing parts. It must be admitted that if the entire composition of a material object is replaced in a single operation, if, for example, a house is demolished and a qualitatively similar structure is put up in the same place, its identity is lost. But if the process of replacing its components is gradual, if only a small proportion of the total composition is replaced at any one time, identity is retained. So although identity of component parts is not wholly unconnected to identity through time it is by no means a necessary condition of that identity. Neither all the parts nor any single part is necessary to the whole. The most that is required for identity is that replacement of parts should be continuous, that at no time is the whole composition of the thing or the greater part of its composition replaced at one time.

It should also be noted that the compositional theory does not provide a sufficient condition of identity, except in a very weak sense. If a knitter makes a scarf out of a large ball of wool the scarf and the ball of wool are not the same thing, nor are the statue and the lump of clay a sculptor makes it out of. Temporally distinct things are only identical under a certain description, as instances of one substantival concept, and a scarf is not a ball of wool nor a ball of wool a scarf. Of course, the scarf and the ball of wool are made of the same stuff and if the scarf is unknitted and the material it was made of rolled into a ball it could perhaps be said that the ball the knitter wound up with was the same ball as the one she started with, but it would be more natural to say simply that it was the same wool. Now these examples are of the type most favourable to the thesis that identity of components is a sufficient condition for the identity of things. Ordinarily where stuff is transformed into a thing the process is irreversible, as in cooking or carving or natural growth. Here there can be no reversion to the state of being a low-grade thing or piece of stuff to provide a link with the earlier state of the same kind. And even where there can be, the decomposed assemblage that results is not identifiable with the decomposed thing. A mechanic who, pointing to a collection of electronic bits and pieces on his bench, says 'that is your radio' is speaking figuratively. Unless I am assured that he can rebuild it I am right to say that I have no radio, that my radio has been destroyed.

There is a practical point about the compositional theory of identity that should be considered. If Locke's account of the identity of inorganic bodies were correct our judgments of identity would all be, to say the least, of a highly conjectural character. We ordinarily know very little about the composition of the material things around us and what we do know is entirely general, relating to the composition of things of that kind and not the composition of those particular things. Our judgments of identity are not in fact based on evidence of ultimate components and we should be very hard put to it if they had to be. We know next to nothing about the individual atoms, in the physical sense, of which the material things around us are made and on some interpretations of their nature, as logical constructions or Machian devices for economy of thought, it is difficult to understand what we could know of them as individuals. In general the kind of physical investigation which would be needed to acquire knowledge about individual atoms would require a kind of continuous attention to material things which would presuppose the ability to identify them through time. The grounds for judgments of identity demanded by the compositional theory are as inaccessible in practice as they are irrelevant in principle.

This is not to say that some judgments of identity are not of a more or less compositional kind. There are some things, rather unstable and impermanent collections of more readily identifiable elements, that we do identify as a result of the prior identification of their constituents. Jones's library, Smith's furniture, Miss Robinson's clothes are all examples of what may be called assemblages. They refer to aggregates of things which are not conceived to be arranged or mutually disposed in any particular way. We may use their usual configuration or position—on Jones's bookshelves, in Smith's flat, on Miss Robinson—as a means of identifying them but this is a very contingent criterion of their identity and it may well mislead us. The elements making up these assemblages, on the other hand, will have a reasonably determinate spatial form and other persisting qualities in virtue of which they are readily identifiable on a second encounter. But compositional judgments of identity do seem restricted to the case of assemblages of this kind and the components involved are not atoms but straightforward material things: books, chairs and undergarments.

I stated the compositional theory as defining the identity of complex things in terms of the identity of their atomic components. The crucial limitation of this theory is that it provides no account of the identity of the atoms themselves. In his account of the identity of inorganic bodies Locke ignores this limitation. The consequence is that his theory is viciously regressive. For the atoms of which ordinary inorganic bodies are composed are inorganic bodies themselves. If they are to do what the theory requires them to do they must persist in time and so an account of their identity through time is required.

Classical atomism conceived its atoms as having a fixed and determinate spatial form. But even if atoms each retained their spatial form throughout their history, and thus remained qualitatively the same at all times, for their only qualities are spatial ones, they would still pose a problem of identity. If each atom had a spatial form which could be shared by other atoms we should need to know how to tell which of two identically shaped atoms existing at one time, if either, should be identified with an atom of the same form existing at a later time. Furthermore it is hard to see how the thesis that atoms are qualitatively stable is to be established, since it would appear to be a contingent matter, unless individual atoms could be identified for the purposes of investigation in this respect in some fashion which did not rely on their qualitative fixity. If atoms were defined as those things which retained their spatial form at all times the weight of the difficulty would merely be shifted. It would now be a very open question as to whether material things were wholly composed of atoms in this sense.

Except, then, in the rather special case of assemblages, identity of composition is neither a necessary nor a sufficient condition for the identity of things. If it were it would follow that judgments about the identity of things would be practically impossible to establish. Finally they would be impossible to establish in principle unless some independent account were given of the identity of atomic components. We must clearly look elsewhere for an adequate theory of the identity of persisting things through time.

Spatial continuity

If the judgments of identity through time that we actually make about things are considered it is clear that something wholly ignored by the compositional theory plays a very important part: the position in space occupied by identical things at different stages of their careers. The simplest case is that of the great natural stabilities like mountains and rivers, the major geographical features which serve as landmarks for our more careful and impersonal judgments of spatial position. The point about these things is that they occur or exist at the same place at all times. But many things move about, so identity of place is not a necessary condition of identity. Mobile things do not, however, have complete freedom of movement. It is required that they should follow a continuous path in space, that, roughly speaking, their position at one time shall be either identical with or very close to their position at closely neighbouring times. Two things can be identical, then, only if there is a continuous spatial path between the places at which they occur.

This requirement is obviously insufficient as it stands since there is an infinite number of continuous spatial paths between any two distinct places in space. The implied further requirement is that the thing in question should have occupied neighbouring positions on some continuous spatial path between the two places at all neighbouring times in the period of time involved. But this way of putting the matter is still unsatisfactory since it refers to the thing in question and thus presupposes that the question of identity can be settled in some independent way. What we should say, perhaps, is that A at t1 at p1 is identical with B at t2 at p2 provided that there is a spatially continuous path between p1 and p2 on every pair of neighbouring

66

points of which there are at neighbouring moments of the interval from t1 to t2 qualitatively identical things.

Some enduring things satisfy this requirement: fortunate and well-cared-for cars, carefully guarded statues or paintings made of durable materials. But many things change in qualities as well as position with the passage of time: all organic things like men and plants, and all inorganic things exposed and sensitive to wear and tear. These cases, perhaps, can be accommodated by replacing the requirement of qualitative identity by one of qualitative continuity modelled on that of spatial continuity. We should then say that A at t1 at p1 is identical with B at t2 at p2 provided that there is a continuous spatial path between p1 and p2 on every pair of neighbouring points of which there are closely qualitatively similar things at neighbouring moments of the interval from t1 to t2.

This is still not quite correct. Suppose I put a log on the fire and it burns away to a small heap of grey ash. For convenience we may assume that all the other combustible materials that went with it to make up the fire turn into a loosely distributed mass of black ash. In this example the limiting case of spatial continuity is exhibited, namely spatial identity. Between the time at which the log was put on the fire and the time when the heap of grey ash is observed in the very same place there is to be found a pair of closely qualitatively similar things at every pair of neighbouring moments during the period of time involved. The log changes into ash continuously. There is no precise moment at which we can say that the log no longer exists and the heap of ash has come into existence. Nevertheless the log has ceased to exist during the process and the heap of ash has come into existence. And the log and the heap of ash are not the same thing. What must be added to the definition at the end of the last paragraph is the condition that A and B and the set of qualitatively similar things that connect them should all be things of the same kind, that they should all fall under the same substantival concept. This has the effect of limiting the range of admissible qualitative variation in a way for which there is no parallel in the condition of spatial continuity. Enduring things have to retain their general substantival nature through time but they may go anywhere, they are not restricted to a particular region of space. The initial assumption that a thing can retain its identity whatever qualitative changes it undergoes, which encouraged the supposition that some transcendent non-qualitative item is the true bearer of identity, is thus mistaken. Descartes's piece of wax is not the same *thing* after it melts; it is only the same *stuff*.

It might be thought that if this condition of identity of substantival kind is introduced the condition of qualitative continuity can be dispensed with since the new condition automatically imposes a limit on the amount of qualitative change consistent with the retention of identity. This is, no doubt, correct in practice. But the range of qualitative variation to be found in the instances of a given substantival concept is often very large. Suppose that at the place where, until this moment, there was a large black limousine of the sort favoured by funeral directors, there is now suddenly a small red sports car of the sort favoured by men anxious to stem the onset of middle age. Now in fact when such an event occurs there is always a spatially continuous path between the parking place occupied by the sports car and some other place where the limousine is trundling away, all points of which are occupied by temporal parts of a limousine and another spatial path connecting the parking place to some place where a sports car was, all points of which are occupied by temporal parts of a sports car. In other words, we can always find a suitable ancestor for the sports car now before us and a descendant for the limousine that was in its place before. But suppose no sports car is to be found before now, and no limousine now or afterwards, anywhere near the parking place in question. If assured of this, and we should take a good deal of assuring, we might say that the limousine had turned into a sports car. But we might just as well say that the limousine had been annihilated and that the sports car had just come into existence. If the requirement of qualitative continuity is dropped this second alternative is closed. We are then compelled to say that the limousine and the sports car are one and the same car. But if the requirement is retained we are not compelled to distinguish between the two. Our doubt about their identity corresponds to the imprecision of the concept of close qualitative similarity. The two cars are, after all, qualitatively similar to a considerable extent. If the limousine turns into a sports car in a qualitatively continuous way, if its shape, size and colour change gradually and not abruptly, we should be content to regard both as phases in the history of one, unusually plastic or organic-seeming car. On the other hand, it could be argued that things can exhibit equally pronounced qualitative discontinuities over short periods of time, as when they are involved in some such catastrophe as an explosion, impact with a very heavy or solid object or a fire. This might seem to settle the matter in favour of abandoning the requirement of qualitative similarity. But that is a rather pedestrian view of the situation. In these catastrophes qualitative change is not discontinuous, it is just more rapid than usual. If the state of the thing at very closely neighbouring times is considered, as it might be with the help of a slow motion film, it will be seen that the qualitative changes taking place are still gradual, they do not have the instantaneous abruptness of the transmogrification of a fairy tale. On the other hand, once again, it may be said that things were identified across incidents of catastrophic change long before the slow motion camera was invented. But even then qualitative continuity was believed in, on analogical grounds, although there was no direct evidence for it. In view of all this it seems not imprudent to claim that the requirement of qualitative continuity can be added to spatial continuity and identity of substantival kind as constitutive of the criterion for the identity of things through time.

It is a consequence of the definition I have given of identity through time that if a thing exists at two distinct times it must exist at all times in between them. Yet there are things which seem to retain their identity across intervals bounded by destruction at one end and reconstitution at the other. Suppose a historic tiara is stolen, its component jewels sold separately and fitted into new settings. During this period the tiara does not exist. Now suppose that the original setting is discovered in the cupboard of some thieves' kitchen and that the original jewels are assembled and put back in their original places in it. The resulting object is, pretty clearly, the original tiara over again. In this case a compositional criterion of identity is employed. The reconstituted tiara is identified with its historic predecessor in virtue of being made of the same components in the same arrangement. The continuity criterion is certainly presupposed by this identification but it is not directly invoked in it. We have already seen that we do use a compositional criterion in practice in the case of what I called assemblages and there would be no objection on the score of regressiveness to adding a compositional criterion to the continuity criterion we already have. (It would be in terms of identical observable parts and not identical atoms.)

We can conceive as an imaginative possibility that there might be things which went wholly out of existence to be replaced at the same position by something qualitatively indistinguishable from them some time afterwards. What makes this easy to conceive is that many small objects of personal use like collar-studs and fountain pens behave, for all practical purposes, as if they were of this nature. But in fact if we really believed what in our exasperation we are sometimes tempted to say, we should not know whether to identify the newly existing thing with its predecessor or not. Our concept of identity is simply not determinate in this respect. We are prepared to accord identity to the temporal parts of an interrupted thing on a compositional basis, that is if its continuously existing parts survive, in the ordinary way, a temporary cessation of the relationships that make a particular whole out of them. But we are not in fact confronted with any cases of temporally discontinuous things which invite us to identify them in which the problem cannot be solved in compositional terms.

In saying earlier that concrete things were extended in space and time it was not strictly implied that they were continuous in either domain. But in both domains, continuity is very much the usual case. To say that things are spatially continuous, in this sense, is not to say that they are what might be called *dense*, that they occupy every point within their spatial boundaries at any one moment in the way that, commonsensically, a cannonball does, but rather that, as with a net, there is a path in space lying wholly within the thing connecting any point in the thing with any other point in it. Generally speaking things that are spatially continuous to this extent move about as wholes, do not change their shape or disintegrate if a force is applied to one particular part of them. We learn from physics that this type of continuity is only apparent, that a tree is as much made up of spatially isolated constituents as the orchard of which it is a part. But there is still a difference between perceptual connectedness and separateness and perceptual connectedness is very highly correlated with independent movability without loss of shape. Likewise there are temporally disconnected things, like the tiara, but they are comparatively exceptional. In both cases the identity of the disconnected whole can be traced to that of its disconnected parts.

We do not ordinarily observe the whole of the spatial and temporal extent of things. Opaque objects have backs and most objects have pasts and futures. But it is not inconceivable that the whole spatial or temporal extent of a thing should be accessible to a single observation. There are decorative spheres of clear glass which conceal nothing from the observer's eye and there are very badly made things which fall to pieces the moment their manufacture has been completed or unfortunately fragile things which meet disaster at the same pathetically early stage in their careers. Now ordinarily when we see some material thing, an umbrella in a stand for example, we could just as truly say that we had seen some part of the umbrella, its handle, say, as that we had seen the thing itself. But to see any *temporal* part of a thing is to see the thing itself. Although we see things only as they are at the moment of observation we do not see temporal parts or slices of things. I suggest that the reason for this convention is that the substantival concept under which a thing falls specifies its spatial form and, in so doing, that of its spatial parts. But nothing is implied about the temporal extent of a thing by the substantival concept in terms of which we identify it through time. Dogs may last from ten minutes to ten years, porcelain bowls from ten seconds to ten centuries. Furthermore the spatial parts of a thing will ordinarily be things of a different substantival kind. The papal crown which is made of crowns is a highly exceptional case. But the temporal parts of a thing are of the same substantival kind as the thing itself, in the sense that had they existed alone a thing of that kind would still have existed. But the handle of an umbrella on its own is not an umbrella. This feature of temporally extended things is, of course, built into our criterion of identity through time.

Hume said that identity through time was a fiction. In the same spirit Whitehead and Russell have said that the notion of persisting things is one of those Aristotelian relics of which philosophy should be purged, that a persisting thing is simply a law-like series of events. In so far as this way of speaking is a protest against the view that identity through time is conferred on things by some unchanging and presumably unobservable identifier, present like a registration number through all qualitative vicissitudes, it is justified. On the other hand, there is nothing illusory or fictitious about enduring continuants. Unless there were such things we should be unable to conceive a spatio-temporally unitary world. We can define a continuant in terms of its temporal parts, as a series of events, thing-slices or momentary individuals, related by identity of substantival kind and continuity in qualities and spatial position. But this is not to define identity, it is to define temporal wholes in terms of relations between their temporal parts which although they are parts of identical things are not identical to each other.

The mutual dependence of things and places

There is a difficulty about this kind of account of the identity of things through time in terms of spatial continuity which we must now consider. It is, very briefly, that places, or at any rate the places involved, are themselves persisting things of a sort. In order to identify two similar things, A' and A'', I have to establish that the places at which they are to be found, p' and p'', are identical or connected by a continuous path. But in order to say anything about the relation of p' and p'' I have to have the notion of a persisting space. It was argued in the first section of this chapter that the only way in which momentary spaces could be unified into a persisting space and sense be given to assertions about spatial relations through time was by defining positions in momentary spaces in terms of persisting continuants, in particular that set of continuants which could be regarded as unmoving in virtue of their preservation of relative contemporaneous position at all times. Thus without enduring things we cannot form the conception of enduring places and without enduring places we cannot identify enduring things. This is unquestionably a vicious circle.

It is natural in the face of this problem to look for some kind of privileged continuant, whose identity can be established without recourse to independently specified identity or continuity of spatial position. Such primary continuants would provide us with a foundation for our conception of a unitary space and this could then be drawn on for further identification of persisting things. In a detailed discussion of this problem Wiggins has considered three possible kinds of primary continuant (Wiggins (1), p. 180). The first of these is myself, or, since we are concerned here with establishment of position in space, myself as a spatial entity, in other words my body. The second is the here-and-now. The third is those things that are continuously observed throughout a period of time during which other things begin and cease to be observed.

The real objection to the first two is that they in fact move about and that since each yields only a single, and of course exactly the same, continuant they do not provide enough material for the fixing of position in three dimensions. Since the here-and-now is the position of my body we can treat these two proposals from now on as the same. In order to arrive at the conception of an enduring space we need stable points of reference. Now I could take the position of my body as fixed and on this basis ascribe at least continuity of position in space to the things, moving or at rest in fact, in my observational environment. The main objection to the resulting notion of space would be that it would produce an exceedingly cumbrous account of the movement of other things, one whose complexity would make it unnecessarily hard to establish laws of motion. The difficulty that the position of my body does not provide enough information to fix the position of other things could be overcome by exploiting the asymmetries of the body itself: up and down, front and back, and that notoriously weak one, left and right. The here-and-now alone would be insufficient for this purpose. What would encourage the identification of my body through time would be its ubiquitous, if somewhat marginal, presence in the field of observation. It is, in fact, a particular case of continuous observation. The fact that it is very seldom at the focus of attention, at least of the kind of visual attention from which the idea of space is derived, is an additional weakness. It is not an objection that without the recognition of other things than my body I should not be in a position to call it 'my body'. For these purposes I do not have to refer to it in this way. I could call it 'the body' or, in a more social setting, 'the largest body' or even 'the nearest body'.

There is, in fact, no fundamental difference of principle between taking my body or any other things I observe continuously as primary continuants. But things other than my body are to be preferred, first, because being plural they allow the application of the majority principle to determine which are stable and afford a sufficiently complex positional scheme to make the precise specification of enduring positions possible and, secondly, because they are more naturally conceived as occupying a central place in the focus of the relevant kind of attention.

We may imagine a conceptual Adam looking out on the world that has been created for him. In his field of view will be a number of things of definite shapes, qualitatively demarcated from their surroundings. At any moment he can distinguish these from one another, and thus individuate them, by their distinct positions in the space of that moment of observation. As he placidly contemplates the scene it varies. Where there were four things arranged as the corners of a square there come to be three things arranged as the corners of an isosceles right-angled triangle and a fourth thing to be found at positions progressively more distant from the group. If there are no interruptions to his survey it is the most natural thing in the world for him to identify the members of the trio as unmoving continuants and the fourth thing as a moving one. Before the fourth thing disappears a new thing moves in and, after the fourth thing has disappeared, comes to occupy what he can now identify as its original place at the fourth corner of the square. Then, when, as we should say, he slightly turns his head, the left hand side of the field of view disappears and new things appear to the right of the remainder. He turns his head back, the newcomers depart and qualitative and positional replicas of the original left hand side appear. It is no large leap of thought for him to suppose that the original left hand side has been reinstated. As time passes none of the original contents of the field remain that have occupied it without interruption. But their successors, or they themselves if they have returned, inherit the positions that their limited persistence in a stable position relative to other such continuously observed things has enabled him to define. First, then, there is direct identification of continuously observed things. These provide a spatial framework for the identification of things over temporal gaps. The primary continuants do, of course, exhibit spatial continuity or identity, but this is directly observed and not determined from their relations to independently identified places. They satisfy the criterion they make possible but it is not required for their own primary identification. In a way the circle remains but the vice is removed from it.

The objection which most concerns Wiggins is that the observer may be mistaken in supposing that his observation is continuous, there may have been a gap in his observation during which deceptively similar things were substituted for those he was originally observing. Any precautions that can be taken against such a possibility of illusion, he argues, presuppose the ability to identify places at different times. To guard against illusion in general we need to observe things from different points of view and this requires separate observations, spread out in time. Secondly, in picking out a candidate for identification we must classify it as of a particular substantival kind and we do not know how to classify unless we know how to rectify misclassifications, which again implies the power to identify the things classified through time. Finally we must be able to count what we distinguish as candidates for identification at any one moment and counting takes time.

These arguments are not directed against the view that it is a criterion of the identity of A and B that they fall within a continuous stretch of observation. They count against the applicability of the criterion rather than its adequacy. What they show is that a claim that the criterion has been satisfied is to some extent conjectural, so that its uncertainty will be transmitted to any identity-statement it entails. But this does not really matter. In the first place the kind of error required if a mistaken belief about continuity of observation is to be formed is, to say the least, unusual. Such an error could be made. Wiggins observes that conjurors trade on our liability to it, but it is not common. Conjurors move the things they manipulate very rapidly and in a region comparatively crowded with other things. But secondly, and more to the point of principle, if such an error is made in one case the spatial framework it leads us to conceive will conflict with that to which we are led by other continuous observations. Our conception of an enduring space occupied by enduring things will not rest on a single bout of continuous observation. We can resort to it at any time to establish the bona fides of the landmarks we use to establish identity across observational gaps. It is a contingent fact that there are continuously observable things and a contingent fact that our assumptions about the continuity of observations of them are generally correct. That these are facts is shown by the coherence of the general system of identifications which results from supposing them to be so. It is not required that every supposition of this kind should be infallible.

Thus we do not need to take precautions beforehand against illusions of continuity, except where the situation is of a kind which experience has shown to be favourable to them, such as a display of conjuring. As for Wiggins's final point, if I have distinguished a number of contemporaneous things from one another it is in principle possible to count them. But I do not have to have counted them if I have distinguished them, though if I have counted them I must have distinguished them. Furthermore not all counting takes time. Or, more correctly, I can tell the number of some, relatively small, groups of things at a glance, and without any temporally extended process of numbering them off.

In things that are accessible to continuous observation, then, we have a class of primary continuants in terms of which the enduring places can be defined that we need for identification in general. They will satisfy the requirement of spatial continuity but it does not have to be invoked for their identification.

Non-temporal identity

The main problem of this chapter has been that of the identification of what is observed at different times as the same enduring thing. Most of the things we observe are continuants in that they endure long enough to raise the question of their identity through time. Furthermore, I have argued, there must be continuants if the momentary spatial arrays which we observe are to be linked together into the all-inclusive unitary space which is the framework of the common world.

I have attempted to show elsewhere that it is not a necessary truth that all real things are in just *one* space (Quinton (2)). The counter-example whose consistency was used to show that the unity of space is not strictly demonstrable had to invoke a fairly fantastic hypothesis: that of two intercalated streams of consciousness which were each internally coherent and connected but which were in certain essential respects unrelated to each other. (The two spatial orders could not be utterly unrelated since the subject, when observing what was going on in one of them, had to be capable of remembering what had gone on in the other. The conditions of the hypothesis ruled out any physical account of the causation of these memories.) But even if there were two, or more, real spaces there would still have to be continuants in each for them to be continuing spaces at all.

I shall conclude this chapter by briefly considering three kinds of non-temporal identity which are of some general interest: spatial, visuo-tactual and qualitative.

(i) *Spatial* There is some measure of analogy between identifications through space and identifications through time. In observing things we no more observe their whole spatial extent, for the most part, than we observe their whole temporal extent. The exceptions in both cases are few and somewhat questionable. In the temporal case it would seem possible to perceive in a single observation the whole temporal extent of a flash of lightning or, to take something more substantival, of a house of cards. In the spatial case there are perfectly transparent balls of coloured glass no part of which may be concealed from a suitably placed observer. But for the most part what we perceive of a thing in any one observation of it is a small tract of its total history and likewise a smallish part of its total spatial extent: the visibly hither end or actually touched part of its surface. Most things are opaque and most have insides.

Commonly, it must be recognised, the spatial identification of things involves temporal identification as well. The man whose feet I see under the partition at one moment is the same as the man whose head I see over the top of it a moment later. The wire attached to the lamp I see now is the same as the wire whose plug I shall discover to have come out of the socket in the wall a few seconds from now. I shall not labour over this complication. In the first place I can ordinarily identify the feet that are observable when the man's head is with the feet that originally attracted my attention and thus carry out my spatial identification on what is contemporaneously observed. Secondly, it would seem that the great fundamental mass of our spatial identifications is carried out on the components of a momentary field of observation. Every time I identify a simultaneously observed head, trunk and legs, in virtue of their spatial juxtaposition, as the head, trunk and legs of a single man I am carrying out a spatial identification. The point is that such identifications are so easy and unproblematic in practice that we are seldom aware of making them.

There is no great obscurity about the criteria for spatial identity. Two tracts of observed matter in a given field of observation are parts of the same thing if they are contiguous, qualitatively homogeneous in respect of the secondary qualities such as colour and texture which flesh out the essential primary qualities of shape and size and make up a dynamical unity in the sense that whatever causes either to move also moves the other. That there are identifiable, countable, substantival things at all is due to the fact that there are qualitatively homogeneous continuities that are ordinarily rather sharply marked off from their spatial environment and which retain their internal positional properties of shape and size when they change their position relative to everything else.

Neither strict qualitative homogeneity nor strict dynamical unity is essential. On the one hand patchwork quilts and hors d'oeuvre trolleys, on the other card-houses and smoke-rings are substantival things all right. But a fair measure of both is usual and one or the other would seem to be necessary.

The substantival concepts with which we primarily classify the manifold of observation into things typically determine with more or less precision the spatial extent, the shape and size, of the instances to which they apply. They do not determine the temporal duration of their instances with anything like the same precision. It could, indeed, be questioned whether they determine it at all. In general, of course, large trees have previously been small trees and, before that, saplings, while saplings have, presumably, come from seeds. If it is doubtful whether this prehistory is a logically necessary condition of a thing's being really a full-sized tree it is simply because, in view of the qualitative differences between real trees and imitation ones, it is a matter that circumstances have not required us to decide.

It is a consequence of this difference that in order to perceive a thing we have to perceive, if not most of its spatial parts, at least enough of them to justify a conjecture about its overall shape and size whereas we do not have to perceive much of its duration. It is to make the same point to say that the temporal parts of an enduring thing would have been a perfectly good thing of that kind if they had existed on their own, without the other phases which in fact preceded and followed them, while this is very seldom true in the analogous spatial case: the spatial parts of a thing, conceived as existing in spatial disconnection from each other, are not things of the same kind. Matter is necessarily extended in space in a way that it is not necessarily extended in time, even though there must be *some* enduring things. Furthermore the discrimination of things into kinds carries necessary implications about the specific form, the shape and size, of their spatial extent as it does not about their temporal duration.

(ii) *Visuo-tactual* The things that extend and endure in our unitary spatio-temporal framework possess, in the very great majority of cases, both visual and tactual qualities. The enduring things that enable us to form the conception of a unitary, enduring space have as their essential, defining characteristics primary qualities that are accessible both to sight and to touch. In fact there is a massive underlying identification here of the spatial order of sight with that of touch. In practice we are not often called upon to carry out an explicit, conscious identification of something presented to one of these senses with something presented to the other. The fact that our words for primary qualities have, for those of us endowed with both the relevant capacities, a visual and a tactual sense conceals the fact that the correlations between the visual and tactual shapes and sizes of things are contingent.

This very fundamental contingency of the correlation between specific visual and specific tactual qualities is brought to attention by Molyneux's problem of the capacity of a man born blind to identify with his restored vision things with which he is tactually familiar and by Whitehead's reference to the leap of hypothesis involved in taking the armchair we see to be the same thing as the armchair which, sitting down in, we touch. The Molyneux problem makes clear that the correlation is contingent since, however rapidly the newly sighted man makes his identifications, however much he can dispense with initial exploratory fumblings, he is still identifying two logically distinct things. Whitehead's example prompts the disconcerting hypothesis that the two spatial orders could conceivably diverge and fail to correlate at all, in that no specific visual quality might be found to accompany a specific tactual quality but an assorted variety of visual qualities each of which was itself associated with a variety of tactual qualities. If this disturbing possibility were actually realised the spatial order of touch would, no doubt, be taken to be the real world. The close connection between the tangible qualities of things and our biological survival would ensure that. The order of sight would be a kind of entertainment, distracting or soothing, that would accompany our serious intercourse with the world, rather in the way that people get on with their practical tasks with the radio on.

This particular form of identification is interesting since it provides an example of identification between things, for example the visual and the tactual armchair, that are not in general, and prior to identifications of this particular kind, in the same space at all. One of the difficulties with which the thesis of the identity of events in the mind with events in the brain has to contend is that, in the examples which are used to explain the kind of contingent identity involved, the terms of the identity, the lightning-flash and the electrical discharge for example, occupy the same position in space, whereas the mental event, if in space at all, is not given as such with anything like the determinacy of the brain event with which the theory identifies it. The remoteness of a mental event and its cerebral correlate from the type of spatial coincidence that is ordinarily required for identification is thus less radical than that between a visual thing and its tactual correlate, yet this latter identification is one that we take so much in our stride that an effort is needed to see that any identification has taken place at all.

(iii) *Qualitative* In order to refer to qualities and thus to turn them into things, of a sort, about which questions of identity arise we have to construct abstract singular terms from the predicates whose senses the qualities are held to be. To attach a predicate to the name (or names) of a thing (or things) is to ascribe a quality (or relation) to it (or them). The name of the quality is formed from the predicate by adding one of the suffixes '-ness', '-hood' or '-ity' to the 'ϕ' in the predicative expression 'is ϕ' or again by prefixing 'ϕ' by 'being'. Thus ugliness, motherhood and muscularity and also being a man are all qualities.

The standard view of the criterion of identity for qualities is that A and B are one and the same quality if 'A' and 'B' are synonymous or, more accessibly, if the corresponding predicative expressions 'α' and 'β' are. But although this is a sufficient condition for the identity of two qualities it is not necessary. If Jim's shirt is red and Joan's dress is red then the colour of Jim's shirt is identical with the colour of Joan's dress. But it does not seem plausible to maintain that the two quality-descriptions used in the identity-statement of the consequent-clause of the preceding sentence are synonymous or that the corresponding predicate-expressions 'is the colour of Jim's shirt' and 'is the colour of Joan's dress' are.

There are, in fact, two ways in which qualities may be referred to. On the one hand they can be referred to by abstract singular terms manufactured from purely predicative expressions in accordance with mechanical rules about suffixes and prefixes; on the other they can be referred to by descriptions which mention some concrete individual which either has the quality in question as in my example or is otherwise related to it, for example 'Jim's favourite colour'. It is tempting to say that abstract singular terms of the first kind are the logically proper names of the qualities to which they refer for it logically follows from the significance of them, and thus of the predicates from which they are derived, that there is a quality to which they refer (it does not matter whether the quality has any instances).

It might be objected, however, that the same is true of the second class of quality-descriptions, or of some of them, at any rate. Jim's shirt must have some colour or other: a shirt is necessarily visible and what is visible is necessarily coloured. But this objection cannot be sustained. Jim's shirt may be of many colours; Jim may have no shirt; there may be no such person as Jim; (as for the other example, there may be no colour Jim prefers to all others). So although these quality-descriptions are significant there is no quality to which they refer in these circumstances; there is no colour which is the colour of Jim's shirt or his favourite colour. It seems reasonable to suppose that expressions ostensibly referring to qualities which although significant nevertheless fail to do so, fail *because*, as well as when, they contain a reference to a concrete individual.

In the light of this the following criterion of identity of qualities when referred to, not by abstract singular terms of a purely predicative sort, but by descriptions that can fail to refer seems a reasonable one: the quality-descriptions 'A' and 'B' refer to the same quality if the purely predicative expression for the quality to which 'A' refers is synonymous with the purely predicative expression for the quality to which 'B' refers. This has the merit of allowing us to say, given that Jim's shirt and Joan's dress are red, both that 'the colour of Jim's shirt' and 'the colour of Joan's dress' refer to the same quality and yet that the expressions quoted are not synonymous.

It will at once appear that this account of the identity of qualities is incomplete. Rules have been provided for identity-statements in which both terms are quality-names and both quality-descriptions. But the rule for the latter type of case cannot cover, because it presupposes, identity-statements in which a quality-name and a quality-description are correlated. But this is not a serious problem. The statement 'the colour of Jim's shirt is red' is a degenerate kind of identity-statement. It follows from the straightforwardly predicative statement that Jim's shirt is red, at least for anyone who acknowledges the necessary truth that red is a colour.

It may be worth mentioning the fact that there is no difficulty in extending this treatment to relations, provided that they are conceived *as* relations and not as (impurely predicative) qualities. 'Arthur is married to Barbara' should be construed as 'marriage relates Arthur to Barbara' or 'Arthur stands to Barbara in the relation of being married' and not as 'Arthur has the quality of being-married-to-Barbara'. The relation mentioned purely predicatively here (viz. marriage), can be referred to, impurely, as the relation in which Charles stands to Diana. Unlike the quality of being-married-to-Barbara it has a great many instances.

4

Ultimates

Most things persist through time and unless some did we should have no conception of a spatio-temporally unitary world. But the things of common observation, pens, dogs, trees, mountains, the earth itself, do not persist forever, their histories are finite at both ends, they come into existence and eventually go out of it again. Philosophers have held that there are or must be eternal things, in particular material atoms and immortal human souls. We have already considered the philosophical notion of an atom in discussing the compositional theory of identity through time. The feature of the atom that concerned us there was its qualitative stability rather than its eternal duration. Even if the compositional theory were correct it would not follow that the unchanging components it invokes are eternal. No complex thing could last longer than the shortest-lived of its atomic constituents. But provided that they were created and annihilated gradually the unity of the world would be preserved. Places could be identified at different times even if none of the atoms existing at one of them were in existence at the other. If there were an intervening time at which some atoms from both sets were in existence the connection could be established. It is not even necessary that any atom from one time should ever be contemporaneous with any atom from the other, as long as the existence of atoms is protracted enough for it to overlap with later atoms to form the beginning of a chain of temporally overlapping existence that terminates with the atoms of the later time. It would be a mistake to infer the existence of eternal things from the presumption that there are eternal places, which is entailed by the principle of the spatio-temporal unity of the world.

It has nevertheless been the general view of philosophical atomists that atoms are eternal as well as qualitatively immutable. The conviction is not confined to materialists. Kant's synthetic *a priori* principle of substance states that the amount of matter in nature is fixed, susceptible of neither increase nor diminution. The successive conservation principles of physical science specify the same point in various ways. In fact the principle of conservation does not involve a full-blooded atomism of eternal things. An active bank-account can remain unchanged if withdrawals are simultaneously compensated for by deposits. The volume of water in a tank can remain the same if the amount that flows out at one end is exactly the same as the amount that flows in at the other. Recent cosmological speculations have made this clear. According to the continuous creation hypothesis although energy is actually annihilated in atomic transformations at high temperatures the loss is compensated for by the creation of new energy elsewhere. But if the ultimate stuff of the world is conceived substantivally, as composed of some sort of particles, it is very natural to run the idea of conservation together with that of eternal things.

Why should it have been supposed that there are eternal things? The first reason for this supposition is that in common experience when things come into existence, most evidently in cases of deliberate manufacture but also when they are the outcome of natural processes, the parts of which they are composed existed beforehand. Similarly when things go out of existence the material of which they were made remains behind in some form or other. Burnt chairs leave ash and smoke, chopped-up chairs leave firewood and splinters. The closer inquiries of the scientist confirm this common experience. Apparent exceptions to the rule that all creation and annihilation is a rearrangement of the elementary parts of complex wholes do not survive closer inspection. Now the immediate parts into which an ordinary thing dissolves or from which it is constructed are themselves liable to annihilation. But it is natural to suppose that the regress must stop somewhere. If all coming into and going out of existence is rearrangement there must be some ultimate rearrangeable elements that are neither created nor annihilated.

The fact remains that even if the principle is universally confirmed by common and scientific experience it is not a necessary truth. It is not inconceivable that ordinary things should be absolutely created and annihilated instead of being composed out of pre-existing elements and resolved into surviving ones. It is perfectly conceivable that in otherwise torpid surroundings an apple should suddenly come into fully-fledged existence on a hitherto empty plate (cf. Stace (2), p. 201). We may suppose that the possibility of its having been thrown or dropped or covertly placed there is ruled out after careful inspection, that witnesses and photographs establish that it was not really there all the time. The apple could just as well go out of existence with the same sort of abruptness. If it came and went in a very short space of time, of course, we should be inclined to pass it off as a trick of the light. But if it lasted long enough for several people to handle it and take bites out of it and if, having slightly quenched their thirst by doing so, they found themselves appreciably thirstier again when the core disappeared the case for its having been absolutely annihilated would be very strong.

Although there would be no contradiction in saying that the apple had been absolutely created and annihilated in these circumstances and although there would be some reason for saying it, it is impossible that the case for doing so could be absolutely conclusive. For there is no limit to the number and kind of conservative explanations that could be given of the puzzling event. The apple's appearance on the scene could be traced to a transformation of the air in the place it came to occupy or, if this were refuted by an appropriate increase in the air pressure of the room, to the intersection of two kinds of radiation or to indefinitely many products of theoretical ingenuity. There is a close similarity between the conservative principle and the principle of causality which Kant perceived in treating them as synthetic *a priori*. They are synthetic in that there is no contradiction in supposing there to be an exception to them. On the other hand, they are *a priori* to the extent that they are not empirically refutable (cf. Watkins (1) & (2)). However unsuccessful we have been so far in finding the material basis of a change of existence or the cause of an event, indefinitely many unrefuted possibilities remain to be examined. The material may be imperceptibly fine just as the cause may be unmanageably complex. Another large synthetic proposition of the same irrefutable kind is the strict, qualitative version of the principle of the identity of indiscernibles.

Kant's principle of substance does not, then, seem to be necessarily true. It does not follow that it cannot be false from the fact that it cannot be conclusively shown to be false. But even if conservation is irrefutable its strength is not directly transferred to atomism. As I mentioned above, although atoms came and went, provided that their overall number remained constant the requirement of conservation would be satisfied. There is also another possibility. It is conceivable that below a certain level of size matter might lose its thing-like or substantial character (cf. Sellars, p. 26; Aune, p. 172). As the work of division proceeded we might arrive at mere stuff, with no definite spatial form at any time and therefore no persistent spatial outline in virtue of which any piece of it could be identified with any other piece existing at another time. The total amount of stuff could remain constant although there would be no clear sense to the assertion that precisely the same stuff persisted. Something like this picture of the material world is conveyed by the view that it is a continuous field of energy rather than an array of discrete particles. The Parmenidean principle lays down that there is no absolute creation or annihilation, that all existential change occurs to or in a fixed stock of pre-existent material. It does not strictly follow that this stock of material should consist of a fixed number of identifiable parts.

This is not to say that tracts or pieces of stuff can never be identified through time. Many of the pieces of stuff we observe have definite spatial form at the time we observe them and may retain it for considerable periods. A puddle of water on a cellar floor may be the object of a long series of increasingly irritable references. But identifiable tracts of stuff are more the exception than the rule. Stuff is essentially formless, in the sense that it is just that kind of matter into whose definition shape does not enter. Tracts of it constantly lose their identity by irreversible mixing or dissipation: the measure of gin becomes inextricably involved with the other contents of the cocktail shaker, the dab of furniture-polish is spread with irredeemable thinness and dispersion over the mahogany surface of the occasional table. Common, observable stuff at least has, for the most part, a reasonably definite spatial form at any one moment. It is clear where the snow leaves off and the garden and the air on either side of it begin. But this is not true of theoretical stuff. A field is a matter of continuously varying intensities and not sharply demarcated presence and absence. Furthermore, two fields may overlap or coincide spatially. Theoretical stuff lacks the primary quality of logical solidity, it does not necessarily exclude other theoretical stuff from the place where it is.

Atoms, then, conceived as eternal and immutable things, identifiable in principle throughout the whole of time, are entailed neither by the spatio-temporal unity of the world nor by the conservative nature of change. It is not necessarily true that change is conservative but it cannot be proved to be false and it is very natural to believe it. The assumption of atomism has played a part in the investigation of nature that is paralleled in its importance only by that of universal causality. But although the belief in eternal things has been a pragmatic condition of the progress of scientific knowledge, their existence is not, like that of enduring things, a logical condition of the possibility of discourse.

Atoms and infinity

There is a third argument, beside the existence of eternal places and the conservative nature of change, that has been influential in securing support for atoms: the argument from division. This seeks to establish atoms more directly than the argument from the nature of change. According to the latter the existence of immutable things, neither created nor annihilated, follows from the premise that things can only come into or go out of existence by reason of a rearrangement of their parts. If that premise is correct there must be ultimate parts which are not themselves complex wholes and are thus not susceptible of existential change. The argument from division asks what the parts of things are and not what they must be if change is, as it seems to be, conservative.

Material things are extended. Anything that is extended in space is in principle capable of being divided since space is infinitely divisible. The natural conclusion from these premises is that there are no physical minima, that the division of material things can continue without end. But it does not follow that material things are infinitely complex. All that is shown is that however far the process of division has gone it is always conceivable that it should go further, there are no material things, however small, that it is logically impossible to resolve into parts. This conceptual truth is perfectly consistent with the hypothesis that material things are only finitely divisible in fact. It asserts that there is a significant and intelligible description of a material thing smaller than, and thus capable of being a part of, any material and thus extended thing whatever. It does not say that there is anything to which such a description actually applies.

The thesis of the finite divisibility in fact of material things could take three forms. The first and simplest is that there are definite termini to the process of division, things of such a kind that whatever is done to them they hold together. A second possibility is that when things reach a certain low level of size the attempt to divide them simply annihilates them. The third is that when things reach a certain low level of size the attempt to divide them turns them into stuff, and so eliminates the substantial character which is required if any further operation is to be described as division.

Interpreted in this way finite and infinite divisibility are entirely compatible. Of any material thing, however small, it is necessarily true that its further division is conceivable, while at the same time it may be contingently true that, in one of the three ways mentioned, it cannot be divided further. In other words, every material thing has an infinity of logically possible parts but it may have a finite number of actual parts. If it is asked what the *ultimate* logically possible parts are like the answer is that there can be no such things, any more than there is a largest cardinal number. There can, then, be no logical atoms of matter. This is a direct consequence of the essential extendedness of material things and the infinite divisibility, in thought, of extension. But there may be physical atoms, in the etymologically primary sense of things that cannot in fact be further divided. If there are they still *could* have been composed of yet smaller things but, *ex hypothesi*, they are not.

A kind of superimposition of the logical thesis of infinite divisibility on the atomistic picture of the world presented by the physical thesis of finite divisibility is familiar in the history of philosophy as the theory of atoms as points. Since 0 is the limit of the descending sequence $\frac{1}{2}\dots\frac{1}{4}\dots\frac{1}{8}\dots$ it is supposed that a thing of zero extension, namely an infinitesimal point, with position but without magnitude, is the terminus of a conceivable process of indefinitely continued division. Part of the trouble with this analogy is that it is not thoroughly carried through. 0 is not a member of the series whose limit it is; it is that to which the members of the series approximate ever more closely without ever reaching it. Points have the merit of being logically guaranteed against the possibility of division, by analogy with the fact that half of zero is zero, but the difficulty is to see how a set of unextended points, even if infinitely large, could constitute a thing of finite extension. It is, of course, logically impossible that any process of division could decompose an extended thing into points. But this may seem a basely technological consideration. The punctual constituents are still there, it might be held, although we have not the time to carve the things we encounter up into them.

Leibniz inferred that the ultimate constituents of things were unextended from the reasonable premises that every complex was made of simples and that everything extended was on that account complex. A reasonable conclusion would have been something like Boscovitch's theory of matter which holds it to be ultimately composed of punctual centres of force. Such a theory rejects the principle that everything material is extended. Leibniz retained this Cartesian doctrine to arrive at his bizarre conclusion that the ultimate simples were monads: Cartesianly spiritual since Cartesianly immaterial.

A theory like Boscovitch's does not follow from the extendedness of ordinary matter together with the principle that the complex must be composed of the simple. An extended thing is conceptually complex to the extent that it is logically possible to distinguish an infinity of points within the region it occupies. But it does not follow that there is a simple part of the thing associated with each of these points. We might ask, however, if a theory like Boscovitch's is possible. On such a theory the problem of accounting for the extension of material complexes of points is solved by regarding the points as separated from one another in space and as interacting with one another by the exercise of repulsive and attractive forces. This way of conceiving the material world is familiar from the formally idealised representations of physical theory in which the mass and other causal properties of a thing are conceived as being concentrated at its centre of gravity. As a useful abstraction or symbolic convenience this mode of representation has much to commend it. It is convenient in the same way that maps on flat pieces of paper with relief shown by differences of colour are handier for the traveller than three-dimensional models in papier-mâché of the ground he is covering. The sun is no more a point than the Alps are uniformly purple. Nevertheless a map is a possible picture. We could come across a flat tract of country with numbered contour lines running sinuously round it, each enclosing an undulating strip of colour. Is Boscovitch's theory a possible picture?

The real difficulty with it is that there seems to be no basis for the distinction between the thing itself, the material point, and its causal activities, the various forces it exerts. These activities pervade a certain extended region of which the supposed material point is just the focus. The point is parasitic on its activities in the sense that the idea of a wholly inert material point seems to be entirely vacuous. The atom might just as well be identified with the extended system of forces it is said to be the source of. Boscovitch's theory is really a field theory in which the substantival notion of a thing is retained in a pensioned state, in recognition of its distinguished past services no doubt, but with no duties that could not be carried out by the bare position at which it is situated. Like Queen Victoria in the eyes of Bagehot, it is decorative rather than functional. Certainly no conceivable observation could distinguish it from the activities going on around it.

The theory of atoms as points is, then, neither a logical consequence of the extendedness of ordinary matter nor a substantial exception to the Cartesian principle that everything material must be extended. Unless a material point has extended manifestations and effects there is no possible ground for asserting its existence and if it has there is no content to the idea that it is distinct from them except as the focus of the region in which they occur and in that case it is not a thing at all but a position.

The other Kantian antinomies of the same kind—those concerning the infinite temporal divisibility of things and the infinite spatial and temporal extent of the world as a whole—can be treated in the same way. A temporally extended process, such as the showing of a film, is composed of temporal parts, the showing of the constituent frames. There is no limit in principle to the brevity of these constituents but it may be impossible in practice to speed a process up beyond a certain point. There may be durations that can perfectly well be described but which are not instantiated by any events. A Boscovitchian hypothesis to the effect that every process is made up of temporally separated instantaneous events is exposed to objections precisely analogous to those brought against the doctrine of material points.

The infinite extent of (Euclidean) space can be invoked to support the infinite size of the material world that occupies it in the way that its infinite divisibility was used to establish the infinitely divisible. At however remote a distance we have found matter to be present it is always possible to describe matter further off still. But it does not follow that there is any matter there. As long as there are some material things we can set up a system of spatial characterisations which allows for the description of possible things at any distance whatever. But it is a contingent question whether these positions are occupied, whether these possibilities are realised. Similarly with time. It has no beginning in the sense that there is no date an earlier date than which cannot be significantly described. But there may be a date at no time earlier than which was anything happening at all. Infinity, we might say, is a necessary feature only of systems of description, not merely those which contain numbers but any which contain such transitive asymmetrical relations as 'smaller than' and 'further than' and 'earlier than'. But this entails neither that there is no limit to the minuteness or remoteness of actual things nor, *a fortiori*, that there are infinitely small or infinitely remote things.

Personal identity

It has been usual in discussions of identity to give special treatment to the identity of persons. There are three reasons for this. The first is a conviction that what is essential about people is, broadly speaking, mental, more precisely their characters and memories. On the usual Cartesian and dualistic view the mind and its contents are altogether non-spatial and so it follows that no criterion of the kind I have argued for in the case of material things that involves spatial continuity can apply in this case. The second reason is the desire for and belief in immortality, or at any rate the survival by persons of the death and dissolution of their bodies. If this requirement is to be met, since bodies do die and dissolve, the criterion of personal identity must make no essential reference to bodily continuity. Furthermore the idea of a spiritual substance, which because simple is indestructible, is attractive in this connection as providing an apparent guarantee of immortality. Finally there is the widespread conviction that experiences or mental states, the more or less short-lived elements of a person's mental life, must have an owner or subject that is distinct from them.

Taken together these three considerations have given strong support to the view that the identity of persons or minds through time must be accounted for in terms of an immutable and perhaps eternal identifier, a spiritual substance. But the support is nowhere conclusive. None of the three considerations strictly requires that people should be or have spiritual substances. As to the first, a purely mental criterion of personal identity is possible in terms of the relations between experiences or mental states. Provided the identification of the experiences, which, as a related series, constitute a person, does not depend on the identification of any particular body a criterion of identity in terms of the relations between them would allow people to be identified after the death and dissolution of their bodies, or, at any rate, after that of their original bodies (though it would not, of course, provide any guarantee of immortality). Finally, the requirement that mental states must have an owner could be satisfied without assigning them to a spiritual substance. The owner might well be the body, perhaps for the time being, of the person in question, or again the related totality of that person's mental states. I shall consider the principle of ownership at the end of the chapter, after personal identity itself has been discussed. The existence of a spiritual substance as the subject or owner of mental states is distinct from its being the criterion of personal identity. It is not therefore refuted by the strong and indeed fatal arguments that can be brought against such a criterion.

The first defect of spiritual substance as a criterion of personal identity is one with which we are already familiar: its regressiveness. It is of no avail to define the identity of an individual thing of a given kind in general in terms of the presence within it of another individual thing of the same kind. In the case under discussion the attempt is made to define the identity of one sort of mental thing, a person, in terms of another, a spiritual substance. It is clear at any rate that spiritual substance poses a problem of identity of its own since it must endure through time, perhaps through all time, and yet it only presents itself as it is at any one moment. To show that the regress is not vicious, that no circularity is involved, a positive account of the nature of spiritual substance must be given, which shows it to be in some way more readily and directly identifiable than the wholes of which it is a component. By analogy with the atoms of speculative cosmology it might be held to differ from persons in being qualitatively immutable. Before any concrete questions are asked about what qualities it can be conceived to have, there is the difficulty that two quite distinct persons might have qualitatively indistinguishable spiritual substances. Since spiritual substances are not in space we cannot make use of their positions to distinguish them.

Secondly, is there any observable mental entity with sufficient stability of character to fill the bill? The only plausible candidate is the dim, inchoate background, largely composed of organic sensations, that envelops the mental states occupying the focus of attention. It is a relatively unchanging environment against which the more dramatic episodes of conscious life stand out. But it is only relatively fixed. It does change from time to time and such fixity as it has can largely be attributed to its being at the periphery of attention. But its peripheral nature makes it practically useless for purposes of public application. Generally speaking we know nothing specific enough about it for it to be used for purposes of identification in any case but our own. It is observable and it is a universal constituent of the momentary cross-sections of a person's experiences. But that is all that there is to be said for it.

The fact that the background of organic feeling does change leads to a third difficulty. It would seem that any permanent and unaltering constituent of a person's conscious life must of necessity be unobservable and thus useless for purposes of identification. If from its very first stirrings my consciousness has contained a continuous whistling sound of unvarying character I should never notice the fact. I can notice only what varies independently of my consciousness: the whistles that start and stop at times other than those at which I wake up and fall asleep. It is this fact that ensured that Hume's search for a self over and above his particular perceptions was bound to fail. The necessary unobservability of spiritual substance, and its consequent uselessness as a criterion of identity, follows even more directly from the desperate and not very intelligible supposition that it is an uncharacterised substratum for qualities and relations to inhere in with no recognisable features of its own, a kind of mental pseudo-position.

The extravagantly unempirical nature of the concept of spiritual substance has combined with the widely prevalent view that the mind is logically dependent on the body to lead many recent philosophers to accept a bodily criterion of identity. But although there is a certain affinity between the two positions the bodily criterion of personal identity neither requires nor is required by the theory that mental states are or necessarily involve bodily behaviour or dispositions to it. On the one hand the most unqualified version of the behavioural theory of mind does not entail that the identity of a person must be defined in terms of the behaviour of a *particular* body. Even if a person's mental states were simply and solely behavioural dispositions, his character a complex property of these dispositions and his memory a particular disposition to make first-person statements in the past tense without inference or reliance on testimony, it would follow only that some body or other, not necessarily human perhaps, would be required for every manifestation of his personality, and not that one particular identifiable body was the seat of all the behaviour identifiable as his. The behavioural theory rules out the wholly disembodied existence of persons but not their reincarnation in new, and possibly very different, bodies. On the other hand a dualist like Ayer, at a time when he accepted the existence of a clear-cut categorial distinction between the mental and the physical, could adopt a strictly bodily criterion of personal identity (cf. Ayer (1), p. 194). In his first treatment of the subject he seems at first to give an account of a person in purely mental terms as a related series of experiences. But the relation which he sees as connecting them involves an indispensable reference to a particular persisting human body. A person is composed of those total mental states that contain an organic sensation belonging to one particular human body, itself to be identified in terms of its continuity of qualities and spatial position.

Ayer drew the conclusion that properly follows from this as from any account of personal identity that involves reference to a particular human body: that the notion of a person's disembodied existence is self-contradictory and, further, that the notion of the association of a personality with different bodies at different times is inconceivable. Before we consider whether these consequences constitute a *reductio ad absurdum* of the theory of a bodily criterion rather than the disproof of the logical possibility of a person's survival of death the virtues of the bodily criterion should be noticed. In the first place it has the theoretical attraction of simplicity. It requires that there should be only a single mode of treatment for the identification through time of all enduring things. Human beings are thus treated as just one variety of concrete objects. Secondly, it has the merit of actual correctness. Its application yields uncontentiously acceptable answers in the very great majority of cases of personal identification with which we are actually called upon to deal. Finally, it is practically realistic, for it is, in fact, the procedure of identification that we most commonly rely on. Even where it is inapplicable for lack of the relevant bodily evidence, as in the case of the Tichborne claimant, no one imagines that the result of applying other criteria such as memory would conflict with what the bodily evidence would have shown if it had been forthcoming. Is there anything better to set against these powerful recommendations in favour of the bodily criterion than its consequence that things many people have very much wanted to say about the survival of death are inconsistent? So much the worse for them, it might be said, their inconsistent assertions are the result of trying at the same moment to assert and to deny that a person no longer exists.

The soul and personality

It does seem unplausible to suppose, as a strictly bodily criterion of personal identity requires, that the notion of a person's survival of the death and dissolution of his body is a self-contradictory one. That such survival occurs, indeed that it lasts for ever, has been an established and consoling conviction of most men in most ages. Against this it may be objected that people can often purport to believe what is in fact self-contradictory. Before Euclid came up with his proof those interested in prime numbers may well have divided into two parties: those who endorsed the necessary truth that there is no largest prime number and those who purported to believe the self-contradictory proposition that there is.

We may consider a less elusively abstract example. More or less engrossing, and to that extent credible, stories have been written about time travel. Yet all such stories, in their Wellsian, pre-Einsteinian forms at any rate, involve contradictions. To travel back to some time t1 in the past implies that the present, t2, is both before t1, since the traveller is there after he is at t2, and after t1, since t1 is in the past relative to t2. It also follows that t2 is before and after, and thus not simultaneous with, itself.

One may suspect that the reader silently reinterprets the narrative so as to make it consistent. The t1 he travels to is a state of things which is in content as like as possible to the historical t1 that preceded t2 but distinct from it and, similarly, that the t2 to which he returns, while more or less like the t2 from which he set out, is different from it, at least in containing memories of having been to the second t1 as well as to the first. (It is sometimes part of the point of the story that the t2 to which the traveller returns should be significantly different from the t2 he set out from.)

Since the most natural way to show that personal survival of bodily death is possible is to describe circumstances in which it would be correct to say that it had occurred it is important to examine the fictions involved very closely. Furthermore, to minimise the risk of admitting inconsistencies, it is desirable that the fiction should depart as little as is possible from circumstances with which we are familiar. This principle of imaginative economy implies that fictions involving totally disembodied existence should be avoided. The point at issue can be less vulnerably made by stories of re-embodiment. The most familiar stories of re-embodiment involve reincarnation. Body A dies; body B comes to exhibit the character-traits exhibited by A and, seemingly, to recollect events that happened to A when it was alive. One weakness of this kind of story is that, in view of the length of the process of human development, there will have to be a long gap between the death of body A and the manifestation of A-like characteristics by body B.

This weakness can be circumvented by a story of what may be called trans-embodiment in which from a certain moment body A manifests the character and memories previously manifested by body B and vice versa. But this still makes an unnecessarily extravagant demand on our powers of belief. Like the idea of reincarnation it flies too violently in the face of our broad psychophysiological assumptions about the causal dependence of character and memories on the body. This unappetising tincture of the miraculous is avoided in Shoemaker's story of the transfer of brains as between the two bodies, which neatly exploits the fact that the causal dependences in question relate character and memories, not to the body as a whole, but to a small if crucial part of it (Shoemaker (2), pp. 22–75).

Not only does this leave our beliefs about the causal order of nature intact, it rests firmly on them, by extrapolating the technique of organ transplantation which is already in use. It does, of course, connect the identity of the person A to an element of his original body. But in this case there is nothing ridiculous about the defence that the impurity involved is only a little one. The identity of body A is not going to be prejudiced by the removal from it of as small a fraction of its total mass and volume as its brain.

The imagined situation is, then, that a surgical exchange of brains is effected between two people A and B. When they come round from the operation the body that was A's exhibits B's character and memories while the body that was B's exhibits A's. When the person who now has A's body is asked who he is he says he is B and the owner or occupier of B's body says he is A. It is generally recognised that it is a necessary condition of the genuineness of a recollection that the event recollected should be rather directly causally related to the recollection of it. (Cf. Martin and Deutscher.) This condition is satisfied here for the assumption that the recollections of A's past history now coming from body B are genuine. The brain that was physically present at the events in question is the immediate source of the memory-claims, is the physical seat of the relevant memory-traces.

There are, in fact, at least three possible responses to the situation produced by the brain-transfer. The first is to take the subject's word for it and to say that the persons A and B have exchanged bodies. For what it is worth this reaction has the support of the great majority of the imaginative literature in which something like such a transfer is described, for example, Anstey's *Vice Versa* and Conan Doyle's *Keinplatz Experiment*. The second is to adhere to a strictly bodily criterion of personal identity and say that A and B have exchanged their characters and memories, or, more accurately, 'memories'. Finally there is the more sophisticated-looking tactic of saying that the original persons A and B have ceased to exist as a result of the operation and that two new, hybrid personages have been brought into existence by it. The ordinary criterion of personal identity, in other words, has broken down. It was not devised for situations of this sort and cannot be expected to apply to them.

Whatever view is taken of the comparative attractions of the first and third options it seems quite obvious that the second is devoid of serious appeal. The persons it identified as A and B would firmly reject the identification. As between the other two proposals it is necessary in order to arrive at a decision to consider what the point of having a criterion of personal identity is. Why should we be so interested in the numerical identification of persons, in picking them out as unique individuals? The answer lies in the character of personal relations. The differences between human beings which render them interestingly unique largely lie in the domain of their characters and memories. It is not unnatural to call these mental aspects of a person his personality and the fact that the word is appropriate suggests something about the essential element in personal identity.

Consider the attitude of those who are most interested in the unique individuality of A and B after the operation, those who know them best and, perhaps, love them most. Who will the mother or wife or son of A want to return to take up the role of son, husband and father: the person with A's body or the person with A's personality? The bodily change brought about may be distressing to those who take the person with A's personality to be A. A massive alteration in appearance or age or a change of sex may be ridiculous or painful to contemplate. But surgery already produces large changes in appearance, in sex, of a slightly dubious sort, and in apparent age without loss of identity. Those who are closely bound up in personal relations with A will plainly want to take up these relations with the person who remembers them and with whose style of behaviour they are familiar, however lavish the change in physical appearance.

To say this is not to suppose that in their personal relations with each other people do not have an interest in the bodily properties of others. The most obvious bodily interest is sexual. But where a person has an exclusively sexual interest in another his requirements can be satisfied by the substitution of another person of the same bodily type while there can be no substitution for a person with memories of experience shared with one.

Two objections to the view that personality, defined as continuity of character and memories, is the basic element in personal identity should be briefly considered. The first of these is that two quite distinct, contemporaneous persons could exhibit all the character-traits and memory of some previous person, say Guy Fawkes, and both claim strenuously and sincerely to be that person. Yet since they are distinct from each other they cannot both be identical with him and the identification of either with him would be arbitrary (cf. Williams pp. 238–9). One limitation of this argument is that it fails to accord with the measure of causal realism involved in the brain-transfer story. A more important weakness is that the disconcerting duplication involved could be perfectly easily paralleled on the bodily plane. Men could be affected by an analogue of amoebic splitting, in which the left and right hand sides of a man stretched away from each other to a point at which two complete bodily replicas split off integrally from each other. Thus if this were a valid objection to a personality criterion of identity it would be an equally valid objection to a bodily criterion. Undoubtedly this conjecture puts our conception of personal identity under a kind of strain which makes the final, non-committal proposal mentioned earlier seem the most appropriate one to adopt. If such duplication, or further multiplication, of personality became common we should perhaps come to think of a personality as an abstraction towards any of whose instances we should have the same personal relationship. But it is hard to imagine that the products of such a multiplication would not soon develop unique individualities after the split, which would preserve their uniqueness until the process was repeated.

Secondly, Shoemaker has argued that bodily continuity is required if we are to be in a position to assess the significance and reliability of the memory-claims of others on which the personality criterion of identity requires us to base our identification of them (Shoemaker (1)). Certainly if people in general switched bodies as rapidly as models working at a fashion show switch clothes we should be in difficulties. But assessment of the apparent memory-claims of the people round us would not be the most pressing of them. We should have lost the most accessible means for recognising other people that we have. Of course the question can arise as to whether what sounds like a memory-claim really is one. To settle it we need to know what the speaker generally has done and said in the past. For this we need some other way of telling where he was in the past than what he now appears to claim. In the brain-transfer case what we really need to know is where his brain was in the past. If he now claims to recollect something which happened where the bulk of his body was but his brain was not we should be in trouble. We might just conceivably say what appears to be a direct piece of personal event-memory is really an ill-expressed piece of factual memory. (Thus, anyone who heard me say 'I remember being born in Kent' would take me to mean 'I remember that I was born in Kent'.) But a much more plausible response would be to question the theory that our capacities of recollection depend on the brain.

A check on the memory-claims of another person does not have to cover the whole range that his recollections purport to cover. An hour of bodily stability could be enough, if he was not aware of being under inspection; a couple of days should be ample. In general one cannot check the reliability of one's own recollections by any other means than their coherence with one another, with the currently observable state of things and the laws of nature, as well, of course, as the ostensible recollections of others. We cannot compare a memory-belief directly with the past event which it reports. Even if, because of body-switching, I do not know who a person now before me was at the time he purports to recollect I am not completely at the mercy of his recollections. I have means independent of them for finding out whether what he claims to recall actually happened. There are then various ways in which I can set about deciding whether he could possibly come to be in a position to know about them in the directly recollective fashion his claim implies.

So far I have argued for the superiority of a mental to a bodily criterion of personal identity in very general terms. I have said that this essential identifying element is personality, conceived as character and memory, but I have not specified at all precisely the nature of the relation between the character and memories of a person existing at one time with those of a person existing at another which makes them one and the same person. This relation is clearly not identity. People's characters change; some memories are lost and new ones are acquired. What is clearly required is continuity. A person could be said to be directly continuous with a person existing at an earlier time provided that the characters of the two are closely similar and that the later person can recollect the bulk of what the earlier person can. Two persons are indirectly continuous if there is a series of persons at intervening times who are each directly continuous with their neighbours in the series and if the two original persons are respectively directly continuous with the latest and earliest members of the series. A, then, is the same person as B if either is directly or indirectly continuous, in the senses defined, with the other.

There is a clear formal analogy with the conditions for the identity of ordinary material things. If C and D exist at closely neighbouring times C is identical with D if and only if C is at or near the position of D and if they share most of their qualities. If C and D are temporally remote from each other they can be very far apart in space and qualitatively very unlike each other without prejudice to their identity so long as they are joined by a sequence of neighbouring things of the same substantival kind each of which is near to and very like its immediate neighbours. Memory is the analogue in the case of persons of position in space and character of qualities.

Ownership and the subject of experience

Spiritual substance, then, conceived as a persistent something, distinct from momentary, introspectible mental states, is not needed to account for personal identity. Yet there is something to the idea that the essence of personal identity is spiritual or mental. However useful and reliable a particular enduring body may be for the practical purpose of identifying a person, it is something that is only contingently related to the particular body that we are using it to identify. There is something to be said for the soul, so long as it is taken to be, not the immutable substratum of mental life but a continuous, related complex of the experiences of which that life is composed.

There is, however, another basis for the theory that a mind or person consists of a spiritual substance as well as particular states or experiences. This is contained in Berkeley's principle that it is inconceivable that an idea should exist that does not inhere in a spirit. It is possible, as with Locke, to deny that spiritual substance is required or able to account for the identity through time of a person or a mind, and yet to insist on the principle of ownership, the thesis that experiences must have an owner, a self or subject or pure ego whose experiences they are.

For McTaggart, for example, this principle was self-evident, as much so as the correlated principle that every experience must belong to only one subject. 'It is impossible', he says, 'that there should be any experience that is not part of a self. . . Nothing that we know, so far as I can see, suggests the existence to us of impersonal experience.' But although beyond doubt this principle is not, according to McTaggart, analytic. It is, he thinks, a synthetic truth about experience (McTaggart (1), pp. 81–2; (2), pp. 91–2).

Ayer takes it to be a consequence of the factual nature of the relations between experiences which constitute a mind or person that 'it is logically conceivable that there should be experiences which were not the experiences of any person'. At the same time he finds the hypothesis of unowned, impersonal experiences unintelligible; 'there would seem to be no conceivable way in which its truth or falsehood could be tested'. He ingeniously reconciles his rejection of both unowned experience and spiritual substance by holding that while it is a contingent matter that an experience is related in a mind-constituting way to the particular experiences to which it is so related it is nevertheless a necessary truth that it should be related to *some* other experiences, no matter what they are (Ayer (5), pp. 223–4).

The foundation of all forms of the ownership principle is the fact that all experiences or states of mind are ascribed. To say that an experience exists is always to say that someone has that experience, either oneself or some other person. We do not have to accept the ownership principle, then, with the unquestioning natural piety of McTaggart. If experiences must be owned there are three main possible candidates for the role of owner: first, spiritual substance or a pure ego, secondly, as in Ayer's theory, the total, internally related set of experiences of which a given experience is a member and, thirdly, the body.

One argument exploits the ordinary concept of ownership to prove that the owner of experiences must be distinct from the experiences that he owns. This, if correct, would rule out Ayer's set of experiences as a candidate for the status of owner. Taken together with the view that a person or mind is only contingently embodied it entails that experiences must be owned by a spiritual substance. But it is, I think, invalid. It holds, very simply, that an owner is necessarily distinct from his possessions. Ownership is an irreflexive relation; one does not own oneself.

There are two levels of objection to this argument. On the first it could be argued that the description of the relation between a person and his experiences as one of ownership is figurative. It is a verbally natural outcome of referring to his experiences, his thoughts, desires, emotions, sensations, as things that he *has*. But although we speak of a whole as having its constituent parts, we are not thereby committed to the conclusion that there is more to the whole than the sum of its parts, suitably arranged. We do, furthermore, speak of a person as having both a mind and a body, but on the most generous view of what a person is there is nothing for him to be than either or both of these.

At the second level it may be questioned whether literal ownership is irreflexive, and if it is not then the need to argue that the ownership by a person of his experiences is merely figurative vanishes. Of course the most obvious examples of items of property—bicycles, fishing-rods, houses and so forth—are clearly distinct from the persons who own them. But, even if it is legally forbidden, selling oneself into slavery is not logically prohibited and one can only sell what one has previously owned. Again, without endorsing Locke's theory of property as a whole, it would seem that one's own labour (and the body *and mind* which are necessarily presupposed by it) is a very fundamental piece of one's property. It does not follow, then, from the fact that a person is the owner of his experiences that he is wholly distinct from them.

Another, and also, I believe, invalid, argument, for the distinctness of a person from his experiences secures this conclusion by conceiving the relation between them as an instance of the relation between a thing and its qualities and then applying the principles of inherence which states that there must be more to a thing than its qualities. Although I have argued that there is an interpretation in which this principle of inherence is correct it does not apply here. An experience is not a quality of a person, any more than a sensible idea or sense-datum is a quality, as Berkeley thought. An experience (and having a sense-datum is an experience) is a particular, which, whether or not it is in space, is appropriated to a particular time. It does not have instances, though it will be an instance of a specific quality or kind.

The idea of the owner or subject of experience, then, as a spiritual substance, wholly distinct from the experiences it owns, receives no support from these general arguments about the irreflexive nature of ownership and the qualitative nature of experiences. It does, formally, provide an answer to the question, what is the subject of experience. But it is an unattractive one since the subject or owner it provides is radically unobservable as was argued in section 3 of this chapter. Is either of the other two alternatives preferable?

Ayer's account of the subject of experience as the whole of which experiences are the constitutive parts, as the total related set of which a given experience is a member is, of course, an application of Hume's account of the self to this particular problem. Empiricist philosophers, Hume himself not excepted, as the Appendix to the *Treatise* shows, have been uncomfortable with this view. Mill, having been led by the general drift of his argument to the conclusion that the self is simply a related series of experiences, pulls himself up with the question: how can a series be aware of itself as a series? (Mill, p. 248). How, in other words, can persons so conceived be credited with their characteristic power of self-consciousness? The answer is surely straightforward. A series can be conscious of itself as a series if it is composed of experiences amongst which recollections of previous tracts of the series are to be found. An answer can be given in the same spirit to Bradley's question to Bain: 'Mr Bain thinks the mind is a collection. Has Mr Bain reflected: who collects Mr Bain?' (Bradley (1).) The answer is that the later Mr Bain collects the earlier Mr Bain by recollecting him.

Certainly Ayer's proposal does have a somewhat arbitrary air. Experiences as he conceives them are necessarily gregarious but quite undiscriminating about their associates. Perhaps some foundation for this necessary but promiscuous sociability can be found if the idea of disembodied existence, with which his account of a mind as a related complex of experiences is consistent, is considered. Although I have rejected a bodily criterion of personal identity earlier in this chapter this was not done in such a way as to imply that wholly disembodied existence is a possibility. All that has been rejected is the view that a person is logically tied to one particular body; it does not follow from this that a person can exist with no body at all.

There are, of course, good factual or causal grounds for holding that all minds or persons are embodied. The possession of an integral brain and nervous system seems to be a causally necessary condition of experience. The only factual considerations that count against this are the purported findings of psychical research about communications from those known to be physically dead. Apart from their evidential weaknesses these findings do not imply that the ostensible communicators are wholly disembodied. If their original bodies have dissolved they still may have been re-embodied somewhere in some other body. But what is needed is a logical argument to show that minds or persons must be embodied.

We can develop such an argument by exploring further the more or less semantic truth from which the principle of ownership is derived, of which indeed the principle of ownership is really a restatement in a different, ontological idiom: all experiences are ascribed either to oneself or to another. The argument has two stages: in the first it is held that all ascription of experiences to others is by way of their bodies; in the second, it is held that no experiences can be ascribed to oneself unless they can also be ascribed to others.

In general I can have no reason to say that someone other than myself is having an experience unless I have reason to think that some body, other than my own, is doing something or is at least disposed to do something. This statement requires two qualifications. In the first place the other body in question does not have to be a human body. No doubt, as Wittgenstein observed, the human body is the best picture of the human soul, but that does not imply, as Malcolm enthusiastically supposes, that it is the *only conceivable* 'picture' of the human soul (cf. Malcolm (2), p. 134). I shall come back to this point in the final section of the chapter. Secondly, there is the alleged existence of telepathy. If there is telepathic awareness of the states of mind of other people it does not rest directly on awareness of their bodies. Might one not, then, be able to become telepathically aware of the experiences of persons who are wholly disembodied?

Telepathy does depend indirectly on awareness of the bodies of others. If I have a habit of coming to believe things about the experiences of others in circumstances in which I am not perceptually aware of their bodies I cannot properly describe this as telepathy, rather than extrospective fantasy, unless these beliefs have successfully been checked against the findings of ordinary, body-based inquiry about their states of mind.

100

However suppose that my tendency to form uninferred beliefs about the experiences of others who are not currently perceived by me passes this test successfully (a) in the case of my beliefs of this sort about a particular person, Jones, and (b) about other people in general. Now suppose that I know Jones's body to have been destroyed and yet find myself with beliefs about experiences of Jones which are appropriate to this situation, that, for example, he is annoyed or distressed at being unable to get in touch with people. One cannot say that this proves that Jones exists in a disembodied state. It is possible that he has been re-embodied in some secluded spot or again that my telepathic powers are malfunctioning (a possibility which, in the circumstances, I cannot exclude). But it is also seemingly conceivable that Jones, disembodied, is having the experiences I take him to have. This array of suppositions provides a possible framework for the disembodied existence of people who have been, and have been known to have been, previously embodied, analogous to the attenuated form of disembodied survival of oneself allowed by Strawson (Strawson (5), pp. 115–16).

More flimsily still, if, as in supposition (b) above, I have substantiated a general telepathic power is it not possible that I should come to believe that there are experiences which are being had by people either whom I have never known when they were embodied or who have never been embodied at all? At least in the case of the purported objects of awareness who have been embodied there is some independent assurance that there is (or was) something for the allegedly telepathic belief to refer to. In the case of the altogether disembodied objects there is nothing outside the allegedly telepathic beliefs to establish that they refer to anything at all. In that case the interpretation of such beliefs as telepathic is the least inviting one and the interpretation of them as just random fantasies overwhelmingly recommends itself.

Others, then, can have experiences ascribed to them when in a disembodied state only if like, Strawson's disembodied selves, they have been previously embodied. And even this concession allows disembodied persons to flourish only in a parasitic way on the margins of the main mass of the embodied. Furthermore, knowledge, like memory, would seem to be a causal notion: the fact that p must be part of the cause of the belief that p which is an ingredient of the knowledge of it. In the case of the embodied persons, remote from ordinary perception, who must exist for beliefs about them to count as telepathic knowledge, the materials for such a causal relationship exist too. But in the case of disembodied persons a new type of causal relationship, radically different from that involved in perception, would have to be invoked.

I conclude from the first stage of this argument, a little untidily,

101

that the only type of persons whom we can readily conceive are embodied and that the circumstances in which disembodied existence is conceivable are at once marginal and susceptible of a less uneconomical interpretation.

The second stage of the argument aims to show that it is impossible to ascribe experiences to oneself unless one can also ascribe them to others. Only in a world in which there are other things in some ways like me is it possible to form the conception of myself. This is not to say that there could not be a world in which I was the only person; only that in such a world the experiences there were would not have a subject or owner. Without the conception of other subjects of experience such experiences as would be known of, those which as we should now say, we are conscious of in ourselves, would not be ascribed at all, though they might be causally correlated with the state and activities of a unique, and ubiquitous, material thing. But, in general, as the first stage of the argument has shown, experiences can be ascribed to others only if they have (or, at the margin, have had) bodies. Hence, in the only, if entirely usual, situation in which the principle of ownership holds, other people must be embodied and I must be (or have been) embodied if there is to be the analogy on which the ascription of experiences of the same sort to both myself and to others must rest. For if I were (and had always been) the only disembodied person in a world of embodied others there would be nothing to connect the classifications I would make of the bodily conduct of others with the experiences I should be conscious of in myself. (I should not, of course, be able to communicate with or otherwise interact with them, it should be remembered.) I can, as Strawson has argued, conceive of myself as disembodied but only if I have previously been embodied and thus been in a position to acquire a conception of myself.

With these qualifications, then, I conclude that persons must be embodied. But this does not imply, as I mentioned earlier, that a person has to have the same body throughout his career, nor again that the body of a person has to be a human body. All that is needed is what Wiggins has called an individuating nucleus of a perceptible kind (Wiggins (2), pp. 51f.). A further reason for this is provided by McTaggart's second principle of the proprietary nature of experience. Unless experiences have a spatial position through their relation to a spatially located subject there could not be two strictly contemporaneous experiences that were identical in content. I shall return to this topic in chapter 11 in a criticism of the Cartesian principle that the mental is not in space. In the final section of this chapter I shall explore further reasons for the possible variety of the embodiment of persons.

Two conceptions of personality

The idea of the soul, as a pure ego or mental substance, persists tenaciously in philosophy. I have argued that it cannot satisfactorily discharge the various tasks for which it has been recruited. The body, with marginal, speculative and dependent exceptions, is all that is required to individuate experiences and to supply them with an owner. An unobservable mental substance cannot individuate and provides a merely formal, because wholly inscrutable, solution to the problem of ownership. It is equally, and even more obviously, inept as an explanation of the identity of a person through time, which rests, not on the body, but on the complex of a person's character and memories, related by continuity.

A possible explanation for the hold of this theoretically unsatisfactory notion is that it is the simplest and most definite way there could be of marking the distinction we draw between persons and things, that is to say mere, non-personal, things. We think of ourselves as primarily and essentially persons and only rather contingently as material objects, mammals, carnivores, husbands and so forth. Of all the contents of the world it is persons to whom we are connected by the strongest bonds of interest and concern. They are the proper objects of love and moral consideration. 'We' and 'I', after all, are *personal* pronouns.

At first glance it may seem that the class of persons is identical in membership with the class of human beings. Even the personal but non-human objects of religious belief and devotion are either ex-human, in the case of the dead, or, in Christianity, capable of incarnation as human. But this, I should contend, is a superficial view. In fact there are two conceptions of personality, of neither of which are all and only human beings the instances actual or possible. The first of these is the complete personality of an adult, sane, human being; the second is the restricted personality of a young child, a mental defective, a higher mammal—to take only actual cases. There are human beings who do not have personality in either of these senses: those in irreversible comas who are still biologically alive, sufferers from senile decay or other defects whom we describe as in a vegetable condition. I should argue, with Aristotle, who attributes personal status to 'another order like man or superior to him' (Aristotle, 4146.20), that there could be non-human beings who are persons in the complete sense: Martians, rational animals in the colloquial sense, even a conceivable kind of mechanically constructed reasoner and agent.

Certainly the dictionary defines a person as 'an individual human being' and even as 'the living body of a human being' but this, although sufficient for most practical purposes, is theoretically inadequate. If there are good moral reasons for treating any human being, however comatose or vegetable, with the concern appropriate to persons (they may recover and our natural ferocity has to be guarded against), they may still in fact be altogether void of personal characteristics. Not all human beings are persons, even in the restricted sense. On the other side there are some beings who have many of the personifying characteristics but who are not human, the higher animals, and non-human beings can be readily conceived who would possess personality in its complete form.

What are these characteristics that are constitutive of personality? There are, I believe, five of them, interrelated in various ways, since some presuppose others, and each of them is susceptible of two interpretations: a stronger one, in which it is a criterion of complete, and a weaker one in which it is a criterion of incomplete, personality. These five characteristics are consciousness, rationality, will, moral status and capacity for personal relations.

A conscious being is always in some sense a self-conscious being. The most elementary form of consciousness has sensations, pre-eminently pain, as its objects. A being that is aware of pain is aware of something in itself, something that constitutes part of itself, but it is not on that account aware of itself as a continuing identity through time, analogous to but distinct from other selves. It is this that is characteristic of a complete personality. But restricted personality must be ascribed to anything that is at least minimally self-conscious in being susceptible of pain.

Rationality, as conceived by the philosophical tradition that stems from Aristotle, is a capacity for abstract reasoning, expressing itself in generalisation, explanation and prediction, which necessarily involve reference to perceptually absent objects and, it would seem reasonable to say, the mastery of language. But there is a weaker form of rationality that is prelinguistic, a concrete and practical rationality that reveals itself in the selection of means to ends, as in those well-judged sequences of animal actions which are not instinctive but based on learning from experience.

There is a comparable duality about the will. A being is an agent, in a restricted sense at any rate, to the extent that its behaviour is motivated, the outcome of desire and not wholly determined by non-mental causal influences. But this level of agency falls short of deliberated choice, which involves the envisagement of alternatives and the application of statable rules of conduct. It is this stronger sense of agency that Kant had in mind when he defined a rational being as one that 'has the power to act in accordance with his idea of laws—that is, in accordance with principles—and only so has he a will' (Kant, p. 29). Full self-consciousness of one's own identity, as well as will or agency in this strong sense, are preconditions of moral responsibility.

This leads to the next characteristic of personality: moral status. On the one hand there are moral agents, those to whom moral injunctions are addressed and who can properly be held responsible for moral lapses; on the other there are what may be called moral patients, those whose interests should be taken into consideration in the formulation of moral principles. These two classes by no means coincide. Although all moral agents are part of the total moral constituency, the converse is not true. It is a widespread conviction (I shall defend it in the final chapter) that mere sentience, the capacity to suffer, is a sufficient condition for moral consideration. But it is not a sufficient condition for responsibility as a moral agent. Infants, defectives and animals are proper objects of moral concern; they are not proper objects of moral praise and blame. This distinction can dispel an unclarity about the way in which moral principles are universal in scope. On the one hand they enjoin conduct *by all moral agents*, on the other they enjoin it *for all moral patients*.

Finally, there is capacity for personal relations. To love someone, in the personal way in which this means more than simply to like them very much, as one might a house or a car, is to identify oneself with the interests of the object of love. So only those beings that literally have interests, in other words persons in the restricted sense, can be loved. But not all those who can be loved are themselves capable of love. To love someone is to conceive him as a continuing being with an identity like one's own. Thus infants and animals can only like very much. Genuinely reciprocal love can exist only between complete personalities. Similarly only complete personalities can enter into genuine relations of co-operation, that is more than a momentary or instinctive coincidence of interests, and communication, that is more than mere incitement to flight or attention.

All five of these personifying characteristics are to be found, then, in a stronger and a weaker form: consciousness may be of one's continuing identity or merely of one's sensations, rationality may be abstract and linguistic or concrete and practical, agency may be deliberate or merely appetitive, moral status may be responsible agency or propriety as an object of moral concern, one's capacity for personal relations may be active or passive, a capacity to return love or merely to receive and be pleased by it. Where the characteristics are present in their stronger form there is a complete personality, where in their weaker form a restricted one. In either case the essence of personality does not lie in the style of its embodiment.

Part II
Knowledge

Knowledge as a system

Throughout its history the philosophical theory of knowledge has been more or less closely bound up with the idea that knowledge as a whole is a hierarchical system. It is, in general, a condition of a truth's being known that the belief in it should rest on good and sufficient reason. In order to justify the claim that something is known, therefore, it must be expounded together with its grounds and the justifying logical relation between them must be specified. Any finite body of knowledge will thus have a set of relative first principles, for which, as far as that body of knowledge is concerned, no ground exists within the body of knowledge in question. Aristotle's theory of the nature of a science is a first generalisation of this idea. In his view there is a set of self-evident first principles for each discriminable topic of knowledge, the development of the science is the logical derivation of the consequences of these first principles and the science as a whole consists of the principles together with their consequences. The model for his theory was clearly geometry, the first body of knowledge to be given a definite logical articulation. The concept of an axiom, as a self-evident or self-justifying first principle, not in need of any support from distinguishable grounds, solves the problem of the infinite regress of justification. As self-evident, an axiom is its own sufficient reason. Without such termini the process of justifying claims to knowledge would be necessarily incompletable. If every truth is known only if it is justified by some other truth, which must itself be known, nothing could be known unless an infinite number of things was known already.

It is clear that some recognised bodies of knowledge presuppose others and this, together with the instinct for simplicity and unification, encourages a further generalisation which brings all partial bodies of knowledge together into the single body of unified knowledge. Some such idea is implicit in Plato's conception of dialectic as a sovereign study in which the relative axioms or assumed postulates of particular bodies of knowledge give up their status as axioms on being derived from an absolute and all-inclusive set of first principles. The idea is to some extent realised in the theory of knowledge of Descartes. *Cogito ergo sum* is not so much a single principle from which the whole of knowledge can be derived as an irresistibly primary example of a self-evident or axiomatic truth. Descartes uses it to exemplify the principle that whatever can be clearly and distinctly conceived is certainly true, rather than as a premise for further deductions. In practice two kinds of truth turn out to be self-evident: necessary truths whose denials would be evidently self-contradictory and descriptions of immediate subjective experience. ('I exist' exemplifies the former class for him, 'I think' the latter.) Spinoza and, with more qualifications, Leibniz develop the more rationalistic side of the Cartesian doctrine: rejecting the ultimacy of singular contingent truths altogether they present an ideal picture of knowledge as a whole as the complete deductive development of a set of fundamental logically necessary principles. Locke and his successors reverse this order of preference. The ultimate, terminal elements of knowledge are singular propositions about immediate experience from which all other substantial knowledge of matters of fact is derived by induction. Necessary truths apply to a realm of their own as asserting the relations of ideas and by Hume, at any rate, are conceived in a more or less functional way as concerned with the internal connections of discourse rather than with the external reality which discourse, in its primary employment, describes.

The logical inquiries initiated by Frege and culminating in the *Principia Mathematica* of Whitehead and Russell seemed, until Gödel at least, a triumphant realisation of the rationalist and ultimately Aristotelian ideal. The system of Whitehead and Russell aimed to set out the whole of rational or *a priori* knowledge, the entire body of necessary truths composing logic and mathematics, in a single, rigorously logical, deductive system in which every truth was derived from a small group of unquestionable axioms and every concept was defined in terms of a small group of elementary formal notions (the holy trinity of the stroke, the universal quantifier and membership). In the logical atomism of Russell and the early Wittgenstein the lessons of this achievement were applied to the systematisation of empirical knowledge. In this field there could be no formal systematisation proper since the class of empirical or synthetic first principles is indefinitely numerous. But the techniques of Russellian logic could be applied to give a complete and logically satisfactory classification of the varieties of empirical truth and a set of elementary concepts and statements could be singled out in terms of which all other concepts could be defined and all other kinds of statement be analysed. Wittgenstein sketched the outline of such a system in the *Tractatus*, Russell identified its elementary components (a matter on which Wittgenstein had been silent) with Cartesian descriptions of immediate experience and Carnap, finally, in his *Logische Aufbau der Welt*, carried the project out in detail. In his 'constitution-system of empirical concepts' he provided an account of the whole apparatus of concepts and statements of empirical discourse in terms of a single concept of the relation of remembered similarity, conceived as holding between sense-impressions. The basic elements of the systems are statements about immediate subjective experience. Out of them can be constructed, with the aid of the formal concepts of logic, the concepts of material things, other minds and 'cultural objects' such as social institutions. The topics of thought and knowledge are conceived as standing on various levels each reducible to its predecessor. Statements about objects of one level are usually analysed as more or less complex generalisations of statements about objects on the level below: material things are regularities in the occurrence of impressions, minds are regularities in the behaviour of certain material things. It follows that higher-level statements are justified by inductive inference from statements on the level below which are, of course, deducible from them. The basic lowest-level statements need and can have no inferential justification. At this point the system of beliefs makes contact, through observation, with the world of empirical fact.

The construction of logical systems of statements can be pursued from two distinct and largely independent motives. The systems I have been discussing have been considered from the point of view of an epistemological interest in the justification of their components and this interest played a large part in the construction of most of them. But system-building can also be undertaken out of a purely formal interest in economy, in system for system's sake. Russell was much struck by the fact that the basic axioms of traditional logic—the laws of identity, contradiction and excluded middle—were derived, consequential theorems in the system of *Principia Mathematica*. Subsequent investigation showed that a particular body of statements could be systematised in quite distinct but each formally adequate ways. Numerous distinct sets of axioms were found, for example, for the logic of statements or propositional calculus which were all consistent, independent and complete. The only objectively logical ground for choice between them was their comparative economy in number of axioms and primitive terms. The idea that one set might be epistemologically preferable to the others, in containing especially indubitable and self-evident members, was lost sight of. This formal relativism about systems of formal truths passed over into the analysis of factual truth. In the late 1930s, in the face

111

of disputes about the nature of the basic factual statements, which some identified with descriptions of immediate experience, others with statements about currently perceived material things, Carnap, with a pacifying intention, put forward a principle of tolerance, allowing that any formally satisfactory systematisation of knowledge was as good as any other (Carnap (2), pp. 51–2). As well as its eirenic virtues this had the apparent merit of conforming to the venerated maxim of Frege that issues of logic and psychology should be kept distinct (Frege, p. x). I shall return to the misuse of this maxim later. For the moment it is sufficient to point out that since the dispute about foundations was resolved in this radical way, by denying the significance of the question at issue, philosophers interested in logical systematisation have in effect abandoned an interest in knowledge. For them knowledge has no foundations, only systems of knowledge have and systems with different foundations can be equally valid and acceptable. Foundations are relative to systems and their choice is a matter of convention. This point of view is most fully expressed in Goodman's *Structure of Appearance*, in which purely formal criteria of adequacy are adopted and the concept of epistemological priority, in terms of which a choice between systems with different foundations could be made on non-formal grounds, is destructively criticised.

While systematisers have lost an interest in knowledge, those who have retained that interest have largely abandoned the view that the theory of knowledge should take the form of a logical system. In part this is due to dissatisfaction with the details of the logical analyses given by systematic epistemology. More important is a rejection of the ability of the logical instruments employed in the analyses to give an adequate interpretation of the actual, ordinary meaning of the concepts and statements they are applied to. On this view formal logic is a simplified caricature of the rules of inference by which our beliefs are actually connected. The meaning and justification of actual discourse must be considered in detail and without formalistic preconceptions; the logic of actual discourse is informal.

These two kinds of rejection of the systematic ideal—formal and conventionalist on the one hand and literal and naturalistic on the other—agree at least that philosophical investigation should be carried on piecemeal. But there is a discernible residue of the systematic conception in a general theory about the nature of philosophical problems which has been independently advanced by three very different philosophers in recent years, these being Waismann, Wisdom and Ayer (Waismann, pp. 28–9; Gasking; Ayer (5), pp. 81–7). According to this general theory philosophical problems are characteristically initiated by a sceptical challenge to some accepted variety of knowledge. The form of this challenge is that knowledge of one kind rests exclusively for its justification on knowledge of another kind and yet essentially goes beyond it. The statements of the first kind whose truth we claim to know rest wholly for their support on statements of the second kind and yet they are quite distinct from them in meaning. There is a group of familiar examples of pairs of objects of knowledge about which it can reasonably be held that the first member of the pair is wholly evidenced by and yet is quite logically distinct from the second: laws of nature and particular events, material objects and sense-impressions, past events and present recollections, mental states and behaviour, the theoretical entities of science and common, observable material things. The list could be enlarged. There is a broadly comparable situation in ethics, in the relation of values to facts, and in the philosophy of religion, in the relation of the supernatural to the natural.

In the face of a sceptical challenge of this form there are at any rate four possible responses. If this fourfold scheme of possibilities is applied to the seven cases I have mentioned the result is a classi-fication of familiar epistemological doctrines which it would be unnecessarily laborious to set out in detail. The first possibility is to admit the validity of the sceptical challenge and to agree that objects of the transcending kind are beyond the reach of possible knowledge. Secondly there is intuitionism, which denies that all evidence for objects of the first kind is provided by objects of the second and holds that there is some sort of direct access to them, as in perceptual naive realism, the theory of a sympathetic awareness of other minds and the doctrine of religious or mystical experience. Thirdly, there is reductionism, which denies the logical distinctness of the two kinds of object and proposes definitions of one in terms of the other, as with phenomenalism, logical behaviourism, ethical natural-ism and religious modernism. Finally there is transcendentalism which admits the premises of the sceptical challenge and thus the existence, as Ayer puts it, of a logical gap between the two kinds of belief but contends that it can be bridged by a rational principle, perhaps of a synthetic *a priori* character, as in the justification of induction by the uniformity of nature, the causal or representative theory of perception, the argument to other minds by analogy and natural or rational theology.

In fact none of the three proponents of this way of considering epistemological problems opts firmly for any of the four solutions recognised as possible, either comprehensively or in particular cases. Waismann's purpose is negative. He sees the gaps as indicating the lines of fracture between various strata in language within which, but not between which, strict logical relations obtain. Rejecting intuitionism and reductionism he allows that evidence from one side of a gap can support, in an unanalysed way, hypotheses about what lies on the other side of it. Wisdom's response is equally inconclusive but in a more positive way. He sees us as the battleground of a permanent conflict between the reductionist and transcendentalist impulses. The gaps exists and cannot be bridged by a general principle, we can cross them only in particular cases and by particular decisions. Ayer, more forthrightly, conceives the possibility of a fifth way of dealing with the situation. This, which he calls 'the method of descriptive analysis', consists, in his words, of 'taking the gaps in our stride'. In effect it is a kind of inarticulate transcendentalism for it proceeds by making clear the forms of inference that are usually employed in the disputed cases and accepting them in a spirit of natural piety towards the established order of things. Where transcendentalism proper proposes a sort of justification of the principles it uses, Ayer's method is content to describe them and use them, while admitting that the only sort of justification they can aspire to is that of ancient prescription.

It should be noticed that the case of induction has a kind of priority to the others which is not fully recognised by placing it first in the list. The possibility of a reductionist solution in any of the other cases presupposes that the simplest kind of extrapolative induction, where the inference involved is to indefinitely many more things of the same kind as those which provide the evidence, is already vindicated as admissible. For the phenomenalist an inference from impressions to material things is an inference to inductive regularities in sense-experience; for the logical behaviourist an inference from behaviour to other minds is an inference to regularities in behaviour. There can, therefore, be no reductionist solution to the problem of induction without obvious circularity. The closest approximation that is possible to it is a descriptive theory like Mach's in which a law of nature is a summary of evidence, from which it is strictly deducible by that perfect or demonstrative induction of old-fashioned logic text-books about which no Humean doubts can arise.

Another point to notice is that there are the makings of a hier-archical system in this scheme since most of the cases following that of perception, by taking facts about material things to be on the hither or evidential side of the gap, assume that the problem of perception has been solved. Other minds, theoretical entities, values and the supernatural are all conceived as dependent for their evidence on facts about the material world. So the outlines of the older unitary system are still discernible through the more up-to-date fragmentariness of the Waismann-Wisdom-Ayer scheme. To adopt it is still to accord a measure of absolute epistemological priority to impressions. The view that problems in the theory of knowledge must be investigated piecemeal is endorsed more in form than in fact.

The idea of epistemological order is an almost inevitable corollary of a philosophical theory of knowledge. Such a theory is not a descriptive account of either the beliefs actually held by a man or a society at a particular time or the historical origin and development of those beliefs. It is necessarily a critical investigation of beliefs since for a statement to count as an item of knowledge it must be true and justified as well as accepted. To say what a man or society knows a critical selection must be made from their beliefs. This point is made by the view that the task of a theory of knowledge is to give a rational reconstruction of the claims to knowledge that are commonly made. Such a reconstruction will, as Reichenbach puts it, be concerned with the logical order of justification of beliefs rather than with the psychological or historical order of their discovery (Reichenbach, pp. 5–8). It will begin by classifying the various distinguishable kinds of claim to knowledge that are made and will specify the nature of the support or justification that these kinds of belief must have if the claim to knowledge in respect of them is to be made good. In many cases, at any rate, this support or justification will consist of other beliefs and the support these other beliefs provide will be conditional on their being justified themselves. If it is found, as it commonly is, that the relations of support between kinds of belief are asymmetrical, that beliefs of a given kind do not or do not ultimately derive their support from the kinds of belief that they themselves justify, the kinds of belief thus related can be arranged in a linear order. It is natural to suppose that such an order will have a beginning, a kind of belief that while supporting others does not owe its justification to any other kind of belief. Such beliefs, as the possessors of absolute epistemological priority, will be the foundations of knowledge.

Theory of knowledge, as a critical account of the logical order of justification, must be governed by Frege's maxim that the logical and the psychological should always be clearly distinguished from one another. The usual causal antecedents of a belief must not be confused with its justification and its customary accompaniments must not be confused with its meaning. Hume made both of these mistakes in his account of the concept of cause. The past conjunctions which in fact justify causal belief he took to be its cause; the sense of compulsive expectation which sometimes accompanies such a belief he took to be its meaning or essence. Again in Popper's critique of inductivism, of the view that our belief in laws of nature is based on the observation of particular instances, a logical and a psychological or genetic interpretation of the thesis under attack are somewhat run together, although both, it should be said, are worthy of criticism (Popper (1), ch. 1). The fact that the general or theoretical hypotheses we accept do not originate psychologically from the successive observation of particular confirming instances, to which a mechanical rule of induction is then applied, does not show that hypotheses are not based on instances in another sense, namely that of owing their justification to them. Indeed what is fairly indubitable is that hypotheses are seldom or never first *entertained* or *envisaged*, in articulate scientific thinking at least, as a result of observed repetitions since for the observation to fasten on the repetitions it must be guided and focused by a tentative hypothesis. But this does not entail that the *acceptance* of hypotheses is universally or largely prior to the discovery of confirming instances. The formation, acceptance and justification of hypotheses must all be kept clearly distinct from one another.

On the other hand the fact that there is a distinction between actual belief on the one hand and justified belief, and in particular knowledge, on the other, does not entail that the psychological relations of actual beliefs have nothing whatever to do with the logical relations of justified ones. For the only way in which the logical relations of support between beliefs can be discovered is by considering those psychological relations between beliefs which are most widely regarded as affording justifications. We are confronted with a bewildering variety of inferences in the psychological sense, passages in thought from one belief to another. Order is introduced into this chaos by the recognition of recurrent patterns in these transitions. It is further evident that some of these patterns have particularly stable results, in that the beliefs in which they issue gain general acceptance when presented in this pattern and that the resulting beliefs are either permanently retained or are abandoned only if the support on which they rested is abandoned as well so that the pattern itself is not invalidated. It is in some such way as this that valid patterns of justifying argument are empirically established. This sets a certain limit to the scope and freedom of rational reconstruction. If a type of belief is rationally reconstructed as depending on a kind of support which it never psychologically or empirically possesses the validity of the reconstruction has the absurd consequence that no belief of the kind in question is ever in fact justified. There is a parallel in political theory. Rousseau's theory of the general will is a rational reconstruction of the justification of government. One is obliged to obey only a government that embodies the general will of its citizens and since no actual government does no actual government has a valid claim to obedience. Hegel's dilution of the theory, which allowed that governments could embody the real will of their citizens, without immediately appearing to and without satisfying Rousseau's conditions of perfect democracy, was a natural response to such a *reductio ad absurdum*.

Rational reconstructions of knowledge, then, should not exploit the fact that their task is logically critical rather than psychologically descriptive by complete indifference to psychological realism. The idea that internal logical consistency is the essential criterion of a reconstruction is implicit in Carnap's tolerant practice. To the extent that this tolerance represents a temporary indecision about the actual nature of the foundations of knowledge there is nothing to complain of. Systems that turn out to be inapplicable may still retain a certain formal interest. But when, as with Goodman, system-building is pursued with the conviction that the problem of foundations is a wholly unreal one since incapable in principle of being decided, the aim that gives a point to the inquiry has been altogether abandoned. Overt rejection of the requirement of applicability is less common than the simple neglect of it. I shall argue that such a neglect is shown in by far the most common account of the foundations of empirical knowledge which identifies them with the immediate impressions of the senses, although it is neither the sole nor the most fatal defect of that theory.

In the introduction to part I, I identified the problem of the foundations of knowledge with the fourth and last of the traditional problems of substance, substance being defined for the purposes of this problem as that which requires nothing but itself in order to exist. To make this identification is to take that which requires nothing but itself to exist as that which requires nothing but itself if it is to be known or, less exigently, if it is to be the object of justified belief. The primary issue here is whether there is any substance at all in the sense in question, whether, in other words, knowledge has foundations. Most of those who have settled this question affirmatively have taken sense-impressions to be the epistemological substances on which knowledge is founded. In doing so they raise the third problem of substance, that of whether the existence of public objective things involves the existence of substrata, unobservable realities transcending given appearances, over and above the appearances themselves. If, however, public material things are taken to be the epistemological substances the problem of an unobservable reality transcending appearances does not arise in this form. Objectivity does not have to be accounted for by substrata if objective things can be directly observed. But the distinction of reality and appearance can still emerge again at another level. One who accepts a direct realist theory of perception is of course committed to the view that objective things can be observed but he may not identify them with the whole of reality for he may accept as well the objective reality of such abstract entities as universals and propositions. A direct realist may also deny ultimate reality to what he regards as the public objects of perception for he may accept the dogmas of theistic religion or some other form of transcendental metaphysics. The only type of metaphysics that is closed to him is idealist, whether transcendent, as with Bradley and McTaggart, or immanent, as with most empiricists, however anti-metaphysical they may profess to be, from Hume to Russell and Ayer. These further issues will be considered in part III. In part II the problem for investigation is that of the existence and nature of the foundations of knowledge.

5

Intuition

The regress of justification

The doctrine that there are foundations to knowledge maintains that there must be intuitive as well as inferred statements. If any beliefs are to be justified at all, and *a fortiori* if any are to qualify as items of knowledge, there must be some terminal beliefs that do not owe their truth or credibility to others. For a belief to be justified it is not enough for it to be accepted, let alone merely entertained: there must also be good reason for accepting it. Furthermore, for an inferential belief to be justified the beliefs that support it must be justified themselves. There must, therefore, be a kind of belief that does not owe its justification to the support provided by others. Unless this were so no belief would be justified at all, for to justify any belief would require the antecedent justification of an infinite series of beliefs. The terminal intuitive beliefs that are needed to bring the regress of justification to a stop need not be strictly self-evident in the sense that they somehow justify themselves. All that is required is that they should not owe their justification to any other beliefs.

To say that a belief is intuitive is not to say that it is in fact uninferred nor again that it is uninferrable. It is rather to say that it does not require the support of other justified beliefs if it is to be justified itself. If, by a somewhat questionable idealisation, we consider the momentary cross-section of the beliefs someone actually holds, it will consist of a body of beliefs some of which owe their credibility, in the eyes of that person, to others within the set and some of which do not. The latter are intuitive only in a psychological sense. They are accepted, and so regarded as justified, by the person in question and their acceptance by him as justified does not rest on their support by other beliefs of his. But it does not follow that they are justified and that his acceptance of them is correct. It is another question altogether as to whether they really are justified and do not need the support of others, as to whether, that is to say, they are logically intuitive.

What makes this idealised cross-section questionable is in part the fact that we may retain a belief while forgetting the support on which it originally rested. Like heartless social climbers we lose touch with those who have helped us in our struggles upward. So a belief that was once psychologically inferred may now be psychologically intuitive. Now if a belief that has become psychologically intuitive in this way is logically inferential in character our forgetfulness may have deprived it of the requisite justification. In that case evidence in support of it must be reassembled. In practice there is an intermediate possibility between wholly forgetting and wholly retaining the grounds of a belief. We may recall, if not the details, the general character of the evidence we had and have good reason for accepting the general principle that evidence of that kind is reliable.

As well as distinguishing between logical and psychological intuitiveness, then, we may also distinguish between two kinds of psychological intuitiveness, which we might call momentary and historical. It would seem that there must be psychologically intuitive beliefs of both these kinds. Unless the set of my beliefs at a given moment is infinitely large they cannot all owe their acceptance by me to the support provided by others. And provided that there is a time at which my beliefs first began and before which I had no beliefs at all, which seems a more reasonable supposition than its opposite, the very first beliefs I accept cannot derive their credibility in my eyes from their relation to other beliefs of mine. But this necessity of momentarily or historically uninferred beliefs does not establish the necessity of logically intuitive ones, of beliefs that do not require the support of others whether they have it or not.

On the other hand logically intuitive beliefs, which do not need support from others, are not necessarily excluded from such support. Indeed there are no beliefs that are strictly uninferable. If I hit my thumb sharply with a hammer I shall form and accept the belief that my thumb hurts, to put the point with a mildness that has led some philosophers to protest that being in pain is not a matter of belief, with its vernacular implication of dubiety, at all. At the same time I may have all the evidence that others have for saying that my thumb hurts. I, like them, may be aware that blood is oozing out under my darkening thumbnail and that I am jumping about and shouting. These public considerations are perfectly good grounds for the statement that my thumb hurts and are so taken by the people around me. They are also, in the case envisaged, available to me but they are, of course entirely superfluous as far as I am concerned.

Let us look at another kind of case. In a murky and ill-lit room I may pick up a book and assert that it is red, not because I see that it is but because this is James's room and I have good reason for thinking that all James's books are red. That this book of James's is red is at any rate a relatively logically intuitive belief to the extent that it does not need to be justified by any general statement about James's books. But it can be justified in that way and in unfavourable circumstances may have to be. What should be noticed is that the kind of support that is given to the belief about this book by the statement about James's books in general cannot suffice to support all beliefs of the same kind. For unless some beliefs of that kind are justified in another way there can be no justification for the general statement about James's books. I shall call the kind of support given by a singular statement to the corresponding generalisation *essential* and that given by the generalisation to a singular statement *accidental*. What essentially supports a belief is epistemologically prior to it; what accidentally supports a belief is not. The only kind of support that a logically intuitive belief can have is accidental. Thus although every logically intuitive belief is capable of being justified by inference it is only accidentally inferable.

The distinction of essential from accidental may also be applied to the consequences of a statement in virtue of which it can be tested. It is sometimes held that the process of empirical testing or verification of beliefs is in principle interminable. From any belief whatever further testable consequences can be derived. The testable consequences of a belief are simply the supporting beliefs from which it can be inferred viewed from the other end, seen as being formulated and justified after and not before the formulation of the hypothesis they are used to justify. If it is held that every factual belief can be tested in the light of its consequences this is only obviously true if accidental as well as essential consequences are included. Logically intuitive beliefs, if there are such things, can have no essential consequences. Every belief, then, is both inferable and testable. But if there are logically intuitive beliefs they will be inferable and testable only in the accidental sense, they will have neither essential support nor essential consequences.

The regress of justification we are concerned with, then, is not intended to show that there must be actually uninferred beliefs, although there must be, nor that there must be uninferable beliefs, for there are none. What it claims is to show that there must be logically intuitive basic statements which do not essentially require the support of other justified beliefs and which are only inferable and testable in the light of their consequences in an accidental way. It poses a familiar problem for the conventional definition of knowledge as that which is believed, is true and is justified. Knowledge so defined is the limiting or perfect case of justified belief. All three elements of the definition have been contested. It has been held that p can be known without being believed on the ground that it is wrong to say that you believe that p when you know it. It is wrong of course to say you believe that p in these circumstances but this is because it is misleading to do so rather than because it is false. It is wrong in the same way as it is wrong to describe your wife as the woman you live with: in both cases the weaker assertion suggests that that is all there is to it. It is also true that you can have conclusive reason for believing that p even though p is in fact false. But if you have conclusive reason for believing that p you ought to say that you know it. However the fact that you ought to say that you know that p does not entail that you really do know it. You ought to say that you know that p if you honestly think that you do. When you say this you plainly imply that p is true, though it may not be. If it is not true then what you said was wrong, in the sense that it was false, but it was the right thing for you to say nevertheless.

The argument for including justification as well as truth and belief in the definition of knowledge goes back to Plato's *Theaetetus*. It is quite possible to arrive at and to be wholly convinced by a belief that is in fact true on absurd or superstitious grounds, as the result, for instance, of a mutually compensating superimposition of fallacious inferences or of a dream or totally irrelevant analogy. But if the justification thus required for a true belief to count as knowledge is a further belief it must itself be known or at least justified. (If ten none too well placed but wholly independent witnesses testify to a certain fact in different ways that fact will be better supported than any of the single items of testimony in its favour. The incompletely justified beliefs of the witnesses can be aggregated into a conclusively justified result.) An inference does not justify its conclusion by reason of its validity alone: its premises must be true as well. This is the most elementary but apparently least absorbable lesson of formal logic and it is summed up in the great truth of common sense that logic isn't everything. So if anything is to be known at all some beliefs must be non-inferentially justifiable, must not owe their justification to other beliefs.

Can the regress of justification be dealt with in any other way than by admitting the existence of logically intuitive beliefs which are not essentially justifiable by other beliefs? There are two possible alternatives which have been pursued. The first is that of Peirce who claims that all belief is inferential but in an as it were continuous way, with no first element and no really, rather than conceptually, discriminable steps, so that the regress argument is a sophism of the same order as Zeno's arguments against the possibility of motion (Peirce (1)). Secondly, there is the position of the coherence theorists, which disputes the linear assumption involved in the concepts of epistemological priority and essential support. On this view beliefs are mutually corroborative, to justify a belief is not to trace out its epistemological ancestry in a single direction but to establish its coherence with other beliefs or judgments of all kinds. These two alternatives will be the topic of chapter 8. For the moment I shall continue with an examination of the concept of intuition in general and go on to consider another kind of argument for the existence of basic statements which sees them as a condition of factual significance rather than of justified belief.

The concept of intuition

Both in its everyday and in its philosophical employment 'intuition' is a word calculated to arouse the suspicions of the empirically-minded. In order to prevent irrelevantly sentimental objections to the idea that it is the foundation of all knowledge of matters of fact something must be said about its customary senses.

In common speech it is used to describe the ability to form reliable beliefs in circumstances where the evidence ordinarily required for beliefs of that kind is not available. Those who confidently prophesy impending disasters without being able to give any grounds for their prophecies and in situations where none of the usual signs of impending disaster is evident may be credited with it. It is not enough for a belief of this kind to count as an intuition that it should be confident and unsupported. It must also be correct. The verb 'intuit', like 'know' and 'remember', implies the truth of the proposition that is its grammatical object.

It follows from this that vernacular intuition, as I shall call it, cannot be the ultimate source of any whole kind of justified beliefs. Before the prediction of an impending disaster can be established as a vernacular intuition the fact that the disaster really was impending when the prediction was made must be assured by the normal method of observing it with the senses. Even this subsequent verification is not enough to settle the question. The prediction might have been an isolated lucky guess. But if a man constantly makes predictions, in the absence of the usual grounds, which turn out to be predominantly correct, he will then be credited with a power of intuition in respect of the type of fact he successfully predicts. Vernacular intuition is inevitably a short cut to knowledge, a psychological economy which can be validated only by some more laborious process of justification. It is closely comparable to telepathy, which is perhaps best regarded as a species of it. If I frequently form beliefs about the state of my twin brother's mind at times when I have no clear idea of where he is or what he is doing and if these beliefs are verified by his diaries and recollections of the time in question and by the recollections of those who were with him, the claim that my beliefs about him are genuinely telepathic is strongly supported. But no kind of vernacular intuition is self-subsistent from the point of view of justification; all such intuition is parasitic on less direct procedures for arriving at beliefs. In the terminology of the preceding section it is psychologically but not logically intuitive.

Stace has drawn attention to the large part that unreasoned beliefs in fact play in our thinking (Stace (1)). His view that very often such beliefs, when correct, are the outcome of associative suggestion seems plausible. For the associative formation of beliefs is an un-conscious equivalent or correlate of deliberate and explicit inductive reasoning. The intuitive woman who mutters to her sceptical husband a few moments after first setting eyes on a neat and composed appli-cant for the post of cook, 'she drinks' and who turns out, after she has given way to his pedestrian empiricism, to be right, may well be using some discriminable feature of the applicant's appearance as an unconscious cue for her judgment. This feature may be regularly associated with the habit of drinking and the intuitive woman can use it as a sign without having given a name to it or having singled it out in any way.

Vernacular intuition is convenient to the extent that it does exist and it would be a help if there were more of it. It is continuous with and not clearly distinguishable from that inarticulate diagnostic skill which is acquired from long-continued experience of a particular kind of subject-matter by garage mechanics, shepherds and fishermen. It is also somewhat perilous since it is not intrinsically distinguishable from wild guess-work. What is important for our purposes is that it is not any sort of necessity of thought, no regress argument can be used to establish its existence, and it does not pick out an inde-pendent class of basic statements as the ultimate terminus of all justifications.

In most modern philosophy intuition is taken to cover all non-empirical varieties of direct knowledge. The most important of these is the direct knowledge of ultimate logical principles. There is a traditional distinction of necessary truths into the intuitive and demonstrative. Intuitive necessary truths are self-evident and thus supply the axioms and the rules of inference required for the deriva-tion of demonstrative ones. The formal relativism that was mentioned in the introduction to part II has abandoned this distinction on the ground that formally satisfactory systems with different axioms and rules of inference can be constructed. But although this suggests that there is no hard and fast line between intuitive and demonstra-tive necessary truths it does not destroy the point of the distinction. Every necessary truth may be demonstrable in some formally adequate system but a system is materially or epistemologically adequate only if its unproved data are acceptable on their own account, in other words if they are intuitive. It would appear that more necessary truths are intuitively self-evident than are needed for purposes of systematisation. If so some of the derived propositions of a formally and materially adequate system will not be essentially demonstrative since they will be qualified to serve as unproved data themselves. But if a system is to have more than a merely formal interest, if, that is to say, it is to provide any reason for accepting the theorems that it proves, its unproved data must be acceptable on their own account and not simply formally sufficient to yield the consequences they do.

Two other varieties of non-empirical intuition should be briefly considered. The first of these is moral intuition. What suggests that there is such a thing is that there are moral convictions which are not merely unreasoned but which seem to their possessors to be insusceptible of justification, their acceptance is taken as a precondition of the rational discussion of moral issues. The second is religious or mystical intuition whose defenders ascribe a logical autonomy to the area of discourse involved comparable to that insisted on by ethical intuitionists.

Logical intuition is more acceptable than the moral or mystical-religious varieties. One theory accounts for it as a direct awareness of the relations between universals, another as a recognition of the fact that the beliefs in question are implicitly definitive of the logical words. I shall examine these competing accounts in detail in chapter 12. For the moment the question to be answered is what grounds are there for supposing that there is such a thing as logical intuition to explain. The admitted psychological intuitiveness of many logical and mathematical beliefs is not enough. Nor again is the fact that the holders of such beliefs do not suppose that any justification of them is necessary or possible. What is significant is the fact of universal agreement, amongst all but the muddled or deliberately perverse, that a particular set of such beliefs are true. Every proposition has been disputed by somebody. But the dialectician who claims to deny the law of contradiction is insincere. In the practical concerns of life he uses this denial only to confuse his opponents, he accords it the fullest possible respect in his dealings with the bank or the income tax authorities.

It is the failure of this third requirement of universal agreement that undermines the claims of moral and mystical intuition. There are primary moral and mystical convictions which are psychologically intuitive and whose defenders feel neither called upon nor able to justify them. But the incompatibility of these convictions shows that not all can be true and there is insufficient general agreement on any one of the contenders for it to be picked out from the rest.

In this book I am following a wider usage of the term than that which defines it as non-empirical direct knowledge. It is familiar from the writings of Kant for whom there is nothing contradictory about the concept of empirical intuition. The problem of whether there is such a thing is precisely the problem of whether there are foundations to knowledge. There is point as well as precedent for this usage. Arguments of the very same form can be used to support the idea of basic truths of fact as to support that of self-evident and essentially axiomatic necessary truths.

Ostensive statements

The regress of justification is intended to show that there must be basic statements which do not owe their justification to inference from any other justified statements. There is an analogous regress argument to show that there must be basic statements of an ostensive rather than intuitive kind which are not introduced into discourse or defined in terms of any other kind of statements. To explain the meaning of a form of words with which statements can be made, in particular to introduce it into discourse in the first place, either generally or for a particular speaker, it is often possible to produce a statement or set of statements whose meaning is already understood with which it is identical in meaning, in other words to produce a translation of it. It is obvious, on regressive grounds, that not all statements can be introduced in this fashion since every employment of this technique presupposes the antecedent understanding of the translation. It follows that there must be an initial class of statements whose meaning is to be explained in some other way. These will be introduced into discourse not by correlation with other statements but by correlation with the world outside language. Adapting a familiar term I shall call them ostensive statements.

The account given of elementary propositions in Wittgenstein's *Tractatus* is a pure theory of ostensive statements. It is argued there that there must be such statements, which directly correspond to the facts of which the world is composed, but no examples are given and no description of their general character. If any statement is to have a definite sense it must either be, or be equivalent and thus reducible to, a statement or set of statements directly correlated with the extra-linguistic world. Wittgenstein's view of this direct correlation as a matter of more or less literal picturing is a peculiarity we may ignore here. What is more significantly original about his position is that it presents the traditional principle of empiricism in a new way, as a theory about statements rather than concepts, the meaning of sentences rather than the meaning of words. The reason for this mode of presentation is not explicitly developed but it is to be found in Wittgenstein's adoption of Frege's maxim that a word has meaning only in the context of a sentence. 'Only propositions have sense' Wittgenstein rather excessively observes, 'only in the nexus of a proposition does a name have meaning' (Wittgenstein (1), 3.3).

It is neither correct to say nor desirable to stipulate that sentences alone, and not their constituent words, have meaning. The requisite point is that sentences are logically prior to words, that to know the meaning of a word is to know the meaning of sentences in which it occurs. This fact is concealed in part by the existence of dictionaries and the practice to which they testify of our commonly explaining meaning in terms of single words (a practice which shows something important about the nature of language) and in part by the existence of significant and intelligible utterances composed of a single word. But these complete one-word utterances are in fact sentences. They are characteristically highly ambiguous. Consider the remark 'fire'. This can mean any of the following: this house is on fire, put some more fuel on the fire, pull your triggers, dismiss rather than reprimand an unsatisfactory employee. Many-word sentences have to be used to guard against the misunderstandings which are ordinarily excluded by the circumstances of utterance. So every complete utterance is a sentence even if it consists of only a single word and in practice there is more to the sentence than that single word, contextual features are involved that could be verbally recognised only in a many-worded sentence. Another consideration that obscures the priority of sentences to words is the fact that the first elements of language instruction are single words. The infant is bombarded with isolated nouns: ball, rattle, mummy and so forth. But here what is being said is 'here is a ball', 'this is Mummy', etc. Since the subject or referring part of these sentences is always the same there is no need to utter it, the predicate can stand alone. To know the meaning of a single word is, for a fully educated speaker, to know about its possibilities of combination with an indefinitely large collection of other words, to know all sorts of different sentence-constructions in which it can figure. It is also to know that there are some associates with which, and some constructions in which, it cannot occur. The infant knows none of this, the first words he learns are all of the same category, being ostensive predicates of the substantival kind. Because the adult has all this categorial knowledge about the words he understands he is able to use dictionaries in which words are correlated with words to extend his understanding. The syntax or categorial nature of the defining terms is carried over to the word defined.

This virtuosity of words within their categories explains how it is that we can understand sentences we have never come across before, provided we are familiar with the words of which they are composed. The possibility of understanding entirely novel combinations of words is a further support for the idea that words are logically prior to sentences. But it does not establish the conclusion: to understand the words composing a wholly novel sentence we must have encountered them in some sentences before. This multiple combinability of words is obviously a great economy, just as a system of writing in which all words are made up of a handful of letters is a vastly economical alternative to an ideographic script in which each word has a unique representation. But although it is convenient it might be questioned whether it was necessary. It might be conjectured that a language was possible in which each sentence was formally unique in the manner of a number code for a system of messages: 1—Happy Christmas; 2—Happy New Year; 3—I hope you are better; 4—I am sorry you are worse, etc., etc. There are many reasons for rejecting this supposition but two will have to suffice here. In the first place a greetings telegram language would have to be very poor in content, if it were an initial or basic language and not a code parasitic on a proper language, for it could consist only of ostensive statements in which substantival concepts were applied to demonstratively indicated things or places. In chapter 2 it was argued that our ordinary apparatus of singular terms must be introduced on a basis of that kind. Analogous arguments apply as far as other structural elements of discourse are concerned. In the third example given above the antecedent understanding of the propositional clause 'you are better' is presupposed by the sentence as a whole. Only someone who understood 'you are better' could be taught to use 'I hope you are better' and some expression meaning the former would have to occur as part of any expression meaning the latter. Secondly, it would seem inevitable that a language should contain a formally uniform convention of negation. To understand any sentence whatever, or at any rate any synthetic sentence, we must know the difference between the kind of situation in which it is to be affirmed and the kind of situation in which it is to be denied. The learning of 'p' is essentially bound up with the learning of 'not-p'. 'I do not hope you are better' should not turn up later in the list as no. 376 since it must be understood if no. 3 is understood.

The thesis that there must be ostensive statements, in terms of which all other statements must be introduced or explained, is, then, an improved version of the traditional empiricist principle, in which the priority of sentences to words is recognised. At this point two questions must be raised. First, does the thesis involve the acceptance of the traditional empiricist conception of experience? Secondly, does the regress of definition or introduction really dispose so easily of the problem of innate ideas or principles? As to the first question: all that the regress argument strictly shows is that there must be sentences that are not introduced in terms of other sentences, it does not entail anything specific about whatever it is that makes possible the introduction of the ultimate sentences. But, provided that the term is interpreted broadly, there can be no objection to saying that experience is the non-verbal something with which ostensive sentences are correlated when they are endowed with meaning. For experience, broadly construed, is simply what we are aware of and unless the basic sentences are correlated with something we can be aware of they can have no meaning for us. This very general formula has no specific implications about the precise nature of experience. Traditional empiricism identified it with sensation and reflection or introspection. This contention makes two disputable exclusions. In the first place experience is taken to consist of the awareness of private entities or states of affairs. This view will be directly contested in chapter 8. For the moment it will be enough to say that the long philosophical tradition behind the doctrine that basic statements report private impressions should not be allowed to obscure the fact that the first sentences we actually learn, and thus the most natural candidates for ostensive status, are about material things. The concept of experience, after all, is closely linked to those of perception and observation and it is still a paradox, even if it is so antique and respectable a paradox as to be hardly noticeable as such, to say that it is impressions and not material things that are really perceived or observed. The second disputable exclusion is one that I, at any rate, shall not dispute. It is that of what might be called non-perceptual experience, for example moral or religious experience. That there is something answering to this description need not be questioned. The problem is: must it be regarded as anything more than moral and religious emotion of a particularly intense kind? The argument against moral and religious intuition, that neither yields anything like universal agreement, applies here too. But there are further considerations. A crucial objection to the notion of moral experience is that the moral characteristics of acts and persons are not logically independent of their ordinary perceptible characteristics. If there were a specific and genuinely cognitive kind of moral experience it would follow that two acts or persons could be identical in all but their morally experienceable respects. But this, as Hare has reasonably argued, is absurd (Hare, pp. 80–1). Goodness, as he puts it, is a consequential or supervenient property. You cannot have two absolutely perceptually indiscriminable pictures one of which is good and the other bad. It might seem that you could have two actions of this sort, that two arm movements in themselves perceptually indistinguishable except in position, could differ in moral character. But actions described in this narrowly muscular way offer no foothold to moral judgment. It is only in the light of their contexts and consequences, the motives that lead to them and the results they bring about, that they have any moral characteristics at all. When these further and essential features are included in the description Hare's argument applies.

Religious assertions, unlike moral ones, do not primarily refer to ordinary perceptible things. No argument like the foregoing can therefore be used to undermine their claim to ostensiveness. It is, however, clear that such understanding as most people have of characteristically religious terms and sentences is verbally acquired. The teacher of religious language does not first evoke a religious experience and then say 'that is the All-Encompassing Unity' or 'that is the Ground of Being'. It is rather the case that an antecedently understood religious vocabulary is mobilised to give expression to powerfully impressive states of mind. An interesting consideration is that mystics are usually dissatisfied with conventional religious language as a means of expression and contend that their experiences can either not be expressed at all in words, or, which comes to much the same thing, can be expressed only in contradictory terms. There is no need to deny the existence of inarticulable experiences. The fact that they cannot be articulated is enough to rule them out as sources of knowledge.

The case of a small sighted minority in what is largely a country of the blind might seem to count against this conclusion. Here the sighted would at least be able to communicate effectively with each other, but then a similar ability is often claimed by or on behalf of mystics. There is an important difference between the two cases. The sighted minority would be able to justify their claim to a special form of experience by making predictions about approaching tangible things in circumstances where their blind compatriots would just have to wait and feel. Mystical experience, on the other hand, is wholly disconnected from the rest of our knowledge. Although these arguments are not by any means sufficient to close the question against the claims of genuinely cognitive mystical experience they seem sufficient to justify ignoring them further in an investigation of this kind.

Innate ideas

The traditional account of the principles of empiricism, both in Locke's assault on innate ideas and in Hume's theory of the origin of ideas, reaches a level of muddle and confusion that almost justifies the exaggerated use some recent philosophers have made of Frege's maxim about the separation of logic and psychology.

Hume is ostensibly concerned with the conditions under which a genuine concept can be said to be possessed, with what it is to have a concept. He maintains that all genuine concepts are either ostensive concepts derived from experience or are derived from such concepts by definition. He interprets the derivation involved in a historical sense but this is not to the point. What makes a concept empirical, and thus for Hume genuine, is not the manner of its acquisition but the rules for its application. To possess an empirical concept is to know in what empirical circumstances to apply and to withhold it, to be able to distinguish between the experiences to which it does and does not apply. In fact many empirical concepts are acquired by confrontation in experience with instances of them but it is not this that makes them empirical. A man possesses the empirical concept of hardness if he is now able to tell of things presented to him whether they are hard or not, whether or not he has ever felt anything hard before.

What shows that there are genuine non-empirical concepts is the manifest failure of attempts to prove that the unquestionably genuine concepts of logic, such as *not* and *and* and *all*, are empirical. Russell has argued that the concept *not* corresponds to the experienceable feeling of rejection and *or* to that of hesitation (Russell (7), pp. 83–7). It may be that such feelings commonly *attend* the use of these concepts, though even this is not obvious, for as Geach has pointed out a threatening feeling is just as natural and proper an associate for *or* as hesitation (Geach (1), pp. 22–7). But even if the suggested associations were universal the feelings would have nothing to do with the meaning of the terms involved. The presence of a feeling of hesitation is not a condition of the correct use of the word 'or'. I may feel sincerely hesitant between the two alternatives mentioned in my statement about a man walking clumsily down the street 'he is drunk or lame', but my remark may well be false, he may be just playing the fool or have a stone in his shoe. The concepts of logic are *a priori* not empirical, they are not learnt by correlation with empirical things or states of affairs nor, which is more to the point, is anything empirical a condition of their correct application. If someone is in fact old and ill there is no additional empirical feature in the situation over and above his being old and his being ill. The concepts of logic are essentially syntactical in character, their function is not to describe the world of experience but to arrange and articulate the descriptions we can give of it.

If empiricists have been generally hostile to *a priori* concepts they have been generally tolerant of *a priori* statements. Locke allows intuitive and demonstrative as well as sensitive knowledge, indeed for him there is only *a priori* knowledge since what we acquire from the senses is really no more than probable opinion, called knowledge by courtesy. Yet while admitting this in book 4 of the *Essay* he devotes book 1 to a demolition of innate ideas and principles and begins book 2 with the main result of this demolition, the thesis that all knowledge is derived from experience.

Despite its name Locke's book 1 is mainly devoted to the destruction of innate knowledge rather than innate ideas. The conclusion he appears to draw from it is that there is no *a priori* knowledge but apart from being inconsistent with his positive account of knowledge this is also not the actual result of his arguments. What these are calculated to show is that there are no universally accepted beliefs and that there are no beliefs held by babies at the moment of birth. His term 'innate' embodies two quite distinct and indeed wholly unrelated concepts, that of the *a priori* or non-empirical and that of the instinctive or non-acquired. Universal agreement is neither a sufficient nor a necessary condition of a belief's having either of these properties. A belief can be universal without being *a priori* if it rests on a universally shared experience, for instance that flames are painful to touch. A belief can be *a priori* without being universal if it rests on an even mildly sophisticated chain of demonstration, for instance that there is no largest prime number. Similarly a belief can be universal without being instinctive, if, like the belief about the painfulness of flames, it is one that everyone is going to pick up. It would seem possible in principle for a belief to be instinctive without being universal since it is only a contingent truth that instincts are common to the species.

Are there, or could there be, genuinely instinctive beliefs? Certainly not if Locke's test for the existence of a belief is accepted. For him the essential test of a person's holding a belief is his readiness to assert it when appropriately questioned. Such a test directly rules out the supposition that babies have any beliefs at all for they are characteristically unable to give a plain answer to a plain question. But a belief can be exhibited just as well by a relevant habit of action as by propositional assent. Many more people accept the law of contraposition than could state it or would assent to it if it were put to them verbally, all those who generally infer *if not-q then not-p* from *if p then q*.

From this point of view it is reasonable to ascribe belief to dogs ('he thinks I am going to take him for a walk') and even, taking a certain amount of liberty, to babies. The new-born infant addresses itself in a purposive way to its mother's breast. This is an instinctive action and goes some way towards displaying the belief that the breast presented will nourish or at least do something to please it. One need not take this supposition very seriously to draw an important conclusion from it. If the baby could really be said to have this belief it would not in the least follow that the belief was *a priori*.

In the case in hand the belief is an obviously empirical one which may well turn out to be false as the baby would discover when he applied that most empirical of precepts: suck it and see.

There is no need to rely on the clearly extravagant supposition that babies literally have beliefs to establish that there can be instinctive beliefs and that such beliefs need not be *a priori*. It is not, after all, a necessary condition of something's being instinctive that it should be evident immediately after birth. Even after Freud we can still regard a definitely focused interest in the opposite sex as at once post-natal and instinctive. Suppose there was a boy brought up by an elderly man in extremely isolated circumstances, protected from the aphrodisiac frenzy of commercial advertisement and the secret lore of other, ordinary, horrible children. When he is fourteen a youthful and personable female piano teacher is secured for him and as she arranges his fingers for the scales he experiences nameless longings. His desire is instinctive and not acquired yet it has not emerged until quite well on in life. It is not necessary that the literally innate should be present in the first stages of infancy. Could there be beliefs that were at once instinctive and mature? A possible example is the belief that one will live forever. It is, after all, a fairly universal surprise and disappointment to discover that this is not the case, which would seem to imply that until the moment of surprise it was believed that it was. To believe that one will never die is by no means the same as not to believe that one will, so this is hardly a clear case of instinctive belief. It could also be argued that in so far as someone does believe he will never die it is a belief acquired inductively from the solid evidence, as far as it goes, that he has never done so yet. But even if it cannot be shown that such a belief is really instinctive it would still be empirical, and false, if it were.

Spencer put forward the theory that necessary truths are really a sort of racial memory, an inheritance of the factual discoveries of ancestors whose apparent indubitability is the result of their instinctiveness (Spencer, vol. 2, pp. 195, 414–20). Some such account of our acceptance of those very general principles which most notably qualify for classification as synthetic *a priori*, such as the Kantian Laws of Conservation and Causation is not altogether unplausible, provided that the inheritance of acquired characteristics is replaced by natural selection. It might be that a tendency to think in causal terms is inheritable and was at one time not universal. The causal disposition would confer a biological advantage on its possessors and in time strains without it would become extinct. But here again origin and validity must be distinguished. A belief could be inherited and so, by implication, be useful for survival without being true at all, let alone necessarily true. To suppose otherwise is to commit the mistake of the pragmatic theory of truth. False optimism about the severity of obstacles to desired ends seems to be a frequent condition of their effective pursuit. The invalid who believes he will probably recover when he probably will not may be assisted in his actual recovery by that mistaken judgment. The society that believes it will defeat its enemies without difficulty may be nerved by this error to efforts it would never have made if its ideas about what lay ahead of it had been more accurate.

It is, then, at least reasonable to conceive that there might be instinctive and inherited beliefs and this is not undermined by the extreme tenuousness of the attribution of any beliefs to babies. If there are any such beliefs, although they will be in a sense natural, they need not be necessarily true since they need not even be true. Innate beliefs in the literal sense of the word are entirely compatible with empiricism. However a belief comes to be accepted it may still be open to empirical testing and if so it will require empirical justification if it is to be justified.

Basic statements

The arguments for intuitive and ostensive statements are connected as well as being similar in their regressive form. The ostensive statement is given its meaning by correlation with some kind of observable state of affairs. It has a meaning to the extent that observable states of affairs are divided into those of which it is true and those of which it is not. To know what it means is to be able to pick out the states of affairs in which it is true, to have been trained to respond to such situations with an inclination to utter it. Now the occurrence of a situation of the appropriate verifying kind will be a logically sufficient reason for the assertion of an intuitive statement and thus the non-inferential kind of justification required to bring an end to the infinite regress. Intuitive statements must be ostensively learnt, for if they were explained in terms of other statements the latter could serve as premises in an inference to them. Ostensive statements must be intuitively justifiable, for the occurrence of a situation of the kind by correlation with which they were introduced would be a sufficient reason of a non-inferential sort for their assertion.

I have not said that all ostensive statements must be intuitively justified in every case in which they are made. The sufficient reason for an ostensive statement does not always have to be non-inferential. If we have found that an ostensive statement q ('this is red') is true whenever another statement p ('this is a book of John's') is true, we can reasonably infer from a new case of p that q is true though we are not aware of the non-inferential sufficient reason for asserting it in the present circumstances (for instance, if John, an honest man, gives us a book he says is his, in the dark).

The point can be clarified by applying the distinction between statement and sentence which has not been kept clearly separate hitherto. Questions of meaning arise about sentences, conceived as forms of words which may have a number of different meanings. Questions of justification and truth arise about statements, conceived, in the first instance, as sentences with a given meaning used with reference to determinate individuals, places and times. (I say in the first instance only, since two different sentences with different meanings—'I am ill' said today by me and 'you will be ill' said yesterday by you—can be used to make the same statement. We may lay down that the utterance of a sentence, in a given meaning, makes the same statement as the sentence which results from replacing all its contextual or token-reflexive terms by non-contextual ones, to be called the corresponding non-contextual sentence. We can then define the utterances of two different sentences as making the same statement if they have the same corresponding non-contextual sentence. Similarly two utterances of the same sentence or form of words will make different statements if their corresponding non-contextual sentences differ. A non-contextual sentence, in a given meaning, can make one and only one statement.)

It follows that what is ostensive is sentences while what is intuitive is statements. But even this does not go far enough, at any rate as long as the ordinary idea that the same statement may be made by different people or at different times and in different words is allowed for in the definition of 'statement'. Consider two men one of whom says 'I am in pain' and the other, hearing what he says and observing his injury and writhings, 'you are in pain'. In the ordinary sense of the term, and by my definition, they make the same statement, yet what the sufferer says is intuitive while what his observer says is not. What is intuitive, then, is a statement made in given circumstances and not just the statement as such.

In the light of this, together with the fact that a statement can be made with an ostensive sentence on indirect, inferential grounds, we cannot say that all ostensive sentences make intuitive statements, though all intuitive statements are made with ostensive sentences. What does seem correct is that every statement made with an ostensive sentence is intuitable by somebody at some time or other. These considerations can now be brought together to define the notion of a basic statement. A basic statement is one that is both ostensive and intuitive or, more precisely, it is a statement made with an ostensive sentence in circumstances where its assertion is intuitive. Basicness, it follows, is not a property of a statement as such since two utterances with the same corresponding non-contextual sentence need not both be intuitive although they are utterances of the same statement: 'I am in pain', 'you are in pain' said to me now and 'I will be in pain tomorrow' said by me yesterday all make the same statement but only the first has any claim to intuitiveness. It would be more strictly correct then to speak not of basic statements but of statements made in circumstances in which they are basic. But it should be enough to recall the reasons that there are for this somewhat long-winded proposal without actually accepting it.

Basic statements are, as it were, the supposed axioms of the system of factual or empirical knowledge and, to be more accurate or inclusive, justified belief. Derived or inferred statements are justified or established by them and non-ostensive sentences are introduced in terms of the ostensive sentences by means of which they are expressed. Ostensive sentences are introduced in the circumstances which would render the making of statements by them intuitive and to understand such a sentence is to know how to make basic statements with them but not all the statements they make are basic.

The usual view of basic statements is that, as well as being intuitively justified and ostensively expressed, they are also certain or incorrigible, and it is commonly agreed furthermore that no non-basic statement is more than probable. Secondly, it has ordinarily been held that basic statements are phenomenal reports of immediate experience, with their subject in the first person singular and their verbs in the present tense. In chapters 6 and 7 I shall examine both of these contentions and reject them. In chapter 8 I shall consider the prior question of whether there are any basic statements at all by tracing the consequences of two theories that are opposed to them: the coherence theory which dispenses with them altogether and the fallibilism which accords them at best a relative and provisional status.

They have certainly played a large part in modern epistemology. They have figured as the atomic propositions of Russell's logical atomism, the elementary propositions of Wittgenstein's *Tractatus*, the protocol propositions of the Vienna Circle, as constatations in Schlick's philosophy (Schlick, p. 221) and as expressive judgments in C. I. Lewis's (Lewis (2), pp. 178–82). In whatever way they may have been named they have been taken to be the ultimate statable evidence for all the factual statements we have any good reason to make and to constitute the ultimate analysis of everything we can significantly assert. They have been held to be the indispensable support of whatever we know or have reason to believe and to be the essential content of whatever we can meaningfully say.

It is desirable that basic statements should not be *defined* as incorrigible and phenomenal. In the first place many philosophers have accepted that there must be basic statements without attributing both of these properties to them. Russell has always been doubtful of the certainty or incorrigibility of any contingent statement whatever and has been content to claim that phenomenal basic statements are less uncertain and corrigible than anything else in the realm of factual belief (Russell (8), pp. 185–6). The idea that there might be basic statements that are no more than probable has been considered by Price and Ayer in a conjectural and exploratory way (Price (2); Ayer (4), pp. 123–4). On the other hand the view that basic statements are phenomenal reports of immediate private experience has been contested by the adherents of physicalism, that left-wing deviation from the positivist orthodoxy of the 1930s. Reichenbach, finally, has explicitly rejected both alleged implications of the view that there are basic statements (Reichenbach, ch. 3).

Secondly, it is at any rate not an immediate consequence of the very general arguments that have been considered here that the statements in which justification terminates and the sentences in which explanation of meaning terminates should be incorrigible and phenomenal. Further argument is needed for this and that it is at least disputable is shown by the dissenting opinions mentioned in the last paragraph.

It might be said that these qualifications do not go far enough if a really general concept of ostension and ostensive sentences is to be formed. Although I have not confined them to the domain of the immediately experienced and incorrigibly known I have introduced some restrictions. In the second section of this chapter I gave some reasons for taking all intuition of matters of fact to be empirical, ruling out moral and religious intuition explicitly and other conceivable forms of intuition of fact (of the mental states of others, for example, or of past events) by implication. Conformably with this in the later part of the third section I connected the theory of ostensive sentences with the traditional principle of empiricism, by saying that while the experience in connection with which ostensive sentences are introduced need not be conceived narrowly as the direct awareness of private impressions it could still be regarded as broadly perceptual on the same grounds that were invoked in support of the parallel account of intuition.

Now to do this is to take sides as between some of the competing theories of knowledge mentioned in the introduction to part II. For it is, in effect, to rule out the intuitionist kind of solution to most of the epistemological problems enumerated there. Such a solution to the problem of other minds, or the past, or theoretical entities or moral or religious knowledge implies that there is a direct and non-inferential awareness of the kind of things or facts involved and, consequently, that there must be ostensive sentences whose primary reference is to those things and which state those facts. There are two reasons for limiting intuition and thus ostension to the broadly perceptual. In the first place I believe such a limitation to be correct and that there is no intuition of the relevant kind that is not broadly perceptual, as I have explicitly argued in the moral and religious cases. Secondly, unless this limitation is introduced the exposition of the subject becomes vague, cumbrous and out of touch with familiar lines of thought. One might put the point by saying that those who believe that there is intuition of the states of other minds or of past events or what have you would be ready to admit that they regard these things as objects of a special kind of perception. So to limit intuition and thus ostension to the perceptual is more to concentrate on a particular kind of example than to rule out, in an illegitimately prejudicial way, the possibility of forms of intuition other than sense-perception and introspection. And in fact some of these possible forms of intuition will be considered on their merits later. So this restriction of generality is more a matter of expository form than of theoretical content, although it does correspond to a theoretical conviction.

It might also be argued that my account of ostension makes another unargued and perhaps unjustifiable assumption beyond its apparent endorsement of something like traditional empiricism. In saying that the meaning of sentences must be introduced either by correlating them with states of affairs outside language or with other sentences already understood I might appear to have surreptitiously embraced reductionism. For the only type of linguistic introduction of sentences I have acknowledged is that in which a sentence is introduced by correlation with a set of sentences with which it is identical in meaning and which are thus a translation of it. To take this view is in effect to rule out the transcendentalist type of solution to epistemological problems. The transcendentalist, as he was defined in the introduction to this part, is one who denies that a certain kind of entity can be the object of any sort of intuition or direct awareness and yet maintains that sentences about them cannot be translated into sentences about the kind of things whose existence is evidence for them. For him, then, sentences about things that are transcendent in this sense will be non-ostensive and so have to be introduced linguistically, but not by explicit and full-blooded translation. In fact the neglect so far of this possibility has had no deleterious effect on the argument which has been concerned with the positive character of ostension and not with the linguistic alternatives to it. But the point is of some independent interest. Is there a method of introducing sentences into discourse that is not reductive or translational? To the extent that transcendentalists address themselves to the problem of the conditions of significance of the statements which they hold to be inferred they ordinarily call upon the notion of analogy. The mental states of others, theoretical entities and God are conceived by Cartesians, scientific realists and natural theologians as more or less like things of which we have some direct awareness: our own mental states, common material, objects and persons. The matter will be considered further, somewhat indirectly, in part III. For the moment it is enough to state that my apparently uncritical adoption of reductionism is only for convenience of exposition.

The correspondence theory

The theory of basic statements is closely connected with the correspondence theory of truth. In its classical form that theory holds that to each true statement, whatever its form may be, a fact of the same form corresponds. The theory of basic statements indicates the point at which the correspondence is established, at which the system of beliefs makes its justifying contact with the world. If it is added that all derived statements are reducible to basic ones then it is only basic statements that properly correspond with reality. Derived statements correspond at best indirectly and with a large and perhaps indefinite number of facts by way of the basic statements into which they can be analysed. It could just as well be said that the truth of derived statements is to be explained in terms of coherence, for a derived statement is true provided that it coheres with the totality of true, corresponding basic statements. The explanation of the truth of derived statements in terms of their coherence can be taken in two different ways in accordance with the familiar distinction between a definition and a criterion of truth. For a derived statement to *be* true it must cohere with basic statements which collectively entail and severally follow from it and thus make up its entire content and these must be true by correspondence. For a derived statement to be *reasonably or justifiably believed* to be true it must be consistent with all other statements in which belief is justified and these must include statements which follow from it directly or in conjunction with yet other justified beliefs and thus conversely confer inductive support on it.

This is, in effect, the theory of truth advanced in Wittgenstein's *Tractatus*. The only facts he admits are those that correspond to elementary or atomic propositions. All other propositions are, if significant, simply equivalent to collections of atomic propositions and if they are contingent their truth or falsity is unequivocally determined by that of their atomic components. (If they are necessary their truth or falsity is determined by their own form and is quite unrelated to what is the case in the world outside discourse.) Russell has been less resolute in drawing out the implications about truth of the theory of basic statements. In his early discussions of the subject he felt compelled to modify the correspondence theory because of the existence of error (Russell (1), pp. 124–30). A satisfactory theory of truth, he maintained, must account for falsehood as well and he thought that the correspondence theory, by taking belief to be a relation between a mind and a single object, made false belief inexplicable. Certainly if that single object is a fact a difficulty does arise. Othello's belief that Desdemona loves Cassio cannot have the fact of Desdemona's love for Cassio as its object since there is no such fact. But the correspondence theory does not require that facts should be the sole objects of belief. If I believe something I stand in some relation to a statement or proposition. When a fact corresponds to this statement my belief is true, when it does not the statement is false. A false statement is not one that corresponds to a non-fact, the 'objective falsehoods' that so much disturbed Russell, but one that does not correspond to a fact. The same mistake underlies his insistence that there must be negative facts for negative statements to correspond to. Although he admits the equivalence that many would question between 'S is not P' and 'it is false that S is P' he is not prepared to admit that both are made true by the absence of the verifying fact that S is P. He argues further that there must be general facts since general statements cannot be identified with open conjunctions, 'everything is F' with 'a is F, b is F, c is F . . . .' on the ground that this can be a correct identification only if a, b, c . . . are all the individuals that there are, so that the general statement that says so must be added to the conjunction. Here he would seem to have confused the conditions under which alone we can have conclusive knowledge of the truth of a general statement with the conditions of its actually being true.

Both Russell and Wittgenstein adopted very questionably concrete views about the nature of the correspondence between a proposition and the fact that makes it true. For Wittgenstein this relation was that of a picture to what it depicted though it is not clear from the cryptic sentences of the *Tractatus* how seriously this is to be taken. On the one hand a figurative interpretation is suggested by his use of the phrase 'logical picture', on the other there is the record of his having undergone a kind of Cartesian revelation about the nature of meaning and truth when once confronted by a scale model of a road accident. If the picture theory is taken literally it is obviously incorrect. The only occasions in which a statement, or, more properly, its verbal expression, has any natural resemblance to the fact that verifies it are those in which the words in a statement about a relationship between objects themselves actually stand in that relationship, such as the written statement 'John is to the left of

James' or the spoken statement 'Caesar's death preceded Christ's birth', and those in which some auditory event is recorded in an onomatopoeic way, a vanishingly small proportion of the totality of true statements. A more general point is that language represents the categorial variety of things in a much more uniform way than literal depiction does. In a sentence objects, qualities and relations are all represented by objects, namely words. But in a picture an object is represented by an object, a particular patch of paint, a quality by a quality, the colour of the patch, and a relation by a relation, that of one patch to another.

Russell's more circumspect theory of a community of form or structure between proposition and fact encouraged the view that the test for the completeness of a philosophical analysis of a statement was its translation into a sentence of the same form as the fact that would make the original statement true. But the conviction came to prevail that correspondence was a conventional relation and that the completeness of an analysis consisted in its having arrived at a verbal expression of the statement being analysed wholly composed of basic sentences. A basic or ostensive sentence acquires its meaning wholly from the establishment of a conventional relationship between itself and the world and not between itself and other sentences. To lay down the meaning of a sentence is to give its truth-conditions, to associate it by a rule with the kind of circumstances in which it is true. Only in the case of basic sentences are these truth-conditions extra-linguistic. It follows that basic sentences can be introduced only in circumstances in which they are true, while there is no such limitation on derived sentences.

Soon after the publication of the *Tractatus* Ramsey said that there was really no philosophical problem of truth on the ground that 'p' and 'p is true' were logically equivalent and meant the same thing (Ramsey, pp. 142–3). To say that p is true is not to say something about the statement 'p', it is simply another way of asserting it. So logically speaking the predicate 'is true' is superfluous. This idea has been taken up and developed by Strawson (Strawson, (1) & (2)). Agreeing with Ramsey that the predicate 'is true' is redundant from a logical point of view since it adds nothing to the statement to which it is attached, he pointed out that it has, nevertheless, a more or less rhetorical point. Its function is to confirm or endorse a statement made or implied by somebody else.

Ramsey's principle that 'p' and 'p is true' are logically equivalent is not in fact correct without qualification. There are many meaningful sentences that can be substitutes for 'p' in his equation, such as questions and commands, which invalidate it by leaving one side of it meaningful but making the other senseless. 'Close the door' does not mean the same as 'close the door is true' for the very simple reason that the first sentence is meaningful and the second is not. There is a certain absurdity about this objection since Ramsey's variable was obviously intended to range over statements or assertions alone. But if this obvious amendment is made to Ramsey's thesis it takes on a somewhat curious appearance. There can be no doubt that if 'p' is an assertion, 'p' and 'p is true' mean the same thing. But what is an assertion? It is a sentence uttered as true. If this is accepted the formula reduces to the vacuous triviality that, if 'p' is a sentence uttered as true, to utter it is to do no more and no less than to say that it is true. The point is that the formula does not really show the dispensability of the predicate 'is true' for in its reliance on the concept of an assertion, brought out explicitly above, it presumes that the concept of truth is already understood.

6

Certainty

The concept of certainty

Those who believe that there are basic statements, that is to say that there are intuitive statements, made by ostensive sentences, whose truth is directly determined by their correspondence with fact, have usually believed that in addition to having these properties basic statements are also certain. Indeed most philosophers would probably take certainty to be a defining characteristic of basic statements. In this chapter I shall examine two kinds of argument designed to justify such a definition. One type of argument seeks to show that some statements must be certain if there is to be any knowledge at all. I shall consider three arguments of this type: one which derives this conclusion from the unacceptability of general scepticism, a second which contends that unless the starting-points of justification are certainly true no belief can be rendered even probable and a third which holds that in learning the meaning of a sentence we have to become acquainted with the kind of circumstance in which statements made by that sentence are certainly true. The other type of argument I shall consider aims to show not that any conceivable kind of basic statement must be certain but rather that the basic statements that our language actually contains, namely 'sense-statements' or direct reports of immediate experience, are as a matter of fact certainly true. I shall conclude that in the relevant sense of 'certain', which is that of incorrigibility, there need not be any contingent, empirical statements that are certain, and indeed, that no contingent statements at all, not even sense-statements are certain in this sense. This is not to deny that nearly all sense-statements and many other statements besides are certain in the everyday sense of being beyond reasonable doubt.

A difficulty about the question, 'are basic statements certain, necessarily or as a matter of fact?' is that there is a number of different senses to the word 'certain' as it appears in philosophical discussions. Until these are distinguished the question has no definite sense. I shall distinguish five such senses.

(i) *Psychologically indubitable* The first of these is simply complete subjective assurance; what we express when we say 'I am certain that p'. We mean more than this, however, when we say 'it is certain that p' even if we often say the latter when we ought to have said only the former. A statement is certain in this sense for a particular person at a particular time. He may be the only person who is wholly assured of its truth and his assurance may be very short-lived. Any statement whatever may be certain in this sense. One person's set of subjective indubitables may be very much larger than another's in which case the former is relatively credulous and the latter relatively sceptical. Psychological indubitability varies quite independently of logical justification. A man's rationality is to be measured by the extent to which they coincide in him. It may be possible to decide fairly definitely whether or not a man believes something with complete assurance at a given moment. But it is harder to determine whether a belief is indubitable by him as against being merely undoubted. What he does not doubt, that is to say, is more determinate than what he cannot bring himself to doubt. Philosophers concerned to allay scepticism have often said that Cartesian doubt is not real doubt. However much a man may play with arguments purporting to show that he has no ground for believing in the external world, the past or other minds, they contend, unless he becomes actually unhinged his doubt will remain pseudo-doubt, an imaginative exercise at most. Hume was at least upset by the doubts for which he prescribed carelessness and in-attention as a remedy. But his doctrine of natural belief, which he applies to the existence of matter when he says ' 'tis in vain to ask whether there be body or not? That is a point we must take for granted in all our reasonings' (Hume, p. 187), was an assertion of the existence of indubitables. Certainty in this sense, whether applied to what is undoubted or to what is indubitable, is, at any rate, subjective. None would deny that most sense-statements are undoubted or that if any statements are indubitable they are. For our purposes it is enough to notice that neither property has any logical connection with justification or truth.

(ii) *Logical necessity* Many philosophers have taken certainty to be the same thing as logical necessity. If this were just a deliberate stipulation of how the word 'certain' is to be used in their writings no great harm would result. Under that stipulation it would be trivially obvious that basic statements are not certain. But most who have made the identification have conceived themselves to be saying what the word really means. One bad argument for this view is perhaps put forward more in diagnosis of it as an error than in support of it as a truth. It might be argued that since it is an evident truth that it is necessary that if I know that p then p, it must be true that if I know that p then p is necessary. The unreliable bridge between premise and conclusion here is the formula, true in one interpretation and false in another: if I know that p then necessarily p. If this argument were correct it would follow that every true proposition is necessary. For it is unquestionably necessary that if p then p. So if the argument were valid it would follow that if p then p is necessary.

In fact, of course, this conception of certainty goes back to Plato's view that knowledge and belief have separate and proprietary objects. The arguments Plato gives for it are not very persuasive. That something now has a property incompatible with a property it had in the past, the common fate of temporal things, does not imply that it did not really have that property then. That it has other properties as well as this one does not imply that it does not really have this one. That no sensible particular does more than approximate to the perfect circularity, triangularity and so on of the objects of geometry is not easy to prove, though it may be true and no comparable reason exists for saying that no such thing is really green or cold.

More to the point is the fact that many necessary truths have been conclusively established: either, where they are intuitively analytic, by simply being understood or else, where they deductively follow from such premises by intuitively acceptable rules of inference, by being proved. There is also a sense in which necessary truths 'cannot be false' in that it is self-contradictory to deny them and this comes near to the underlying conception that the certain is that which cannot be doubted. But, of course, necessary truths can perfectly well be doubted and they ought to be doubted when they are neither intuitive nor proved. In whatever precise terms the ordinary concept of certainty should be defined there is a certain general feature of the concept which ensures that there can be no logical connection between it and necessity. This is that certainty is a historical notion. The proposition that there is no largest prime number acquired its certainty at the moment a proof for it was discovered; before that it was not certain and if civilisation were to collapse it might become uncertain again. But its necessity is a timeless characteristic which it possesses quite independently of its relations to human thought and of the vicissitudes of intellectual history. It can be admitted that necessary truths are, in general, dramatically certifiable but this is not to say that they are one and all certain.

(iii) *Self-authentication* By a self-authenticating statement I mean one whose truth is guaranteed by the way in which it is expressed. It is not a sense that anyone actually has given to certainty but it is the one Descartes ought to have given it. For it is the characteristic feature of the primal certainties that survive the application of his method of doubt: I think and I exist. What he said when he said these things could have been said by others in ways that did not guarantee their truth. 'Descartes is thinking' and 'Descartes exists' are, of course, contingent statements, once true but now no doubt false. Descartes failed to discern the special reason for the indubitability of his statements. The criterion of certainty he extracted from them, clarity and distinctness, is wholly uninformative as it stands. It can be fleshed out only by seeing the use he puts it to. It is invoked to establish the premises of his first proof of the existence of God. One of these, that he has a clear and distinct idea of God, is acceptable for the reason that makes 'I think' acceptable, namely that it is a report of the current contents of his mind. The other main premise, that every event must have an adequate cause, we may suppose he took, like 'I exist', to be a necessary truth. Together with the thesis that God himself is the only cause adequate to his having an idea of him they entail that God exists. For Descartes, then, the only truths that were quite certainly certain were those of the same kind as 'I think' and 'I exist'. As it turned out he did not identify their kind correctly. Its instances are for the most part rather uninteresting: I am awake, I am here, it is now, I am speaking/ writing in English and so on. Few of what are ordinarily regarded as basic statements are certain in this peculiar sense. In particular although one or two self-authenticating truths fall into the class of sense-statements, the great majority of sense-statements do not have this property.

(iv) *Incorrigibility* We now come to the concept of certainty which has been most widely thought to attach specially to basic statements and will thus concern us most closely in this chapter. This is the notion of infallibility or incorrigibility. A statement is incorrigible if its truth follows from the fact that it is believed. An incorrigible statement is one which is wholly verified by the experience that prompts its assertion, whose claim coincides with the evidence on which it is based. It has no predictive consequences whose failure to occur might refute it.

The notion is usually confined in its application to contingent statements, but if it is defined as the entailment of truth by belief it would seem to apply to some necessary propositions as well. There are and must be certain basic and intuitive necessary truths if any such truth is to be shown to be necessary. These are the intuitive analytic truths one's acceptance of which is a condition of one's being held to understand them and the words in which they are expressed. Nothing can count against them since it is only if they are accepted that anything can count against anything.

146

Incorrigible contingent statements, if there are any, differ from incorrigible necessary truths, and just in virtue of their being contingent, in that they can be denied without self-contradiction. But they cannot be sincerely denied. If a false statement of this kind is made it must be a deliberate untruth. The only other way in which they can go wrong, one cannot exactly say be false, is if the words in them are misused or misunderstood, if the speaker makes some verbal slip or mistake.

Philosophers have not distinguished carefully between incorrigibility and another supposed property of statements of a closely similar and related kind: self-intimation. By this I mean a statement's truth entailing its being known. If, for example, 'I am in pain' is incorrigible it is possible for me to be in pain and not to believe that I am. What is ruled out is that I should believe that I am not in pain (assuming that the denial of 'I am in pain' is incorrigible too) when I really am. But if 'I am in pain' is self-intimating, and its negation also, this possibility is excluded. If I am in pain I must know that I am and therefore believe that I am. Consider the possibility left open by incorrigibility but excluded by self-intimation a little more closely: that I may not believe I am in pain when I in fact am. If not believing were the same thing as disbelieving, as believing that not, this possibility would be ruled out by incorrigibility. For in that case I should both be in pain, *ex hypothesi*, and also, contradictorily, be not in pain by reason of the incorrigibility of my belief that I am not. Now in general not believing is not the same as disbelieving, though we often express our disbelief by saying 'I don't believe that'. Incorrigibility, then, does not entail self-intimation.

Does self-intimation entail incorrigibility? The possibility it leaves open is that I should not be in pain but believe that I am. In other words while requiring that true statements of the relevant kind should intimate themselves it appears to allow false ones to intimate themselves falsely as well. Now if my in fact not being in pain is self-intimating it follows that in the circumstances I should know, and believe, that I am not in pain as well as, *ex hypothesi*, believing that I am. This looks very like a contradiction. But is it? What is certainly a contradiction is that I should both believe and not believe that I am in pain. But that is not the case before us which is of my believing both that I am in pain and that I am not. The fact is that people often do hold contradictory beliefs though not usually about quite such elemental subject-matter. So that although self-intimation does not strictly entail incorrigibility it does seem to involve it in practice.

Although there are good reasons for denying that the concept of incorrigibility is the correct account of what certainty really is, it is, nevertheless, a logically coherent concept in its own right. And it is, generally, the particular kind of certainty which basic statements or sense-statements are supposed to have. I shall consider this claim in detail in the last two sections of the chapter.

(v) *Beyond reasonable doubt* In recent times a number of philosophers have followed Moore, most notably Wittgenstein, Austin and Malcolm, in saying that the certain is that which has been established beyond reasonable doubt and that to hold only the incorrigible to be certain is to set an excessively stringent standard of certainty which severely distorts settled linguistic practice. The conclusion they arrive at is better than many of the arguments they employ. Moore suggests that the word 'certain' acquires its meaning from such a situation as that in which a man raises his hand and says 'I know for certain that this is a hand' (Moore (2), ch. 7). The false implication of this argument is that 'certain' is a wholly ostensive word, an echo of Cook Wilson's doctrine that knowledge is indefinable. Another argument is that 'certain' owes its meaning to the contrast it makes with 'uncertain' or 'probable' and that in order to effect this contrast there must be cases of the application of both sides of the contrast. This is doubly erroneous. In the first place we can contrast the perfectly virtuous or circular with the imperfectly virtuous or circular without supposing that there actually are any perfectly virtuous people or perfectly circular things. Secondly, those who identify certainty with incorrigibility can produce actual instances of their kind of certainty, or so they contend, in sense-statements like *I am in pain*.

The real point is, simply, that when we use the word 'certain' in ordinary speech we do not mean incorrigible; we mean beyond reasonable doubt. There is a normative element about the word, it asserts that the statements it is applied to do not *need* any further justification, that it is *right* to act on them with complete confidence, that it would be *irrational* to doubt them. Here as elsewhere the standard of rationality is set by past experience. If statements of just this kind and made in circumstances just like these have not turned out to be false in the past there is no reason to doubt this one. The fact that it is not logically necessary and so can be denied without self-contradiction is not such a reason, nor is the fact that we can imagine a future course of events which would lead us to withdraw it. Even if it is logically possible that it is false and it is conceivable that it should turn out that it is false it does not follow that there is any reason to think that it actually is false.

Ayer, whose general tendency has been to take the certain and the incorrigible as one and the same, is prepared to give a qualified acceptance to Moore's view; 'it is good English' he says 'to use the words "know" and "certain" in the way that [Moore and his followers] encourage us to do' (Ayer (4), p. 108). But he claims that there is point to the incorrigibilist's procedure. In the first place there is the point 'that from the fact that someone is convinced that a proposition is true it never follows that it is true' (Ayer (5), p. 151). Or, in another place, 'no act of intuition can constitute knowledge .... it is never self-contradictory to say A believes p and p is false' (Ayer (4), p. 111). This is a very strange position for one who holds that there are incorrigible statements to adopt, for an incorrigible statement is defined as one whose truth follows from the fact that it is believed. Ayer's position here is a direct rejection of the possibility of incorrigible propositions. The second point is that no statement about material things of the kind Moore holds to be capable of certainty ever follows from any accumulation of basic sense-statements, however large. This is no doubt correct and if all our evidence for Moore's certainties rests on sense-statements, as Ayer believes, which have a much greater degree of certainty than the material-thing-statements they support, then there is good reason for introducing a special term to indicate the special kind of certainty that they have, 'incorrigibility', for example. But it is not a reason for denying that any of the corrigible statements they are used to support are certain.

In what follows I shall use the word 'certain' in its ordinary sense to mean 'beyond reasonable doubt' and use 'incorrigible' to refer to the solider kind of certainty often ascribed to basic statements and in the sense I have defined. The problem of this chapter can now be more clearly specified. The main question is: are basic statements incorrigible? I shall first consider arguments designed to show that basic statements must be incorrigible and then go on to argue that in fact no contingent statements are incorrigible. If the latter conclusion were correct but it was true that if there are any basic statements they must be incorrigible it would follow that there are no basic statements. But I shall argue that the hypothetical is not correct and thus that there are basic statements, that is to say intuitive statements made by ostensive sentences which owe their truth to correspondence, which are nevertheless corrigible, though many of them are, in the ordinary sense, quite certainly true.

Scepticism and fallibilism

Most of the arguments that have been brought against the validity of claims to certain knowledge are to be found in the Greek sceptics who flourished from the 4th century B.C. to the 2nd century A.D. and whose ideas are recorded in the works of Sextus Empiricus. Three dogmatic schools were the objects of their criticism: the Platonic Academy who maintained the rational self-evidence of the *a priori*, the Stoics who anticipated one strand in the philosophy of Descartes by taking subjective conviction to be the criterion of certainty, and the Epicureans who followed the tradition of Protagoras, as represented by Plato, by asserting the infallibility and immediate evidence of sensation. In the ten tropes of Aenesidemus the relativity of perception to the perceiver's state of mind, bodily condition and surrounding circumstances is set out in detail. Agrippa added four more general grounds for doubt to the relativity of perception: (i) the conflict of opinions between men, (ii) the unproved and hypothetical nature of any ultimate premises used in proof, (iii) the infinite regress in proof that is encountered if unproved premises are to be avoided and (iv) the essential circularity of the syllogism where the truth of the conclusion must be already assumed in the premises, an anticipation of Mill. The upshot of these arguments is that there can be no certain knowledge, immediate or inferred: none immediate because of the relativity of perception and the conflict of opinions, none inferred because all proof is circular and must either hang in the air from unproved premises or be infinitely regressive.

An obvious objection to the kind of comprehensive scepticism towards which these arguments point is that it is self-refuting. If the conclusion drawn is the extreme one to which the earliest sceptics were attracted, that no statement is justified to any degree whatever, that there is no more reason for asserting any belief than for denying it, scepticism would appear to entail its own unacceptability. And if scepticism refutes itself it might seem to follow that there must be some items of certain knowledge. But the falsity of this kind of comprehensive scepticism does not entail anything as strong as this. The falsity of the view that every belief is no more worthy of assertion than of denial entails only that some belief is more worthy of assertion than of denial, which falls some way short of the claim that any belief is certainly true. This weaker conclusion from comprehensive scepticism is quite compatible with the kind of modified scepticism that is often called fallibilism, which maintains, not that no belief is to any degree justified, but that no belief is finally and conclusively justified, that no belief, in other words, is incorrigible.

The fallibilist thesis that all beliefs are corrigible is not self-refuting though it is, perhaps, mildly self-enfeebling. 'It must itself be corrigible', says Price, 'And if it is, then it may not after all be the case that all judgements are corrigible. Shall we say then that the thesis is *not* corrigible? But then again it refutes itself. For it is maintained that all judgements are corrigible and it is itself a judgement' (Price (2), p. 5). The second horn of this dilemma is sharp enough to be worth avoiding but the possibility that fallibilism may be false is not a self-refutation; it no more constitutes a reason for asserting fallibilism than it does for any other corrigible but well-supported belief. Corrigibility and justification are perfectly compatible. 'All generalisations are false' refutes itself but 'all generalisations are less than certain' does not.

It has been widely believed since Russell formulated the theory of types to deal with the logical paradoxes that all statements like the sceptical and fallibilist principles we have been discussing are ill-formed and without meaning by reason of the fact that they refer to themselves. It is true that self-reference is a general feature of logically paradoxical utterances and that if it is ruled out as senseless they cannot be formulated. But the acceptance of Russell's prohibition does not materially alter the situation. Suppose that, for the kind of reasons given by Aenesidemus and Agrippa, we assert the second-order statement 'all first-order statements are corrigible'. This assertion leaves the status of the second-order statement itself indeterminate. In order to establish it we can assemble third-order statements about second-order ones, such as that there is conflict of opinion about second-order statements, which there undoubtedly is, that the proofs on which second-order statements rest are circular and regressive or hypothetical. From these we can infer the third-order conclusion that second-order statements are corrigible and can go on to repeat the process indefinitely. Indeed as far as conflict of opinions goes there would seem to be more of a reason for doubt the higher the order of the statements considered.

It often appears to be supposed that the ban on self-reference shows the statements it excludes to be false and to establish the truth of their negations. But although the negation of a self-referring statement is not always a self-referring statement too (the negation of 'all statements are corrigible' is 'some statements are incorrigible' which does not necessarily include itself in its scope) it would seem that the negation of a meaningless statement must be meaningless. In other words if 'some statements are incorrigible' is to make sense it must be taken to apply to a range of statements which does not include itself. But in that case it is the denial of 'all first-order state-ments are corrigible' and the falsity of this is not established by showing that 'all statements whatever are corrigible' is without meaning. The same argument holds if 'no more worthy of assertion than denial' is substituted for 'corrigible'. 'No first-order statement is more worthy of assertion than denial' is left an open question by the ruling that the utterance that results from removing the qualification 'first-order' from it is meaningless. Russell's restriction then, does not have the consequence of establishing the opposite of either scepticism or fallibilism. What it does do is ensure that the form-ulation and development of either view will be a complicated and strictly incompletable business. In the case of fallibilism, at any rate, the reasons that exist for asserting it in first-order statements apply even more forcibly to asserting it for statements of higher orders. In the case of comprehensive scepticism, however, the situation is rather different. If we are to have any ground for saying that no first-order statement is more worthy of assertion than denial we must accept that some second-order statements (e.g. concerning the conflict of opinions that there is about first-order statements) are worthy of assertion.

It is, in general, an objection to comprehensive scepticism that, allowing that it has been formulated in a meaningful way, it must rest on grounds which are regarded as worthy of acceptance. This is equally true of and damaging to various more localised forms of scepticism. A complete distrust of memory is incoherent since it is only through some degree of reliance on memory that we have any reason to suppose that memory ever plays us false. Any reasonable doubt that I have of the reliability of my memory now must rest on my recollections of past occasions when my memory has proved mistaken. A similar argument applies to Descartes's sceptical inferences from the possibility that he is dreaming. There is, of course, no certain mark by which one can tell whether one is dreaming or awake. But why should this be a cause of concern? It is because I accept the principle that most of what I dream to be the case is not the case. But how do I know this? There is no direct logical connection in general between 'I dreamed that p' and 'not-p'. It is perfectly possible for any belief that I form in a dream, except perhaps some beliefs about what I am currently physically doing, to be true. And even that qualification may be questioned in view of the ancient pleasantry about the man who, dreaming that he was addressing the House of Lords, awoke to find that he was. It is just because I have in the past been able to distinguish dreaming from waking states and have discovered that most of what I dreamt did not really happen that the supposition that I am dreaming now affords any reason for doubting what I now believe. This is not to say that it is simply an empirical generalisation that most of what one dreams is false. We only have the concept of dreaming because there are identifiable tracts of our biographies in which an exceptionally high proportion of the beliefs we form are mistaken.

It may be questioned whether Russell's contention that all self-referring utterances are meaningless is correct. His procedure is not unlike that of a man who has a leg amputated to be rid of his corns. Certainly logically paradoxical utterances are characteristically self-referring and if self-reference is prohibited the paradoxes cannot arise. But, as Popper has argued (Popper (3), ch. 14), many self-referring utterances are apparently true (e.g. 'this statement contains five words') and many are apparently false (e.g. 'this statement contains six words'). But if they are true or false they must be significant. Furthermore it is only a very small class of self-referring utterances that are strictly paradoxical. 'All generalisations are false' and 'all Cretans are (complete) liars', said by a Cretan, are only necessarily false and not, like Russell's original paradox of 'this statement is false', necessarily both true and false. 'No statement is more worthy of acceptance than denial' is rather like 'all Cretans are liars'. If there is any reason for asserting it there is no reason for asserting it and equally, and trivially, if there is no reason for asserting it. Though not strictly self-refuting, for it does not entail its own falsehood, it is anyway self-destructive.

I conclude then that both comprehensive scepticism and fallibilism can be significantly formulated, that the former but not the latter is, in a broad sense, self-refuting and that its rejection does not establish that there are any incorrigible statements, although the rejection of fallibilism would. Even if Russell's prohibition of self-reference is followed the situation is not materially changed. The reasons that exist for holding all first-order statements to be corrigible apply *a fortiori* to all second- and higher-order statements while the sceptical view that no first-order statement is more worthy of assertion than denial is inconsistent with the corresponding view about second-order statements both because it is a second-order statement itself whose worthiness to be asserted is implied by asserting it and because there can be no rational ground for it unless some other second-order statements (e.g. about the conflict of first-order opinions) are worthy of assertion. The existence of incorrigible statements, then, is not established by the self-refuting nature of scepticism. For the only kind of scepticism which is self-refuting proves by its failure only that there must be statements more worthy of assertion than denial.

In fact something rather more specific than this conclusion can be derived from a critical examination of sceptical arguments, although it does not prove the incorrigibility of anything. The three specific arguments that Descartes advances in the first of his *Meditations* can be recruited for this purpose. They have the advantages of being at once familiar and broad in scope.

In the first of them he infers the untrustworthiness of the senses from the fact that he has been sometimes deceived by them. Secondly, he holds that since there is no certain mark whereby dreams can be distinguished from waking life any belief may be false. Finally, since it is possible that all my beliefs are caused by a malignant demon it may be that none of them is true. He does not, in fact, swallow these arguments whole. The senses deceive me about what is remote or unfamiliar, not about the near and usual. The indiscernibility of dreams, although it puts all contingent beliefs in question, does not cast doubt on necessary truths since I can demonstrate such a truth in a dream. The malignant demon, of course, is brought up short by the absolute indubitability of *cogito ergo sum*.

The first thing to notice here is that the first two arguments rest on factual considerations. In the second argument about dreaming two premises are invoked: that there is no certain mark to distinguish dreaming from waking life, which is no doubt true, and the implicit premise, to which I drew attention earlier, that most of what one dreams to be the case is not. This second premise is not only contingent; it presupposes the ability to distinguish dreams from waking life, if only after the event. Unless beliefs to the effect that I am or was awake or was asleep are sometimes, indeed often, justified I should be in no position to use the possibility that I am dreaming to cast doubt on what I am now inclined to believe.

Some further consequences may be extracted from the very reasonable contention that my senses have sometimes deceived me. In the first place I can have no reason to assert this unless memory is generally and preponderantly reliable. Secondly, it might reasonably be held to assume the general reliability of induction. For, unless it is reasonable to project the pattern of the observed into the unobserved, why should the fact that my senses have deceived me in the past create any presumption whatever that they are going to continue doing so in the future?

Most important, however, is the fact that my belief that the senses sometimes err presupposes that the senses themselves are generally reliable. I can detect errors of perception only by relying on my senses. I think I see a man crouching outside the window in the twilight. I go out to explore and find a bush. I conclude that there was no man there, just because I am now convinced that there is a bush. Unless this conviction is justified I have no good reason to think that there was no man.

Ayer has objected to this line of reasoning that, in effect, all we need if we are to find out that the senses are unreliable is logic and a knowledge of what the senses incline us to believe (Ayer (5)). If I believe that something is F, on the basis of perception, and then that the same thing is G, where being G is logically incompatible with being F, then I can tell on logical grounds alone that at least one of 'a is F' and 'a is G' is false, without having to suppose either is true. But this is incorrect because the argument involves a hidden premise as did the argument about dreams. This is that whatever is F does not rapidly turn into something that is G (in the case where the two beliefs are acquired at different times) or that a physical thing with the visual properties of an F never has the tactual properties of a G (where senses operating simultaneously supply us with apparently incompatible beliefs). Men do not turn into bushes: things with the visible shape, size and colour of men do not have the tangible texture and density of bushes. These truths are obvious enough, but they are not necessary truths. They rest on massive and largely unnoticed accretions of perceptual knowledge. In other words a premise essential to the proof that perception is unreliable is not available unless the general reliability of perception is assumed. The moral is that no form of scepticism that is based on contingent premises can reach very far if it is not to erode its own support.

A priori scepticism, as we may describe the kind of argument exemplified by Descartes' malignant demon, in which only the logical possibility of something is assumed, is not exposed to this kind of objection about self-destructiveness. But it has weaknesses of its own. There is no obvious contradiction in the supposition that instead of sitting at my typewriter after forty-odd years of ordinary life, I am and have always been in fact a brain in a bottle being supplied with quasiperceptual stimuli by a technologically advanced Dr Frankenstein. But from the fact that p is not obviously self-contradictory it does not in the least follow that p may well be true. It does follow that it could logically be true if it is not self-contradictory. But, as Moore elaborately argued, there is a great deal of difference between what logically could be true and what there is the smallest reason to suppose is true (Moore (2), ch. 10).

As for Descartes' specific example in this mode: if the malignant demon suddenly chooses to reveal himself by stripping aside the flimsy veil of appearance one would feel something like the annoyance Russell said he would feel towards God were he to find that he did exist after all after having provided such inadequate grounds for thinking he did. But even then the distinction between reality and mere appearance with which he had operated until the moment of revelation would not be retrospectively impugned. Within the total scheme of the demonic shadow-play the distinction between real and imaginary happenings would still obtain.

Two arguments for certainty

There are two further general arguments for the certainty of basic statements which rest respectively on the intuitiveness and ostensiveness which are the defining characteristics of such statements. In the first argument, which is developed in the two chief works of C. I. Lewis, it is held that certainly true premises are required if any belief is to be justified as probable. In the second, expounded by Hampshire, it is argued that to endow a sentence with meaning is to specify the conditions in which statements made by it would be certainly true.

'Probability' says Lewis 'is relative to the data on which it is based . . . it concerns the relation between the judgement and whatever are the relevant data upon which it is based. . . . Unless this backward-leading chain comes to rest finally in certainty, no probability-judgement can be valid at all.' And again: 'If anything is to be probable, something must be certain. The data which support a genuine probability must themselves be certainties.' One merely probable statement may support another but 'such confirmation is only provisional and hypothetical, and it must have reference eventually to confirmations by direct experience, which alone is capable of being decisive and providing any sure foundation' (Lewis (2), pp. 186–7).

Lewis's argument appears to be a version of the regress of justification. No statement is probable in itself but only in relation to its evidence, the presumed truth of some other statement. If every statement owes its probability to some other statement it cannot be the case that every statement is probable. The point can be expressed in terms of a distinction drawn by Price between hypothetical and categorical probability (Price (2), p. 23). A statement of hypothetical probability is non-committal with regard to the acceptability of its evidence. 'If he has caught the train he will probably be there by six' leaves the question of his having caught the train open and says only that he will probably arrive at six *if* he has caught it. A statement of categorical probability, set out in full, is of the form 'since he has caught the train he will probably be there by six' and any such statement as 'he will probably be there by six' presupposes the acceptance of some such since-clause. Thus for any belief to be actually and categorically rendered probable or justified some categorical statement of evidence must be accepted. But if this is itself probable yet further accepted evidence must be available and so on *ad infinitum*.

The crucial weakness of this argument is that certainty is as much relevant to evidence as probability. No more than probability is it an intrinsic property of statements. As has been shown, it is a temporally variable feature of our beliefs; coming and going with the increase and decrease of our grounds of belief. What was only probable yesterday, for example, that I should have breakfast before 9 today, is this morning quite certain. In a few weeks' time it will be only probable again. If there is an infinite regress of justification, then, it cannot be stopped by statements that are certainly true. The regress is a regress of justification and of this both certainty and probability are forms.

This embarrassment is very similar to one that is encountered by the familiar definition of knowledge as justified true belief. Plato, considering this definition in the *Theaetetus*, and assuming that the only thing that could justify a belief is another justified belief, pointed out its regressiveness. But the difficulty can be avoided by abandoning his assumption that all justifying support must be provided by further statements. As well as propositional support we may also admit experiential support, the kind of support that is given to a belief by experience itself and not by antecedently established statements. If this extended conception of support or justification is admitted, in other words if intuitive statements are allowed, the requirement that every acceptable statement must rest on evidence does not generate a regress. The relevant point with regard to Lewis is that he does accept the notion of experiential support or justification as far as the expressive judgments which report the immediate deliverances of sense are concerned. But if he admits that experience can certify our terminal empirical beliefs why should he not allow that it could support them partially or render them probable as well?

At one point he remarks: 'If what is to confirm the objective belief and thus show it probable, were itself an objective belief and hence no more than probable, then the objective belief to be confirmed would only probably be rendered probable' (Lewis (2), p. 186). The suggestion here seems to be that beliefs resting on a merely probable basis would be so little supported as to be never worth accepting. If so it is mistaken. An interesting piece of information h is rendered less probable by being communicated to one by a moderately reliable informant A than the assumed evidence for it, namely that A believes h. For even if he believes it, which is, of course, not certified by the fact that he says it, it does not follow that it is true. But if the same news is imparted by a series of similar informants, whom we have reason to believe are not in any sort of collusion or dependent on one another for what they say, it will be more probable than is the belief that any particular one of them believes it. Supporting evidence can make up in bulk for what its individual constituents lack in strength.

It should be noticed that even if it were valid Lewis's argument would not establish that there must be incorrigible statements. What it is designed to prove is that there must be statements at the foundations of knowledge that do not rest for their acceptability on other statements. Since he holds that all probable beliefs do rest on others he concludes that basic statements cannot be merely probable. But this, as we have seen in the previous section, does not imply that they are incorrigible, only that they are beyond reasonable doubt. For Lewis, of course, certainty and incorrigibility are one and the same. Perhaps a version of his argument could be constructed in which it did yield the conclusion he is after. It might be said that a corrigible statement, since it is one exposed to the possibility of falsification by other beliefs, is one which would derive confirmation from their falsehood. But that a belief *can* be confirmed in this way does not entail that its only confirmation must be of this kind. Its main confirmation could still come from experience rather than other beliefs which would merely strengthen its acceptability.

Lewis, then, runs together the probable, what is less than certain, with the corrigible, what could be less than certain, whether it is in fact or not. But his regress argument shows neither that probability must start from certainty, since both are relative to evidence, nor that corrigible statements must rest on incorrigible ones. What his argument does show is that not all statements can owe their acceptability to other acceptable statements; there must be non-propositional or experiential grounds for accepting basic statements. That basic statements must have experiential grounds does not entail that these grounds must always be sufficient to certify them, to justify them completely; it is enough if they are partially justified or rendered probable by experience. Even less does it entail that these experiential grounds are the only things that could bear on their justification at all and thus that they are incorrigible.

Hampshire contends that 'one understands a statement, if, and only if, one can think of some conditions, however unattainable in fact, in which the statement in question might be known to be true or might be known to be false: and to clarify the meaning of an expression is to specify the conditions in which it could be used with the greatest possible confidence' (Hampshire (3), p. 230). He goes on: 'to study the conditions for the proper use of "know" and "certain" in conjunction with sentences of different types is to learn how these sentences are typically used.' It follows that for every statement whose meaning is understood there must be some conditions in which it can be known for certain to be true, namely conditions of the sort that are standard for introducing someone to the meaning of the sentence used to make it. And he concludes that there is no class of statements that is pre-eminently capable of certainty since every kind of statement has its own way of being certain. This does indeed follow from his premises but its evident incorrectness must refute them. To say that a material object is infinitely divisible has an intelligible meaning (perhaps several) but, unless it is interpreted as analytic, it is not possible to envisage circumstances in which it was certainly true. If it means the object can be actually divided into ever smaller parts without end it can, of course, be refuted by reaching a point at which further endeavours to divide it simply fail or cause the parts reached to go out of existence altogether. It would be more plausible to say that for every kind of statement there are conditions which would justify its assertion, though even this is questionable. Familiar arguments about contingent statements of unrestricted generality are sufficient to disprove his thesis in its comprehensive form: however many

A's we find to be B it is always possible that some future A will turn out not to be B. And to say this is not just to say that empirical generalisations are corrigible in principle. There is always precedent for reasonable doubt in this field since the number of general hypotheses that are confirmed and at some time accepted is much greater than that of those that have never come to grief on a negative instance.

Hampshire's argument is an apparently inevitable development of the principle that the meaning of a statement is given by its truth-conditions. But at best it can apply only to ostensive sentences, those whose meaning is introduced by correlating them with experienced reality. For other types of sentence will be introduced by rules which connect them with open sets of ostensive sentences. But is it necessary that ostensive sentences should be introduced by correlation with experienceable states of affairs whose occurrence is sufficient to certify them incorrigibly? Ayer says that in affirming basic propositions about our immediate experience we describe it 'by indicating that a certain word applies to it in virtue of a meaning-rule of the language' (Ayer (4), p. 120). Such ostensive meaning-rules are necessary for any language that can be used for empirical description. 'Unless one knows how to apply [these rules], one does not understand the language. Thus I understand a word if I know in what situations to apply it. For this it is essential that I should be able to recognise the situations when I come upon them' (ibid., pp. 120-1). But, he goes on, although a language must have ostensive meaning-rules, they do not have to be of the kind which conclusively establish the truth or falsehood of the statements they are used to introduce. Meaning-rules, he holds, can be of this certifying kind and he believes that the rules governing the use of such statements as 'this looks green' and 'I am in pain' actually are. But they do not have to be. They could be merely probabilifying. 'It might be that the rules were such that every correct description of an empirical situation involved some reference beyond it; and in that case, while the use of the sentence which was dictated by the given meaning rule could be justified in the given situation, its truth would not be conclusively established' (ibid., p. 123). In such circumstances, then, ostensive meaning-rules would determine the conditions in which it would be correct to make a statement but not those in which it was known, for certain and incorrigibly, to be true.

There is a similar conjecture in Price's discussion of the thesis that all beliefs are corrigible (Price (2), pp. 24-7). He suggests that the only way in which its supporters could avoid the regress that follows from the relational nature of probability is if they reject the assumption that all probability is relative and assert the existence of intrinsically probable beliefs, citing judgments of perception, introspection and memory as examples. He is, not unreasonably, worried about the notion of intrinsic probability. It has, in fact, the same defect as the corresponding view that incorrigible basic statements are self-evident. For these two kinds of assertion are not held by their defenders to be probable or certain in themselves and out of all relation to everything else. It is rather that their justification, whether partial or complete, does not depend on other beliefs. We should not, then, seek to deny that probability is relational (or that certainty is either) but rather that it is always a relation to belief, to other statements, is propositional in nature. What Price's 'corrigibilist' needs is the notion of experiential probability and this would be possessed by those statements which had been introduced by meaning-rules of the second, justifying but not certifying, kind that Ayer describes.

These, as Price put it, would be 'corrigent' as well as, like all other statements, corrigible. They would serve as the categorical but still merely probable premises which, in conjunction with hypothetical statements of probability, would enable us to assign categorical probabilities to other beliefs and they would be the point at which the whole structure of our beliefs would make its justifying contact with empirical reality. But this structure would not, as it is usually represented as doing, rest on the immovable foundation stones of incorrigible certainty; rather, in Popper's image, it would be supported by piles, driven more or less securely into the river-bed of experience (Popper (1), p. 111).

I shall argue that not only are the basic elements of our system of empirical beliefs like this but also that they must be since there are, and indeed could be, no incorrigible empirical statements. In chapter 7 I shall try to show that the first of Price's three examples, judgments of perception, satisfy the conditions he lays down for 'intrinsic probability', in that they are corrigible and yet do not owe their whole justification to other beliefs. I shall also try to show that the meaning-rules which govern their use are of the second, probabilifying kind envisaged by Ayer. The essential point here is that we first learn the use of simple perceptual sentences like 'that is a horse' or just 'horse' in carefully prepared situations. Our teachers make sure that the object we can see really is a horse. The skill we acquire from these elementary lessons does not, however, protect us against all possibility of error. Our learning of 'this is a horse' is not over until we have been equipped to cope with statues of horses, large cardboard horses, cows seen in fog, the vaulting-horses of ill-lit gymnasiums and so on. Experiences like those of our first prepared encounters with horses thus come, when we have more fully mastered the use of the word, only to support and not to certify the judgment that this is a horse in front of us. A full understanding of 'that is a horse' involves an unlearning of part of our first over-simple lessons. This view does not imply that we are not often quite reasonably certain of the truth of such judgments, both where we subsequently arrive at some other supporting beliefs and where the judgment first occurs to us in circumstances where other things we reasonably believe are such as to put it beyond reasonable doubt. Nor does it imply that the experience which prompts our judgment is not itself describable. But I shall argue that such direct, phenomenological descriptions of experience are not incorrigible themselves and are not, anyway, available to us in the ordinary case where we make judgments of perception.

Incorrigibility and language

I have now considered and rejected such general arguments as are known to me that seek to prove that there must be incorrigible statements at the foundations of knowledge. But from the fact that there do not have to be incorrigible statements it does not follow that there are not, let alone cannot be, any. The simplest argument for their existence consists in the production of what are held to be actual instances of incorrigible statements. These, of course, are the sense-statements which directly report present immediate experience. They are of two kinds: first, statements of the form 'there appears to me now to be a ϕ here', which I shall call appearance-statements, and, secondly, statements which report current states of mind such as 'I am in pain', 'I feel cold' and 'I wish that noise would stop', which I shall call feeling-statements.

It is widely maintained that sense-statements of these two kinds are strictly incorrigible, in the sense of my definition of an incorrigible statement as one whose truth follows from the fact that it is believed to be true. Such a statement can be made falsely only if the speaker is aware that it is false; there is no possibility of his being honestly mistaken about it. The only other way in which they can go wrong is if the speaker makes a verbal mistake. This is usually seen as a verbal slip of the sort the speaker would immediately correct if it were brought to his attention, as when one says 'it's on the wireless' meaning that it's on the television set. Here we can say that the statement the man intended to make is true even if the one he formally made was not and there is an acceptable way of settling doubt about what he meant to say. Another possibility is where a man does not make a single inattentive slip but uses a word in an idiosyncratic way. Here again his intended statement is identifiable and is not refuted by the falsehood of what he said under its common interpretation. Someone might say 'I feel very nostalgic' when visiting a place he had never been to before and which did not remind him of anywhere he had been but which simply made him feel vaguely melancholy. He is under the not uncommon but mistaken impression that 'nostalgic' means 'sad'. He may mislead us but what he meant may be quite true. One further point that should be mentioned is that a statement that I make about what appears to me or what I feel now may be rejected by me for good reasons later on. I may have a clear recollection of the circumstances, which is authenticated by the testimony of others, and on this basis reject a very faint memory of what I felt at the time if this was incongruous with the circumstances. Yet my faint recollection may be correct despite its faintness, incongruities of this sort do occur and so the 'correction', though reasonable, is in fact mistaken. But my belief at the later date that I felt appropriately mournful at the funeral is not, like my realisation at the funeral that I feel perfectly cheerful, held in conditions that make it basic and, despite its identity of content with what could be held to be incorrigible, is not incorrigible itself on any view.

The simplest rejoinder to this simple kind of argument for incorrigible statements would be to produce instances of the two kinds of sense-statement which are in fact corrigible. And I shall, in fact, suggest cases in which such statements are not incorrigible and not self-intimating. But it would be more satisfactory to produce a general argument to show that no statements of this kind can be guaranteed as true by the fact that they are believed. There are several arguments of this kind and in this section I shall consider a group of them which turn on the fact that every statement must contain a general predicative term. The general form of these arguments is that predicative concepts are applied to things in accordance with a rule and the mastery of this rule is something that we may not wholly possess. As Mackie puts it, those who hold sense-statements to be incorrigible rest their case on the fact that sense-statements are not predicative, are not open to subsequent refutation, for with them the claim made does not in any way go beyond the evidence on which it rests. But, he adds, the gap between claim and evidence need not be the only source of error. We may attempt to put conceptual garments that fit their owners perfectly on to the wrong people (Mackie).

One well-known version of this argument from the fallibility of predication was given by Ayer (Ayer (1), pp. 126–7). A purely ostensive statement, he says, one that consisted wholly of demonstrative terms, would indeed be logically indubitable, but it would not really be a statement, it could communicate nothing. 'One cannot in language point to an object without describing it. If a sentence is to express a proposition, it cannot merely name a situation; it must say something about it. And in describing a situation, one is not merely "registering" a sense-content; one is classifying it in some way or other, and this means going beyond what is immediately given.' What Ayer is saying is that a significant statement must contain a general, predicative, classificatory term, which is not disputable, and, more controversially, that in using such a term we are going beyond what is immediately given. His ground for this second, controversial claim is that when, for example, I call something immediately present to my mind 'white' I am saying that it is an element in the class of immediately given things that are white for me or that it is similar in colour to those that I should call or have called white. A special version of the argument would hold that in calling it white I am implicitly comparing it to the things by reference to which I learnt the word 'white' in the first place. But since memory is fallible my comparison, my judgment that the given thing is similar to the remembered ones, may well be mistaken.

The first weakness of this argument is that it seems to be empirically false. I can confidently call things white even if I have no recollection whatever, and in fact I have none, of the things by reference to which the word was taught me. No doubt they stand in a causal relation to my current ability to use the word 'white' but I do not have to think, or even to be able to think, of them when I use it. A familiar argument against the existence of universals can also be applied here to show that my use of general terms could not generally be the result of a comparison between something given and the things by means of which my use of the term was originally acquired. For to make such a comparison would be to judge that this given thing is similar to some formerly observed thing or things. But in order to apply the general term 'similar' here I must first judge that the relation between the given thing and the exemplar or exemplars of the concept of whiteness resembles the relation present in the exemplary cases of similarity. And so on *ad infinitum*. Thus every judgment in which a general term was applied to something would have to be the end-term of an infinite sequence of such judgments, a clear logical impossibility. In fact what I acquire from being shown exemplary white things is the capacity I now have to tell directly whether some given thing is white or not. Lewis gives a cryptic version of the same argument when he holds that all conceptualisation is interpretative. Popper, again, says that we can make no statement 'that does not go far beyond what can be known with certainty "on the basis of immediate experience" '. He refers to this fact as the 'transcendence inherent in any description'. It sometimes looks as if he is merely saying this of public, objective statements for at one stage he confines it to 'scientific statements' and the example he uses is 'here is a glass of water'. But the reason he offers is more widely applicable. It is that 'every description uses *universal* names (or symbols, or ideas); every statement has the character of a theory, of a hypothesis', whereas 'an "immediate experience" is *only once* "immediately given"; it is unique . . . universals cannot be reduced to classes of experiences; they cannot be *constituted*.' And again 'even ordinary singular statements are always *interpretations of "the facts" in the light of theories*. (And the same holds even for "the facts" of the case. They contain *universals*; and universals always entail a *law-like* behaviour.)' (Popper (1), pp. 94–5.) Popper seems to be saying that since every statement involves a universal or predicative concept, which cannot be identified with any class of its instances, it must have the character of a theoretical interpretation and thus be corrigible. His view that all predicates are dispositional and imply law-like behaviour seems unplausible when applied to the predicates of sense-statements such as 'appears to me to be red' or 'pain' (said of oneself). But, as we shall see, it is not unreasonable to hold that the statements they occur in can enter into systematic logical connections with other statements our acceptance of which can have a bearing on their own rejection.

In later discussions Ayer has come round to accepting incorrigible statements (cf. Ayer (2), pp. 53–4 and (4)). Against the view that when I state the colour of a thing I am saying that it resembles some other objects he argues that it does not follow from the thing's being the colour it is that anything else exists at all. This is not really relevant. The fact to be explained is not that the thing is of a certain colour but the fact that I believe and say that it is. But his point is correct for although my ability to believe and say what I do depends as a matter of fact on my having seen things of that colour before, it does not logically presuppose this. I might, in principle, have been endowed with this skill by brain-surgery. And he is right, as the regress argument shows, when he says that 'if I use a sensory predicate to describe what I am now experiencing I need not be making any claim about a situation other than the one before me'. This does not entail that I am simply and uninformatively naming the situation; what I am doing is 'indicating that a word applies to it in virtue of a meaning-rule of the language', one that lays down that the statement in question is conclusively and indubitably verified by the situation to which it refers.

More recently still Ayer has reverted to his first view that there are no incorrigible statements. He still thinks, for the rather unsatisfactory reason mentioned in the last paragraph, but correctly, in my view, that predication is not, in general, comparison with what may be faultily remembered. But he argues that there are cases in which we are positively uncertain about what sense-statement to make which it is unreasonable to treat as cases of uncertainty about the meaning of the words involved. 'Suppose that two lines of approximately the same length are drawn so that they both come within my field of vision and I am then asked whether either of them looks to be the longer and if so which. I think I might very well be uncertain how to answer.' But this uncertainty does not relate to the meaning of the expression 'longer than', it concerns the facts of the case (Ayer (5), p. 69).

It can be replied to this, as it is by Mackie, that in such a case we should not let ourselves be bullied into giving a definite answer one way or the other: neither line looks longer than the other and that is what we should say. But if we add that the lines do not look equal either we will be in a difficulty. For what the line looks, the appearance or impression of the line, it is held, actually is. And in this case the two line-appearances would actually have contradictory characters, being neither different nor equal in length.

A weakness of most discussions of the incorrigibility of sense-statements is that they assume an unrealistically sharp distinction between mistakes of fact and language. Certainly a simple verbal slip is just a verbal mistake and so is the use of a wholly incorrect word to express a clearly apprehended and otherwise ordinarily expressible meaning. But there are, as Ayer's last example shows, cases where we are uncertain what to say, such as those mentioned by Austin, where a taste strikes us as quite unique and unprecedented or, again, where it is very like something familiar but there is also something odd about it (Austin (1), pp. 60–1). The point that these possibilities emphasise is that the application of descriptive general terms to things, even to our immediate experiences, is a learnt skill our command of which may vary a very great deal. Even if we suppose that the words we know are sufficient to cater for any experience we may have, and it is hard to see how this could be shown and indeed, by reason of open texture, clear that it is in general false, we may well be less than perfectly efficient in applying them and very often are. Since words are governed by rules there is always the formal possibility of a mistake. Where immediate experience is concerned such a mistake may be taken to show, with considerable plausibility in some cases, that the speaker has a less than complete command of the words he is using. But such a failure is not a simple verbal mistake. He may be fully competent in following the logical connections of the word, in being able to tell with what the statements it figures in are inconsistent and what they entail and he may in easy cases be able to apply it without hesitation. In that case he is likely to know the meaning of the word as well as anyone, yet he is not guaranteed against all misuse of it that is not just a verbal slip. In other words the fact that sense-statements do necessarily contain predicative general terms does count against their incorrigibility: not because it shows them to involve a comparison with what may be misrecalled but because for these terms to be used with meaning they must be used in accordance with rules. These rules may not specify how the word is to be used in all the situations that arise; even where they do we may well be less than perfectly competent in handling them without being remotely exposed to the charge that we do not know their meaning at all or again that we have made a verbal slip.

The falsification of sense-statements

The last section has, I hope, provided a firmer foundation for the view that sense-statements are capable of falsehood, where there is no intent to deceive on the speaker's part, than it is usually given. This conclusion would be much strengthened if it could be shown that such statements, as well as being capable of being false in this way, can also be shown to be false. I shall consider three arguments that bear on this point.

The first of them has been most effectively presented by Goodman (Goodman (2)). It is possible, he says, for the following situation to arise: at t1 I hold that something appears blue to me, at t2 I recall this judgment and also hold that what I am now looking at appears green to me, finally, still at t2, I cannot recall any difference in colour between what now appears to me and what appeared to me at t1. In a case like this I can preserve the incorrigibility of the two sense-statements involved ('at t1 blue appeared', 'at t2 green appeared') by rejecting one of the judgments of memory. I can suppose either that my recollection of the sense-statement I accepted at t1 is mistaken (and that, in fact, what I held at t1 was that something appeared green to me) or that my recollective judgment of identity of colour is mistaken. But a firm determination always to resolve the inconsistency in this way seems gratuitous. Suppose that the object in both cases, presented in a good light and so forth, is a turquoise ring and that there is independent evidence, as there perfectly well may be, that at t1 I judged it to look blue. It is, surely, not uncommon in cases of this kind for the second look to function as a corrector of the judgment prompted by the first; to remind one, as it were, of what green really is. To insist on abandoning only one or other of the memory-judgments is, Goodman holds, to turn the sense-statements into mere decrees, into expressions of a kind of ostensively definitional resolve and to deprive them of their power to describe.

An analogous possibility, considered by Ayer and Armstrong, is to allow other circumstances about oneself than one's sense-statements and memories as having a bearing on the sense-statements one accepts. Ayer supposes that there might have been a uniform association hitherto between something's looking green to one and one's making a certain bodily reaction. If I now sincerely say 'this looks green' and fail to make the bodily reaction, abandonment of the generalisation is not the only possibility open to me (Ayer (5)). Armstrong considers the possibility of a brain investigator who establishes a uniform relationship between a man's belief that something looks green and a recognisable state of his brain. If the belief now occurs in conjunction with the brain-state associated hitherto with things looking blue we are, once again, not compelled to abandon the generalisation (Armstrong (2)).

To say this is not to say that sense-statements often are falsely believed or that they are often less than certain in the ordinary sense. To allow an option which defenders of the incorrigibility of sense-statements rule out is not to imply that it should be chosen very frequently.

Armstrong has constructed an ingenious argument for the corrigibility of sense-statements which has, perhaps, a slightly scholastic flavour considered on its own but which has more force when combined with the previous considerations (ibid., p. 420). This is that the formation of a judgment takes time, that it cannot begin before the experience to which it refers takes place and that it is, therefore, unlikely to be completed until after the experience in question is over. It is clear enough that the public assertion of a statement must occupy a period of time comparatively great in relation to a perceptual or introspective instant but it is not so clear that the judgment it expresses will be so deliberate about coming into existence. But it should be noticed that if the fallibility of memory destroys the incorrigibility of any belief which to any extent rests upon it then sense-statements can possess their incorrigibility only for an instant, the moment of occurrence of the experiences to which they refer. By the time we get round to using them to justify or refute any other beliefs they will already be infected with enfeebling historicity. It would appear, in general, that the more we seek to protect sense-statements by cutting them off logically from other beliefs that might count against them the less they can be conceived as doing. Like other valetudinarians they pay for their security with a loss of general usefulness. Armstrong's argument here is that since memory is fallible and all sense-statements rest on it they must be fallible too. I suggest rather that these considerations confront the defenders of incorrigibility with a dilemma. If they insist on the fallibility of memory sense-statements can have, at best and ignoring the arguments of the last section, an instantaneous and evidentially wholly infertile kind of incorrigibility. If they do not insist on it they cannot maintain that where there is an inconsistency between a sense-statement, the recollection of an immediately previous statement and a recollection of identity of apparent character one of the latter two must always be rejected.

The last general argument I shall consider has been put forward by both Mackie and Armstrong. It contends that the distinction between having the experience reported in a sense-statement and noticing it or reflecting on it in a way that would make possible a judgment about it cannot be obliterated. To be in pain is one thing; to be aware that one is is another. It might be true that whenever I am in pain I am aware of the fact but this could be only a contingent and empirical truth. Mackie observes that in general we have little or no occasion to doubt past sense-statements and we may find it psychologically impossible to doubt present ones but this, he goes on, is a guarantee not against the possibility of error but rather against the possibility of its detection (Mackie, pp. 26–7). In fact, I should argue, we do have some occasion to doubt past sense-statements and, again, can for various reasons feel uncertain about present ones, although what he says is no doubt true in the vast majority of cases. Their argument here is that to identify pain with being aware of it involves an infinite regress. To be in pain is to be aware of being in pain and to be aware of being in pain is to be aware that one is aware that one is in pain and so on. But the defender of incorrigibility could reply that the regress is harmless since every member of the infinite set means precisely the same as every other. The regress is comparable in its harmlessness, they could say, to that which follows from the view that 'p' and 'p is true' are logically equivalent, namely, 'p', 'p is true', 'it is true that p is true', 'it is true that p is true is true', etc., etc. What makes this comparison unplausible is that there seems to be a clear difference between having a sensation and having a belief about a sensation. Those who make it often follow Wittgenstein in saying that the utterances produced by prefixing phrases like 'I am aware that' and 'I know that' to sense-statements are meaningless, presumably because they suggest a difference between the prefixed and unprefixed form which does not exist. The prefixed form makes a vacuous but misleadingly suggestive addition.

We must admit that, although in general 'I am aware that p' and 'p' do not mean the same thing, if they do in cases where p is a sense-statement like 'I am in pain', no vicious regress is generated. The only effective way of establishing the opposite opinion is to produce instances in which a sense-statement *s* is true although 'I am aware that *s*' is not (which would show *s* to be not self-intimating) and instances in which 'I believe that *s*' is true although *s* is not (which would show *s* to be not incorrigible in the strict sense defined earlier). I believe that this can be done. Suppose I am suffering from toothache and someone tells me an extremely complicated and fascinating piece of gossip which entirely engrosses my attention for the duration of his narrative but at the end of which the pain once again secures my attention. Would it be natural to say here that his recital acted as an anaesthetic in the sense that it eliminated the pain for the period of its duration altogether? The situation is quite different from one in which a pain definitely comes and goes as when my wife at an exciting film intermittently seizes my upper arm in a tight grip. We should naturally be inclined to say that his story had caused us to forget the pain, had distracted our attention from it but this plainly implies that the pain is still there, waiting to recapture our attention. It would even seem possible for our grimaces and clenched fists to continue, testifying to the continuation of the pain, while our minds were far away from it. The same sort of thing can happen in more perceptual cases. To explain an illusory belief about a material object, or again an intuition in the vernacular sense, we may have to call on some sensible feature of the object in question that was not consciously perceived, one which we did not realise that the object possessed, as would be shown in the latter case especially by our inability to give any reason for our hunch.

To turn to the other side of the problem: there is a conjuring trick whose equipment is one ordinary nail and another contraption whose outer thirds are just like the head and point of the ordinary nail but which has a D-shaped piece of wire in the intervening gap which can be fitted round the back of the finger. At the points where the wire is joined to the outer thirds there is glistening red paint to simulate blood. Slipped on to the finger and presented to someone so that the wire is out of sight it looks as if a nail has been painfully driven through the finger. Now suppose I shake someone's hand with this appliance concealed in my palm and in doing so slip it on to his finger which I then hold sharply up in front of his face. He is very likely to imagine that he is in acute pain, let out a cry and grip the apparently injured hand. It is highly probable that he will feel some referred pain in the finger but it will be much milder than the pain that he thinks he is having. The same thing would occur if one were suddenly to run a concealed lipstick down someone's cheek in circumstances where he could see his face in a mirror. He would suppose that he had been slashed with a razor. A more familiar case is that in which one puts one's hand under the flowing bath tap and withdraws it believing it to be very hot when in fact it is very cold. Admittedly there is some pain present in all these cases and it is also true that there is a lively expectation of pain to come but can this really be distinguished from the belief that one is in pain now in this sort of circumstance?

Those who hold pain-statements to be incorrigible have elaborated a theory of avowals from Wittgenstein's suggestion that such statements are conventional developments of pain-behaviour, that they are learnt alternatives and supplements to natural and instinctive cries and gestures (Wittgenstein (2), p. 89). According to this theory our pain-statements do not describe our pains; they express them. It would seem to follow that, like other expressive utterances, they can be neither true nor false. The use of the word 'damn' is, after all, a conventional development and extension of our annoyance-behaviour. We have to learn how to use it. There could be failures of learning here: someone might get the idea that 'damn' is used to express elation. There can be insincerity, as when we use the word to suggest an annoyance we do not feel at some third party whose actions have prevented the person we are speaking to from making a threatened and dreaded visit. There would seem to be a fairly complete analogy between swear-words and sense-statements conceived as avowals. They cannot be false but they can be inappropriate either by reason of insincerity, where the feeling is not present though we speak as if it were, or by reason of misunderstanding.

There are, however, two vital differences between the two forms of speech. The first is that if 'I am in pain' is an avowal, and thus neither true nor false, it cannot be incompatible with the statement made to one by another at the same time: 'you are not in pain', which is clearly true or false. The singular consequence is that on this view we cannot actually say anything about our pains, but can only express them, while others can. In particular we cannot directly contradict what another says about our pain. Secondly, we can explain what it is for a man to use the word 'damn' sincerely. It is for him to utter it when he is annoyed, or believes that he is. In other words something he can know or believe is the condition of the appropriateness of his utterance, something, furthermore, that he can state in the words 'I am annoyed', as well as express. But what can play this part in the pain case if 'I am in pain' is an avowal? In other words it is impossible for him to know or say what he is expressing.

Another point to be noticed is that there is a third way in which expressive utterances can go wrong. There are, for example, unconsciously insincere apologies. I may say 'sorry' without conscious insincerity, thinking that I regret what has happened, when in fact, as others may now realise and as I may come to realise, I do not really regret it at all. In this case as well as being liable to deceive others I am myself deceived. If 'I am in pain' is an avowal the same thing should be possible. Others would say: he is not really in pain though he thinks he is. But what sense, on this theory, can we attach to 'he thinks he is in pain (but he is not)' where I say that I am in

170

pain without conscious insincerity? The fact is that 'I am in pain' does not mean the same as 'ow' even though one would do as well as the other in most circumstances. For 'ow', which really is an expressive utterance, to be part of the language and not an instinctive response its user must connect it with being in pain, in the sense that he must be able to recognise the occasions on which it is appropriate to use it. Unless this is so he will not be able to misuse it, that is with insincerity, or in a sophisticated sympathetic way, as when someone we are with hits his thumb with a hammer. There is, then, no adequate reason to ignore the grammatical appearances. 'I am in pain' is what it looks like, a report of the mental state that 'ow' expresses. Unless it were we could not introduce the convention that governs 'ow'.

It might seem to be a difficulty for the view that sense-statements are corrigible that if so we should be driven back to admitting sense-statements of the second order, as it were, to admitting the propriety of such locutions as 'I think I'm in pain', 'I think this looks green' and 'It seems to me that this looks green'. The short answer to this is that we can admit them, for those cases where for one reason or other we are uncertain what to say, such as Ayer's two lines example or Austin's unprecedented taste, though it does seem a bit excessive to hold that these watery affirmations are corrigible too. But in general we can agree with Mackie that there is no occasion for them. If I think I am in pain or that something looks green I have the best reason I can ask for in the circumstances for saying that I am in pain or that it does look green. But although these statements are justified it does not follow that they are true. Others may say truly that I think I am in pain but am not and I may come to admit, and not as a piece of mistaken 'correction', that I thought I was but was not. The point is that sense-statements are almost universally certain in the ordinary sense of being beyond reasonable doubt. It very seldom happens that we have occasion to correct them. But this does not show that they cannot in principle be corrected. They are still logically corrigible even if they are seldom theoretically in need of, and hardly ever practically open to, correction.

7

Perception

Theories of perception

Until fairly recent years it has been taken for granted by most theorists of knowledge that our beliefs about the material world are based on immediate experience, or, at any rate, that they ought to be, if we are to be justified in holding them. Now this particular but central application of the general empiricist principle that knowledge, or justified belief about matters of fact, must rest on experience, can be interpreted in three different ways. Two of these interpretations are hardly controversial but the third is very much open to question and I hope to refute it in this chapter. First, it may be taken to mean that factual knowledge must rest in the end on observation, that if anyone is to have good reason for accepting any factual belief it must, in the end, be because someone has discovered something by means of observation with the senses. It is through the exercise of the senses that the fabric of our beliefs makes its justifying contact with the world of fact. To accept this thesis is not to accept any particular account of the precise nature of these observations, that, for example, the empirical hard core of observation is the direct awareness of the character of the observer's private sense-fields. It is compatible with direct observation of material things.

Secondly, it may be taken to mean that the occurrence of sensations is a *causally* necessary condition of our having justified beliefs about matters of fact. Unless, that is to say, there were certain physical transactions between the material environment and our nervous systems we should have no perceptual, and, in consequence, no empirical, knowledge. To admit this obvious truth is to say nothing about the logical prerequisites of justified perceptual belief. It does not imply that in order to support any claim we make about the material world we have to bring forward knowledge about the causal background, physiological and psychological, of the claim. In this sense the causal theory of perception is almost a truism.

It is wholly distinct from the representationist doctrine that a belief about the material world is, if justified, the outcome of some kind of causal inference from perceived events within our minds or nervous systems to the causes of those events in the external world.

It is the third interpretation of the principle that has received most attention and had the most surprising consequences. This is that we can have only indirect, inferred knowledge of material things, which is always in some sense less than fully certain, whereas we have a direct, certain and uninferred acquaintance with our sense-experience, with our sense-data or impressions, and it affords the indispensable justifying support for our beliefs about material things. This is the first and most important exemplification of the pattern of given foundations and inferred superstructure that is held to articulate all our knowledge. Impressions or appearances are one of the two kinds of immediate experience, the other being directly introspected thoughts and feelings, which are held to be reported in the sense-statements that are usually regarded as alone truly basic.

In the fifth chapter I defined a basic statement as an intuitive statement, expressed by an ostensive sentence and owing its truth to correspondence. In the sixth chapter I argued that basic statements, so understood, were not certain in any special way. They were often beyond reasonable doubt but they were not always so or uniquely so. On the other hand they were not incorrigible because no empirical and contingent statement could be. In this chapter my aim is to show that they are not necessarily subjective, private and phenomenological, that they are not confined in their reference to the personal states of mind of their assertors. Positively I shall contend that some statements about material objects are basic and thus that we can have direct and non-inferential perception of material things.

One way of casting doubt on the doctrine that private impressions alone are the direct and immediate objects of perception is to consider the unappetising consequences that it has for our knowledge of the external world. If impressions are all we directly know in perception then either we must embrace a more or less Humean scepticism about the external world and admit that although we do not seem able to help forming beliefs about it we cannot offer any justification for them or else we must give some account of the support given to beliefs about objects by beliefs about impressions. Such an account could take either of two possible forms: it can either, as in the representationism of Descartes and Locke, take the relation between them to be contingent and see objects and impressions to be distinct but causally connected existences or it can, as in the phenomenalism of Mill, Russell and Ayer, take it to be necessary and interpret objects as constructions out of impressions, statements about objects being compact ways of making highly complicated statements about persistent regularities among impressions, actual and possible. The difficulty is that all three alternatives are extremely unpalatable. The sceptical position is absurdly defeatist and collides with Reid's common-sense observation that our conviction of having genuine knowledge about the external world is 'older and of more authority than all the arguments of philosophers'. The objection to the representative theory is that it fails to explain how beliefs about objects can be even intelligible, let alone justified. Phenomenalism is certainly the most reasonable development of the idea that impressions alone are directly perceived but it is unacceptable for a number of reasons.

The view of Descartes and Locke that objects must be inferred from impressions as their causes is derived by them from the conviction which they share with Berkeley that impressions, being independent of our wills, must have causes external to us. The trouble with this conviction is that it is not wholly true, since dreams and hallucinations are just as much impressions as veridical perceptions of objects are, and yet are not caused by anything outside us, and, furthermore, even if it were true its proponents would be unable to explain how they came to know it. Descartes argues that we find, introspectively, within us an irresistible natural propensity to suppose that our impressions have external causes. Since God is necessarily veracious he would not have equipped us with such a propensity unless it was right for us to indulge it. In fact his theological assumptions support a very different conclusion, for we have no such propensity as he alleges. What we are naturally disposed to believe is that we really do perceive material things. If this is something we are endowed with by a veracious God it follows that direct realism is true. The propensity of which Descartes speaks is rather a fundamental empirical discovery, subsequent and not prior to the establishment of beliefs about material things. Locke conjures from nowhere in particular the principle that the external causes of our impressions partially resemble them. This again cannot logically precede knowledge of objects because it is an instance of such knowledge. Any representationist theory requires us to accept some contingent proposition asserting relations of causation, and perhaps resemblance, between objects and impressions. In requiring this proposition to be accepted prior to the justification of any beliefs about objects it rules out its own justification. What is more it destroys the conditions of its own intelligibility. How can any theory about the nature of objects or their relation to impressions be understood if the only words we can understand are those which refer to impressions and it is assumed that words for objects cannot be defined in terms of them? Representationism could only be intelligible or justifiable if there was some direct access to or acquaintance with objects. But if there is such access the assumption that all knowledge of objects is derived from impressions must be abandoned.

Phenomenalism interprets the belief that there is an object here as asserting that certain impressions would be forthcoming if certain conditions of observation were realised, if I opened my eyes, turned my head, put out my hand and so forth. If I actually do perceive the objects then some of these possible impressions must be actualised. A favourite objection to the theory has been that it reduces actualities to possibilities; as Berlin puts it, a hypothetical statement can be true even though nothing exists at all, and he concludes that no categorical statement can be analysed in wholly hypothetical terms (Berlin, p. 312). This conclusion is clearly false. 'This piece of sugar is soluble' is plainly categorical but it is exactly equivalent in meaning to the hypothetical 'if this piece of sugar is put in water it will dissolve'. But there is a difference between this elementary reduction and that proposed by the phenomenalist. In the first case the piece of sugar survives the translation; what is assumed to exist by the categorical is still assumed to exist by the hypothetical. But the phenomenalised object disappears. Nevertheless there are acceptable reductions of the latter kind. 'There is a readiness for a change of government' means roughly that if people are given the opportunity they will vote for a change of government. Here a statement about a society is interpreted as a hypothetical statement about citizens and the procedure is comparable to the phenomenalist interpretation of a statement about an object as a hypothetical statement about a particular perceiver. A statement that is categorical in form, about one kind of thing can, then, be reduced to a hypothetical statement about things of another kind.

What of Berlin's premise that a hypothetical statement can be true although nothing exists? It seems to suggest that he is working on the assumption that hypothetical statements are material conditionals, false only if their antecedents are true and their consequents false. The incorrectness of such an assumption is proved by the paradoxes of material implication (whatever p and q may be, if p is false or q true then p materially implies q is true), and by the connected consequence that every counterfactual conditional is true. There are two respects in which hypothetical statements must have, as it were, a categorical basis. In the first place every hypothetical, whether simple (if p then q), counterfactual (if p had been the case then q would have been) or explanatory (q because p), presupposes the acceptance of a general statement which there can be no reason to accept unless it either has positive confirming instances itself or is derived from some yet more general statement with positive confirming instances. If a hypothetical form of words is to make a statement, true or false, something must exist, then, to provide the essential confirming instances. Secondly, there is the less well-established requirement that a disposition must have what may be called an explanatory basis. The solubility of a piece of sugar or the elasticity of a rubber band is not just accepted with natural piety as a brute fact. The tendency of these things to react in particular ways in particular circumstances has to be explained in terms of some peculiarities of their fine structure, the way their material constituents are arranged.

The first of these considerations rules out Berlin's objection. The phenomenalist can answer that his hypotheticals have their categorical basis in observed correlations between actual impressions. Unless there are some actual impressions no hypothetical can be asserted as true. But there is an embarrassing consequence for phenomenalism in that it renders the hypothesis of a material world which is never perceived by anyone, in which there is no sentence whatever, unintelligible. The second, more controversial consideration bears against the phenomenalist view of an object as a temporary disposition of a perceiver. In realistic terms these dispositions can readily be explained as due to the perceptual capacities of the perceiver together with the character of his physical environment. But for the phenomenalist this environment *is* his dispositions.

These objections to the hypothetical character of the phenomenalist account of beliefs about objects are somewhat inconclusive. The real fault of the theory is that the equivalences it alleges simply do not obtain. No hypothetical statement about impressions, however complicated, is logically connected to any statement about objects. There is something to be said for the view that 'there is a table in the next room' entails and is supported by 'if I go into the next room and look I shall have impressions of a table'. But this, of course, is an incomplete translation; it should read 'if I have the impression of going into the next room and of looking, I shall have the impression of a table' and that, since the impressions mentioned in the antecedent may be delusive, is neither here nor there. The only hypotheticals which even look as if they follow from statements about objects are those that mention the conditions of observation in objective terms in their antecedents. To suppose that the requirements of phenomenalism could be satisfied by replacing these antecedents with ones in which only impressions figure is to beg the very question at issue, namely whether statements about objects can be translated into statements about impressions. In fact it is highly doubtful if even these hybrid hypotheticals with objective antecedents follow from statements about objects. The number of conditions that have to be mentioned is very large, even if to a great extent negative, and almost certainly not known in its entirety, since

176

we do not know all the circumstances which might prevent an observer from having an impression of a table that is right in front of him. We do, indeed, know a good deal about the empirical conditions of having impressions of what is in front of us, concerned with the medium and the physical and mental state of the perceiver. But we have only discovered this because we have a lot of information, independently acquired, about objects on the one hand and the impressions perceivers have of them on the other.

It is sometimes supposed that something like phenomenalism can be saved by making some judicious concessions to the representative theory. We can, it is said, regard our beliefs about objects as a kind of explanatory theory, which, as Ayer puts it in his particularly ingenious version of the doctrine, 'is richer than anything that could be yielded by an attempt to reformulate it at the sensory level. But this does not mean that it has any other supply of wealth than the phenomena over which it ranges' (Ayer (5), p. 147). His point is that no set of statements about impressions does more than count in favour of or count against a statement about an object, except in the conceivable limiting cases that there are no impressions of the object in any circumstances, which entails that it does not exist, or that, *in the relevant setting*, as he puts it, there are impressions of the object whatever the circumstances. He admits that there are few cases in which the former negative limiting case stands much chance of being true, because of the manifold possibilities of illusion, and that he cannot think of any instance in which there is even the least likelihood of a statement of the positive kind being true, since no object could be as obtrusive as it requires objects to be. But since in these unrealisable limiting cases statements about impressions *would* entail the truth or falsity of statements about objects the essential principle of phenomenalism is established. But even here, in the qualification I have italicised, the inevitable impurity of the phenomenalist translation persists. The virtue of Ayer's position here is that he does not hide behind the eirenic principle that belief in objects is a theory designed to explain the order of our impressions. For by itself that thesis is an evasion of the problem rather than a solution of it. The point is: what sort of theory? Is it a substantial explanation in terms of independent existences, like the atomic theory of matter, or a logical construction, like theories of electrical and magnetic fields? To choose between these possibilities is to opt for the representative theory or for phenomenalism.

Illusions and appearances

We may now turn to the common assumption of the theories of perception I have been examining: the proposition that what we really perceive, the direct and immediate objects of perception, are appearances (impressions, sensations, presentations, sense-data etc.). This is sometimes recommended as the plain consequence of any resolute and unprejudiced attempt to answer the question: what do you really perceive, what is actually given or presented to the mind in perception? From this point of view it is just an inescapable matter of fact that what we really see are patches of colour, what we hear are sounds, what we smell are smells. This account of what we hear and smell is hardly disputable. And it does in a way have the consequence that we do not always perceive material objects, strictly speaking. But although a smell or a sound is not a material object, since it does not have a definite spatial outline, a determinate shape or size, it is, nevertheless, a public, objective, physical existence; it can be perceived by more than one person and it has a position, at least, in public space. In practice, furthermore, we can just as properly speak of hearing bells and smelling roses as of hearing the sound of bells or smelling the smell of roses, though the former claims are more adventurous than the latter and may be wrong in cases where the latter are right, where, for example, the smell of roses comes from some distilled essence and the sound of bells from a gramophone record.

But it is far from indisputable that all that we really see is patches of colour. We may be said to do this when we are looking at a kitchen wall with which a decorator has been experimenting but it is a ludicrously unapt account of what we see when we are looking at a brand new car in a brightly lit showroom. But even if it were an acceptable account of what we really see, of what is actually given to sight in perception, it would not follow that the patches of colour in question were private to the perceiver, that they were patches of colour in his personal field of vision rather than patches of colour in public space on walls, screens and so forth. It is, in fact, generally recognised that argument is needed to show that appearances are the immediate objects of perception, rather than an appeal to the innocent eye.

Most reasonable arguments for this theory turn out in the end to be variants of the argument from illusion. It starts from the uncontentious premise that public, material things do not always appear, seem or look to be what they really are. The next step is to say that there is no intrinsic difference between veridical and delusive appearances, between those that do and those that do not correspond to reality. What I really or directly see when I am confronted, in favourable conditions, by a shotgun may be indistinguishable by me from what I see when I am dreaming about or having a hallucination of a shotgun. Again suppose I am standing in front of a circular plaque fixed in a wall and then move steadily away and to one side. When I am in the first, optimum position the plaque appears to me to be exactly what it is, appearance and reality perfectly correspond. But as I move away the appearance of the plaque steadily changes; appearance and reality increasingly diverge. Yet, it is argued, there is no sharp break in the series of appearances and thus no distinguishing mark to separate the perception of reality from the perception of appearance. The conclusion is drawn that since there is no perceptible distinction between what I see in veridical and in delusive cases and since, in the delusive cases at any rate, I cannot be seeing the real object, I cannot be seeing it in the veridical case either.

There are some unsympathetically direct answers to the argument as so far presented which can hardly be thought to settle the question but have the merit of making the issue more definite. Against the first example it can be said that one who has a dream or hallucination of a shotgun does not see anything at all. Of course, he *thinks* he sees a shotgun, but there is no reason whatever to suppose that any-one who thinks wrongly that he sees something must really be seeing something else. In dreams, at any rate, nobody really sees anything at all. The answer to this is that even if it is incorrect to say that the dreamer sees something shotgun-like he is, nevertheless, directly aware of something shotgun-like, he knows that there appears to him to be a shotgun there. Against the second example it can be said that in fact the plaque will not look any different as we move away from it, all that will change is the shape of the patch on one's retina affected by the light coming from the plaque. But this, it can be replied, exploits the fact that we know what shape the plaque really is already, before we start moving away. Suppose we come towards the plaque from a distance and from an angle, though we do not realise this. It will then inevitably appear to us to be elliptical. And this appearance is still there in cases where collateral information enables us to counteract its possibly misleading tendency.

The main point of the argument of illusion is that in every per-ceptual situation, by which I mean any situation in which we are inclined to suppose that we are perceiving something, we do know what appears to be there, whether or not it really is. So, it is argued, what we really know in perception is only appearances and any justified belief we are to have in objects must be derived from them. At various times philosophers have protested against the last step in the argument, from 'all we really know is what appears' to 'all we really know are appearances'. Prichard described it as the sense-datum fallacy (Prichard (2)). But these objectors have not explained in what precisely its error consists. I shall argue that it is not so much the linguistic move from talking of what appears to appearances that is at fault but rather the assumption, which the

179

linguistic move certainly facilitates, that the appearances that we are directly aware of in perception are always private, subjective entities, states or contents of personal sense-fields.

This mistake arises from failure to recognise that there are at least three different ways in which the verb 'appear' is used. In the sense in which they are present in every perceptual situation appearances are not private objects and in the sense in which they are private objects they are not present in every perceptual situation, indeed they are present in hardly any. The three uses or senses of 'appear' are as follows.

(i) *Epistemic* When I say, in front of a house whose bell has not been answered and whose curtains are drawn in the middle of the day, 'they appear to be away' (or 'they seem to be away' or 'it looks as if they are away') I am simply asserting in a guarded, tentative, qualified fashion that they are away. I could just as well have said 'they are probably away' or 'they are away, I think'. In this case I can actually state the evidence on which I am going: the unanswered bell, the pulled curtains. Now suppose I am looking at what I take to be a cow in moderately unfavourable conditions, through a light mist say, or at a considerable distance, and say 'it appears to be a cow' or 'it looks like a cow'. Here, too, my utterance expresses hesitation and less than full confidence. 'It's probably a cow' or 'it's a cow, I think' would have served my purposes just as well. But in this case I cannot give much of an answer to why I said what I did. The best I can do is to say that it is shaped like a cow, or appears to be, but to say this is to make another public, objective statement, with or without hesitation. I maintain that this is the most common use of the word 'appear' and its cognates 'seem' and 'look', namely to express a less than fully confident belief or an inclination to believe. It should be noticed that in speaking in this way I am not reporting or describing my state of mind; the focus of interest is the thing believed not the believing of it.

(ii) *Perceptually minimal* Suppose I see what I take to be a cow and answer the question 'what's that' by saying 'that's a cow'. If I am asked 'are you quite sure' I may well, knowing that there are such things as dummies, stuffed cows, flat posters of a convincingly *trompe l'oeil* character and so forth, answer 'well, it looks like a cow' or 'it appears to be a cow'. What I mean here is that it has the more or less directly visible properties of a cow, that it is cow-shaped and cow-coloured. But more than this has to be true of a cow proper. It must have been born to another cow, move itself about, moo, eat grass and so on. And these implications of my original judgment I may have had no opportunity yet to check. It is vitally important to realise that this too is a public, objective statement and not a phenomenological description of my immediate experience. This use is closely related to but not quite identical with that in which 'it looks like a ϕ' means 'anyone would (be inclined to) say it is a cow'. They are not identical because adjectival concepts can be put to the second of these uses but not the first. If I say of a piece of cloth held up in a poor light that it looks, appears or seems to be green I may well mean that anyone would be inclined to say that that was its colour rather than be expressing my own inclination to believe that it is green. But I shall not be saying that it has the directly visible properties that green things usually have for there are no such properties except actually being green which is what I have already, tentatively, said it is.

(iii) *Phenomenological* Finally I may say that there appears, looks or seems to me to be a cow, or something green, here, now. Only in this sense is it justifiable to reify the appearance, to identify the apparent cow or green thing with a cow-shaped or green-coloured patch in my private visual field. We tend to make tentative judgments of perception and make an epistemic use of the word 'appear' in circumstances where we know or believe that the conditions of observation are somehow abnormal and such as to cause us to be misled. We say 'it appears to be a cow' or 'it looks like a cow' if it is far away, if the light is bad, if it is misty, if one's glasses are smeared, if one is preoccupied with something else, if one is frightened, if one has had more than usual to drink. Where we have a confident belief either that the conditions are normal or that they are abnormal in a way that we know how to compensate for we say without qualification that it is a cow. In the phenomenological use of 'appear' and its cognates we suppose a set of conventional, idealised conditions of observation to obtain even though we may know that they do not, because we do not, for these purposes, care whether they do or not. In the case of vision we suppose that what we see is on a flat surface a few feet directly in front of us in broad daylight. In other words we treat what we see as if it were a picture viewed under ideal conditions. The ability to look at things in this way and to describe them accordingly is a learnt and rather sophisticated skill which we acquire only after we have learnt to perceive and describe things in the ordinary, natural, non-phenomenological way (Collingwood, pp. 68–9). It is a skill that has not been acquired by primitive painters and it justifies the existence of art teachers. To acquire it is to learn how to adopt an unnatural attitude to the world around us which involves the suppression of the framework of our ordinary beliefs about it. And to adopt the phenomenological attitude is to abandon the attitude, psychologically incompatible with it, in which we normally look at the world.

Now it is only in this phenomenological use that statements like 'there appears to be a cow, or something green, here' can be regarded as descriptions of private, immediate experience. So only here can what appears be substantively referred to, without misleading suggestions, as appearances. To interpret 'there appears to be a cow here', in its epistemic use, as 'there is here the appearance of a cow' is comparable to interpreting 'he will probably marry her' as asserting the unquestioned existence of a mysterious entity called his probable-marriage to her. In the perceptually minimal use 'there appears to be a cow here' means 'there is something with the directly visible properties, e.g. the shape and colour, of a cow here'. This is a public objective thing and on this account it would be radically misleading to call it the appearance of a cow.

I defined a perceptual situation, not, I hope, in an arbitrary or idiosyncratic way, as one in which one was inclined to believe that one was perceiving something. It is an obvious logical consequence of this definition that in every perceptual situation something appears to be present in the epistemic sense of the word, since for something to appear to one epistemically is for one to be inclined to believe that one perceives it. It is not true that in every perceptual situation something appears to one in the perceptually minimal sense. Situations occur in which one is inclined to believe no more than that there is something green before one. But one does not here, except in a vacuous and degenerate sense, believe that there is something here with the directly visible properties ordinarily possessed by green things. However it is no doubt true that in every perceptual situation in which one is inclined to believe that there is an object of a determinate kind present, one also believes that there is something present that has the directly perceptible properties, visible or other (though one might say 'there appears to be a goat here' on merely olfactory grounds), which objects of that kind usually possess.

But it is quite false that in every perceptual situation there is something that appears in the phenomenological sense, something that presents a reifiable appearance that we are aware of. If this were to be so we should have to be constantly in a phenomenological frame of mind, which in fact we are very seldom in, and which we can learn how to adopt only when we have already mastered the ordinary, straightforwardly perceptual frame of mind. The argument from illusion draws attention to the necessary truth that we know anyway what epistemically appears to be the case. It is also true that in most perceptual situations we know what appears to be present in the perceptually minimal sense. But the argument from illusion does not, and cannot, show that in every perceptual situation we know what phenomenologically appears, that we are directly aware of private appearances, the states and contents of our personal sense-fields.

Consider the somewhat bizarre example of the hallucinatory

shotgun. I say 'there appears to be a shotgun in the corner of the room', though in fact there is nothing there at all. Here I am expressing an inclination to believe which ought in fact not to be given way to. If challenged I may say, none too informatively, 'well, it looks like a shotgun' in so doing making the false, perceptually minimal statement that there is something there with the directly visible properties of a shotgun. What I am not saying, because I am not aware of the fact, is that there is a shotgun-shaped patch of colour in my visual field in the midst of the patches of colour that correspond to the corner of the room.

It may indeed be true that there is, in a way, such a patch of colour in my private visual field. That is, if I were to redirect my attention appropriately, if I were to adopt the special, sophisticated phenomenological frame of mind, I might be in a position to describe it. But I am not in this position when I am first hallucinated. The hypothetical phenomenological colour-patch can be invoked to explain why I came to adopt the false belief about what was really there. But it is not referred to in any belief I have at the time of hallucination which can serve as a premise from which my mistaken conclusion is inferred. The relation between the colour-patch and my false belief about the shotgun is at best causal; it is not logical.

That well-loved old epistemological favourite, the stick that looks bent in water, brings the point out more clearly. If I say it is bent I am just wrong. If I say it looks or appears to be bent I may be expressing my inclination to believe or saying that anyone would have some inclination to believe that it is bent. But I am not saying that there is a bent brown strip in the middle of my visual field. Nevertheless there almost certainly is such a strip there as I should discover if I were to shift my attention appropriately. But it is not in general true that if I see something that looks ϕ there is something that is ϕ, present or discoverable, in my visual field. I may see one end of a small tray that is in fact flat-sided and with semi-circular ends, the rest being obscured, and say, when asked what shape I think it is, that it is or looks round. But there is no corresponding round patch in my visual field, only a semi-circular one. So in saying that it looked round I must have been speaking epistemically, not phenomenologically.

It may be objected that in such a case, even if the private semi-circular patch or whatever is not reported, it must somehow be *there*. Have I not admitted this in allowing that it can be called upon to explain the mistaken perceptual beliefs that we form? But to hold that it is there is not to hold that one is aware of it unless it is also maintained that it is self-intimating, that one cannot have an experience of this kind without being aware that one has. This is an assumption that, in its general form, I have examined and rejected in the preceding chapter. An empirical consideration which supports this rejection in the present case is that if I am asked to recall the state of my sense-field a few moments ago, a time when I was not in a consciously phenomenological frame of mind, I cannot simply report it as I should be able to do if I really had then been aware of it; I have to reconstruct it, more or less conjecturally and in the light of various familiar rules correlating what is actually present with what is in the sense-field, from what I remember of the actual physical circumstances and my place in them.

In every perceptual situation, then, we know appearances only in the sense that we know what we think or are inclined to think and that we know or think we know what directly perceptible characteristics the thing in question possesses. But we do not, in general, know what the current state of our sense-fields is, though we can find out by making an appropriate shift of attention and we can often infer it afterwards, with some confidence, from what we know of our physical surroundings at the time and our place in them. I should maintain that in fact we much more often know what is physically present than we know what is phenomenologically present.

Certainty and inference

So far I have been considering the question whether we are always aware of appearances in a straightforwardly commonsensical manner and without inquiring too closely into the concept of awareness itself. My effective criterion of awareness has been that one is aware that p provided that one is ready to assert p if the need arises. The result of the inquiry so far is that we are not aware of our immediate experiences in every perceptual situation though we are, trivially, aware of what epistemically appears. But nothing has so far shown that we are not often aware in perceptual situations of material things or again that whenever this kind of awareness takes place it is the outcome of inference from impressions or sense-data, from what appears phenomenologically. But the appearance theory of perception holds not only that we are aware of appearances in the phenomenological sense in every perceptual situation but also that they are the *only* things we are *directly* aware of and thus that any awareness we may have of public things must be indirect and somehow derived from our direct awareness of appearances.

Before this view can be considered the new and clearly technical notion of direct awareness must be explained. It is ordinarily defined in terms of certainty or inference or both. I am directly aware of whatever I find out for certain to exist or of whatever I find out to exist without inference. As Ayer puts it: 'The meaning of the expression "direct awareness" is such that, whenever we are directly aware of a sense-datum, it follows that we know some proposition which describes the sense-datum to be true' (Ayer (2), p. 80). The qualification of the awareness as direct clearly suggests that no inference is involved, perhaps because none is possible. I shall consider these two accounts of the notion separately, although they are usually run together, as a result of the mistaken assumption that a belief that is less than certain can be accepted only on the ground of one that is certain. The purpose of this section is to inquire whether appearances, and particularly appearances in the phenomenological sense, impressions, sense-data, colour-patches and other contents of sense-fields, are the sole objects of direct awareness in any sense, while material objects and other public, physical things never are but are always objects of indirect awareness of some kind or other.

(i) *Direct awareness as certain knowledge* We should begin here by recalling the various conceptions of certainty that were distinguished in the previous chapter. The relevance of the conception of certainty as logical necessity can be eliminated right away since the knowledge perception gives us of material things and appearances is empirical. If the logically necessary alone were certain neither things nor appearances could be the objects of direct awareness. If, as in ordinary speech, to have certain knowledge of something is to know its existence beyond reasonable doubt then both appearances and material things are objects of direct awareness and no fundamental difference of kind distinguishes them. If, finally, to have certain knowledge of something is to have incorrigible knowledge of it then neither appearances nor material things are the objects of direct awareness and nor is anything else, the concept of direct awareness can have no application.

It could be argued that we are *more* certain of appearances than we are of material things and in consequence that we are more directly aware of the one than of the other. It is undoubtedly true that there are kinds of mistakes that we can make about material things that we cannot make about our immediate experiences of them. But for the most part, since we are very seldom in the phenomenological frame of mind, we have no beliefs at all, and therefore neither knowledge nor supposed knowledge, about appearances in the phenomenological sense. But even when we are in that frame of mind we are not immune from justified hesitation and error. Immediate experiences are vulnerable because of their fleeting and momentary character, the very feature which preserves them from the liability to error which beliefs about material things have in virtue of their predictive nature (cf. Quine (5), pp. 211–12). There is, of course, a kind of incorrigibility about epistemic appearances. But it is spurious since it arises not from the unquestionable truth of the assertion involved but from the incompleteness and tentativeness of the assertion. Finally, appearances in the perceptually minimal sense are obviously known with greater certainty than the corresponding statements about material things as being of a determinate substantival kind. In most perceptual situations in which we have grounds for saying 'that thing is a cow' we will have better grounds for saying 'that thing is cow-shaped'. But perceptually minimal appearance-statements are (qualitative) statements about material things and their greater certainty than substantival statements about material things has, therefore, no bearing on the point at issue.

It is often said that statements about material things are less certain than statements about impressions or appearances in the phenomenological sense, that, indeed, they are not certain at all because they have indefinitely or infinitely extensive implications about future fact. It is true that at no time, however far in the future it may be, is it inconceivable that there should be evidence for or, more to the point, against some statement about a material thing. But then this is also true of statements about impressions. Seeing a photograph of some scene at which I was present I may subsequently reject my recollection of how the scene looked, phenomenologically, to me, in the highly unlikely event of my having any such recollection. In either case the supposed correction of the earlier belief may be no correction at all but equally in either case it may be. In fact, of course, we do not connect such phenomenological beliefs as we have with the rest of our beliefs to anything like the extent we do with beliefs in material things, so in their case this kind of correction, whether valid or not, seldom occurs. But in principle it could.

What makes this consideration about indefinitely extensive future consequences less than fatal for the certainty of beliefs about material things is that such a belief p will only entail some statement about the future q if it is conjoined with a great mass of other information which we may call r. Thus the falsification of q does not simply falsify p, only the conjunction of p and r. But the remoter the subject-matter of q is from that of p the more questionable r will be. Beliefs about material things commonly are predictive, especially if they are of the substantival kind but even if they are of the adjectival or perceptually minimal variety. But these predictions will in fact be further statements about material things and they need not be strictly predictive at all. If I have been working on the lawn-mower in the garden shed for half an hour I shall have at my disposal all the collateral information I can reasonably demand for supposing that this thing, which I am inclined to think is a sparking-plug, really is a sparking-plug. At various times in the last half-hour I have handled the sparking-plug I took out of the machine for cleaning, I have reason to think there is only one sparking-plug or object remotely like one in the shed, nobody has interrupted my activities since I started on them. If I now pick it up and feel it to be solid and it looks, in the perceptually minimal sense, like a sparking-plug then I should be a fool to think that it was not one.

Beliefs about things and appearances, then, are not incorrigible, though both are capable of certainty. We are no doubt more certain of our beliefs about our immediate experiences, where we actually have any, than we are of our beliefs about material things taken as a whole. For we have frequent good reason to be hesitant in expressing our beliefs about material things: whenever we are not sure about the conditions of observation or know or suppose them to be in some way abnormal. We seldom have occasion to qualify descriptions of immediate experience, though, as we have seen, such occasions do arise. When they do we will not say 'it appears to me now that it appears to me now that there is something mauve here' though we could. We might say 'it appears to me now that there is a mauve patch in my visual field' or 'there is a mauve patch in my visual field, I think', where the perhaps wholly reasonable doubt is as to its being actually *mauve*. The linguistic fact that we do not in such cases reiterate 'appears to me now' does not, then, show that the kind of qualification such a reiteration would be used to introduce is never conceivably called for. Mistakes that do not arise from some kind of error about the conditions of observation are still mistakes. Ayer says that 'all one can properly mean . . . by saying that one doubts whether this (sense-datum) is green is that one is doubting whether "green" is the correct word to use' (Ayer (2), p. 83). In a way this is true of one's situation when one doubts whether a material thing is green. The meaning-rules of which he writes do not, in their practical employment, operate with quite the foolproof obviousness of their 'semantic' formulation: the word 'red' applies to red things. All empirical, descriptive terms have a margin of uncertain application and some of them are hard to master in any application, for example the less usual colour-words. We are, then, neither *only* directly aware of appearances or sense-data nor are we *more* directly aware of them, in this sense, than we are of material things.

(ii) *Direct awareness as uninferred knowledge* The theory that appearances alone are the objects of direct awareness is usually taken to *entail* that beliefs about material things, if they are to be justified, must be inferred from beliefs about appearances. If direct awareness is defined in terms of certain knowledge the additional premise is required that whatever is probable or less than certain but still in some measure justified must rest on what is certain. For if, as the original premise implies, beliefs about material things are less than certain their justification must be sought in some other certain beliefs. In the preceding section the view that appearances, in the relevant, phenomenological sense, are the sole objects of direct awareness has been rejected. If certainty is understood in its everyday sense, material things are often objects of direct awareness; if it is understood as incorrigibility then there are no such objects, or, at any rate, no empirical objects. The additional premise that probability must rest on certainty has also been refuted. But the doctrine that all justified belief in material things is derived from logically antecedent beliefs about impressions remains to be considered on its merits. Even if it is deprived of the support promised it by the various arguments that hinge on the notion of certainty, whose downfall ensures that the notion of direct awareness we have been examining so far has either too wide an application or none at all, the thesis that we are directly aware of appearances or impressions alone can be considered in a different interpretation. This is that only beliefs about appearances are uninferred, while all beliefs about material things, to the extent that they are justified, are based on inference from them.

This doctrine is not a creation of my own. It has always been maintained by Russell who has never ascribed an indestructible hardness to hard data but has been content to say that we have more certainty about our sense-impressions than we do about anything else. It is indeed the position that must, for consistency, be adopted by anyone who, like the early Ayer, wants to define material things in terms of sense-experience and derive all our knowledge of them from it and yet at the same time denies that any empirical, contingent statement, including statements about immediate experience, is incorrigible.

It may be agreed that many beliefs about immediate experience are uninferred. The most obvious examples of those that are not are irrelevant since they are not candidates for basic status, namely beliefs about the impressions of others or beliefs about our own impressions at other times than the present. It is not easy, however, to find examples of beliefs about the believer's own present experience which it is plausible to suggest are inferred. The best that can be offered is the example of the conjurer's nail in the preceding chapter where the apparent visible condition of one's finger is taken as a reason for thinking that one must be in pain. In general, we may admit, that if one knows anything at all about one's current experience one knows it, with the rarest and most far-fetched exceptions, without inference. But it seems equally clear that one has good reason to believe a great many things about one's current physical situation without having inferred what one believes from anything else and simply in virtue of perceiving the material things around one. The difficulty here is on what principle we are to decide whether or not a belief is inferential.

It is clear that many beliefs are the result of inference which have not been formed at the end of a discernible interval for reflection between them and the formation of some logically distinct belief at an earlier moment. As a criterion of inference a reflective pause is intolerably vague. It also gives unacceptable results even where it applies unequivocally. A girl, sitting in the drawing-room, hears the front door slam and says 'Father's home'. I hear a pattering on the roof and say 'it's raining'. I see a small pool on the kitchen floor and say 'the dog has misbehaved itself again'. In none of these cases is there the kind of conscious inference that involves a reflective pause. We make conscious inferences only in situations that are unfamiliar or complex, when in the predicament of the weekend guest or the new boy on the first day of term, or going about our professional tasks as detectives or scientists. Conscious and deliberate thinking is both exhausting and infrequent, a last resort to be appealed to when all habitual capacities have failed. A more inclusive and satisfactory criterion of inferential character is that we can or could or think we should be able to state the evidence from which the supposedly inferential belief is derived.

There is a continuum of possible cases here. At one end is the conscious derivation of one belief from another that has already been consciously affirmed, as when it dawns on me that I must have come away from the dinner-party with somebody else's umbrella since here is my umbrella in its usual place at home. Next there is the case like the examples of the last paragraph where I can give a reason without the least hesitation for what I say although I can recollect no conscious process of inferring. Thirdly, I may take some time over producing my grounds or require some assistance in the task. Fourthly, I may be unable to produce any reason of my own and be unwilling to accept any reasons suggested by others for what I believe, that, for example, X really dislikes his brother. Yet I may be quite sure that a reason does exist for my belief, may be extremely confident of the truth of my belief and may turn out, in the end, to be quite right. But now, finally, consider some belief about a material thing formed in optimally favourable conditions. I am standing in broad daylight three feet away from a large and perfectly normal chestnut cart-horse. I say 'that is a horse' or, more adventurously, 'that horse is brown'. Like the fourth case above one would here be quite unable to give or accept any reason whatever for one's assertion. But one would in this case be not in the least abashed or apologetic about one's incapacity. In these conditions the request for a statable justification seems simply devoid of sense.

Nevertheless if such a request were made, if one were asked

'how do you know' or 'how can you tell' one might answer 'well, it looks like a horse'. There are, as we have seen, three ways in which this remark could be interpreted: (i) epistemic: 'it's a horse, I think', (ii) perceptually minimal: 'it's horse-shaped and horse-coloured, i.e. has the directly visible properties that horses usually have' and (iii) phenomenological: 'there is a horse-shaped patch in the middle of my visual field'. Very much the most natural of these interpretations for the present case is the second. Things that in this sense look like horses are sometimes not horses. If someone challenges my claim that what I see is a horse I may suspect that he has special information which I, having only looked at the thing briefly, may lack. So I reduce the scope of my claim; but it is still a claim about a public material thing. It is also possible, however, to interpret what I say in the first, epistemic way, much as if I had said 'isn't it a horse?' Worried by the challenge, which suggests a doubt without specifying a reason for it, I retreat to a tentative, hesitant reaffirmation of what I have already said. I might even be taken to be not *expressing* my inclination to believe but reporting it. The one thing I am clearly not doing is reporting on the current contents of my visual field, although it is no doubt true, as I can infer from what I actually see and what I know of my present circumstances, that among those contents there is a horse-shaped patch of colour and that if I were to redirect my attention appropriately I should become directly aware of it.

An appearance-statement can, then, serve as a reason for a statement about a material thing, most obviously in its perceptually minimal interpretation in which it is also a statement about a public, material thing. An epistemic appearance-statement is more questionably a reason or piece of statable evidence in support of my claim; it is a guarded, qualified reiteration of the claim. In their phenomenological sense, appearance-statements are not offered as reasons. What has led people to suppose that they are is that they have confused this interpretation of such statements with the perceptually minimal one in which they can be given as reasons, or perhaps with the epistemic one.

I conclude that we do not in fact regard descriptions of immediate experience as evidence from which beliefs about material things can be inferred. The only possible circumstances in which they could be are those in which, waking up from an anaesthetic or some other state of unconsciousness in featureless and wholly unfamiliar surroundings, I might attempt to infer from the character of my immediate experience together with various conjectured premises about the general nature of my surroundings what was really in front of me. But I should be able to do this only if I already had a stock of contingent information about what sort of immediate experiences one has in various physical situations and this I must have accumulated through independent observation both of immediate experience and of the material world. This, it must be admitted, is a pretty far-fetched exception to the general rule and in no way counts against the general conclusion I have drawn.

There is a further reason for saying that our justified beliefs about material things are not inferred from logically antecedent beliefs about our immediate experiences. For one belief to rest for its justification on being inferred from another, not only must the latter count in favour of the former, it must also be held, and with justification, by the believer. Beliefs about immediate experience no more satisfy the second requirement of availability as premises than they satisfy the first one of being recognised as a support. For as we have seen, although there is a sense in which we know something about appearances in every perceptual situation, this is only generally, because trivially, true of appearances in the epistemic sense. In most perceptual situations the phenomenological evidence which the inference theory demands is simply not there to be made use of. So either we must hold that our beliefs about material things are only in very exceptional circumstances in any way justified or we must admit that they need not be inferred from beliefs about immediate experience.

I have considered what we might say if an ordinary statement about a straightforwardly perceived material thing was challenged. But in favourable, standard conditions if we are asked how do we know, how can we tell, what reason, ground or evidence have we for supposing, that the thing we are looking at is green, we really do not know what to say. In such circumstances there is almost no sense in asking for a reason. All we can do in reply is to reiterate what we have already said, perhaps qualifying it, for such claims are not, even in standard conditions, incorrigible, perhaps in such a way as to show, in cases like that of 'round' or other such visuo-tactual properties, by which sense we have ascertained the fact we are stating: 'I see that it's round'.

The explanation of this fact is quite simple. The standard conditions for the use of some sentence reporting the existence and perceptible character of a material thing are those in which its use was first learnt. To the extent that the sentence is ostensive this is how its meaning is first introduced to us. But, of course, we soon find that not all conditions are standard. Wherever we are inclined to believe what it says but know or suspect that the conditions are not standard we make our assertion guardedly, if we are careful. Now most of the time, when we are in our usual perceptual, and not phenomenological, frame of mind, we face the surrounding physical world armoured with a mass of background knowledge about where we are and the general circumstances of our observation. In other words we do not, generally, have to set an inquiry on foot to establish what the conditions of observation are each time we think we perceive anything. Thus, if I already know that the conditions are standard and I am inclined to believe that there is a cow here, I just express my inclination categorically and without qualification. I do not first discover that I have the inclination, recognise that the conditions are standard and then infer the perceptual judgment. To know how to use the sentence that makes the judgment is, in part, to be able to come out with it in an unqualified way in just these circumstances.

If we must give an answer to the question: what do we really see in any perceptual situation, it should be in terms of standard conditions thus defined. What I really see is what the conditions I am in are standard for. It is for a standard description in this sense that the lawyer who asks 'what did you actually see' is seeking, not an account of the state of our visual field at the time in question.

For some sentences there are no standard conditions, the main examples of these are generalisations; some conditions are not standard for the description of any material things, such as the case of waking up in featureless and unfamiliar surroundings. Any sentence describing a material thing can be asserted in a vast variety of circumstances in many of which it will not be a standard description but only assertible with qualification, as when the object is at a distance in twilight, or arrived at as the result of an inference, where, perhaps, only a part, its tail or legs, or a characteristic perceptible effect, its sound or its smell, is 'really perceived'.

Standard conditions do not guarantee the truth of a statement made in them. There is always a certain risk involved since deceptions can be very life-like. But to retreat to the description of immediate experience, for which, of course, the conditions are, in a somewhat degenerate sense, always standard, would be an excessive response to this residual imperfection. We should guard against one kind of uncertainty only to be exposed to another. For the very thing that imparts this uncertainty to statements about material things, the fact that they can be looked at again from another angle, for instance, is necessarily lacking in the case of descriptions of immediate experience which ensures that they will be fleeting and evanescent. Immediate experience, I have argued, is not the sole uninferred object of awareness in perception, so the sense-datum theory is not a description of how we actually do form our perceptual beliefs. The fact that one uncertainty would be replaced by another is just one of many reasons for rejecting it as a proposal of how we should form them. The systematic and mutually corroborative character of our beliefs about material things is, in fact a strength and the atomic, disconnected character of experiences is a corresponding weakness.

The relation between immediate experience and our beliefs about material things is not logical but causal, a matter of psychological fact which explains but does not justify those beliefs. The view that it is logical is an outcome of the apparently regressive nature of the requirement of justification. A belief or statement can be justified, it seems, only if it rests on another justified belief or statement. Either the body of knowledge, or, more properly of justified statements, hangs unsupported in mid-air, or it must stand in some justifying relation to the extra-linguistic world. If the ultimate support of the whole structure is logically related to it, as premise to conclusion, it must be contained within it and the problem of its justification arises or it is not so related and the acceptability of the ultimate supporting statements cannot be explained in terms of inference. Philosophers have attempted to overcome this difficulty by taking experience as the ultimate support, this being conceived as something we cannot have unless we are aware of it and thus as at once a statement, capable of standing in logical relations to the rest of the structure, and as a part, perhaps the only ultimate kind of part there is, of the extra-linguistic world. I have argued that there are no such self-describing entities, that the dilemma would recur in exactly the same form for a language whose basic statements were phenomenological descriptions of immediate experience. Basic statements about material things are, indeed, justified by experience but they are neither, in general, descriptions of that experience nor are they inferred from such descriptions. They are justified, though not certified, by the fact of being made in circumstances like those in which the use of the sentences that make them were originally learnt. The perception of material things is an intelligent activity; that is a reason for its fallibility. But it is not, on that account, a matter of reasoning. We cannot set out the logical relation of an assertion about material things with the experiences that occasion it because there is no such relation. This is not, as with the coherence theory, to disjoin language from the world altogether. It is simply to say that the relations that obtain within the body of knowledge do not connect it with what lies outside it. The only real alternative to a theory of this kind is one which holds that the world entirely consists of judgments or beliefs, a view openly accepted by the absolute idealists but also an unrecognised consequence of any empiricist development of the sense-datum theory such as phenomenalism.

There is one further surprising and unpalatable consequence to the view that immediate experience alone is the object of direct, non-inferential awareness. This is that only phenomenological statements are ostensive; and therefore all statements about public objects must acquire their empirical meaning from correlation with statements in an antecedently understood private language. One does not have to accept the somewhat inconclusive arguments of Wittgenstein against the logical possibility of a private language to find this conclusion unattractive. It is clear that the nearest thing to a private language that we actually use, that in which we report our own sensations and emotions, is taught to us by others on the basis of our publicly observable behaviour and that we have to draw on the public language in developing it: a stabbing pain is the sort of pain caused by a knife, anger is the emotion that typically expresses itself in aggressive behaviour. The theory that phenomenological statements are ostensive implies that they must be originally private in a double sense, since they must be expressed in some internal symbolism, such as imagery, as well as referring to private entities and that we must have acquired the capacity to use this language not from teaching by others but by our own devices. The teaching of language as a public, social activity clearly begins with statements about material things. If phenomenological statements alone are basic we must come to understand the statements about material things that others teach us by correlating them with the already understood phenomenological statements of our inner language which are present to our minds in the circumstances in which the teaching takes place.

Science and perception: space-gap and time-gap

So far I have confined myself to those arguments for the thesis that material things are never the direct objects of perception which seek to derive it from the obvious, common-sense ways in which perception is fallible, in which there is a divergence between how things appear to us and how they really are. There is another set of arguments which arrive at the conclusion from certain scientific findings that I shall examine in this section and the next. The first two arise from the fact that there is both a spatial and a temporal gap between the public object ostensibly perceived and the perceiving of it, or, at any rate, the immediate physical antecedents of the perceiving. The third is based on the apparent conflict between the account of the physical world provided by science, which excluded secondary qualities, and what we ordinarily take our senses to tell us about the physical world.

Both of these styles of scientifically-based reasoning are to be found in Locke. They figure prominently in the writings of Russell and Broad about perception, but, until the last few years, in which they have been reanimated by Smart, Armstrong and Pitcher, they have been under something of a cloud. I suspect that this discredit can be attributed to the effect of an argument, developed early in the course of Price's *Perception*, that, since these scientific premises must rest on perceptual knowledge of material things, they cannot be consistently used to deny that there is any such knowledge (Price (1), pp. 36–7).

It is true that these scientific considerations cannot be used to show that perception gives us no knowledge of the material world at all without undermining themselves. But it is only that rare, if not wholly fictitious, creature the radical sceptic, exemplified, at most, by Hume in some of his moods, who makes such a use of them. Their usual purpose is to show, not that the kind of minimal realism, which takes perception to give us, how even indirectly, some knowledge of the material world, is mistaken, but that something much more controversial, namely naive or direct realism is. Their conclusion that we have no *direct* knowledge of the material world through perception is entirely consistent with the assumption that we have *some* perceptual knowledge and thus a support for the scientific findings they invoke.

Sense-datum philosophers typically describe the position they are criticising, which they take to be the point of view of unreflective common sense, as naive realism. The mild adjectival slur is wholly appropriate to the view to which they give this name, but it is far from clear that it has any appeal to common sense. Naive realism they define as the theory that in every perceptual situation the direct object of perception is a material thing, or at least part of its surface. The man in the street is not quite as naive as that. He does not suppose that every perceptual belief that his senses prompt him to hold about his physical surroundings is true. What he might well be credited with is *direct* realism, the assumption that in at least *some*, and as a matter of fact in *most*, situations in which his senses incline him to believe something about the physical world the belief is both true and not inferred from any antecedent belief about something non-physical. (Direct realism, so defined, should be distinguished from the minimal realism I mentioned earlier, which holds that in most perceptual situations material things are actually perceived. For this leaves open the question whether the perception is direct. What it rules out is not the sense-datum theory as direct realism does, but radical scepticism about perception. And that is not a controversial issue.)

Arguments from science are, then, relevant to the dispute between direct realism and the sense-datum theory. There is an abstract and peremptory argument of Russell's which makes the scientific case against direct realism in very general terms. Direct, or, as he calls it, naive, realism leads to physics and physics implies that direct realism is false. Therefore direct realism implies its own falsity. Therefore it is false (Russell (7), p. 15). The logic of the final stages of this argument is impeccable, although it has been questioned. What are dubious are the premises and, in particular, Russell's interpretation of the vague remark that direct realism 'leads to' physics as meaning that direct realism implies, or is a sufficient condition of, physics. It would be much more plausible to hold that physics presupposes direct realism, and thus implies it as its necessary condition. This is, in effect, the assumption made by Price and is, for the reasons I have given, in fact incorrect. If it were not, and if Russell's second premise that physics implies the falsity of direct realism were true, it would follow, not that direct realism was false, but that physics was, as implying a contradiction. But since all that physics presupposes is the truth of what I have called minimal realism there is no problem here.

The best way to show that direct realism does not, as Russell supposes, imply physics is to show that it would be possible for direct realism to be true and yet physics false. The chief difficulty here is to know what is meant by 'physics' in this connection. The hard, historic Galilean core of physics, after all, is classical mechanics and this is primarily based on the behaviour of common material objects, such as cannon-balls and rolling stones, whose existence is assured if direct realism is true. At this level, initially at any rate, physics does not have a different subject-matter from ordinary perception. What differentiates it is the mathematical precision with which it is formulated and the fact that its formulations take the form of strict universal laws, not singular observation-reports or vague qualitative statements of general tendency (e.g. 'if you let things go they usually fall to the ground').

However it could be argued that the part of physics which is used to show the falsity of direct realism is the theoretical part, in which are to be found the crucial facts that light has a finite velocity and that the ultimate constituents of matter have no secondary qualities. It could only be if direct realism implied this theoretical part of physics that it would imply its own falsity. Now since a natural way of defining the theoretical entities of physics is as those physical things which cannot be perceived in the way that ordinary material things are at all, it is evident that direct realism cannot imply theoretical physics. I shall argue in chapter 10 that the theoretical entities of physics are not, in fact, necessarily unperceivable. Even so I should agree that such entities are not perceived in the ordinary way and this is enough to show that direct realism does not, in fact, imply the truth of theoretical physics.

It is important to make a distinction within physics in connection with Russell's argument since there is a sense, I believe, in which direct realism does imply physics, where physics is taken, very loosely, to mean a measure of regularity or orderliness in nature. According to direct realism perception supplies us with a mass of uninferred beliefs about the external world. If we are to determine which of these beliefs are true we have to select from the total presented mass by criteria that are, so to speak, internal to it. In general, the majority of these beliefs exhibit a lawful order by reference to which the residue can be ejected as false. Furthermore, to ratify these ejections it is desirable, and, as it happens, possible, to explain why the ejected beliefs are false, in terms, for example, of the law-like connection between abnormal conditions of observation and the falsity of the perceptual beliefs formed in them. We are, of course, able to exploit the commonsensical part of this body of explanatory theory in inhibiting our perceptual inclinations to believe falsehoods.

A final point about the bearing of theoretical physics on the falsity of direct realism is that it presupposes that the propositions of theoretical physics invoked are taken literally. If, as positivism, instrumentalism or conventionalism maintain, these propositions are merely symbolic conveniences or *façons de parler* there can be no clash between them and the findings of perception of the sort the scientific arguments require. Duhem was consistently a direct realist about common material objects.

I conclude that the only sense of 'physics' in which Russell's first premise is true is a different one from that in which it occurs in his second premise. The physical facts from which the falsity of direct realism is derived are the finite velocity of the causal processes involved in perception, in particular the finite velocity of light, and the absence of secondary qualities from the fine structure of matter. But these are themselves well enough established to provide a sufficient refutation of direct realism if they really do entail its falsity without the help of Russell's elusive assertion that direct realism leads to physics. The question now is: do they really entail that direct realism is false?

The first scientific argument against direct realism is the weakest and, perhaps on that account, is seldom formulated very explicitly. It starts from the fact that perception, as an act of the mind, is the last element in a causal process which originates in the ostensible object of the perception. The object, in being perceived, must exert some influence on a sense-organ of the perceiver, and by way of some medium if it is at a distance from the sense-organ in question. From the sense-organ the stimulus is transmitted to the brain so that some brain-event is either the proximate cause of, or else identical with, the act of perception. The conclusion usually drawn from this is that the direct object of perception is either the mental event caused by the terminal brain-event or, according to Russell, is the terminal brain-event itself. Russell's view that what we directly perceive is in our brains occasioned general consternation (Russell (5), p. 146). But it was not a new idea: it had been anticipated in the 'physical realism' of Thomas Case some forty years earlier (Case, p. 66).

Reid discerned a reliance on this argument in the philosophy of Locke and reasonably objected that it rested on the absurd assumption 'that the mind can operate only where it is' (Reid). As against dualists like Locke who hold that the mind is not in space this objection is entirely valid. But even if, with Case and Russell, the mental act of perception in which the causal sequence comes to an end is identified with a brain-event the thesis still has little to recommend it. For what it holds is that the direct object of perception can only be where the perception itself, or, for a consistent dualist, its immediate physical cause is. There are three considerations that may have contributed to the endowment of this assumption with a plausibility which it does not deserve. The first is that by far the greater part of what we perceive is spatially close to us. But this broad truth cannot be sharpened into the view that the real objects of perception must be, so to speak, absolutely contiguous to us. In fact objects can be too close to us to be seen at all.

Secondly, because the concept of direct perception is a philosophical technicality it is readily confused with that of what may be called direct, or, more naturally, immediate, causation. Because of the spatial gap between a perception and its ostensible object there is a certain lack of directness or immediacy about the relation between the two. But the directness that is lacking is not of the philosophically relevant kind. It does not in the least show that the existence of the object has to be inferred from the uninferred perception of something else in absolute proximity to the act of perception.

Finally, the indirectness of the causal link between an object and the perception of it provides a further foothold for the argument from illusion. When we take ourselves to perceive something that is not actually there a state of affairs not containing that object has brought about a state of mind (and, presumably, brain) in us that is indistinguishable from that brought about by a state of affairs in which the object in question is present. The causal account of the mechanism of perception suggests that such a misleading state of of mind could be brought about deliberately by direct interference with the brain, rather than by the natural action of unpropitious circumstances on it. This introduces no new theoretical consideration. Science is not used here to introduce a new argument against the direct perception of material objects, but only to conceive another, more sophisticated way in which the false perceptual beliefs can arise on which the argument from illusion depends.

A more persuasive argument from scientific facts to show that all perception of material things is indirect draws attention to the temporal gap between perception and the event or state of an object that is perceived. This time-gap between perception and object is easily enough discerned without benefit of science. Frequently the sight and sound of an event, which are believed to occur simultaneously, are perceived at different times. A cricket bat is seen to hit a ball before it is heard to do so; lightning precedes thunder; the flash of a gunshot precedes the hearing of the report. But these cases can be accommodated to the underlying assumption of simultaneity between perception and what is perceived by reason of the somewhat amorphous character of the delayed element in such situations: the sound. This can be conceived as a temporally and spatially extended process, only the later and hither end of which is actually perceived.

This treatment does not suffice to deal with the more dramatic facts about non-simultaneity implied by the finite velocity of light as regards our perception of remote celestial objects. The events we see on the sun have taken place eight minutes before we see them; stellar explosions seen in outer space may have happened millions, even thousands of millions of years ago.

There is a further delay to be taken into account. There is a time-gap between the impact of the external stimulus on our sense-organs and the arrival of a message from them in the brain. The conveyance of nervous impulses that is involved takes place at a speed much slower than that of light. So even when we touch something there is still a lapse of time between its coming into contact with our organs of touch and the corresponding brain-event which is, or immediately causes, our perception of the object touched. In every perception, then, the perceiving itself clearly occurs later than the event or state of a material object that is taken to be perceived.

Could it not be argued here, as it was in the previous case of a spatial gap between perception and object perceived, that the temporal indirectness involved in the perception of material objects is something quite distinct from the logical indirectness of their perception which it is held to demonstrate? More generally, must we accept the principle that what is really perceived must be simultaneous with the perception of it?

Certainly those who have subscribed to the principle of simultaneity seem to take it to be self-evident for they provide no justification of it. Pap, for example, says 'if you use the phrase "x sees y" in such a way that seeing y implies the simultaneous existence of the act of seeing and y the conclusion that physical things are not really seen necessarily follows' (Pap (1), p. 125). But he does not inquire whether 'see' and other verbs of perception are in fact used with this implication of simultaneity or whether there is any good reason why they should be. To this Chisholm's cheerful but un-argued dismissal of the principle is quite appropriate. 'We tend to assume' he says 'that S can perceive a at t only if a exists at t'. But this, he goes on, 'is no more reasonable than to assume that S can receive or reflect light from a at t only if a exists at t' (Chisholm (1), 153).

But there is a ground for the simultaneity-principle which is not paralleled in the case of the spatial gap between perception and the perceived. This is that we define the present or 'now' in terms of simultaneity with perception. If a report of perception explicitly indicates that what is perceived is in the past, as with 'I see that George has been here', the report is plainly inferential in an ordinary, philosophically uncontroversial sense. In the example, I see a state of affairs now for which George's presence at an earlier time seems the best explanation. The present tense, one might say, is logically tied to non-inferential judgments of perception. The primary use of the past tense is tied in the same way to judgments of memory. But although in fact our non-inferential judgments are allocated to perception and memory by reason of being in the present and past tenses respectively it seems conceivable that we should verbally mark the distinction in a different way: 'he was just now in the garden' and 'he was some time ago in the garden'. The use of current perceivability as a criterion of presentness might lead, indeed has led in a way, to difficulties which this new convention would circum-vent. There would still be judgments of introspection in which strictly current events were reported.

But for two reasons heroic steps of this kind can, I believe, be avoided. These are that the sense of 'now' or 'present' in which the material objects and events we take ourselves to perceive are in existence or occurring now or at this present moment is such that in the great majority of our perceptual claims the gap is not of such a kind as to rule out their application. Secondly, the remaining cases, where there is a substantial gap between perception and event perceived, can still be reckoned genuine cases of direct per-ception of material objects although part of what is involved in the belief that expresses them is simply false.

If an astronomer says 'there is an explosion at the north-west corner of the sun at the moment' what he says is false, or at best an accidentally true prediction about an explosion he will be in a position to see in eight minutes' time but is not the explosion he takes himself to perceive. But most public objects of perception are much nearer than the sun and the time-gap involved is very small. Only if the present tense is taken to refer to an instant or a very small tract of time indeed do non-astronomical time-gaps imply that reports of perception couched in it are incorrect.

To what do 'now' and the tensed verb 'is' refer? In non-perceptual discourse the present can be very large, as in 'England is not now joined to the continent by a land-bridge', though even here the time of utterance has to be included in the vaguely delineated now. But an utterance, even a thought, takes time. Must the now or present that corresponds to it contain its whole length or that of its tensed verb or its beginning or its end?

There is no fixed answer to the question. If I say 'he is putting his hat on' my statement would not be regarded as false if it began half a second after he had completed the operation. But if someone is relying on me to tell him when a sentry is looking the other way so he can make a dash for freedom and I say 'now' half a second after the sentry has ceased to do so I could be held to have spoken falsely.

What is clear is that the epistemological present is not an instant without duration. Unless a state of affairs lasts for more than such an instant it will not be perceived at all. Furthermore the perceptible world is not all that busy, unlike the theoretical world of ultimate particles. Light takes a hundred-millionth of a second to reach the eye from an object ten feet away. Even allowing for the comparatively sluggish movement of nervous impulses to the brain the whole sequence must fall well inside a second. Now as far as most of the ordinary world is concerned what is happening is still going on a second later at the same place, at the moment when we actually perceive it. As Armstrong observes there would be no perceptible difference if the causal process involved in perception had an infinite velocity (Armstrong (1), p. 145). Simultaneity ascribed on the basis of perception can only be perceptible simultaneity. Thus the existence of an imperceptibly small interval between the events we perceive and our perception of them does not disprove their simultaneity in the appropriate sense. Perception does not have to tell us everything there is to know about its objects to be direct. No doubt most of the things we perceive to be identical in size or weight are theoretically different to some minute extent in these respects. But this would not show our perceptual judgments to be mistaken in such cases. It is perceptible not theoretical simultaneity we are claiming to obtain. Aristotle's licence for appropriate imprecision is applicable here.

There remain the astronomical cases where perception does lead us to make false judgments, which we can correct only by inference. Does this show that in such cases our perception of the celestial event in question is not direct? There seems no reason why it should. If my perception of an object involves some false beliefs about it, it does not follow that my perception is illusory as a whole. If I take a blue flag in the distance to be green it does not follow that I did not see the flag. Why should the temporal properties of a thing be treated differently from its colour? In seeing the sun I see a roughly spherical, luminous object lying in the heavens in a certain direction from where I am standing. I also think I perceive, but do not, that this thing has a certain temporal property, that of being contemporaneous with my act of seeing. Though I am right to believe that there still is such a thing out there this is not justified by that perception. Only inference can justify what I correctly believe on the basis of a misperception. But I do still see the sun, even if it is the sun of eight minutes ago.

Secondary qualities and the fine structure of matter

The two previous scientific arguments against the view that material objects can be directly perceived relied on the scientifically established gaps, spatial and temporal, between the object and the perception of it to show that the perception could not be direct. The third and final scientific argument starts from the fact that the conception of material objects supplied by physical theory does not assign secondary qualities like colour to them, perhaps, indeed, logically excludes their possession of secondary qualities. Thus, what we take ourselves to perceive does have secondary qualities; what is really there does not, and perhaps cannot, have them; therefore, we do not perceive what really exists in the physical world.

This argument does seem to come perilously close to the self-destructive undermining of its own support in implying that ordinary perception is infected with error. It will not do to say that it indicts ordinary perception to the extent that it is concerned with secondary qualities, since primary qualities like shape and size are perceived only as manifested through secondary qualities. However, the user of this argument could preserve consistency by saying that what is actually perceived is subjective, mental effects on the perceiver of physical states of affairs outside him, from which the existence and nature of these physical causes is somehow inferred.

Physics is thus seen as a methodical and systematic extension of ordinary perception, in the light of which it is possible to correct the errors which unsophisticated perception initially inspires in us. Just as science shows us that the sky is not, as it might at first seem, a pale blue ceiling, it also shows us that nothing at all is really coloured or solid or aromatic.

For some time the Berkeleyan thesis that there is no essential difference, from an epistemological point of view, between primary and secondary qualities has been widely taken for granted. One factor in this consensus was Susan Stebbing's exemplary refutation of Eddington's assertion that the solid table we suppose to exist in everyday life is not really solid, but is in fact a swarm of rapidly moving particles which are at great distances from each other relative to their diameters. Stebbing argued that the word 'solid', in the sense in which it is ordinarily applied to such things as tables, does not mean 'composed of a dense or continuous array of ultimate constituents' but 'without perceptible gaps between its perceptible components' (Stebbing, pp. 47–60).

The acceptance of this dismissal of the argument from the fine structure of matter was reinforced by the prevalence of a positivist or instrumentalist interpretation of physical theory. It is only if the propositions of physical theory are taken as literally true, and not as figurative devices for the abridged representation of regularities in what is straightforwardly observable, that they can conflict with the deliverances of common perception. An economy can be overheated without the men and plant which compose it having temperatures above normal. But the revival in recent years of the literal and realistic interpretation of physical theory has reanimated the idea that there is a conflict between the findings of physics with those of everyday perception.

I shall conclude this chapter on perception by examining two arguments of this kind. The first, due to Sellars, maintains that our ordinary perceptual beliefs about the colour of things imply that all their parts are coloured which is directly inconsistent with the account of their ultimate constituents provided by physics (Sellars, p. 26). The second, due to Smart, rather more elusively, holds that colour does not figure in the physicist's account of the material world, that, indeed, it does not *fit in* with that account and that, finally, it is anthropocentric in a way that undermines the claim that it is an objective feature of the physical world (Smart (2), p. 69).

With Sellars's premise that the ultimate constituents of material things are colourless, or even must be, since there is no sense in the ascription of colour to them, I do not wish to quarrel here, although I shall question the truth of at least its stronger form in chapter 10. What I do question is his assumption that in asserting that a material object is coloured we are committed to the conclusion that all its parts are coloured too. This Anaxagorean principle contends, in Goodman's convenient term, that colour is dissective (Goodman (1), p. 48). Generally speaking substantival properties, like being a horse, are undissective while stuff-properties like being silver or milk are dissective down to a certain level of dissection. One of the few properties which it is plausible to say are absolutely dissective is extension in the Cartesian sense, a thesis denied by Leibniz.

Sellars's argument should be quoted at length. 'There is no trouble', he says, 'about systems having properties which their parts do not have *if their properties are a matter of the parts having such-and-such qualities and being related in such-and-such ways*. But the case of a pink ice cube, it would seem clear, cannot be treated in this way. It does not seem plausible to say that for a system of particles to be a pink ice cube is for them to have such-and-such unperceptible qualities and to be related to one another so as to make up an approximate cube. Pink does not seem to be made up of unperceptible qualities in the way in which being a ladder is made up of being cylindrical (the rungs), rectangular (the frame), wooden etc. The manifest ice cube presents itself to us as something which is pink through and through, as a pink continuum, all the regions of which, however small, are pink. It presents itself to us as *ultimately homogeneous*' (op. cit., p. 26).

But the only sense in which an ice cube can *present itself* to us as continuously pink is that in which all its *perceptible* parts are pink. What Sellars calls 'ultimate homogeneity' is not a perceptible property at all, only perceptible homogeneity is and that is something an ice cube may be perceived to possess. To perceive that a thing is pink all through is to perceive that every perceivable part of it is pink, not that every conceivable part of it is.

Sellars rests his case on the principle that 'every property of a system of objects consists of properties of and relations between its constituents'. If 'consists of' as it occurs in this formula means 'can be causally explained in terms of' it seems reasonable enough in an indeterminate way. But it cannot mean 'can be logically analysed in terms of'. There is a long and respectable tradition that colour-properties are logically primitive. They cannot be defined in terms of the primary qualities of the surfaces that have them, since we know the meaning of colour-words before we learn anything about the fine structure of coloured surfaces. Nor can they be defined in terms of their possessors without making such synthetic statements as that Jim's shirt or ripe tomatoes are red analytic.

Some perceptible properties of 'systems', i.e. objects with parts, must be primitive if any perceptible thing has imperceptible parts. No doubt the logically primitive colour-properties of 'systems' can be causally explained in terms of the primary qualities of the imperceptible particles on their surfaces. But Sellars's principle, although a reasonable methodological canon, is not an obvious necessary truth. It would seem to be rejected by the Copenhagen interpretation of quantum mechanics.

At any rate if colour is an exception to Sellars's principle in its logical interpretation this should cause no disquiet since, if perceptible things have imperceptible parts, there must be some exceptions to it. On the other hand colour does conform to the causal interpretation of the principle in which alone it has any claim to be acceptable. But in that causal interpretation it is not required that the property to be explained should be identical with any of the qualities of, or relations between, the imperceptible ultimate constituents of its possessors which are invoked to explain it. That requirement is brought in only by Sellars's unacceptable claim to perceive imperceptible continuity.

So far I have not questioned the assumption that colour is at least perceptibly dissective. But this, too, is open to question. A piece of cloth which everyone agrees to be green may prove on very close inspection to be entirely composed of fibres each of which is either wholly yellow or wholly blue. The non-green fibres are perceptible if only in an abnormal or unusual way. In this case below a level of size greater than the perceptual minimum none of the thing's parts are the same colour as it is. If this cloth is green then the relevant principle of dissectiveness is that all the ordinarily perceived parts of a thing are identical in colour with it.

Smart's argument against the objective reality of colour is that colour does not figure in the physicist's account of the material world, that it does not fit in with that account, that it is so anthropocentric as to be subjective.

The fact that colour does not figure in the physicist's account of the world does not amount to much. The scientist's attitude to nature resembles in its selectiveness that of a bursar to a college library as described by Ryle (Ryle (2), pp. 75–7). Where others see the precious life-blood of master-spirits, the bursar sees depreciating assets in hand, but they still are accumulations of precious life-blood. Bursars, and scientists, are men of limited interests; their vision is narrowed by their respective concerns with accountancy and causal explanation. It is a cost exacted by their effectiveness. For most purposes colour is causally uninteresting.

The claim that colour does not fit in with the physicist's account of the world has been disposed of to the extent that it rests on the over-extrapolated dissectiveness of colour. What Smart has in mind is something different: the rather loose relation between the colours things are ordinarily taken to have and the conditions of their surfaces which determine their light-reflecting powers. It is a philosopher's illusion, Smart says, to suppose that there is a simple correlation between the colour perceived and the wave-length of the light that causes the perception (op. cit., p. 69). But although the plurality of the causes of a particular kind of colour-perception may be too great to be subsumed under a manageable unifying formula it is not denied by Smart that the complex relationships involved are causal. There still are causal relations between the colour-perception and the surface of the supposedly coloured object. That they are so complex may help to explain the generally causally uninteresting character of colour.

Vision, by which colour is perceived, operates at a distance and is strongly dependent on conditions of illumination which are in fact very varied. The distance allows distorting factors like mist to intrude; the varying illumination of our environment compounds the difficulty. There is nothing quite comparable in the case of sound, since we spend most of our time in air: we are never in vacuums and seldom wholly immersed in water. In the face of these relativising factors we lay down, fairly implicit, normalising conventions in terms of which the real colour of things is defined. Standard illumination is noon daylight, but this varies from place to place. Standard distance varies with the kind of object involved. In general our conventions seem to result from the intersection of two considerations: the normal situations should be both optimal, in that they are those in which the finest agreed discriminations are made, and frequent, those in which the object is most commonly encountered.

The object of the conventions is to ensure that the colour we actually ascribe to objects shall be the same as long as the surface of the object is. They filter out all the interloping factors, external to the object itself, which might influence our colour-judgment. Armstrong says that when an object appears to change in colour because of a change in the conditions of illumination we must admit that a real change in quality occurs at the surface (Armstrong (3), p. 284). Certainly a real change does occur at the surface. But our conventions are designed to ensure that in such cases it is not the colour but the nature of the light reflected by it. The conventions ensure that our colour-judgments embody the largest number (because optimal) of reasonably achievable (because frequent) discriminations possible about the properties of the surfaces of things, independent of what is going on between that surface and the perceiver. Our ordinary conception of colour is, then, protected against anthropocentricity, the subjectivizing effect of the large variability as between different perceivers and occasions of perception in which colour is perceived.

A final point made by Smart to show the anthropocentric nature of colour perception is the, as it were, arbitrary and contingent character of our visual apparatus. The cones of the retina act in the manner of light-sensitive cells and our perception of colour depends on the balance of stimulation between them. Our vision works on a three-cell principle; that of Martians might be five-cell or thirty-cell and might lead them to identify and distinguish things in respect of colour in a very different way from ours (op. cit., p. 72).

But provided that our colour-discriminations correlate with the primary qualities of the fine structure of the surfaces of things this does not matter. It would be a field for the further application of the principle that consensus about some range of qualities establishes their objectivity as long as there is a causal explanation of deviations from the consensus. The conjectured, more discriminating Martians would be a group of deviants exhibiting more solidarity and *esprit de corps* than the colour-blind do at present, a body of people who seem reconciled to their relegation to an inferior cognitive status. The contingency of our visual apparatus suggests that our present system of colour-concepts could be shown to be rather superficially selective in what they are used to state about the surfaces of material objects. But it does not in the least show that colour is not really an objective property of the surfaces of things at all.

In sum, then, the loose relation between colour-perception and the primary qualities of the surfaces of objects shows only that the causally efficacious differences in question are not theoretically important or explanatorily fruitful, not that they do not exist. The variability of our unreflective colour-judgments due to variation in the conditions of observation and not in the objects themselves is filtered out by our normalising conventions. The somewhat arbitrary and readily changeable, nature of our visual apparatus shows at most that our colour-perception is selective, not that the qualities do not exist or are not intrinsic to the objects to which we ascribe them. Colour-perception lacks explanatory interest, is particularly liable to error and is in principle selective. But none of these deficiencies justifies the conclusion that colour is not a real property of material things.

8

Coherence

Against foundations

In the first chapter of this part of the book I have set out the most general arguments for the existence of basic statements; the traditional argument that there must be some beliefs that do not owe their justification to others if any beliefs are to be justified and the more recent argument that there must be some sentences which are introduced ostensively and not by correlation with other, antecedently understood, sentences if any are to have factual, descriptive, empirical meaning. In the next two chapters I went on to argue that it did not follow from the existence of basic statements in this very general sense either that such statements must be certain in some special way, since inferred statements may be beyond reasonable doubt and no statements are incorrigible, or that they should be reports of immediate experience.

In this chapter I shall consider more fundamental criticisms of the theory that knowledge has foundations than those I have so far examined, criticisms that seek to overthrow the whole idea that there are basic statements, even in the general and unrestricted sense that I have so far accepted. Defenders of basic statements have often been fortified in their opinion by the presumption that the only alternative to it is some form of the coherence theory, most familiar as a principle of the absolute idealists of the nineteenth century, which, it is widely supposed, has been irrevocably refuted. I shall consider the coherence theory in the next section but first I shall examine two less elaborate rejections of the theory of basic statements, those of Austin and Goodman.

What makes their views comparatively simple is that they do not think that the question to which the doctrine of foundations gives one answer and the coherence theory another is a question that needs an answer at all. Goodman, at any rate, regards the concept of epistemological priority, in terms of which basic statements may be defined as those to which no other statements are epistemologically prior, as too confused to be useful. Austin's position is a little more ambiguous. It may be that he is rejecting much less than he appears to be. The view about knowledge that he regards as *'radically* and *in principle* misconceived' is one in which basicness in the general sense and incorrigibility are run together (Austin (1), p. 124). The theory that knowledge 'is a structure the upper tiers of which are reached by inferences [while] the foundations are the *data* on which these inferences are based' is held to include the view that the upper tiers are to be identified by our ability to be mistaken about them and the data by their incorrigibility. His penetrating arguments against incorrigibility, on which I have drawn with advantage in the sixth chapter, do not count against the idea of basic statements in the general sense. To undermine that he must also show that 'there is indeed no special sub-class of sentences whose business it is to count as evidence for, or to be taken as verifying, other sentences' (op. cit., p. 110). We may agree with him that there is no kind of *sentence*, understood as a form of words in a given meaning, which could do this job. A given sentence can be used to express the conclusion of an inference or to report a direct observation. A, straining and heaving at a large chest, says 'it's too heavy to lift' as a direct report; B says the same thing on the basis of the agonised grimaces of A that he observes. But this, as we have seen, is neither here nor there. It is not even sufficient, strictly speaking, if we replace 'sentence' by 'statement' since two people can make the same statement in circumstances where it is basic for only one of them: A says 'I feel ill' and B says 'A feels ill'. To the extent that the doctrine of foundations has been expressed in terms of sentences it is because of the peculiarities of the German word 'Satz'. What Austin needs to show is that there is no class of statements and no kinds of circumstance such that statements made in those circumstances are the ultimate statable evidence for, or verification of, others.

His first argument is that in general we do not have to produce or even have evidence for our assertions about material things (op. cit., p. 115). If this is taken to refer to propositional evidence only it is, I have argued, correct. But it is not a criticism of the theory of basic statements, only of the version of that theory which identifies them with reports of immediate experience. If it is taken to refer to experiential evidence as well it is simply false. For we cannot, as it suggests, make justified assertions about material things by mere whim. What he perhaps intended to say is that we do not ordinarily call the experience that justifies a statement about material things evidence for it. This would not be very interesting even if it were true. But it is not true and there is no reason to alter our way of speaking in order to make it so. If a man who, looking into a room, says 'there's a fire in here', is asked if he has any evidence for saying so, when he has in fact seen the fire, although he might feel that the question was a bit cumbrously expressed in the circumstances, it would be ridiculous for him to answer 'no'. The proper answer would be 'yes, I can see it'. (For him to do so is for him to say that the circumstances are sufficient to justify his assertion experientially, not to state his propositional evidence for it.)

The curious thing about Austin's position is that he concedes the greater part of what the defender of basic statements in the general sense would wish to claim. He agrees with those like Schlick and Ayer who hold that the truth of some statements must be determined by non-verbal reality, in other words that there must be statements that are justified other than propositionally, and he maintains that most words are learnt ostensively, a more generous concession than the doctrine of foundations, which requires only that there should be some ostensive words and sentences, requires.

The real point of his criticism seems to be his claim that 'in general. . . *any* kind of statement could state evidence for *any* other kind'. 'It is not true, in general,' he goes on, 'that general statements are "based on" singular statements and not vice versa; my belief that *this* animal will eat turnips may be based on the belief that most pigs eat turnips; though certainly, in different circumstances, I might have supported the claim that most pigs eat turnips by saying that this pig eats them at any rate' (op. cit., p. 116). It is quite true that the belief of a particular man that a given pig, now before him, eats turnips may be based on and owe what justification it has to his antecedent conviction that most pigs eat turnips. But there is an obvious asymmetry in the logical relation between the two beliefs. For the general belief, although formally or hypothetically evidence for the singular one, by itself and independently of there being any reason for accepting it, will actually confirm and justify the singular belief only if it is itself already supported. Such support will ordinarily be provided by the establishment of a number of statements of the form 'this pig eats turnips' and of not more than a very few of the form 'this pig does not eat turnips'. This recourse to the empirical may be postponed. That most pigs eat turnips may be inferred from the further generalisations that most curly-tailed animals eat turnips and that all pigs are curly-tailed. But these, if they are really to support it, must themselves rest either on singular statements about particular curly-tailed animals eating turnips and particular pigs being curly-tailed or else on yet further generalisations which possess, at some finite remove, singular evidence of the same kind. On the other hand the singular belief that this pig eats turnips stands in no such relation to the general belief about most pigs or to any other general statement. Thus general statements can be only contingently or derivatively evidence for singular ones, whereas singular statements are the primary and indispensable evidence for generalisations. We can have sufficient reason for thinking that this pig eats turnips without having any justified belief about what pigs in general do; but we cannot have reason for thinking that most pigs eat turnips unless we have some justified beliefs about the eating-habits of particular pigs. Austin's argument here has the negative utility that without it the priority of singular statements to general ones might have seemed too obvious to need demonstration.

In part Goodman's rejection of the concept of epistemological priority stems from a formal relativism about the logical systematisation of concepts and statements that adds up to a refusal to endorse the rapprochement of logic and psychology implied by the doctrine of foundations (Goodman (1), pp. 102–3). For him there is only the *formally* logical priority that relates the primitive and defined or inferred elements of a particular way of systematising a body of such elements. But any such body of elements can be systematised in a plurality of different ways. It is a matter of free choice for the system-builder which elements he selects as primitive, a choice in which he should be guided by such strictly formal considerations as that of the simplicity, economy or elegance of one choice as compared with another. Although there is a purely formal sense of priority in which it is relative to a given way of systematising a body of statements, philosophers should be concerned with more than the construction of formally consistent systems. Their aim is to set out, as systematically as possible, the order of logical dependence of the apparatus of concepts and statements that we actually possess. A formally consistent system might be epistemologically inconsistent. If Wittgenstein's argument against the possibility of a private language is valid, a system in which physical concepts are defined in terms of phenomenological ones, though it might be perfectly consistent as a formal system, would be epistemologically inconsistent in being incapable of being used as a language.

Goodman's chief direct argument against the existence of a clear concept of epistemological priority takes the form of a challenge to its defenders to give a reasoned justification of their ascription of epistemological priority to one of the three statements 'that is a moving patch of red', 'that is a cardinal bird', 'that is the 37th bird in the tree this morning' as compared with the other two. He considers the argument that the third is ruled out since, although it is true, the speaker would not know it to be true at the time he spoke. But in that case, he goes on, why not allow 'that thing is lighter than Aristotle' as basic since it will be known at the time (op. cit., p. 104). The collateral information that supports the judgment about the bird's weight is very near the surface. To say anything as odd as that in the circumstance one would certainly have to have reviewed it consciously, to have recognised that that is a bird and to have recalled that all garden birds are lighter than men and that Aristotle was a man. In any such case as this another possible candidate for priority would have to be brought in as support. The serious candidates, therefore, are 'that is a moving patch of red' and 'that is a cardinal bird' or some other statement about it as a material thing.

Now the meaning of 'that is a moving patch of red' is not clear. It may mean 'there is something red that moves here', a very cautious, perceptually minimal, material-thing statement, in which case the competition is confined to a restricted class of candidates, or, on the other hand, and this is clearly what Goodman had in mind, it can mean 'there is a moving red patch in my visual field'. The arguments against the priority of the latter have been considered at length in the preceding chapter and do not need to be repeated. In summary they are that unless we are in a special frame of mind we shall not be aware of the phenomenological fact it states and that we do not regard it as called for by a request to justify some perceptually minimal statement about a material thing.

The survivors of the competition do pose a residual problem, however. Which of these three statements is prior to the other: there is a cardinal bird in the tree, there is bird in the tree, there is something bird-shaped in the tree (a statement, it will be remembered, that we might use the words 'that looks like a bird' to express)? I am not at all sure that there is a definite answer to this question. Which it would be correct to assert without feeling obliged to be ready to support it will depend on the circumstances: how far one is from the tree, whether one has seen it alight on the branch (to rule out its being a bird-shaped dummy), how familiar one is with American garden birds. Of the third, perceptually minimal, statement it can be said that it never requires further support. But is this a sufficient reason for treating perceptually minimal statements alone as basic? In the first place the fact that there is an X here does not entail that there is something here with the visible properties characteristic of Xs. A very misshapen human being may have the usual visible properties of monkeys. So although 'that looks like an X' (in the perceptually minimal sense) may claim less than the corresponding straight material-thing statement, 'that is an X', it sometimes makes a different claim rather than a logical part of the same one. Secondly, I may be justified in thinking that there is an X here without thinking myself, or being, in a position to make the corresponding perceptually minimal claim. Suppose I see a small brown thing of no perceptibly determinate shape in a tree from whose direction a cascade of bird-song is coming. I shall say, without reflection, that it is a bird (from its colour, its position and its sound) but I shall not be aware of a bird-shaped thing and shall only believe that there is a bird-shaped thing there on the strength of my belief that there is a bird there. Of course the latter belief is not basic in these circumstances either, for these circumstances are mildly unfavourable, I can only just see it and will be able and willing to give my reasons for saying there is a bird there.

My conclusion is, then, that there is no particular class of material-thing statements that are basic. Rather, for any material-thing statement expressed by an ostensively learnt sentence (which rules out statements about lungs, germs and molecules) there will be circumstances in which it can be basic. This conclusion leaves open the possibility that there are basic statements that are not about material things, that is to say that there are experiences other than perception not merely in our ordinary way of speaking, by which perception and introspection or self-knowledge are contrasted, but also more fundamentally, in that they have a radically different subject-matter: material things in one case, inner mental states in the other.

The coherence theory

Three main arguments have been persistently advanced against the coherence theory. The first and most effective is that there can be a plurality of internally coherent systems of statements, each of which has members that are incompatible with some members of the others. In effect this is to say that either one must begin the assemblage of one's system of accepted beliefs with some beliefs that owe their acceptability to something other than coherence or one must start from some arbitrary selection, in which case there are many alternative but mutually incoherent arbitrary sets to choose from. The mere coherence of a statement with others is not enough unless these others deserve to be accepted themselves. The second argument is that the rules of logic and evidence by which coherence is defined cannot, without another infinite regress, be held to owe their acceptability to coherence. If 'p coheres with q' is to mean anything definite *some* principles of coherence must be admitted on other grounds, for until they are accepted the question 'does this cohere' can have no definite sense. Finally, it is argued that the coherence theory is self-refuting. Like other beliefs of finite minds it is not, or is not at any rate known to be, completely coherent. The coherence theory implies the doctrine of degrees of truth which holds that no statement is more than partially true. In applying to itself, then, the coherence theory undermines itself. I do not think this third argument is very powerful. The sceptical implications of the coherence theory are not radical enough to do more than mildly weaken it.

It is often said that the coherence theory is not an account of the nature of truth but is rather a criterion of truth. This modification of the theory's claims is not as clear as it might be. It could be a way of saying that coherence is a logically necessary condition of truth or a way of saying that it is the correct procedure for finding out what is true. On the first interpretation it is, of course, obviously correct if coherence is identified with mere consistency. Every true statement must be consistent with every other true statement. It is not so obvious, though it may be true, that every true statement stands in some stronger relation, one of mutual support or corroboration, to all other truths. But to affirm this would be to accept some form of determinism. The description of a purely chance event is not inferable, deductively or inductively, from the set of statements describing the rest of the universe together with the laws of nature. It can be anticipated only by guesswork and must be accepted with natural piety.

On the second interpretation the coherence theory becomes a theory of knowledge or justification rather than a theory of truth. In this guise it is more plausible. For many statements are justified on the basis of their logical and evidential relations to others. It was such a theory of confirmation rather than truth that the left-wing positivists of the 1930s were driven to by their hostility to the seemingly metaphysical consequence of a theory of basic statements like Schlick's which held that the relations between language and reality could be grasped. In so far as Quine's holism is a coherence theory, it too is a theory of confirmation not truth.

A persistent obscurity in all coherence theories has enveloped the concept of coherence itself. To identify it with mere consistency is far too weak. An indefinitely large number of statements inconsistent with each other are consistent with any given statement. At the other extreme it is far too much to identify it with mutual entailment, as many who recognise the previous difficulty are inclined to do. Two statements that entail each other have the same meaning, so, if every true statement entailed every other and was entailed by it, there could only be one statement. In terms of confirmation this would imply that there could be no new knowledge, for no justified statement could assert anything not already contained in the statements on which it was based. Sometimes what are thought to be weaker senses of mutual entailment are introduced. Woozley defines a set of statements as related by mutual entailment as one in which each is deducible from all the rest and in which none could be true if any of the others were false (Woozley, p. 157). If the first half of this definition is taken to mean that each is deducible from all the rest *distributively*, taken one by one, we are back where we started. It must mean that each is deducible from all the rest *collectively*, taken as a group or conjunction (p and q and . . . and y entail z; p and q and . . . and z entail y . . . q and r and . . . and z entail p). But the second condition, added to this, has the consequence that each member of the set entails and is entailed by the conjunction of the remainder. For it simply reverses the entailments of the previous conditon (z entails p and q and . . . and y; y entails p and q and . . . and z; . . . p entails q and r and . . . and z). But in that case every member of the set entails and is entailed by every other, and we have returned to the ordinary, original sense of mutual entailment by a roundabout route.

What is clearly intended is not that the elements of a coherent set entail one another, singly or in groups, but that they support each other or render each other more probable. But how does one statement support another? There seem to be two main ways: one direct, the other indirect. A statement directly supports any statement from which it follows but which it does not entail. Thus 'this cat is black' supports, very weakly, 'all cats are black'. It indirectly supports any statement which follows from it and some such directly supported statement or again any statement on which it and some directly supported statement confer some proportional statistical likelihood. In this way 'this cat is black' supports 'that cat is black', very weakly, by way of 'all cats are black' and 'these four cats are black and that fifth one is grey' supports 'that cat is black' by way of 'most cats are black'. But, in default of other information 'this cat is black' confers no more support on 'that cat is black' than it does on 'that cat is grey'. For it follows from 'this cat is black and that cat is grey' just as much as it does from 'all cats are black' or 'this cat is black and that cat is black'. The point of this exceedingly schematic exercise is that no statement supports another from which it is logically independent except by way of the directly supported statements from which it follows but which it does not entail. But to have any support for these indispensable intermediaries an initial source of supply is required; a stock of information that does not owe its support to other accepted information. Of course the body of directly supported general knowledge can react back, as it were, on the primary evidence on which it is based. The only reason for preferring a rather complicated law to a simpler one might be some early observation, anomalous with respect to the simpler law and of a kind which has never been repeated. But this founding father can only be disfranchised by a democratic process. It is not the simpler law itself, by virtue of its mere simplicity, that has the authority to expel it from the ranks of accepted statements; it is the mass of lawful instances that the simpler law represents. Attempts

P

to define coherence in terms of support or justification tend to have a somewhat nebulous quality, to produce a kind of mist in which questionable deeds can be perpetrated unobserved. But even the most rough and ready dispersal of the mist reveals that an overall theory of justification in terms of support is confronted not only with the old difficulty of the regress of justification, which the notion of mutual support might seem to overcome, but also with the difficulty that the other premise of the supporting inference, the essential intermediary as I have called it, requires independent support itself.

I suggested earlier that the third argument against the coherence theory, that it undermined itself, was not a very serious objection to it. It should be recognised that the second argument does not apply to a coherence theory which is limited in its application to the domain of factual or empirical knowledge. For the principles of logic are not within the scope of such a limited coherence theory nor need the basic principles of evidential support be regarded as empirical. But the second argument does apply to a doctrine like Quine's holism, in which the laws of logic are exposed to the test of coherence with all other beliefs (Quine (3), pp. 42–3). In such a system it is hard to see what incoherence can possibly be. Believing that all cats are black I encounter what I am inclined to believe is a grey cat, have what Quine calls a 'refractory experience'. But what is refractory about it; why should I not accommodate it alongside my belief that all cats are black? Because, we instinctively reply, the two beliefs are inconsistent. But for the holist this means because they are inconsistent with the further belief I hold that if all A are B then there is not an A which is not B, which I could, no doubt inconveniently, drop instead of either of them. But are these three, now, really inconsistent? Only if it is accepted that if all A are B only if there is not an A which is not B then not both all A are B and there is an A which is not B. And so Achilles hobbles after the tortoise *ad infinitum*.

Quine writes of the fabric of our beliefs colliding with experience but as he represents it that fabric is indefinitely elastic. For him every collision between a new empirical belief and the body of hitherto accepted beliefs is hypothetical in the sense that there is an infinite set of elements in the accepted structure from amongst which we can select which one we are going to abandon if we do not choose to rule out the new empirical belief as an illusion or mistake. Accepting ordinary logic and all X are Y, I find myself inclined to believe that this X is not Y. I can suppress the inclination or drop the law or drop 'if all X are Y then there is not an X which is not Y' or drop the conditional whose antecedent is the last conditional and whose consequent is the conjunction of the law and the new belief or the next conditional formed in the same way or the next or the next. . . . But until I accept some conditional in the series there is no inconsistency between its predecessor and the conjunction of what has gone before.

The laws of logic are not on the same footing as our factual beliefs. Only by accepting them do we fix the sense of those beliefs. That there is not an X which is not Y is part of what we believe when we believe that all X are Y. A belief cannot be severed from its logical implications and its relation to them be regarded as something determined by a further belief that is independent of them both except in the light of a yet further belief and so on. Quine says that we are reluctant to reject statements at the empirical periphery of our beliefs and admits that without this reluctance our beliefs would have no empirical content. He also admits that we are reluctant to reject the logical laws that are at the centre of the whole structure. The reason he gives for this second reluctance is that it would be inconvenient to make such amendments. But he does not explain the nature of this inconvenience. If I allow that 'all X are Y' and 'this X is not Y' are consistent I must retrospectively cancel a vast mass of past rejections, made on the assumption of their inconsistency. An immense logical amnesty is declared, permitting the return of a horde of hitherto rejected, because supposedly refuted, hypotheses to scientific respectability. In such a free-for-all intellectual order would break down altogether: we should not know what to believe and we should not understand what we were believing if we tried to believe anything.

But it is possible to advance a coherence theory of knowledge or justification which, being limited to statements of non-logical fact, is not exposed to the objection that, since an essential part of the sense of coherence is defined by logic, the statement that one belief coheres or fails to cohere with another is without any definite meaning unless some logical laws are accepted on grounds independent of their coherence with the beliefs whose coherence with one another they determine. Firth has recently suggested a sophisticated coherence theory of this limited kind (Firth). He observes that acceptance of what he calls the central thesis of epistemological priority, that there are some beliefs that do not owe all their justification to others, does not entail Lewis's strong position that there must be incorrigible basic statements, whose justification is neither derived from nor defeasible by other statements. This is the point I argued for in the sixth chapter. There are, he goes on, three weaker possibilities. The first is that basic statements have some justification which is not derived from other statements and which other statements can strengthen or weaken but never to the point that their denials are more justified than they are. Secondly, basic statements, although falsifiable through failure to cohere with other statements, always have some independent and undefeasible measure of justification. Finally, there is the minimal position that basic statements always have some independent justification although this may be wholly 'defeated' by their failure to cohere with other statements. I find the first and third of these positions a little strange. As to the first, it would be odd for basic statements to be weakened by other statements if those other statements could never weaken them to such a point that their rejection was justified. How, for example, could a statement about the circumstances (such as that I am in a panic or had my attention rapidly distracted or that the colour in question is unfamiliar) weaken a basic statement (whether physical or phenomenological) unless such basic statements had *sometimes* turned out to be false in such circumstances? As to the third, is there any difference between the defeasibility of justification spoken of here and the falsification spoken of under the second heading? At any rate, Firth agrees that there can be basic, or epistemically prior, statements that have intrinsic or non-propositional probability or support. These, he contends, might be those statements describing our immediate experience which we believe to be true.

But, he continues, might it not be possible to identify a class of statements which owed all their justification to their coherence with each other and which were the indispensable ultimate support for all other statements? He admits that if every statement owes what justification it has to its coherence with other justified statements then it is not possible to explain why one system of statements is justified and another system, to some extent inconsistent with the former, is not. But if some class of statements, those, perhaps, which a man believes at a particular time, can be identified without reference to coherence and those in the class that cohere best with rest of the class (or those that cohere with the largest number of other members of the class) are picked out as 'initially' justified, then they can be used to decide which other statements or possible beliefs are justified and which are not.

I find it very hard to distinguish this highly qualified version of the coherence theory from the almost as highly qualified version of the theory of basic statements to which it is offered as an alternative. To accord a primary status to statements that are believed is surely to regard them as intrinsically justified in a way that other statements are not.

Peirce on intuition and inquiry

In this section and the next I shall consider two comprehensive versions of the fallibilist theory of knowledge, those of Peirce and

Popper, in which knowledge is admitted to have foundations—perceptual judgments for Peirce, basic statements for Popper—but in which these foundations are not held to be incorrigible or (in Popper's case at any rate, there is no clear decision on this point in Peirce) to be phenomenological. There is a striking similarity between their two doctrines: both hold that the task of inquiry is to eliminate false hypotheses, that new hypotheses are found by insight not induction, that the conceptual nature of belief entails its corrigibility, that a regress of justification should not be a cause of concern. This correspondence is not due to any direct influence of the earlier philosopher on the later, there is no reference, or obvious occasion for reference, to Peirce in Popper's *Logik der Forschung*, but rather to the fact that the ideas of both these philosophers about knowledge are derived from a close study of the growth of science.

Peirce's account of the foundations of knowledge, of the perceptual judgments that are the practical terminus of justification but not the objects of any kind of infallible intuition, is a consequence of his general view of the nature of factual or scientific inquiry (Peirce (1) & (2)). Knowledge, he contends, is not the result of methodical, inductive accumulation, as the empiricist tradition has represented it; method comes in with the critical examination of beliefs that we already have. To know something is to believe it, which, following Bain, he regards as the possession of a fixed habit of action, and to believe it truly, the truth of what we believe being indicated by the fact that the habit in question does not lead to disappointment or surprise. When a habit is surprised or disappointed, when an expectation fails to be realised, it becomes unfixed, we are put into a state of doubt, which is an unpleasant, uneasy condition, a desire for the peace and comfort of belief. The uneasy desire to replace doubt by belief inspires inquiry, the conscious resolve to form a habit of action that shall be proof against surprises. Insight, not any mechanical rule, suggests hypotheses alternative to the belief that surprise has compelled us to abandon. These are tested, in the first instance, by their plausibility, their consonance with existing knowledge, but, more importantly, by the verification of their observable consequences, as stated in perceptual judgments. Most hypotheses, Peirce observes, are false, but there is a gradual social convergence on the truth.

Peirce sets himself squarely against Descartes' precept that the philosopher should start by doubting everything he can. Philosophers' doubts are only paper doubts. There can be no real doubt without surprise and no surprise without a general framework of beliefs. The Cartesian uncommitted mind is an impossibility, for there is in fact a large range of common-sense beliefs which are not seriously dubitable as a matter of psychological fact. Among these psychological indubitables are perceptual judgments and the belief that there is some intelligible order in nature (though Peirce, like Popper, is an indeterminist). To say this is not to say that no single common-sense belief can be doubted, only that such beliefs cannot be doubted as an entire group. It is, indeed, according to Peirce, a belief of common sense that some common-sense beliefs are false.

The apparent termini of empirical justification are perceptual judgments. What suggests that they are to be understood as statements about material things is the fact that Peirce distinguishes the percepts they refer to from sense-impressions, conceived as the hard sensory core of our percepts, which we can only subsequently elicit by means of analysis and inference. Although practically terminable, perceptual judgments are not intuitive apprehensions of the truth. They are hypotheses too, like the conjectures they are used to test, but they are unconscious hypotheses which just crop up in our minds and are not the result of a controlled process of conjecture. He gives two reasons for their fallibility, both of which have been considered earlier. First, they have to be expressed in classificatory words, whose use embodies a learnt skill we may not be fully masters of, and, secondly, they take time to make and thus rest on memory, whose fallibility is generally admitted.

Peirce's view that perceptual judgments are not infallible is part of a general assault on the notion of intuitive cognition, which he defines, not too helpfully, as cognition not determined by previous cognitions. In his view all apparent intuition is hypothesis, which is accessible to testing by way of its consequences. All the knowledge we possess rests on previous learning of the symbols in which it is expressed and of the method by which it is acquired and our credentials in both of these respects can be criticised. He does not deny, therefore, that there are beliefs that are not the outcome of any conscious process of inference. But articulate reasonings, as he calls them, are not the only inferential cognitions. There are what he calls 'acritical inferences' and 'unconscious analogies of inference'. The logical reconstruction of our beliefs as inferences is an artificial and highly conventionalised affair. In effect, his view that induction is a method of testing, and not of discovery, comes to the view that any belief with testable consequences is inferential and all beliefs, he maintains, have such consequences.

He devotes some attention to the Cartesian doctrine that self-knowledge is intuitive. In so far as self-knowledge is knowledge of the self as a thinking substance he observes that its certainty does not rule out its being a 'telescoped inference' and that a child knows many things before he is able to distinguish himself from the world around him. In so far as it is knowledge of our own mental states he argues that to know what we believe must be a hypothesis, since a belief is a habit of action, and that our emotions come before us primarily as beliefs about the external world: 'I am angry' is a sophisticated reinterpretation of 'this thing is vile'. Again we acquire the ability to discern facts about ourselves by way of our ability to discern the same sort of facts in others.

Two general arguments he brings against intuition are of some interest. The first takes the form of a question. Is the intuitiveness of a belief, he asks, intuitive or inferred? It cannot be intuited because there is so much disagreement as to what is intuitive. The apparent implication of this is that since we cannot know intuitively that a belief is intuitive we cannot be justified in treating it as if it were, that is to say in accepting it without putting its consequences to the test. Here we could distinguish between practical and theoretical knowledge of the intuitiveness of a belief. To have practical knowledge of a belief's intuitiveness is for it just not to occur to one that it needs testing. We could have this while having no theoretical opinion at all, or a conflicting one, as to whether inferential justification was logically required for beliefs of that kind. Difference of theoretical opinion on the point could then be attributed to limited self-knowledge. In what sense, after all, would we need to know that an intuitive belief was in fact intuitive, in order to treat it, confidently and correctly, as if it were? All that would be necessary, in fact, would be for us to have learnt to use the statement expressing it in the appropriate circumstances, without having acquired any inclination to suppose that beliefs of its kind need any justification by inference. All we should need, in other words, is what I have called practical knowledge of its intuitiveness. We could know *how* to treat it, without having any clear knowledge *that* our way of treating it is the correct one.

Peirce's second general argument against intuition is that the infinite regress with which it threatens those who reject it is not to be feared. Why, he asks, should the series of cognitions that determine a given cognition not be strictly continuous, like the series: $\frac{1}{2} \ldots \frac{3}{4} \ldots \frac{7}{8} \ldots \frac{15}{16} \ldots \ldots 1$? The suggestion seems to be that the series of determining cognitions could have an unlimited number of members without being of unlimited (temporal?) extent. A comparison he uses is that of a triangle whose apex is immersed in water. Beneath the actual waterline is an infinite series of possible waterlines, but the apex is not infinitely far below the surface. This could be a way of saying that the in itself more or less undifferentiated mass of cognition *actually preceding* a given cognition is capable of being conventionally carved up into an infinite number of artificially distinguished cognitions. This view would be a development of his idea that not all inferences are pieces of articulate reasoning. But this, on Peirce's own assumptions, is beside the point. He should be concerned with the logic of a belief's justification and not with the psychology of its apprehension. Looked at from this point of view it is not clear how his hypothesis of strict continuity is to be applied. Would it mean that an infinite series of justifying consequences could be inferred from a given belief but that they could all be tested with a finite amount of observational effort? This seems absurd, even allowing for his view that there is a marked conventional element in the partitioning of the ground from which a belief is justifyingly inferred into separate premises.

He finally sums up the case against Cartesian intuitionism by listing four errors which he takes it to embody. First, we should not attempt to subject all our beliefs to scrutiny by methodical doubt for we cannot doubt unless we have some reason to. Secondly, we should not assume that whatever survives the impact of doubt is certain; objective certainty is something social, the convergence to agreement of mutually critical inquirers. Thirdly, we should not be bemused by the irrelevant example of Euclid into supposing that knowledge grows in a linear fashion, step by step; our beliefs should rest on as wide and various a range of arguments as possible. Finally, the process of explanation and justification does not end in self-evident simple elements; ultimates, he says in a characteristic phrase, block the road of inquiry (on Peirce cf. Chisholm (2)).

There is much of interest in this body of suggestive but far from fully worked-out ideas. In Popper's theory of knowledge, as we shall see in the next section, definite answers are given at a number of strategically crucial points in the argument to questions that Peirce leaves open. Popper's basic statements are about observable, medium-sized material things, not immediate experiences. Any such statement has a potentially infinite set of testable consequences, of the same kind as itself and derived from it with the help of accepted laws and theories. But this potential regress of justification is not actualised. We accept some basic statements as true by a kind of convention, which can always be revised if their acceptance is challenged.

Peirce exhibits with particular clarity a widespread error about the foundations of knowledge which it was one of the aims of the fifth and sixth chapters to expose. This is that either there must be strongly intuitive and incorrigible beliefs at the foundations of knowledge or else all beliefs must owe their entire justification to inference from others. Peirce perceives that there are two distinct forms of the second alternative: the full-blooded coherence theory, which he rejects, and the doctrine of a relative basis of perceptual judgments, which he accepts. He does not see that there are also two distinct forms of the first alternative: full-blooded Cartesianism, which takes the foundations of knowledge to be incorrigible and self-evident statements about immediate experience and the doctrine, put forward as a conceivable possibility, but not endorsed, by Price and Ayer, that there are basic statements which owe part of their justification or support to experience and not to other beliefs, which have, in Price's rather puzzling phrase, 'intrinsic probability', and yet which can be further supported, or, on the other hand, weakened, by other beliefs, with which they are more or less coherent or congruent. The examination of Popper's theory of knowledge, to which I now turn, will show how close his chastened version of the coherence theory is to the chastened version of Cartesianism that I wish to defend and also produce reasons for preferring that doctrine to his.

Popper's theory of knowledge

Popper's philosophy might be said to have developed from an unprecedentedly resolute attempt to take Hume's problem of induction seriously. Science consists of hypotheses, laws or theories, of general statements that do not follow logically from the singular reports of observation which constitute the evidence for them. But theories can be falsified by singular observation-statements. Popper's theory of knowledge arises from an unqualified acceptance of this logical asymmetry between theories and their evidence and takes the form of a thorough exploitation of the possibilities it leaves open. Three central doctrines are derived from the principle that theories can be falsified but not verified by observation. The first is that verifiability cannot be used as a criterion for the demarcation of science from what is not science, and it is even less appropriate as a criterion for the demarcation of sense from nonsense. In general Popper dismisses the problem of finding a criterion of significance, holding that all attempts to find one have been intolerably restrictive and have rested, in any case, on nothing better than the arbitrary decisions of their proposers. In the place of such a criterion he proposes falsifiability as a way of distinguishing science from other forms of discourse: from pseudo-science, whether ancient like alchemy and astrology or modern like Marx's theory of history and society and Freudian psychoanalysis, which can be confirmed but cannot be refuted, and from non-science, in other words from metaphysics proper, which can be neither confirmed nor refuted. He has had to endure an amazingly persistent incapacity among his critics to realise that his criterion is one of scientific status and not of meaningfulness. A corollary of this first doctrine is that falsifiability can vary in degree and that statements can to some extent be compared in the extent to which they possess it. Although every general statement has an infinite class of potential singular falsifiers one may be more falsifiable than another, when everything that falsifies the former falsifies the latter but some things falsify the former that do not falsify the latter. This will be the case wherever the former entails the latter but not vice versa. He further shows that the more falsifiable a theory the greater its empirical content, the greater its simplicity and the less its logical or *a priori* probability. The scientific theorist should seek to put forward the most falsifiable hypotheses consistent with the knowledge he has. These will involve the greatest degree of risk but they will be more informative and simpler than any logically more probable alternative. And if they are in fact false this will be discovered sooner than it would otherwise have been (Popper (1), ch. 4).

The second central doctrine is that theories are not in fact found or first hit upon by any mechanical routine of inductive generalisation but are first propounded as a result of creative and imaginative insight of a kind which cannot be reduced to rule. Nor can theories be proved or even justified by observation of confirming instances. Positive confirmation can establish only an infinitesimal portion of the infinite set of a theory's singular, observable consequences. All that can be achieved is the corroboration of theories by their successful exposure to the most stringent tests that can be devised. The rational pursuit of scientific knowledge is an essentially critical undertaking: a theory is rationally acceptable, and never this more than provisionally, if it has survived the most persistent and energetic attempts to falsify it. It follows that the more falsifiable a hypothesis is in the first place the higher the degree of corroboration it can secure. In this doctrine Popper presents a theory of the growth of knowledge together with a theory of its justification. The process begins with free, imaginative conjecture, the more falsifiable the better. From such conjectural hypotheses observable consequences are derived by ordinary deductive logic. If the hypothesis escapes falsification it is to some extent corroborated, if not it must be rejected and imagination must be relied on to provide another to replace it. It remains acceptable as long as it continues to resist our endeavours to refute it.

His third central doctrine is his account of the logical, if not psychological, foundations of the whole system, the basic singular statements which falsify or corroborate our hypotheses (Popper (1), ch. 5). In form these basic statements are existential statements of a circumscribed and not unrestrictedly general variety which assert the existence at a definite place and time of an observable thing or state of affairs. They are public and intersubjective, not descriptions of immediate experience. Furthermore they are corrigible. Just as they are deducible from hypotheses taken together with other, accepted basic statements (the initial conditions), so further basic statements can be derived from them taken together with accepted laws and theories. They can be further tested and perhaps refuted in this way but, Popper maintains, the infinite regress involved is an innocuous one since it is only potential. We *can* always test basic statements further, but we only *need* to do so if they are challenged. In practice we must accept them as true by a kind of convention. But the dogmatism implicit in such a convention is not vicious since it is only provisional. It is this theory of the empirical basis of scientific knowledge with which I shall be most closely concerned here.

A general consequence of the three doctrines is that all accepted empirical statements, whether singular or general, are only provisionally accepted. Every theory has an open class of observable consequences among the unchecked part of which a falsifier may be contained. Every basic statement may, together with accepted theory, entail some basic statement which we will accept as false. Furthermore, since the theories used in these derivations are only provisional, only provisional falsification of basic statements can be achieved in this way. Equally it would appear that the falsification of theories is none too conclusive an operation since the basic statements that effect it are open to revision.

On this challenging and original foundation Popper erects a large number of philosophical theories, which need only be listed here. (i) He puts forward a view of the mind as active in the search for knowledge as against the passive conception of its working to be found in ordinary empiricism. The pursuit of knowledge begins with free conjecture and proceeds by resolute criticism, both active processes. It does not start from the passive reception of perceptual experience and proceed to the level of theory by mechanical inductive generalisation. There is, Popper says, no such thing as pure observation untainted by anticipatory prejudice; all observation is made from the point of view of some theory or hypothesis (Popper (2), vol. 2, pp. 246–8). (ii) The empiricist account of concept formation suffers from the same defects as the corresponding theory of the growth of knowledge. Concepts are not acquired by the passive registration of recurrent similar experiences. Similarity is always ascribed to things from some point of view. The world is indefinitely patient of our classificatory activities and these reflect the interested, theory-guided presumptions with which we approach it (Popper (3), pp. 42–6). (iii) In order to test a theory we must use a body of accepted basic statements as initial conditions and basic statements can be tested only in the light of accepted theories. Knowledge cannot start, then from a *tabula rasa*; anti-traditionalist epistemologies which propose a clean sweep of accepted beliefs are incoherent. The pursuit of knowledge must always begin from a body of presumptions, whether reasonable or not, which we can progressively improve by resolute critical endeavour to eliminate falsehood. Here as elsewhere we have to start from where we are (Popper (3), introduction). (iv) Scientific theory, in particular the more sophisticated layers of it which refer to unobservable entities, is neither an account of the hidden essence of things, lurking behind observable appearances, nor, at the opposite extreme, is it simply a convenient conceptual instrument for the prediction of future experience. Essentialism errs in implying that the task of scientific inquiry is in principle completable; instrumentalism in holding that we aim with our hypotheses at convenience or utility rather than truth (Popper (3), ch. 3). (v) Empirical probability is not a measure of ignorance, it is an objective propensity of physical things, expressed in statistical laws. These laws must be interpreted so as to render them accessible to falsification. This kind of probability must be distinguished from the logical probability of hypotheses which is the exact and necessary opposite of empirical content or falsifiability; and again from the empirical probability of a theory in the light of its actual evidence, which is better called corroboration (Popper (4)). (vi) The essentially active character of mind in the pursuit of knowledge has a host of more general consequences: mind-body dualism (which is argued for on the ground that the simplest intellectual operation, naming, cannot be understood as a causal process); indeterminism (an admittedly metaphysical but none the less reasonable assumption); anti-historicism (the view that since future discoveries are unpredictable and yet strongly influence the historical development of society that development cannot be made the subject of any large-scale prediction) and a dualism of facts on the one hand, which are discovered, and decisions or proposals on the other, which are made or proposed.

There is a number of difficulties in the first two doctrines of falsifiability as a criterion of demarcation and of the non-inductive nature of the formulation and corroboration of theories. Laws of the instantial kind which assert the connection of observable things and properties seem more straightforwardly falsifiable than the theories, more characteristic of developed sciences, which refer to unobservables. Such theories do not entail instantial laws by themselves but only in conjunction with laws correlating observables and unobservables. It could, however, be replied that these laws of correlation can be corroborated by ordinary observations since it is not an essential feature of them that part of their reference is to unobservables. For example, the laws that correlate gas molecules to the collective phenomena described by the gas laws could be, and indeed must be, corroborated by examination of the behaviour of large masses of small but still observable objects.

Popper does not generally distinguish very clearly between his non-inductive accounts of the historical growth and the logical justification of theories. But the two are logically independent. Inductive theory-formulation is compatible with non-inductive corroboration and non-inductive theory-formation with inductive justification. Non-inductive theorising would seem to be more characteristic of the more advanced sciences or the more advanced phases of a science than of the less: it is more obviously present in physics than in biology and in molecular biology than in entomology. Furthermore it is generally more evident in science, which is, after all, a deliberate pursuit of knowledge, than it is in common life, where our beliefs about the character of persons or nations, about the colour-range of a particular kind of animal or flower or about the characteristic weights of different kinds of things are gradually 'borne in upon us' rather than conjectured and then critically tested. But the non-inductiveness of theorising is not a readily falsifiable doctrine since any apparent counter-example can be ruled out as a case of implicit conjecture. More to the point is the question whether corroboration is really non-inductive. In it, after all, the observable fact that a theory has survived tests is regarded as a reason for accepting it. To do this is very hard to distinguish from taking past survival to be an inductive ground for expecting future survival. It will not do to say that a corroborated theory is simply one that it is reasonable to act on, since the reasonableness of acting on it stands and falls with that of the expectation that it will not be falsified. Nor again is it a peculiar virtue of the non-inductive approach that it insists on the provisional and revisable character of theories, for this is asserted, even if not so emphatically, by 'inductivism' with its view that theories are never more than probable.

But the part of Popper's theory of knowledge which is, I think, most open to criticism and is also most relevant to my concerns here, is his account of the foundations of knowledge, his theory of basic statements. He formulates the problem of the acceptability of basic statements in terms of a threefold distinction due to J. F. Fries. The foundations of knowledge must be dogmatically accepted as somehow self-evident or they must be held to be justified by perceptual experience, the procedure of what he calls 'psychologism' or, finally, the idea of a foundation must be abandoned and an infinite regress accepted. Against psychologism he argues that it makes knowledge intolerably subjective, turning it into a system of private convictions. Furthermore all description transcends experience since it necessarily embodies universals which cannot, as he puts it, be constituted out of experience. Experience can, then, never certify any empirical statement. Now what this kind of argument shows is that statements based on experience are corrigible. It does not entail that basic statements must be about public things and not immediate experiences. Popper does not, in fact, give transcendence of all description as a reason for choosing a public basis. His defence of the choice could be partly empirical, public statements are the basis we actually use, and partly logical, private, phenomenological statements would be no more secure than the basis we already use and would import further problems of their own. What is more important is that the corrigibility of basic statements does not entail that they are not supported or to some extent justified by experience. This is an alternative to his much weaker conclusion that at best experience *motivates* our acceptance of basic statements.

He recommends his own view as doing justice to all three sides of Fries's 'trilemma'. The acceptance of basic statements has an element of dogmatism about it, in that it involves a conventional decision; since every basic statement can be subjected to critical testing it involves a potential infinite regress; basic statements do depend causally on perceptual experience in being motivated by it even if they are not justified by it. But none of these three elements, he believes, is involved to an objectionable degree. The dogmatism of our conventions here is only provisional; the infinite regress involved is only potential; the psychologism is, as it should be, causal and not logical.

There is, then, no absolute basis to knowledge, but only a relative one. In building up a system of accepted statements we are not starting from scratch by putting absolutely trustworthy foundation-stones on an unencumbered surface; rather we are rendering an existing structure more secure by driving piles into the swamp above which it more or less precariously rises. In writings subsequent to the *Logik der Forschung* the implications of this point of view have been further developed. The notion of an absolutely secure basis for knowledge, whether it is intellectual intuition or sense-experience, is no more than an internalised version of the epistemological authoritarianism which would accept the ultimate authority of some person, institution, text or tradition. Such authoritarianism leads to an excessive optimism about knowledge (corresponding to the equal and opposite pessimistic error of scepticism) which takes truth to be manifest and any failure to find it to be due to error or intellectual sin, perhaps to the collective sin of a conspiracy. There can be no tracing of beliefs to their ultimately justifying foundations. Most of what we believe rests on testimony which we acquire from other people who themselves depend on a great deal of collateral information. We cannot fully check the sources of our beliefs, therefore, we can only test them directly for ourselves. The central problem of epistemology is to devise procedures that will eliminate falsehood, not to discover absolutely reliable sources of truth, just as that of politics is to devise institutions for controlling and eliminating bad rulers rather than to decide positively who should rule. Intuition plays a part in the growth of knowledge, but as a suggester of hypotheses not as a source of authoritative truth. It is only useful against a background of traditionally accepted beliefs and in conjunction with a resolutely followed procedure of critical testing.

Popper does not imply that the perceptual experiences that motivate our acceptance of basic statements do so inexorably and cannot be resisted, even by those who have reflected on the principles of rational belief. If they were irresistible there would be no place for a theory of knowledge telling us how we ought to manage our beliefs. It will perhaps be most *natural* for us to accept the basic statements to which our experiences motivate us, but is there any justifying ground or reason why we should do so? Why should we not accept the basic statements which we should most like to be true or again those which are most compatible with our beliefs or yet again those which allow us to form the most economical overall system of beliefs? In short, if we cannot resist motivated basic statements the only problem is that of making our theories compatible with them. But if we can accept others in their place the question inevitably arises: why should we accept them in preference to one of the alternative possibilities? One is inclined to reply that basic statements chosen on a principle of wishful thinking or compatibility with existing knowledge or systematic economy would clash with experience but in Popper's view this is no more than to say that different procedures for accepting basic statements are likely to lead to mutually inconsistent overall systems of belief. But unless experience supports as well as motivates the acceptance of basic statements, why show this partiality between different emotional determinants of belief? If the mere fact that they are conjectured does nothing, in itself, to justify the acceptance of a hypothesis, but merely makes it available for critical examination, why should not the same be true of basic statements? Furthermore we have subjective convictions about theories as well as basic statements, so why should we not accept them as conventionally true, since both types of belief are testable in the light of their consequences? We might also ask why it is that we are motivated to accept some possible basic statements but not others. A plausible explanation is that we have been taught to accept them in circumstances just like those in which we find ourselves motivated to accept them.

As a matter of fact there is a further requirement beyond motivation by experience that Popper requires a basic statement to satisfy if it is to be acceptable, even provisionally. This is that it shall not conflict with the basic statements of others. Now this further condition will, no doubt, be more readily satisfied in the case of basic statements motivated by experience than in the case of those to which hope, laziness or a love of order might prompt us. There is, of course, a difficulty about how the rather theoretical-looking belief that the basic statements accepted by others agree with mine is to be rendered acceptable, but this may be waived, since we could adopt the rule never to accept a basic statement b where we also accept a basic statement of the form 'X says "not-b"', without further testing. But now the question arises: why should we let our choice of basic statements for acceptance be dictated by the aim of securing the widest social harmony about subjective convictions? This convention will perhaps accelerate the corroboration of theories and make it a more sociable affair. But can it be shown to have more chance of approximating to the truth than the convention of accepting basic statements on the ground of their euphony or some other emotionally attractive quality?

The crucial point is that unless motivation by experience lends some support to basic statements and given, as it must be, that we have some element of free choice in the matter of which basic statements to accept, there can be no reason for preferring experientially motivated basic statements from those motivated in some other way. A conventionally adopted basic statement is really in much the same position as a conjectured theory. Any theory that it is incompatible with is only, as it were, conventionally and provisionally falsified. Really to expose a theory to testing is to see if it conflicts with any basic statements we have reason to accept, not just with those we provisionally choose to accept. Popper has not, in fact, escaped from the dilemma of dogmatism or an infinite regress. If experience in no way justifies basic statements then their acceptance is inevitably an arbitrary piece of dogmatism which is only deferred if they are accepted because we do not choose to accept the negation of any basic statement that can be deduced from them in conjunction with accepted theories.

The only alternative is for him to allow himself to be impaled, to a moderate extent, on the remaining, third, 'psychologistic' horn of his trilemma by admitting that basic statements derive some support, though not certification, from the experiences that motivate them and are not entirely dependent for justification on the consequences that can be derived from them. This theory that basic statements acquire some, perhaps small, initial probability from experience is, in effect, the corrigibilist theory conceived as a possibility by Price with his doctrine of intrinsic probability and by Ayer in his conception of meaning-rules by which experience renders basic statements probable but does not certify them. It is entirely consistent with the fallibilist conviction that no statement of fact is ever finally and unalterably established and that every statement, basic or theoretical, can be corroborated by its consequences. It does maintain that knowledge has foundations but it does not regard them as absolutely solid and incorrigible and, while it asserts that it is through their connection with experience that basic statements acquire that initial support without which no statement of fact whatever would have any justification, it does not require them to be phenomenological descriptions of experience.

Part III

Ideas

Introduction

Metaphysics

The concept of metaphysics is large, controversial and, in consequence, somewhat indeterminate in outline. Always abstract, and so an object of suspicion to the practical, it has been for many philosophers in recent times a residual category to which all the more grandiloquent kinds of seemingly insignificant speech can be consigned. But perhaps a more positive definition, acceptable to both its practitioners and its opponents, can be found. Both parties, I think, would agree that, in its most ordinary interpretation, metaphysics is the attempt to arrive by rational means at a general picture of the world.

Both parts of this definition, the idea of rational means and the idea of a general picture of the world, need explanation. The requirement that a picture of the world should be arrived at by rational means has, at any rate, some clear negative implications. To start with it rules out from metaphysics any picture of the world that has been acquired by mere absorption from the surrounding intellectual atmosphere. Nor again can beliefs be truly metaphysical in this sense if they rest simply on tradition or authority. Most people, no doubt, have some general picture of the world. But although this picture consists of metaphysical beliefs it has not usually been metaphysically arrived at. It has come into existence in a passive, non-rational way. Such people are the clients of metaphysics, but they are not metaphysicians, any more than I am a biochemist or a solid state physicist because I have some rather vague, general and probably out-of-date beliefs about the subject-matter of these disciplines which I have acquired from hearsay, popularisations and encyclopedias.

The claims of intuition present a slightly more complicated problem for the definition. In relation to metaphysics intuition can be of two forms: plain and fancy. By plain intuition I mean the apprehension of self-evident, necessary truths, a species of the kind of logical intuition that was the topic of chapter 5. Examples of metaphysical beliefs intuited in the plain sense are Leibniz's principle that what is complex must have simple parts or McTaggart's basic doctrines of infinite divisibility and the dissimilarity of the diverse. By fancy intuition I mean the varied forms of more or less mystical insight whose literary by-products, lumped together with works of rational philosophy, cause bouts of occupational nausea to philosophers surveying the philosophy sections of public libraries. The large propositions about the transcendent Beyond to which fancy intuition gives rise are at best intuitive in the psychological sense, the outcomes of 'just knowing'.

An infinite regress argument was used earlier to show that there must be logically intuitive first principles of demonstration in the domain of necessary knowledge, truths like the law of contradiction. These are justified by universal acceptance together with general recognition that they do not admit of justification by argument. They are explained as implicitly definitive of the very fundamental concepts they contain, their acceptance being a criterion of the genuine possession of these concepts. If any necessary truth is to be susceptible of demonstration there must be some intuitive necessary truths of this kind. Plain intuition, then, is a limiting case of rational method, since it is a direct way of arriving at truths. As such it can be admitted to strictly metaphysical reasoning. But the psychologically intuitive insights into the nature of things that constitute fancy intuition require the authentication of the kind of experience from which they arise. This problem of authentication can be ignored here since in fact the doctrines of traditional metaphysics, although sometimes suggested by some kind of mystical experience or vision, are ordinarily supported by rational argument.

The general picture of the world that forms the content of a metaphysical system needs to be distinguished from the kind of detailed account of what there is that is provided by an encyclopedia. It usually takes the form of a list of the main categories of things to be found in the world and of the relations between them. The main categories discussed by recognised metaphysicians are (i) material objects and events, whether observable or theoretical, (ii) minds, finite and infinite, and their states, in particular sense-impressions, (iii) abstract entities such as qualities, relations, numbers and propositions, and, finally, (iv) values. A metaphysical system will arrange these categories in some sort of hierarchy, the members of the preferred category or categories being held to be what really or ultimately exists and the remainder regarded as either dependent in some way on the ultimate existences or else as altogether illusory. Such a hierarchy of categories has an obvious title to the name 'ontology'. It is reasonable to mark it out within metaphysics as a whole by means of the traditional name for the fundamental part of the subject since a metaphysical system will usually go on to take a position, not as ontology does, about the logical relations of the categories, but about the causal relations to one another of their members, as to whether or not all existences fall under causal law and as to whether things of one category can stand in causal relations with things in another.

To show that this is not a gratuitous account of the nature of metaphysics we may consider the main kinds of ontological theory. First there is the Platonic view that only abstract entities or essences are truly real, in which values are obscurely identified with essences, minds are held real to the extent that they are concerned with essences and matter is disregarded as merely apparent. Secondly, there is the other kind of idealism, which I shall refer to, with apologies, as 'mentalism', expounded in various forms by Leibniz, Berkeley and Hegel, in which only minds, and derivatively their states, are truly real. Thirdly, there is the materialism of Hobbes which takes mind to be a special kind of material motion and which reduces essences to names and names to sounds. Fourthly, there is the kind of phenomenalistic or neutral monist theory intimated by Hume and Mill, set out more articulately by Russell and the early Wittgenstein, and most systematically expressed in Carnap's *Logische Aufbau der Welt*. Here sense-impressions are the only fundamental existences, minds and material things are defined in terms of them, institutions are constructed out of the activity of persons and essences out of the words they use. These are all monistic ontologies in which a single category is picked out as fundamental. But there are also various pluralistic possibilities. The most historically important of these is the compound of scientific transcendentalism with mentalism advanced by Descartes and Locke in which what is truly real is the order of theoretical material things and the order of minds. A more comprehensive pluralism is the realistic ontology of the early Russell and Moore in their books of 1912 and 1910–11. Here matter, mind, essence and value are held to be equally real or independently and self-subsistently existent. These examples suggest that the main varieties of recognised metaphysical position offer pictures of the world of the kind my definition proposes.

Metaphysics as I have defined it is not identical with the undertaking against which most recent criticisms of metaphysics have been directed. Its positivistic critics, to take the most explicit and notorious of anti-metaphysicians, have understood the *rational means* in question to be those of strict demonstration and the *picture of the world* to be arrived at to be a picture of another world than this, a transcendent and in principle unobservable reality underlying the world that appears to us in experience. On this view the aim of metaphysics is to arrive at necessary and demonstrable truths about existences that transcend all possible experience. Against such a project it has been persuasively argued that no assertions of real existence are necessarily true and susceptible of valid demonstration and, on the other hand, that statements about what is in principle transcendent are neither true nor false and so vacuous or devoid of meaning.

Although this conception of metaphysics is, I believe, mistaken it is not gratuitously so. For, even if it does not apply to the greater part of what are generally recognised as metaphysical theories, it does apply at least to one very fundamental metaphysical argument: the ontological proof of the existence of God. That proof does assert that the existence of one transcendent thing is demonstrably necessary. It provides an answer, furthermore, to what Heidegger sees as the central problem of metaphysics: why should there be anything at all rather than nothing? In showing that there logically must be something, namely God, it implies that the existence of nothing at all is a self-contradiction. But for all its reputation the ontological proof is not a typical or characteristic piece of metaphysical reasoning. The usual procedure of the metaphysician is not pure demonstration but deductive inference from substantial premises already given and the realities whose existence he is concerned to establish are not inaccessibly beyond the world but are already within it.

In reasoning deductively, but not in a purely demonstrative way, the metaphysician is, it is sometimes said, trying to elicit the presuppositions of something, some matter of fact that he takes for granted. Two distinct activities can be regarded as the pursuit of presuppositions. In the first what is sought is the logically sufficient conditions of the data to be explained. Given some admitted fact q it looks for some p from which q follows. This, of course, is the method of hypothesis typical of the empirical sciences. An argument of this kind does not establish the truth of the hypothesis involved, at best it confers on it some degree of confirmation. There are some metaphysical theories that satisfy this description. Herbert Spencer's very general evolutionary doctrine and Alexander's comparable theory of emergence are large-scale, imprecise and minimally testable inductions of this kind. It may also be true that some metaphysical theories are no more strongly founded than such hypotheses in spite of their more ambitious claims. The conclusion that they are the indispensable, and not merely a possible, explanation of the admitted facts may rest on an insufficient elimination of alternatives.

But even if some metaphysical theories are in fact no more than hypotheses confirmed to some limited extent by the data they are introduced to explain they are usually intended to be something more. They are advanced as strong presuppositions of their data, as necessary and not just sufficient conditions. In other words they are claimed to be logical consequences of the admitted data and to that extent metaphysics is a strictly deductive enterprise. But this does not make it a purely demonstrative one. Even McTaggart, the most *a priori* of modern metaphysicians, admitted that one empirical premise was indispensable, the rather modest assumption that something exists. Kant's idea of the data of metaphysics is at once more comprehensive and more characteristic. He took it for granted that we had certain knowledge of mathematics, the natural world and moral obligation. Even Descartes, whose philosophy has a thoroughly demonstrative appearance, can be seen as having made at least one, not very controversial assumption, namely that he was sometimes conscious.

So even if the first general criticism of metaphysics, that there can be no demonstrative proof of substantial assertions of fact and existence, is valid only a small and unrepresentative part of metaphysics is undermined. The refutation of the ontological proof does not carry down as well less ambitious but more usual forms of metaphysical reasoning.

One way of meeting the second general criticism, by showing that the things to which metaphysical theories ascribe reality or ultimate existence are not transcendent in a discreditable way, can be derived from the previous argument about the logical character of metaphysical reasoning. If metaphysical conclusions are, as they purport to be, logical consequences of data which are taken to be true and significant, they must themselves be true and significant. For q can follow from p only if q asserts part of what p asserts. This argument is valid only to the extent that the conclusions are the direct logical consequences of the data. In fact such reasonings very often invoke additional premises, transcendental principles that are held to be both necessary and synthetic. Consider the arguments of Descartes and Berkeley for the existence of God and Locke for the existence of material objects.

Much metaphysics is, admittedly, transcendentalist in this way. In so far as some form of verificationism is accepted it will be to that extent illegitimate. In chapter 5 section 3 I have argued for a generalised form of the verification principle which has the consequence that unless a sentence is itself ostensive it must be introduced or defined in terms of sentences that are if it is to be capable of making statements true or false, if it is to be a possible expression of knowledge. (My departure from the empiricist tradition concerned the subject-matter of ostensive statements which I held to be not private impressions but public material things.) But although this commits me to admitting the force of the positivist criticism of transcendental metaphysics I should maintain that although much

239

metaphysics is in fact exposed to this criticism not all of it need be and not all of it is.

It is possible, in other words, that there should be such a thing as immanent metaphysics (to borrow, and adapt, a phrase of W. H. Walsh's) (Walsh, pp. 84–6). I have said that it is characteristic of ontological theories to distinguish between a category, or some categories, of things that are ultimate and basic and other categories that are, by contrast, dependent or derived. Now the relation of dependence involved may rest on transcendental principles. Descartes and Locke make impressions dependent on material objects, theoretically conceived, with the aid of the causal principle; Berkeley makes ideas dependent on spiritual substance with the aid of the, to him, self-evident proposition that every experience must have an owner. But there is another alternative. The relation of dependence can be conceived as the converse of epistemological priority. It is by appeal to this that phenomenalists reverse the dependence-relation between impressions and material things. For Descartes and Locke there cannot be coherent and passively received impressions unless there are unobservable material causes for them. For Mill and Russell no object can be said or known to exist unless sense-impressions can be said or known to exist, to equip statements about objects with meaning and with justification.

An immanent metaphysics, so conceived, is thus a development of a reductionist theory of knowledge. Such a theory of knowledge arranges the various broad categories of things in a hierarchy ordered in respect of epistemological priority. At the base of the hierarchy are the truly concrete, self-subsistent entities, which can be said and known to exist without reference to things of any other category. Things in the residual categories are introduced into discourse in terms of the concrete, basic entities and established statements about such basic entities provide the justification for claims about the existence of dependent ones in the residual categories.

The process of arriving at such a system must begin with a *prima facie* set of categories, each composed of things whose existence is established or refuted in the same way. (But as the process continues the set of categories may well undergo some modification.) To discover the relations between the different categories we must consider, first, how sentences about things in a given category are introduced into discourse, endowed with meaning and empowered to make statements, and, secondly, we must consider what, and whether, beliefs about things in other categories are required to justify or refute beliefs about the existence of things in the given category, the nature, that is to say, of the logically direct evidence on which their affirmation or rejection depends.

The outcome of a successfully completed undertaking of this kind will be a hierarchy of logically related categories. It will constitute a *general picture of the world*, particularly in picking out some category or categories of things as basic. The members of the basic category or categories are the truly concrete things, the substance of the world in the fourth, Cartesian sense in that they logically require nothing but themselves in order to exist. The dependent categories will fall into two classes. Those which are found to stand in epistemologically satisfactory relations to the basic entities, to be definable in terms of them and to owe their logically direct evidence to them, will be accepted as dependent, derived existences. Those which do not, which could not be defined or supported, at some remove or other, by basic entities, will be discarded as fictitious and illusory. Furthermore the picture of the world in question will have been arrived at by *rational means*, namely by considering the logically necessary conditions, the presuppositions in the strong, not merely hypothetical, sense, of the meaning and justification of statements about the types of thing we are most strongly inclined to suppose there are.

This supposition about which types of thing actually exist is the substantial premise which metaphysics as a deductive, but non-demonstrative, enterprise must begin from. Without it the logical relations of inter-categorial equivalence of meaning and of support will remain hypothetical. Behaviourism, as an account of the relation of behaviour and feelings, says only that *if* there are (said to be or known to be) feelings there must be behaviour. Only if it is further agreed that there *are* mental states can it be inferred that there then *must be* behaviour. If it is agreed that there is behaviour then it can be inferred that there *may be* mental states.

How is this substantial premise, this indispensable factual presupposition of any ontology that is to be more than hypothetical to be arrived at? A generally favoured court of appeal has been common sense. The categories unequivocally endorsed by this criterion no doubt provide an acceptable minimum assumption, a set of appearances that must be saved. But there can well be dispute about how far its endorsement extends. Are gods and disembodied spirits common-sense entities? They certainly figure quite prominently in common speech. Common sense's predecessor in this position was science, mathematical and empirical. Here too there are indeterminacies. Is sociology a science? Or psychoanalysis? Or dogmatic theology?

Each claimant has something powerful to be said in its favour. To doubt the central beliefs of common sense looks either insincere or unhinged. To doubt the conclusions of science is to disdain the most methodically arrived at claims to knowledge and those about which there is least serious disagreement among the informed, those, that is to say, who know how the conclusions were reached. At least we can say that both make a very strong *prima facie* claim to consideration. Any ontology that discards the main beliefs of either as *illusory* is difficult to take seriously. For here, as with the discrimination of logically intuitive beliefs, what have we to rely on but widespread general agreement as to what is true? Where common sense has width, science has closeness, of agreement.

It is important to realise that the substantial premise, specifying which appearances are to be saved, requires only that the existences it endorses shall find a place in *the basic or the derived* categories of the system. What it rules out is the dismissal of the things it affirms as illusory or fictitious. It does not determine which entities are to be basic. Metaphysics as I have conceived it recognises three ontological grades or statuses: (i) the basic, concrete or ultimate, (ii) the derived, abstract or dependent and (iii) the illusory or fictitious. Basic entities are those to which nothing is logically prior and which can be ostensively introduced and intuitively known. Derived entities are those which are epistemologically related to the basic things, can be defined in terms of them and evidenced by them. Pseudo-entities are those which are epistemologically disconnected altogether from the basis.

But very often metaphysicians work with the presumption that there are only two ontological grades: the real on the one hand and the imaginary, the merely apparent on the other. This error I shall christen metaphysical hyperbole. Examples of it are such theses as: only sense-data exist, nothing is real but matter and motion, material things are fictions, matter is in the same position as the Gorgons and the Harpies. In such remarks the ontological distinction between the basic and the derived is superimposed on the common-sense distinction between the existent and the non-existent. That both sides of the ontological distinction fall within the existent side of the common-sense one is shown by the frequent recourse of the hyperbolical to such qualified idioms as *real* existence and *logical* fiction. There is a compensating error in the other direction: metaphysical litotes. This denies that there is any difference between the the kind of existence possessed by basic entities and that possessed by derived ones. It is committed by positivists anxious to conceal the fact that they are metaphysicians. I shall return to it shortly.

I would claim, then, that an interpretation can be found for many of the surprising-looking assertions of metaphysics which treats them as true or false statements but as neither demonstrative nor transcendental. They are very general statements about the logical relations between concepts (and, in the case of basic ones, between

242

concepts and the world) established by deductive reasoning from revisable data provided by common sense, science or any other widespread area of agreement. Not every metaphysical proposition can be interpreted in this way. Some are not ontological, some are argued for on the basis of transcendental principles. But a considerable part of what has traditionally been described as metaphysics is covered by it.

Metaphysics so conceived is exposed, then, to neither of the ordinary positivist criticisms. It is equally immune to the objection of post-positivist linguistic philosophers that metaphysics is plainly incompatible with common sense, with what we all know perfectly well to be true. What this objection really applies to is metaphysical hyperbole of the kind exemplified by McTaggart's remark about matter being in the same position as the Gorgons and the Harpies. Moore's dogged pedestrianism served a useful purpose in deflating the dramatic postures of idealist metaphysicians. But there is a better way. For it does not follow from the fact that a statement is plainly false on a literal interpretation that it is, therefore, not a statement at all but rather a symptom of conceptual disease or a kind of strangulated poetic outburst. Carnap's exemplary treatment of Kronecker's aphorism 'God made the natural numbers; all else is the work of man', which he translated as 'natural-number symbols are primitive, other number-expressions are introduced by definition' (Carnap (2), pp. 304–5), is the model to follow here. An ontological statement about the relations of categories, may lurk behind an unfortunately overdramatic form of words. About a complex and intricate conceptual issue of this kind, which in so far as it deals with the relations of the basic and the derived does not deny the existence of anything but only specifies the kind of existence involved, common sense has no more to say than it has about the denumerability of the real numbers or the irreducibly statistical character of the laws of quantum mechanics.

It follows from this account of immanent metaphysics that positivists in fact pursue it. In a way it is odd that they should ever have denied it. For the main lines of their ontology were derived from Russell's *Philosophy of Logical Atomism* (whose last chapter is called, without irony, 'excursus into metaphysics: what there is') and from Wittgenstein's *Tractatus* (whose opening pages are explicitly ontological). Positivism, indeed, differs from its logical atomist predecessor less in its content than in the view its propounders took of what they were doing.

The original positivist ontology took sense-impressions, reported in Schlick's 'constations' and Carnap's protocol statements, to be basic and defined material things, the theoretical entities of science, the minds of other people and institutions in terms of them (most fully in Carnap's *Aufbau*). Later Carnap and Neurath took ordinary material things as basic and constructed mental states and theoretical entities out of them. Only in a final stage of Carnap's development was a kind of antinomianism reached which made priority relative to a particular systematisation of concepts. His 'principle of tolerance' encouraged the construction of alternative systems and denied that there was any incompatibility between them. Goodman argues from much this position when, in his *Structure of Appearance*, he gives a left-handed justification of his free choice, for purposes of investigation, of a phenomenal basis by saying that he can make nothing of the confused notion of epistemological priority.

But although the positivists could formally support their claim to be non-metaphysicians by making the employment of transcendent principles a defining condition of metaphysics they were in fact aware that their conclusions had a metaphysical flavour and they took pains to deny that their doctrines really had metaphysical implications. Schlick, in *Positivism and Realism*, and Carnap, in *Scheinprobleme in der Philosophie*, argue that positivism does not assert the ontological formula of phenomenalism: only sense-impressions are real. To ascribe this conviction to them, they contend, is to confuse an empirical question about reality with a metaphysical one. The empirical issue about the reality of material objects is to be decided by observation; they are empirically real if observation discloses lawful systems of regularly connected impressions. But the metaphysical question of the reality of an entire category of things is, they maintain, senseless. Yet it is not hard to give such questions a clear sense in their terms, namely, are entities of the kind involved logically connected to the empirical basis? There are three metaphysical possibilities with regard to material things. First, that they are basic (the realistic doctrine of part 2 of this book); secondly, that they are derived (the phenomenalism of Schlick and the early Carnap); thirdly, that they are logically disconnected from experience (the solipsism to which Hume at times approximates and which McTaggart proclaims without perhaps meaning to). Schlick was so convinced that only sense-impressions were given and that transcendental argument was invalid that he failed to perceive the metaphysical nature of the one and the metaphysical implications of the other.

Schlick's defensive manoeuvre has a point, however. By insisting that existence can be ascribed just as much to derived as to basic entities he enters an appropriate protest against metaphysical hyperbole. But the distinction overdramatised by the hyperbolical metaphysician between the basic and the derived should not, as by Schlick, be obliterated altogether. If it is a mistake to assimilate the derived to the illusory it is equally a mistake to assimilate the derived to the basic. For there is something to be said for the view that the existence of the derived is somehow inferior to that of the basic. Descartes's definition of substance formulates the idea that there is a significant difference between dependent and independent existence. Guidance can be found here in the character of our response to the discovery, in philosophically uncontroversial cases, that something which we had thought to exist independently is in fact dependent on something else. Invited to visit a man in order to find out about his organisation one discovers on arrival that it is all in his head, that he and his administrative practices are all that it comes to, and that there is no large apparatus of secretaries, telephones, IBM machines and filing-cabinets. We might well say here that his organisation was nothing more than, was really only, was just or simply him. This way of speaking registers the fact that his organisation has fallen short of our expectations. What engenders expectations of this kind, in general as much as in this particular case, is that logically distinct kinds of existence are referred to in a grammatically uniform manner.

The claim of standard positivism, then, to be non-metaphysical rests partly on a prejudicial restriction of the concept to doctrines with transcendental support and partly on a misinterpretation of the distinction they draw between basic and derived or constructed existence, one that all but obliterated it. This second error is assisted by their assumption that the highly complex and controversial matter of identifying the basic category of things is something quite obvious and indisputable.

Ontology is more deeply embedded or concealed in the work of the positivists' linguistic successors. In Ryle's *Concept of Mind* it takes the form of a rough and ready common-sense materialism in which mental states and abstract entities are derived from straightforwardly material things and happenings. Ryle's position has affinities to the more positivistic, or at any rate formalistic, point of view of Quine's *Word and Object*, with its sustained assault on the idea of the independent existence of meanings, and of Kotarbinski's reism, with its direct realist account of perception, its 'pansomatist' interpretation of statements about minds as statements about bodies and its nominalist rejection of ideal objects (Kotarbinski, pp. 420–8). A comparable view is to be found in Anderson's *Studies in Empirical Philosophy* which holds that there is only one 'way of being', that of observable things in space and time.

To ascribe a reistic ontology to the later Wittgenstein and to Austin would be to fly in the face of their most measured protestations and of the resolute ontological indeterminacy of their practice. Yet Wittgenstein's denial of the possibility of a private language undermines phenomenalism and his view that inner states need outward criteria is incompatible with dualism. Austin insists that his rejection of the sense-datum theory is not made in the interests of some other theory of what the direct objects of perception are and in the course of it he attacks, in a way I have already criticised, the concept of foundations to knowledge. At most, then, these two influential philosophers have very latent ontologies whose characterisation would be so speculative as to make their detailed pursuit unprofitable. It would be tendentiously diagnostic to say more than that they share to some extent the hostility to philosopher's entities (impressions, inner states, abstract essences and so forth) which is the motive power of reism.

In his *Introduction to Logical Theory* Strawson dismisses the project of identifying a basic type or category of things, by reference to which statements about things of all other kinds can be interpreted, as metaphysical in an obviously pejorative sense. He implies that the selection of the basic category must be gratuitous and holds that the translations required if the project is to be brought to a successful completion cannot be carried out. Yet in *Individuals* he introduces a hierarchy of categories of his own: basic particulars (material things and embodied persons), non-basic particulars (events, mental states, theoretical constructs) and non-particulars (qualities, relations). But there is no inconsistency here since the categories in his hierarchy are related in a novel way. He does not argue that, say, bodies are *epistemologically* prior to mental states, but that they are *referentially* prior. He does not hold that discourse about mental states owes its significance and justification to discourse about bodies but rather that there can be no identifying reference to mental states unless a technique for identifying reference to bodies has been mastered. Unless his referential priority can be shown to entail priority of the more familiar epistemological kind there is no more than a formal parallelism between his system and the kind of ontology I have ascribed to Ryle.

Two of Strawson's general points about metaphysics may be mentioned here. In the last chapter of *Individuals* he considers what he calls 'reductionist pressure on non-particulars', that nominalistic 'category-preference' which would ascribe existence, or 'real' existence, only to one favoured category of things. His argument here is, in a sense, purely formal, being concerned to show that a statement of the form 'a is F', where 'a' is a logical subject and 'F' a predicate of any kind, may be regarded as implying the existence of F-ness just as much as it implies the existence of a. He observes that we need not be confused by the ambiguity of 'F-ness exists' which may mean that there are some Fs or that the term 'F' has a meaning. Now in the first of these interpretations 'F-ness exists' is clearly implied by 'a is F', in the strict logical sense of entailment. But what it comes to is no more than that a, and things like it, exist. That 'F' has a meaning is not entailed by 'a is F' but only by the more complicated assertion that 'a is F' is a meaningful sentence. The epistemological question is whether the abstract entities referred to in metalinguistic statements of this order must be accorded basic, independent existence or whether they can be explained in terms of, for example, the observable linguistic activities of concrete human beings. But Strawson does not consider epistemological 'pressures' here.

The other point arises out of the widely-discussed distinction he draws in the introduction to *Individuals* between descriptive metaphysics, exemplified by Aristotle and Kant, and the more usual 'revisionary' kind. Is immanent metaphysics of the sort I have outlined descriptive or revisionary? In so far as it must be based on generally accepted procedures of definition and justification it must be descriptive. To the extent that it 'saves the appearances', and I have argued that it must save some of them, it will underwrite some region of existing discourse. But if it holds some part of existing discourse to be logically disconnected from the basis that confers factual significance and justification, the way of crusading, pristine positivism with theology, it is revisionary. What has often happened is that metaphysical hyperbole has given a revisionary appearance to an articulation of concepts that is in fact descriptive. To the extent that Berkeley's protests that his doctrines are conformable to common sense are acceptable he must be taken to be saying that they are descriptive despite their revisionary appearance. Strawson's distinction applies to the intentions of philosophers at a very abstract level, one at which the relevance of intention to achievement is not perhaps very great. Even when Wittgenstein says that 'ordinary language is all right as it is', seemingly the most resolute of commitments to descriptiveness, there is a concealed revisionary element in the word 'ordinary', a proscription of the unordinary, but undeniably actual, discourse of confused philosophers. At the other extreme, Carnap, the creator of artificial languages, locates their philosophical point in explication, in the clarification and general tidying-up of the better-established part of our current conceptual practices (Carnap (3), ch. 1).

Strawson's notion of revisionary metaphysics is one version of a quite common view that metaphysics is a prescriptive activity, the modern successor of Kant's concept of the regulative. Another version is given by Carnap, in *Empiricism, Semantics and Ontology*, where he says that assertions about the existence of a given type of entity can be understood either as internal to a linguistic framework which contains expressions for them, in which case they are trivially true, or else as proposals or decisions, external to the framework, to the effect that the framework should be adopted. However these proposals have theoretical correlates. For if they are to be rational it must in fact be the case that the framework in question is simple, fruitful and efficient. One might add to his list of requirements the more fundamental condition that the nature of the world is such that the framework should be usable at all to make statements whose truth can be decided, but perhaps this is implied by 'efficient'.

I do not find it easy to take this suggestion very seriously. We may pass over the incoherence involved in Carnap's regarding as theoretical the ascription of plainly evaluative predicates like 'fruitful' and 'efficient' as simply another expression of the special animus of some philosophers towards the rational status of morality which is often left to bear the full brunt of the doctrine that judgments of value are not cognitive. Waiving this *ad hominem* point, why should not metaphysical answers to external questions about linguistic frameworks be identified, not with the proposals to adopt them, but with the theoretical justifications of those proposals; not with 'let us adopt the number-system' but with 'the world is numerable'? But really the whole idea of proposing and deciding to adopt or reject such massive tracts of our conceptual apparatus as the thing-language or the number-system is impossible to accept. These are not open questions. But if we do ask such questions, in an experimental spirit, what we have to do is either to show how the proposed framework can be logically related to some accepted part of our conceptual apparatus, and in particular to its basis, or else establish that it is basic itself. The external question, in other words, is not 'shall we accept this category' but rather 'how does this category work'.

In this final part I shall be concerned with four main categories of things: (i) essences or ideal, abstract objects, (ii) theoretical entities and causal connections, (iii) minds and mental states and (iv) values. These are the principal categories of non-material things to which independent existence has been ascribed by some substantial body of philosophical opinion. It is their non-material character which has led me to bring them together under the heading of 'ideas' in this part of the book. In part 2 I endeavoured to show that common, publicly observable material things were basic or independent existences by showing statements about them to be ostensive and intuitive although not infallible. The target there was the almost universal conviction of philosophers since the earliest times that sense-impressions or appearances are epistemologically prior to material objects. The main argument of part 1 could also be seen as fulfilling a comparable purpose. For if the bundle theory that a material thing is no more than a collection of genuinely qualitative properties were correct it would follow that qualities, which are abstract and non-material even if they are possessed by material things, are prior to material objects.

But, even if I have succeeded in showing that material things are basic, logically independent existences, it does not follow that nothing else is basic. There is no general argument to prove the incoherence of any ontology which asserts a plurality of basic categories. To show that material things alone are logically independent existences the claims made to this status by the main types of non-material things, by ideas in my extended sense, must be defeated. To achieve this purpose I shall follow two procedures. In one type of case, namely ideal objects, causal connections and values, I shall argue that the ideas in question are in a broad sense *reducible* to material things; in another type of case, namely the theoretical entities of science and mental entities, I shall argue that the things in question are not 'ideas' but are in fact material, are, that is to say, *identifiable* with material things.

By essences, ideal objects or abstract entities I mean 'universals' (i.e. qualities and relations), numbers, meanings and propositions. The simplest way of showing their dependent status is the elimination by paraphrase of explicit reference to them, the replacement of statements in which abstract reference occurs by statements in which there is explicit reference only to concrete things. But this is a little too easy and much of my attention will be given to the criticism of two general arguments for the substantive independence of essences which combine great antiquity with current vitality. The first of these is the Platonic derivation of substantive essences from the fact of necessary knowledge. Plato held that necessary knowledge, which was for him the only true knowledge, must have its proper objects, eternal or at any rate timeless. Secondly, there is the more usual argument for the independent existence of universals which is derived from the fact of predication. I shall also be concerned to rebut arguments designed to identify essences with some variety of concrete things, whether material (a possible interpretation of the Aristotelian doctrine of *universalia in rebus*) or mental (the conceptualism or imagism of many seventeenth- and eighteenth-century philosophers). This will be the topic of chapter 9.

By theoretical entities I mean the not ordinarily observable things whose existence is asserted by natural science such as the fundamental particles of physics. One view, that of Locke, holds them to be substantively independent but unknowable. At the other extreme is the instrumentalist or conventionalist theory of Mach and many subsequent philosophers of science which regards them as reducible to ordinary material objects (and these, in turn, to sense-impressions, a view often hyperbolically expressed in the contention that they are 'symbolic conveniences' or 'logical fictions'). Causal connections, on the other hand, I shall argue to be reducible by a defence of a regularity theory of causation that is the heart of Hume's contribution to the subject.

Since most philosophers have held that material objects are dependent on sense-impressions it is not surprising that they should also have been mind-body dualists, holding that introspective statements about the speaker's mind are as basic as statements about his sense-impressions. For both views, I shall contend, rest on the same ultimate conviction: that the foundations of knowledge must be infallible. The main available alternative to dualism is behaviourism, which attempts to reduce statements about mind to logically more complex statements about behaviour. This leads in the first instance to a factually unacceptable account of much self-knowledge, which its defenders have sought to avoid by a theory of avowals which I shall criticise. The remaining possibility is the identity theory which says that mental states are in fact states of the brain. There are conclusive objections to the notion of the older materialism that there is any logical equivalence between statements about things of the two kinds. But the identity theory holds only that as a matter of contingent fact events with mental characteristics are identical with the events with cerebral characteristics with which they are usually associated. Neurophysiology suggests the association but could not establish the identity. To establish this we must seek a principle of identifiability exemplified by other accepted cases of identification.

In the philosophy of Plato the ideal objects or forms are also values: a thing is good of its kind the more perfectly it approximates to its abstract archetype. Something of this idea persists in Aristotle's tendency to assimilate formal and final causes and, since his time, in a tradition of ethical rationalism which ascribes to men a capacity for rational insight into the value-properties of things. It was in the interests of a theory of this kind that Moore elaborated the anti-naturalist principle that has dominated recent moral philosophy. Moore's successors have put his principle to very different uses, in particular to the task of showing that judgments of value are not statements at all, and thus not possible expressions of knowledge, but are really commands or expressions of desire and emotion. The most persistent variety of naturalism can also claim an Aristotelian ancestry, the type of theory that defines value in terms of human satisfaction and suffering. A view of this kind will be defended in chapter 12. If this reduction of value to the mental is correct, and also the doctrine of chapter 11 that mental entities are a particular kind of material ones, the dependence of value on the basic category of matter will have been established.

The final outcome of my inquiry into the concept of substance is, then, a version of a familiar ontology: the materialism of Democritus,

Epicurus, Lucretius, Gassendi, Hobbes and Holbach. This has always been the least well regarded of the major philosophical traditions, despite its fundamental place in the thinking of many scientists and ordinary men. Some obstacles to its acceptance have been external to philosophy, in particular the hold of religious belief on men through institutional pressure and, where that has been absent, through its appeal to their wishes and emotions. Others have been more strictly intellectual, most notably through the theory, almost as old as European thought, that we do not perceive material things directly with our senses but only through the mediation of subjective states of our own minds. The result of this presumption has been that a naturalistic view of the world has had to find its chief philosophical expression through doctrines of a sceptical and subjectivistic kind, such as Hume's, which have a tendency to undermine the naturalistic presumptions which inspired them. In this book I have tried to equip materialism with solid philosophical credentials. In part 1 the general character of material things in space and time was expounded. In part 2 it was argued that such things are basic and primary objects of knowledge. In this part, finally, the attempt is made to show that all the other main kinds of thing it is reasonable to claim we know of are logically dependent upon them.

9

Essence

Abstract reference

The simplest argument for the existence of an order of abstract entities or ideal objects, existing independently of the concrete things in space and time which in various ways exemplify or substantiate them, is based on the fact of abstract reference. There are, that is to say, statements known to be true whose subjects are abstract nouns. Just as the truth of 'the field is green' requires the existence of the field that it refers to, so, it seems, is the existence of infantile mortality in the abstract required by the truth of 'infantile mortality is decreasing'.

It seems equally simple to show that the existence of abstract entities established by this argument is not of an independent, substantial kind. The use of abstract nouns as logical subjects is a convenient but formally dispensable idiom. In general, an abstractly-referring statement can be replaced, without change of meaning, by a statement in which reference is made only to concrete individuals. In the example mentioned the concretely-referring paraphrase would be 'children who die in infancy form a smaller proportion of total births than used to be the case'.

What makes it reasonable to suppose that this kind of reduction can be generally effected is that our ability to use abstract nouns would appear to be derived from our antecedent mastery of the corresponding predicative terms. Before we can understand what cleanliness is we have to understand what it is for a person (or thing) to be clean.

Abstractly-referring statements may be contingent or necessary. 'The dog is a loyal creature' (where it is the species and not a particular animal that is in question) is an example of the first kind, 'the triangle is a plane figure' is an example of the second. 'All (or, perhaps, most) dogs are loyal' reports a factual uniformity. But 'all triangles are plane figures' does not. The latter rests on a rule of language to the effect that the application of the predicate 'triangle' to anything requires that the application of 'plane figure' to it be accepted. But this second-order remark about predicative terms is not a translation of the original, abstractly-referring statement. Nor, *a fortiori*, is the third-order statement to the effect that the rule is a rule. This last could be interpreted as a theoretical assertion about the practices of a given linguistic community. The distinction is parallel to that between moving a king in chess only one square at a time, affirming the rule that it may only be so moved (with which the move itself is a compliance) and asserting that it is a rule of chess so to move the king. An abstractly-referring necessary truth is not, then, a statement *about* words though a statement of this kind asserts the fact that it is necessary.

Statements about words, although they are not required for the reduction to concrete terms of abstractly-referring necessary truths, figure largely, nevertheless, in philosophy and in ordinary discourse. And they themselves make abstract references. The words they explicitly refer to are abstractions, types not tokens as a familiar distinction has it. What helps us to forget this is partly the fact that the name of a word-type in any particular act of reference to it is, or more properly contains, a token of it and partly the fact that nearly all reference to words is reference to word-types. Furthermore the very same expression may be used indifferently to refer to type or token. In 'that remark was uncalled-for' a token is the object of reference, but in 'that remark is ungrammatical' a type is.

But there does not seem to be any objection in principle to the reduction of discourse about types to discourse about tokens. An empirical statement about the way in which a type is used can be seen as a generalisation about sounds and marks, utterances and 'inscriptions'. The project may occasion aesthetic repulsion in the fastidious (Strawson says the suggestion 'is apt . . . to produce nothing but nausea') (Strawson (5), p. 231), but it has its point. Discourse *about* language is, after all, a somewhat sophisticated operation, at once difficult and essential for many purposes to distinguish from discourse in it about other things.

Critics of essentialism, the theory that abstract entities have an independent existence, often object that it ultimately derives from the simple mistake of supposing, as they put it, that general words are proper names. One trouble with this claim is that the notion of a general word is unclear. If it means predicative term, applicable in principle to a multiplicity of things, then it would indeed be a very elementary error to suppose that because we can truly say 'this is heavy' of many things there must be such a thing as heaviness for the word 'heavy' to refer to. In fact it is not because the predicate 'heavy' is supposed to be a proper name that our ability to use it is believed by essentialists to involve the existence of an abstract entity. As we shall see, the argument from predication to abstract entities rests on the inability of a certain extreme kind of nominalism to explain our capacity to apply predicates to things we have never encountered before. But there is another sense of 'general word', namely 'abstract noun', in which, if not exactly proper names, its instances are referring expressions which serve as the logical subjects of true statements.

There remain two connected varieties of abstract reference which offer serious resistance to the project of paraphrase in concrete terms. The first of these is shown in the kind of statement which refers indefinitely to qualities or properties, such, to take a familiar example, as 'Napoleon had all the qualities of a great general'. The trivialising interpretation which construes this as saying that Napoleon had the defining properties, the logically necessary and sufficient conditions, of being a great general may be rejected out of hand. For on this view the original statement is just a pleonastic way of saying 'Napoleon was a great general'. Now if the connection between the qualities in question and being a great general is contingent they may be the necessary or the sufficient condition of great generalhood (or, of course, both). If every great general is FGH then being FGH is the necessary condition of being a great general; if everyone who is FGH is a great general then FGH is the sufficient condition.

Now if the original statement is interpreted as saying that Napoleon had the qualities necessary to being a great general we are not, of course, saying that he actually was one. There is, then, a definite point to the statement. But if we interpret it in the other way it approximates to the assertion that he simply was a great general. There may be, however, a residual point to the more long-winded mode of expression. It could be a way of showing that the judgment of his greatness as a general rested on inductive and not on logically conclusive criteria. And, arising out of that, it may be a way of qualifying the judgment by drawing attention to the imperfection of its grounds.

In either case the statement must, if reasonable, be an inference from a premise about Napoleon, that he was FGH, and a premise about great generals or possessors of FGH, that all great generals have these properties or that all who have them are great generals. The truth of some such generalisation is presupposed by the reference to 'the qualities of a great general'. That there is anything answering to this description would seem to be a presumption of fact, which could only be taken for granted in the absence of a relevant specific generalisation on the basis of some deterministic principle. But if determinism is a matter of fact, and not a conceptual necessity, it must rest on the truth of specific generalisations. If, on the other hand, it is a conceptual necessity then the original statement turns out to be equivalent to 'Napoleon was a great general'.

I conclude that reference to properties of this indefinite kind, if it is not simply a pleonastic idiom, is in principle dispensable, that it must derive its sense from statements in which the properties in question occur predicatively and must derive its justification in any particular case from such statements.

The other, and much more important, kind of abstract reference which offers resistance to concrete paraphrase is reference to mathematical entities. In its historically most distinguished form, as Plato's theory of ideas, essentialism drew much of its support from our pre-eminently certain and indisputable knowledge of geometrical truths. In the truths of geometry reference is made to entities which have no exact concrete instances. Yet there is no logical obstacle to their having instances. If any plot of land were perfectly, geometrically square, a diagonal straight line would divide it into two congruent right-angled triangles. Thus geometrical propositions can be interpreted as subjunctive conditionals about ordinary concrete objects. The concepts in them are idealised, complex concepts of whose applicability to concrete things we can never be sure. But they could, in principle, be properties of concrete things.

The apparent absence of this last possibility constitutes the crucial ontological problem about numbers. Certainly statements about the number 3 can be translated into statements about trios. To say that $3 + 2 = 5$ is to say that every set composed of a trio and a duet with distinct membership is a quintet, quaintly musical though this sounds. But to talk of trios, duets and so forth is to talk of sets or classes and classes are not collections or aggregates. There are two familiar arguments for this distinction. First, membership of a class is not transitive, whereas being part of a collection is. A man can be a member of a football club which is itself a member of a federation of football clubs without being himself a member of that federation. On the other hand if a brick is a part of a wall and the wall is part of a house then the brick is a part of the house. Secondly, a given object or concrete tract of stuff does not have a number in the way that it has a colour or a mass. A particular animal is one horse, many cells and very many molecules. The concrete object is identical with the whole composed of the membership of many different classes and it is classes to which the propositions of arithmetic seem ultimately to refer.

One, rather defeatist, way of attempting to deal with this problem is to insist that classes are a very modest kind of abstract entities, ontological housemaid's babies, as it were. For, with the exception of that slightly marginal entity the null class, they are logically dependent for their existence on that of their members. Identity of membership is the criterion for class identity and a class is wholly and unequivocally specified by the specification of its members.

There is, however, a more forthright way with the difficulty. This is to deny the received view that elementary number-statements (such as 'there are two policemen in the hall') ascribe number-predicates ('two') to classes ('policemen-in-the-hall'). The view is attractive because it is obviously wrong to regard numbers as predicates of the individuals mentioned in the way we can regard 'enormous' as the predicate of the policemen in 'there are some enormous policemen in the hall'. The last statement can be re-phrased 'the policemen in the hall are enormous'. The received view invites us to construe the original statement as 'the class of policemen-in-the-hall is two-membered'.

Benacerraf has pointed out, in an important article, that statements like 'the policemen in the hall are two' are exceedingly artificial and that while 'being two-membered' is a predicate of classes 'two' is not (Benacerraf, p. 59). The closest logical relatives of number-words are, not surprisingly when one reflects on it, the quantifiers: 'all', 'some' and their civilian colleagues 'most', 'few', 'several', 'many', etc. This affinity is further emphasised if we consider the simplest formal analysis of number-statements. 'There are two policemen in the hall' comes out, reading 'P' as 'being a policeman in the hall', '$(Ex) (Ey) Px. Py. x \neq y$' in which nothing but 'P' and formal words occur. (We do not need to add '$(z)Pz \rightarrow z = x.v.z = y$' since the original statement does not strictly imply that there are no more than two policemen in the hall though to do so would not affect the argument.) The natural inference, though Benacerraf does not explicitly draw it, is that number-words are formal words, definite quantifiers to be ranged alongside the indefinite quantifiers of familiar logic.

Drawing on the arguments of chapter 2 it can be pointed out that the concept of one number, namely the number one, occurs in some of the most elementary statements we make. Any statement reporting the presence and existence of a bounded, individuated concrete object, such as 'here is a door', asserts, through the indefinite article, that there is *one* thing of the appropriate kind here. It is from the fact that we have concepts of objects of this kind, and not merely concepts of features or stuffs, that makes counting possible, the primary application of arithmetic.

Benacerraf argues most ingeniously that we should be well advised not to infer from the fact that the number-system can be identified with any of an indefinitely large number of systems of sets which have in common the property of being recursive sequences, in respect, simply, of being such a sequence itself, that number-words are the names of sets. For these identifications have inconsistent (non-arithmetical) consequences yet there is no argument for preferring one of the identifications (that of Frege, say, which holds a number to be a set of sets whose members correspond one-to-one) to the rest. What this special kind of identifiability shows is that the number-system and sets of a certain kind have an analogy of abstract structure in being recursive progressions. As he puts it 'Arithmetic is, therefore, the science that elaborates the abstract structure that all progressions have in common merely in virtue of being progressions' (op. cit., p. 70).

Number-words, then, are not ultimately predicates, so they are not predicates of classes, any more than existence is ultimately a predicate of concepts. To say this is neither to rule out classes nor to deny the heuristic utility of interpreting existential statements as asserting a concept to have the property of being instantiated. Classes or sets can be introduced extensionally through the enumeration of their members ($x = (a, b \ldots n)$) or intensionally through a property ($k = xFx$). But they do not have to be accepted as part of the ultimate furniture of the world if arithmetic is to be sustained. Number-words are formal words and these, as will be argued later, have no ontological implications.

Universals

Arguments for the irreducible existence of abstract entities, outside the philosophy of mathematics and the diagnostic imaginations of some nominalistically-inclined philosophers with their slogan 'general words are not proper names', are based not on abstract reference but on predication. General words, in the more natural sense of predicates, words for qualities and relations, are indispensable to discourse. But they have a problematic feature. We can apply them to things we have never encountered before, once our attention has been drawn to a number of instances both of their application and of their non-application, without hesitation and in a way that agrees with the applications of other people who have been through much the same course of training. How, it is natural to ask, is this possible?

Theories of universals attempt to answer this question. We are able to recognise red things that we have never seen before as red because they and the things we have been authoritatively told are red, the representative instances of the teaching process, have a property in common, that of redness, and this common property is something with which we are familiar and of whose relation to the particular red things in question we are somehow aware. For a thing to be red it has to stand in some relation to the universal redness and for us to tell that it is red we have to be aware of the thing, the universal and the relation between them.

Platonism (essentialism, realism) takes these assertions at their explanatory face value as giving a substantial account of the presuppositions of the possession of qualities by things and of our ability to discover that they possess them. So the question arises: what sort of thing is a universal? There are two quite persuasive reasons for taking it to be an abstract entity, neither in time nor space. The first is that if it were in time and space it would flout the laws of thinghood. It would possess the logically intolerable properties of being in many different places at the same time and of sharing the positions it occupies with other things of its own sort, or bits of them. Redness is dotted about all over space and time, or instances of it are, in a disconnected fashion, and wherever it is to be found there are other universals present as well: coldness or hardness or roughness. The second reason is that there are predicates we understand, and thus properties with which we are acquainted, which have no concrete instances in space and time at all.

The best argument against universals as independent abstract existences is, of course, due to their most renowned exponent. If, in order to find out that something I have just come across for the first time is red, I must first ascertain that it stands in a certain relation to the universal redness, then, before I can ascertain that, I must discover that it stands in a no doubt similar relation to the universal being-related-to-redness. For being-related-to-redness is just as much a universal as redness is and, oddly enough, it is instantiated by the very same things. Since the thing in question is one which, *ex hypothesi*, I have never met before it cannot be one of the authoritative instances of being-related-to-redness. That it has this sophisticated-looking property is something that I have to find out. In doing so I set out on a vicious infinite regress. Nothing, on this view, can ever be found to be red except as the terminus of a logically impossible series of classificatory operations.

Another argument develops a consequence of the theory that has not yet been mentioned. My awareness of the original coloured object is perceptual, but my awareness of the abstract universal redness cannot be since redness is not in space and time. It must, then, be some sort of purely intellectual apprehension. So much for the consequence. But now we must ask what sort of awareness do I have of the categorially hybrid relation between the two? I cannot perceive it with my senses since one of its terms is purely intellectual, but for an analogous reason I cannot be aware of it in an exclusively intellectual way (cf. Passmore, ch. 3).

Against the rather strictly Platonic view that universals alone are real, independently existing entities the arguments of chapter 1 can be brought which sought to show that a thing cannot be simply a complex of qualities.

The original infinite regress argument of Plato's *Parmenides*, the Third Man, is fatal to any theory which tries to account for our ability to ascribe general predicative terms to things by reference to our awareness of some antecedent relation between the thing to be classified and an intermediary, predication-guiding, object. Whatever the intermediary may be, essence, concept or image (or even standard concrete thing), to discover that the thing is so related is to ascribe a further predicate to it, involving a regressive sequence of further explanation.

The only way in which to render such a regress innocuous is to recognise that it is trivial. The purported explanations are in fact only cumbrous restatements of the facts they were introduced to explain. 'This is an instance of redness' says no more than that this is red. Far from the former explaining the latter, the former would not be intelligible unless the latter were already understood. Unnecessary prolixity is not the main weakness of such restatements; they are positively misleading in their spurious suggestions of being informative or explanatory. What makes them look substantial, as Pears has argued, is that they are commonly expressed as giving an account in general terms of something specific (Pears). 'We can recognise all these things as red because they have a common property' loses its informative appearance if the status of its clauses is equalised: 'we can recognise these things as red because they all are red' or 'we can recognise that these things have a given property because they all have that property in common'.

Ordinary empirical predication, then, does not require an antecedent awareness of independently existing abstract entities. It is not the case that we are first shown some authoritatively red things, then somehow become acquainted with the abstract universal redness and finally apply this knowledge by discerning the relation between new concrete things and the universal in question. We are simply shown some red things and then are able to pick out more. To talk of our apprehension of the universal redness is just a confusing way of referring to this ability.

Nominalism

Philosophers critical of Platonism have often proposed as a nominalistic alternative to it the view that the things to which a general predicative term applies are related by similarity. Sometimes this is done explicitly, as a consequence of the principle that general words are not proper names. Sometimes the similarity theory is accepted almost by inadvertence, as by Locke, who, after giving our possession of abstract ideas as his official account of our ability to predicate, goes on to say that our abstract ideas are 'rooted in the similitudes of things'.

There is a familiar argument of Russell's which shows that this manoeuvre is simply a repetition in new terminology of the essentialist doctrine it was designed to replace. It interprets 'a is red' as meaning 'a is similar to the exemplary red things: x, y and z' instead of 'a is related to the universal redness'. But although the things of the exemplary group are more concrete than the universal redness, being similar to them is as much a property as being related to the universal. To find out that a and x are similar we must find out that they resemble the exemplary pair of similar objects etc. Russell carries the argument this far without seeing that it can be applied again to the platonistic doctrine with which he identifies the similarity theory. Not only do the two views stand or fall together; they are both either empty reiterations of the matter to be explained or viciously regressive.

Similarity is, indeed, neither more nor less than the possession of a common property. As Bradley put it, similarity is partial identity. Two things are identical if they have all their properties in common, they are similar if they have at least one in common (and they are exactly similar, qualitatively but not numerically identical, if they have all their strictly qualitative properties in common but differ in position). We may of course recognise that two or more things are similar without being able to put an established name to the respect in which they are similar. But its capacity to provide for this situation is not an advantage peculiar to the similarity theory. For we could just as well say in circumstances of this kind that things have an as yet nameless common property.

Another advantage that has been claimed for the similarity theory over its more ancient rival is that it is well equipped to accommodate the fact that things can be classified together more or less closely, that it allows for differences in degree in a way that the theory of common properties does not. But we can perfectly well speak of things as fairly or nearly or almost or on the whole round, as rather or mostly or predominantly green, as roughly or approximately or up to a point flat and so on. When these possibilities of qualification are ignored it may be that the terminology of common properties is more suggestive than the terminology of resemblances of an unplausible fixity of class-membership. But the common property theory does not entail that the contents of the world are sorted out into a final and definite repertoire of nature kinds that an ideal vocabulary might be used to distinguish.

Full-blooded nominalism is traditionally described in histories of philosophy as the view that the things to which a predicate is applied have nothing more in common than the fact that this predicate is applied to them. One modern version of this is the blunt doctrine that singular words stand for single things and general words for pluralities of things and that that is all there is to it. The trouble with this view is that it fails to notice and account for a distinction between the different ways in which proper names and predicates are related to their extensions. A primary way of acquiring the capacity to use a proper name correctly is to be introduced to its bearer. But I cannot be introduced to the entire extension of a predicate. Even if it in fact has a finite and empirically available extension this is always a contingent matter; in principle predicates are applicable to an indefinitely large multiplicity of things. Not only are we not in fact acquainted with the whole extension of the great majority of the predicates we use, it would be impossible for us to use them in the way we do if we were so acquainted. If a predicate is simply an abbreviation for a list of the names of the things it applies to, every true predication would be analytic and every false one contradictory. Properties can no more be identified with collections of things than things can be identified with collections of qualities.

An unusually articulate exposition of full-blooded nominalism has been given by Hampshire (Hampshire (1)). He rejects the similarity theory, not on the ordinary grounds that it is a merely verbal alternative to platonism, as Russell showed, or that, if taken as substantial, it is regressive, but because he believes that resemblance must always be in a certain respect. 'Resemblance', he says, is not the name of a relation, it is not a descriptive symbol but an incomplete expression. If we say two things are similar without specifying in what respect, we must, if we are saying anything at all, be speaking elliptically, some respect of resemblance must be implied or understood. He holds that it is vacuous to say that two things are similar without having any respect of resemblance in mind because there must always be *some* respect in which any two things are similar. Indefinite judgments of similarity are thus always trivially true.

Now although it is correct to say that any two things must have some respect of resemblance, or, in other words, common property, it must be recognised that these resemblances will vary very greatly as between different pairs in their obviousness or naturalness. For some pairs of things we may have to hunt around with energy and ingenuity to find a respect of resemblance, in other cases it stares us in the face. It is this consideration which undermines Hampshire's generalisation of his claim about the emptiness of judgments of similarity from pairs to collections of any size. 'We may be inclined to think' he says 'that we can conceive a collection of objects, a sufficiently large collection, of which it might not be true that they all resemble each other in some one respect. But could we? That is what I question. Of any finite group of objects, however numerous and apparently heterogeneous they may be, it is always meaningless to deny, and in that sense also meaningless to assert, that they all resemble each other in some one respect' (op. cit., p. 240).

What this contention comes to is that every collection of things, however arbitrarily assembled, is the extension or field of application of some possible predicate. If this were correct it would have disastrous consequences. Suppose I show somebody a large collection of objects a, b, c . . . m and say 'get me another of these'. Whatever he produces must be right since it, let us call it n, will fall into all of the indefinitely numerous collections which have a, b, c . . . m and n among their members and equally whatever he produces will be wrong since it will not be included in all the collections which have a, b, c . . . m in their extension but not n. In these circumstances significant predication would be impossible. It would be impossible to teach anyone the meaning of a general word unless seeing the exemplary instances of its application led him to associate some other things with them and dissociate others from them. In other words the members of some of the collections of things which it is formally possible to construct must have a natural affinity for each other, there must be some collections of things which it is natural to class together in contrast to other collections whose association is arbitrary.

There are two positive arguments for this view. The first is arithmetical in character. For any collection of n things there are $2^n - 1$ non-empty classes of varying size from 1 to n members in which they can be arranged: the class composed of all n of them, the n classes of $n - 1$ of them and so on. 7 things can be arranged in over 100 classes, 10 things in over a thousand, 20 things in over a million. But can 20 things really have a million common properties or respects of resemblance?

A more directly persuasive argument is empirical. Compare a dozen red things with the first dozen things you happen to select in a random way from a cluttered attic or the things in someone's right-hand trouser-pocket (all coins) with the things in his left-hand trouser-pocket (handkerchief, car-key, packet of ten cigarettes, stub of a cinema ticket, piece of string, small pencil, top of a toothpaste tube etc.).

It is surely a fact that some possible classes of things, such as the red or right-hand pocket ones, go naturally together in a way that other possible classes, such the attic or left-hand pocket things, do not. The authoritative exemplification of a predicate with a collection of the first, natural, kind would genuinely serve to introduce it, would make it genuinely reapplicable, in that those to whom it was thus introduced would go on to identify other things as being of the same kind without hesitation and in agreement with each other. Whereas those introduced to a predicate linked authoritatively with a collection of things of the second, arbitrary kind, would either be unable to identify with confidence any other things as having a property in common with, or a similarity to, the members of the original set or, to the extent that they did pick out further things, would not agree with one another as to which they were.

It is the special characteristic of predicates to be reapplicable. But unless some ways of classifying the totality of things were more natural, in the way I have described, than others this would be impossible. It follows that the existence of natural classes is a necessary precondition of our ability to think and speak about the world.

Natural classes

To say that there are properties, then, is to say that there are natural classes, classes introduction to some of whose members enables people to pick out others without hesitation and in agreement. Not all the classes into which concrete things could be arranged are natural. That there are natural classes is entailed by the existence of reapplicable predicates but does not entail it. For there to be a reapplicable predicate the naturalness of some class, a common property or a resemblance, has to be noticed and to be named. That there are unnoticed natural classes is something we may believe on inductive grounds: the richness of our descriptive vocabulary has increased in the past and there is no reason to suppose that it could not be enriched further. That there are noticed but unnamed natural classes is suggested by the difficulty we find in communicating to each other such things as the facial likeness between generally very different people.

The existence of natural classes is, I believe, the very general fact about the world that it is part of the point of platonism to stress, as against the idea that our classificatory apparatus is a wholly conventional fabrication. But conceptualism makes a point too, one that is easier to recognise if the matter is expressed in terms of natural classes rather than common properties. The naturalness of a class depends as essentially on the nature of the observers who classify as it does on the nature of the objects that they classify. Naturalness and arbitrariness should not be conceived either as sharply marked off from each other nor again as wholly determined by factors external to men. What we find natural will depend partly on our relatively fixed perceptual apparatus and partly on our relatively mutable needs and interests.

The point of nominalism is to deny to natural classes or properties an existence independent of the concrete things they respectively comprise or belong to. For some natural classes must have members. Properties that have no concrete instances must be defined in terms of those that have. Furthermore the basic natural classes must have a fair number of members. We cannot learn the meaning of a predicative term ostensively without being shown several instances of its application and the lesson will be pointless if there are not further instances for us to apply it to on our own.

One of the sources of strength of platonism has been the existence of significant predicates that have no application, of properties without instances. That there are such properties must be explained in terms of their reducibility to properties that are actually exemplified. That there are properties without instances does not entail that any particular property could have had no instances, for though there are explicitly definable predicates it does not follow that any predicate could be explicitly defined in a verbal way. There might be intrinsically ostensive predicates. But even if this were false and if simplicity or ostensiveness of predicates were not intrinsic or absolute, but relative rather to which of a number of alternative modes of introducing a system of concepts happened to be selected, it would still not follow that all properties could be uninstantiated. We return here to the conclusion of chapter 1. Both properties and positions are abstract or dependent existences, necessarily encountered in the first instance together, in concrete individuals. Unqualified or empty positions must be defined in terms of occupied ones (in other words there can be no absolute or wholly unoccupied time and space) and equally uninstantiated qualities must be defined in terms of instantiated ones.

Positive theories of universals are not gratuitous exercises in ontological inflation. The protest they enter against the pure, extreme nominalism that sees all classification as the product of arbitrary convention is correct. But in taking a realm of abstract entities to be the factual basis of classification platonism goes too far in the opposite direction, with regressive results. Our ability to use predicates does depend on a fact about the world: that it contains natural classes. But this fact is not logically independent of predication; it can be discovered only through, and stated only in terms of, the use of reapplicable predicates. To say that a class is natural is to say that when some of its members are shown to people they pick out others without hesitation and in agreement. Generalising we can say that there are natural classes that have not yet been noticed or named, classes whose further members *would* be agreed upon without hesitation if some members *were* picked out. That the world is articulated in this way, that it (and we) are so constructed, is a necessary condition of thought and speech. It is an empirical fact that a particular class of things is natural, for not all classes are; one to be established by a test of agreed reapplication. It is even an empirical fact that there are any natural classes at all, though not one that needs investigation for its discovery, any more than that something exists is.

The distinction between natural and arbitrary classes has a number of more detailed uses. It can be used to explain the difference between sets which have a common property and sets related by a family resemblance, the difference between positive and negative properties (the reason for including the formal sign of negation in the predicate for things that are not blue rather than to the predicate for things that are), the difference between projectible predicates, in Goodman's sense, like '*blue*' and non-projectible ones, like '*bleen*' (= blue until next Christmas and green from then on). It applies further to various questions that arise about induction. It explains the intuitive judgments of simplicity for which no satisfactory formal criterion can be provided. It prevents the trivialisation of determinism which ensues from allowing laws to be of any degree of complexity or couched in terms of predicates of any degree of arbitrariness. Finally it resolves certain problems about the analysis of causal statements and counterfactuals which will be mentioned in the next chapter (cf. Quinton (1), pp. 53–8)

Necessary truth

The existence of essences or abstract universals has been thought to explain more than our ability to apply predicates to concrete, perceptible objects. It has seemed particularly apt for the explanation of our knowledge of necessary truth in logic, mathematics and elsewhere, including philosophy itself. On this view an exact parallel is held to obtain between necessary and contingent knowledge. Contingent beliefs have the properties and relations of concrete objects as their subject-matter and are to be verified by observation with the senses. Likewise necessary beliefs state the relations between timeless essences and are to be verified by means of a purely intellectual scrutiny of these supposed entities.

The principle that all necessary truths are analytic is generally intended and understood as a rejection of this account of the nature of necessity. But the issue is complicated by the fact that the technical term 'analytic' is used by philosophers in a variety of different senses. A weakness of the principle, or of the way in which it is usually defended, is that it is treated, in practice, as if it were an inductive generalisation. It is shown or argued that particular specimens, whose necessity is recognised, are analytic in the defender's favoured sense of the term and apparent counter-examples are disposed of by arguing either that they are not, as they seem, necessary or that they are, despite appearances, analytic.

Thirty years ago, when this controversy was at its most active, critics would ask whether the principle was itself analytic. It is put forward as being a necessary truth itself, so if it is not analytic, it refutes itself. Its defenders usually took the view that it is, despite appearances, analytic; but they did not treat it as if it were. Instead of trying to prove it they approached it as if it were a factual hypothesis, to be supported with representative pieces of favourable evidence and by the elimination of apparent counter-examples.

The traditional view that necessary truths must be rationally established by intuition or demonstration is the analogue in this domain of knowledge of the principle defended in chapter 5 that contingent truths of fact must be either intuitive or inferred. In each case an infinite regress argument proves that if a belief is to be known to be true it must be seen or be shown to be so. To prove that a statement is necessarily true it must be inferred from necessary premises, intuited as self-evident, if the regress of demonstration is to be halted. This notion of logically intuitive first principles of demonstration has been brought into disfavour by the discovery that a given body of necessary truths can be derived equally well from distinct sets of axioms. But that several distinct sets of axioms are formally sufficient for the purpose leaves open the question of their material adequacy. That the theorems follow from the axioms is one thing, that the axioms are true is another. But unless they are the theorems are not established as true by derivation from them. A formally sufficient axiom will be materially adequate, in the end, only if it is intuitive. If all necessary truths are analytic a necessary truth is intuitive if its acceptance as true is a criterion of the understanding of the terms it contains.

The analytic principle does not seem to be intuitive in any of its interpretations. That there is controversy about it does not show this conclusively. It is abstractly possible that the upholders of the principle attach a different sense to the word 'analytic', one in which it is a bare synonym of 'necessary', from the sense it is given by their opponents. But if this were the case it could not go undetected: for it would be the only way in which the principle's defenders, seeing it as intuitive, could explain the obvious fact of hostility to it. In fact there are familiar explicit definitions of the words involved, in none of which is either word straightforwardly defined in terms of the other so it is clear that no such general misunderstanding prevails in practice.

To say that a statement is necessarily true is to say that it must be true, cannot be false, is true no matter what is otherwise the case. What it means to say, that a statement is analytic, is more difficult to state because of the multiple interpretations of the term. There are, I suggest, four main, *prima facie* distinct, conceptions of the analytic. (i) In the largest and loosest an analytic statement is one that is true in virtue of the meaning of the terms it contains. (ii) As understood by Leibniz and Kant, an analytic statement is a tautology that repeats itself, asserts no more than it assumes, is an instance of the law of identity whose denial is a contradiction. (iii) As understood by Hobbes, an analytic statement is true in virtue of the conventions of language. (iv) Finally, as understood by Frege and many subsequent logicians, an analytic statement is a truth of logic or is reducible to one with the help of definitions. The identity of these four senses of 'analytic' with necessity is not intuitively obvious, nor is their identity with each other.

There is a general argument to prove that all necessary truths are analytic in the first sense, are true in virtue of the meaning of the terms they contain. But its ease and simplicity suggest that it is non-controversial to the point of triviality. No defender of essences need object to it. A necessary truth is one that is true in itself, true in C. I. Lewis's phrase, 'no matter what'. A contingent truth, as etymology suggests, is one that is true because of or dependently on something else, something outside itself. Now the first concept of the analytic is simply a development or exposition of this idea of the necessary. If a truth is necessary it is true in itself and independently of everything outside it. The statement consists of a form of words with a meaning attached. But the truth of the statement is not determined by the form of words. If 'lie' is defined as 'false statement made with intent to deceive' the words 'every lie is a falsehood' express a necessary truth; but if 'lie' is defined as 'statement believed false made with intent to deceive' then the words express a contingent falsehood. Since there is nothing more to the statement than the words it is composed of and the meaning they are given and since the words alone do not determine its truth, if it is true in itself it must be true in virtue of its meaning. Equally if it is true in virtue of its meaning it does not matter what happens outside it, it must be necessarily true in itself, no matter what.

What shows that the analytic principle in this interpretation is not controversial is the fact that most defenders of synthetic necessary truth, of the possibility of substantive rational knowledge, implicitly subscribe to it. Russell says 'all *a priori* knowledge deals exclusively with the relations of universals' (Russell (1), p. 103). Since universals are the meanings of general terms this amounts to an acceptance of the analytic principle in its widest form. Broad says that a necessary proposition is either one that can be seen to be true 'by merely inspecting it and reflecting on its terms and their mode of combination' or else the logical consequence of such a proposition (Broad, p. 102). Ewing says that the truth of a necessary proposition 'depends wholly on the meanings of the terms used' (Ewing, p. 231). Kneale, finally, says that 'anything we come to know *a priori* . . . is learnt by reflection on the meanings of words or other symbols' (Kneale, p. 636). Pap sums the matter up in a criticism of C. I. Lewis. 'The term "analytic" is sometimes used in the strict sense of demonstrability on the basis of definitions and principles of logic, sometimes in a broader sense which is often expressed as "certifiable as true by reflection upon meanings alone". . . . The broader sense of "analytic" is not distinguishable at all from the sense of "*a priori*" so that by this interpretation the empiricist thesis is true but trivial.'

Pap's last remark is a little exaggerated (Pap (2), p. 89). The move from '*a priori*' or 'necessary' to 'analytic' is not to an obvious synonym, a matter simply of inelegant variation. Although 'necessary' and 'true in virtue of meaning' do mean the same, the identity is not quite intuitively obvious. A simple argument is needed to license the step from one to the other and the notion of being true in virtue of meaning gives a little more clarity of outline to the comparatively amorphous notion of a statement's being true in itself, no matter what.

It is clearly not in this interpretation that rationalists have objected to the principle that all necessary truth is analytic. The real issue between them and their opponents concerns the conceptions they respectively adopt about the nature of the meanings whose relationships determine necessary truth. For the rationalist these meanings are independently existing essences whose nature and relations are to be apprehended by intellectual scrutiny. For the adherents of the analytic principle in its stronger, disputable form the relations of meanings are bare identities and exclusions, determined by linguistic convention. This emerges most clearly in the quotation from Russell, with its explicit reference to universals, but the same conviction underlies the other positions mentioned.

I have argued in earlier sections of this chapter that predicates or general words can have meaning without there being independently existing abstract entities which are their meanings. That argument is an objection to the interpretation given by rationalists to the weak, inclusive sense of the analytic principle. It is desirable all the same to examine their criticisms of the stronger forms of the analytic principle. For if these cannot be countered the theory of essences is to that extent restored. Furthermore in rejecting platonism I conceded that it made a point, if in an ontologically extravagant way, against the kind of extreme nominalism which takes all classification to be arbitrarily conventional. If I admit that the existence of reapplicable predicates implies a non-conventional fact about the world it might seem that I cannot consistently maintain that the relations of predicates to one another, as stated in necessary truths, are a matter of convention.

In fact the inconsistency is only apparent. Necessary truths, I shall argue, rest on identity of meaning, partial or total, between different predicates. Predicates with the same meaning express the same property. That there is a property to express is not a matter of convention but the choice of predicates to express it is and so is the fact that more than one predicate does so. The synonymy of predicates may be brought about either by verbal definition or by their having been ostensively introduced by members of the same natural class. The naturalness of the relevant class is not conventional but the nature, and the multiplicity, of the predicates introduced to pick out its members are. I shall try to justify this claim in the next section.

But before I turn to the stronger forms of the analytic principle I must say something about the distinction between the *a priori* and the empirical which I have so far largely ignored. For Kant this distinction coincided with that between the necessary and the contingent. But here again the coincidence is not quite intuitively obvious, if only because necessity and contingency are kinds of truth (or falsehood) while to distinguish statements as *a priori* and empirical is to divide them in accordance with the way which they are *found* to be true (or false). Nevertheless for anyone who accepts the generalised form of the verification principle discussed in the introduction to part 3 the connection between the two distinctions is very close. If a statement is contingent, if it depends for its truth (or falsity) on something other than itself then this external determinant of truth-value must be accessible in principle, an object of possible experience or at least something to the issue of whose existence experience is relevant.

However there is some reason to accept a concept of the empirical which does not make all contingent statements empirically decidable in principle. Popper maintains that no statement containing an unrestricted existential quantifier is empirical on the ground that no such statement can be conclusively falsified (Popper (1), p. 69). He prefers conclusively falsifiability by experience over confirmability or disconfirmability by experience as the criterion of the empirical for two main reasons. The first is that science consists mainly of universal statements, essential for prediction and explanation. The only existential statements it contains are restricted or circumscribed. These assert that something of a given kind exists, not at some unspecified place and time, but in a circumscribed spatio-temporal region and can thus be conclusively falsified. Secondly, an empirical statement is one that can be empirically tested. But to test something is to see how much it can stand, to see whether it can be destroyed. So the empirical test of a statement is its exposure to the possibility of refutation, of elimination as a rational belief. What cannot in principle be refuted cannot be genuinely tested.

If this proposal is accepted it follows that all unrestrictedly existential statements are *a priori*. Yet many such statements are obviously synthetic. However these are not the synthetic *a priori* propositions of ordinary rationalism, for there is nothing to suggest that they are anything but contingent. Popper agrees that they cannot be shown to be either true or false so they are clearly not necessary. There is thus no conflict between this version of the view that there are synthetic *a priori* statements and the principle that all necessary truths are analytic.

If the *a priori*-empirical and analytic-synthetic distinctions are both seen as attempts to elucidate the primary distinction between the necessary and the contingent it is not hard to see why the idea that there are synthetic *a priori* propositions should constantly recur, although there is no parallel attraction about the idea of propositions at once analytic and empirical. For the terms 'analytic' and 'empirical' are the positively defined members of their respective pairs, while the notions of the synthetic and the *a priori* are residual or complementary. If a statement is analytic it is true in virtue of its meaning, if empirical its truth can be established only by recourse to experience. So these two properties are plainly exclusive of one another. But a synthetic statement is one whose meaning does not determine its truth and an *a priori* statement is one whose truth or falsity is not determined by experience. There is no obtrusive impropriety in supposing there to be statements which have both characteristics, their truth-value being determined neither by meaning nor experience. If, as Popper's concept of the empirical implies, there are statements whose truth-value is not determinable at all, it follows that they will be of this kind.

Tautologies and convention

The claim of the weak analytic principle that we discover the necessary truth of a statement by reflecting on the meaning of its terms, a claim, as I have shown, that is not seriously disputed, is more suggestive than explanatory. What are we supposed to look for in this process of reflection? How can meanings be so connected or related in a statement that its falsity is ruled out and its truth, therefore, certified?

The answer proposed by Leibniz can be seen to rest on a general account of the nature of statements embodying two kinds of factor (I shall call them the assumption and the assertion) which generalises the familiar idea that every statement has a subject or referring element and a predicate or describing element. This duality of factors has a categorical and a hypothetical form. In a categorical statement 'S is P' to utter the subject-expression 'S' is to assume the existence of what it refers to. The statement then goes on to assert the predicate 'P' of the S that has been assumed to exist. In a hypothetical statement 'if p then q' the antecedent makes the hypothetical assumption that the fact obtains which 'p' by itself could be used to state categorically. According to the Leibnizian view a categorical necessary truth is of the form 'the F is F' and a hypothetical necessary truth is of the form 'if p then p'. In either case denial involves contradiction: 'the F is not F' and 'p and not-p'.

On this view the meaning of a statement rules out the possibility of its falsehood and so makes it necessarily true if the statement makes some assumption, categorical or hypothetical, as to how things are and then does no more than assert all or part of what has been assumed. It thus runs no risk of falsification. It guarantees that what the statement asserts is correct by assuming it. Unless the occurrence of something incompatible with what is asserted is ruled out by the assumption of the statement the assertion may turn out to be false. Necessary truth, then, depends on repetition.

There will be no objection to the claim that if a statement is repetitive or tautologous in this way it is necessarily true. It is the converse claim that is controversial. But those who reject it give no clear account of the relation between meanings other than identity that they have in mind. Blanshard, for example, says that 'elements really different may be intelligibly connected' (Blanshard, vol. 2, p. 408). Certainly elements that are verbally different may be identical in meaning. And elements that differ in meaning may be intelligibly connected to the extent that a reason can be given for the fact that one applies to everything to which the other applies. But these admissions do not conflict with Leibniz's version of the analytic principle. In the first necessity remains grounded in identity of meaning; in the second the 'intelligible connection' is not an identity of meaning but it is not a necessary connection either.

Ewing (op. cit.) has attempted to explain the alleged difference between necessary connections that do and do not rest on identity of meaning by distinguishing two senses in which the conclusion of a valid deductive inference may be contained in its premises. It may be contained as a part of the premises or it may be merely entailed by them. An example of entailment not resting upon identity that he offers is that of q by the conjunction of p and if p then q. Admittedly the categorical assertion of q is not explicitly present in the premises nor is there an explicit self-contradiction in the joint assertion of the premises together with the negation of the conclusion. But we can easily turn the formula '(if p then q) and p and not q' into an explicit contradiction by substituting 'not (p and not q)' for 'if p then q', a substitution licensed by the fact that the substitute is at least part of the meaning of 'if p then q'. And the same is true of all other formal entailments.

The conception of necessary truths as descriptive of the structure of a timeless realm of independently existing essences encourages this idea of intelligible connections. Concrete things have a multitude of distinct kinds of relations to one another, so it is natural to think that the same is true of the realm of essences. But this conception owes its appeal to its indefiniteness. When its defenders are called on to specify the relations, other than identity, total or partial, that necessary truths describe, what they give can either be shown to be reducible to identity, as is logical entailment, or are question-begging, like necessary connection, which describes the relation in terms of the logical properties of its description, in other words as a relation, other than identity, whose description is a necessary truth.

If the necessity of a statement arises from the meaning of the words that compose it, it is easy to see why necessity should be regarded as the outcome of linguistic convention. For it is to convention that words owe their meanings. The Hobbesian version of the analytic principle makes necessity unmysterious by treating it, not as something objectively discoverable in the nature of things, but as a matter of human decision. The impossibility of falsification that is characteristic of necessary truths is not a brute fact, it is brought about by our refusal from the start to let any falsification occur.

One objection to this view is of an emotional character. Those who know the difficulty of mathematical work from direct experience resent what they see as an insult to mathematicians. The theorems of mathematics are not arbitrary whims; mathematicians do not just decide that they are true, they find it out after heavy labour. The Leibnizian idea that mathematical propositions are tautologies, with its apparent implication of obviousness and triviality, calls forth the same kind of response. In fact neither offensive implication follows from the versions of the analytic principle in question. It is often easy to verify a complex mathematical proposition by progressive tautologous substitutions which reduce it to an obvious and explicit identity. But it may be very hard to discover the proposition in the first place. It is hard to discover the general formula for the solution of quadratic equations, but it is a simple matter to verify it by substituting the complex expression it equates to x for the occurrences of 'x' in the formula $ax^2 + bx + c = 0$. An identity is none the less an identity for being deeply hidden. Similarly the view that necessary truth is conventional does not trivialise it, any more than chess is rendered trivial and intellectually negligible by the indubitable fact that it is conventional. To say that it is a game is not to assimilate it to the activity of a child idly kicking a stone down a road.

If necessity is conventional it follows that the conventions actually in force could have been different from what they are. It is generally agreed that the meanings of many non-logical words have changed in the course of time. But it is argued that there is a limit to this alterability. Some would say that no logical law can be replaced by some other rule for the use of logical words. Others, more cautiously, would say that the law of contradiction, at least, is indispensable. The existence of alternative logics with no law of excluded middle is a difficulty for the wider view about the limits of convention. The defence that they are only called logics by courtesy is too like obscurantist resistances to non-Euclidean geometries to be very convincing. But there is a sense in which the law of contradiction is unalterable. No system that rejected it could be used as a logic, a system of the general rules of inference of a language, since no practice of utterance that failed to abide by the law would be a language.

If an utterance has meaning there must, in general, be occasions on which it is correct and occasions on which it is incorrect to make it. For this to be so is for there to be a rule for its use. To impart such rules to others we must be able to correct their errors and for our own use to be critical we must be able to cancel our mistakes. Language is rule-governed utterance and conventions of affirmation and negation are the indispensable minimum of rules. The difference between a language and a practice of making arbitrary noises is that the former embodies a concept of negation. The law of contradiction is an essential part of all definitions of negation, even if the law of excluded middle is not. But this does not show that the law of contradiction is not conventional. It shows, rather, that it is a convention we have to adopt if we are to have a language, if we are to speak rather than babble. But to speak a language is still a choice and the law of contradiction still a convention, even if their abandonment would ensure that we should be unable to say, or even to realise, what we had done.

Most arguments against the view that necessity is conventional start by misstating it. Broad (op. cit.) says that if necessary truths report the existence of linguistic conventions they must be synthetic and empirical. If that is what they did they would be; but what the conventionalist thesis says is that they are made necessary by convention, not that they describe the conventions that prevail. To move your knight in accordance with the relevant rule of chess is not to say that that rule obtains. It is argued again that if the assertion of a necessary truth were a matter of convention it would be a free choice. But, according to the conventionalist thesis, although the necessity of a statement *reflects* the existence of a convention its assertion is not ordinarily a way of *instituting* it. A man who moves his knight in accordance with the rules of chess is not reinventing the game and when he moves it in a way the rules forbid he is not setting up a new game of his own. From time to time new conventions are introduced in this comparatively inarticulate way. William Webb Ellis invented rugby football, by being the first man to pick up the ball and run with it. The performance of a counter-conventional act may be striking enough to recommend a new convention by a concrete display of its possibilities.

C. I. Lewis raises the more serious objection that conventionalism fails to distinguish sentences from the propositions they express (Lewis (2), pp. 107–10). Since the meaning that a sentence has is due to convention, it is convention that determines the fact that a sentence expresses a necessary proposition. But, he goes on, it does not follow, and is not true, that the necessity of the proposition expressed is conventional. The relation of meanings in which it consists is an objective and timeless necessity which obtains whether or not anyone is aware of it or has conventionally instituted any terms to express it.

This argument is incompatible with the aim of most defenders of synthetic necessity to distinguish between trifling, verbal, analytic necessities, like 'all bald men are bald' and serious, substantial, synthetic ones, such as 'nothing can be red and green all over' or 'there is no largest prime number'. But if the latter two owe their necessity to non-conventional relations of meanings which they are used by convention to express so does the former. If the convention governing 'all' were exchanged for that now governing 'not all' the sentence would come to express a contradiction but the proposition it originally expressed would remain, on Lewis's view, necessarily true. So those who accept Lewis's argument must admit that no necessary propositions whatever are true by convention and, in consequence, that there is no basic difference of logical character between the most blatant tautology and the most elaborate mathematical theorem, something which it is part of the point of the analytic principle to establish.

I want to argue that the distinction Lewis's argument draws between the conventionally introduced relations between words in virtue of the meanings they have been given and the supposedly non-conventional relations between the meanings themselves cannot be drawn. The reason for this is, very briefly, that there is no way of identifying the meanings that words have that does not refer to the words that have them. Here, as elsewhere, identity does not relate objects in themselves but only objects under a certain description.

It is easiest to consider this issue in connection with the exactly parallel problem about the conventionality of verbal definitions. Both sides agree that the identity of meaning of two synonymous *words* is established by convention. But the anti-conventionalist maintains that there is also a non-conventional identity of concepts, lying behind the conventional synonymy of words, which would still exist even if no means of expressing the concepts had ever been devised. The actual use of the expressions 'bachelor' and 'unmarried man' is something that has been set up by convention in the course of history. But it is only because there is a non-conventional identity between the timeless and objective concepts in question that the expressions are synonymous.

There is a suggestive incoherence here. On the one hand there are said to be two concepts involved, one corresponding to each of the synonymous expressions; on the other there is said to be only a single concept which is the meaning common to both. The anti-conventionalist detects two senses in statements of identity of meaning where in fact there is only one. He wants to say that it is a matter of convention that the meaning of 'bachelor' is the same as the meaning of 'unmarried man' but that it is an objective, non-conventional fact that *this* concept (the one conventionally expressed by the word 'bachelor' as it happens) is identical with *that* one (the one conventionally expressed by the phrase 'unmarried man'). But identity-statements do not correlate objects considered in themselves, they can correlate objects only under a certain description. The only way in which concepts can be identifyingly referred to is by means of the words that express them. Of course every concept, like everything else, is what it is. But we can only say what it is by correlating one description of it with another.

I can know what the meaning of 'F' is and know what the meaning of 'G' is without realising that 'F' and 'G' have the same meaning. But this does not imply that there is an objective relation of self-identity, over and above the identity asserted of the concept under two descriptions. The reason for this is that I can know what the meaning of 'F' is without knowing everything about the meaning of 'F'. To know the meaning of a non-logical term is to be able to decide about any particular thing, actual or possible, whether or not the term applies to it. To decide whether two terms are the same in meaning I have to exercise this capacity by considering whether there is any particular thing, actual or possible, to which I would apply one term but not the other. The meaning is not some kind of wholly transparent object present to consciousness in all its details.

The object referred to in a true identity-statement does not have, in itself, the duality which makes identification possible. Duality arises only through the ways in which the object is described and conceived. One identity-statement can be grounded in another, for identity is transitive. But inferences of this kind will only replace some descriptions by others. They will never terminate in statements in which the object, innocent of all description, will be identified with itself.

It is perhaps worth saying that this argument does not have the disconcerting consequence that all statements of identity are conventional. In statements of identity of meaning the correlated terms (of the form 'the meaning of x') presuppose a fact (that 'x' has a meaning) which obtains wholly by reason of a convention (to understand 'x' in that way). But the facts presupposed by 'the man I met' and 'her best friend' (viz. that I met someone and that she has a preferred friend), the correlates of a typical identity-statement, are ordinary empirical facts.

Logical truths

In recent discussions of the subject the most favoured concept of the analytic has been Frege's which defines an analytic statement as one for whose proof nothing is required beyond logical laws and definitions of non-logical terms (Frege, p. 4). Whatever its explanatory merits this account of the analytic does not have the view that all necessity is logical as a direct consequence. Frege thought that geometry was necessary but, in this sense, synthetic. However there is a general argument, present in outline in Wittgenstein's *Tractatus*, to show that every statement true in virtue of its meaning (and I have argued that this is uncontroversially a feature of all necessary truths) depends for its truth on logic and definitions.

The argument starts with the question: how are expressions given the meanings from which the necessity of statements arises? It must be either indirectly, by definition in terms of other expressions already understood, or in a direct way. The direct definition of non-logical terms is effected by ostension, by their correlation with observable features of the world. Logical terms, on the other hand, are implicitly defined by means of logical laws. The logical laws that are implicitly definitive of the basic logical terms supply an initial stock of necessary truths. Others are generated by substitution in them in accordance with explicit definitions. Two non-logical terms with the same ostensive definition can be explicitly defined in terms of each other (that follows from the theory of natural classes). Two such terms with different ostensive definitions are distinct in meaning and are thus not related in the way that gives rise to necessity. Therefore the only conventions of meaning that can render necessary the statements that concern the terms they apply to are (i) logical laws that implicitly define logical terms, (ii) explicit definitions and (iii) identical ostensive definitions of non-logical terms which could be replaced by explicit definitions of either in terms of the other.

This argument can be criticised for assuming that the expressions of our language can be exclusively separated into the logical and the non-logical. Although this assumption looks reasonable enough at first glance the argument does not in fact represent logical and non-logical terms as the assumption requires in a necessarily exclusive way. For it takes a logical term to be one whose meaning is *wholly* determined, in the end and after explicit definitions have been applied, by logical laws and a non-logical term to be one whose meaning is *wholly* determined, in the end, by ostension. It ignores the possibility that there are mixed terms whose meaning is partly fixed by ostension and partly by the kind of implicit definition given for the basic logical terms. Simple descriptive predicates like 'red' suggest that this possibility is realised. It is not sufficient for an understanding of 'red' to have been shown enough red things to be able to tell whether further things are red or not. The use of the word must also be circumscribed by the realisation that if a thing is red it cannot also be of another colour as well. Must we then admit that some necessities depend on non-logical laws, implicitly definitive of non-logical terms, as well as logical laws and explicit definitions? To decide the question we need a criterion for distinguishing between logical and non-logical laws and terms. But whatever the answer may be it will affect only the number of types of convention that have to be distinguished, it will not affect the view that if a statement is true in virtue of its meaning it is true by convention.

Before considering this obscurity in the Fregean definition of analytic, and thus in the principle that all necessity is logical, there are three preliminary points that should be noticed. First, Frege's definition derives some of its attraction from the idea that it improves on the Leibnizian definition in terms of identity and contradiction in that it does not accord any specially elevated place to the traditional laws of thought. Russell and others believed this elevation to be a mistake because the ancient laws did not figure in any of the recognised sets of axioms sufficiently powerful for the derivation of ordinary logic. But perhaps the laws of thought were dethroned prematurely. One good reason for giving a special place to the law of contradiction has emerged already: no system without it is a logic. Furthermore it plays a crucial part in two non-axiomatic methods of demonstration by *reductio ad absurdum* and it is presupposed by the mechanical method of truth-tables in the rule that a sentence-element cannot have more than one truth-value.

Secondly, the contracted version of Frege's definition now in general currency which holds a statement to be analytic if it is true in virtue of logical laws alone or if it is reducible with the help of definitions to a law of logic has led some philosophers to conclude that logical laws are, therefore, not themselves analytic. This is, of course, a misunderstanding. Whatever is thus reducible to a law of logic is identical in meaning to it and must have the same logical status as it has.

But, thirdly, this mistaken inference does point to a weakness of the Fregean definition which is that it wholly trivialises the statement that logical truths are analytic. It would certainly be an achievement to show that all necessity is logical. But to do so does not throw any light on the nature of logical truths themselves and, furthermore, it can be done only after it has first been shown that all necessary truths are analytic in the wider sense that they depend for their truth on their meaning.

The main defect of the Fregean definition, one that must infect the corresponding version of the analytic principle, remains to be discussed: the fact that the concept of a logical law or truth on which it turns is thoroughly indeterminate. At one end the concept is fixed firmly enough by highly abstract elementary principles which would be universally accepted as laws of logic. But how far down into the body of truths as a whole does the class of logical truths extend?

A familiar and reasonable criterion for a statement's being a logical truth is that logical terms alone should occur essentially in it. When Russell made this suggestion he was aware of its limitations: it provides a necessary, but not a sufficient, condition of being a logical truth (Russell (3), pp. 202–3). In the plainly contingent statements that something exists $((Ex)x = x)$, that at least two things exist $((Ex)(Ey)x \neq y)$ . . . logical terms alone occur essentially. The further necessary condition required to exclude such cases is that logical truths are necessary. If logical truth is thus defined as a necessary truth in which only logical terms occur essentially, the Fregean version of the analytic principle takes the form: every necessary truth in which non-logical terms occur essentially can be reduced with the help of definitions to one in which they do not.

If this principle is to be effectively discussed a precise account of what it is for a term to be logical is needed. It would be obviously circular to define a logical term as one that occurs essentially in a logical truth. Essential occurrence in necessary truths is not much better. In the first place it would make every term logical since every term occurs essentially in some necessary truth: 'bachelor' in 'all bachelors are unmarried', 'red' in 'nothing can be red and green all over'. Secondly, this proposal would trivialise the principle under discussion in equating logical and necessary truth by fiat.

The influence of Tarski has led to a widespread scepticism about the possibility of arriving at any general criterion for logical terms. Quine simply enumerates a set of logical primitives, regarding these and anything wholly definable in terms of them as logical (Quine (1), pp. 1–5). In assembling his list of primitives he adheres to a roughly conformist principle of selection: the list consists of the smallest set of terms capable of yielding the vocabulary of what has traditionally passed as logic.

Is there a more explanatory and less passive alternative to this procedure? It is an agreed and obvious feature of admitted logical terms that they are neutral as between topics, that they can figure in discourse about any sort of subject-matter. The essential character of logical terms can be made clearer if the reasons for this virtuosity are considered. For it is a consequence of the particular way in which logical terms are endowed with meaning. Whereas topical, non-logical terms are introduced, directly or indirectly, by some kind of ostension, which correlates them with particular regions or features of the extra-linguistic world, the topic-neutral terms of logic are introduced by implicit definition. The ordinary concept of negation, for example, is introduced by the laws of contradiction and excluded middle, which are general formulae whose variable elements can take statements about any subject-matter whatever as their values. Logical terms are, it could be said, purely syntactical. Their function is to arrange or organise discourse, not to refer to anything in the extra-linguistic world. We can thus define a logical term as one whose meaning is wholly specified by implicit definitions.

In his *Truth By Convention* Quine makes an objection to this proposal, which has been very influential but is, I believe, mistaken. Comparing various ways in which mathematics might be reduced to logic he comes finally to the view that the two disciplines might be identified as containing only terms whose sense is wholly introducible by conventional assignment of truth to implicit definitions. His objection is that this criterion is entirely undiscriminating. Certainly sense can be given by implicit definition to 'not', 'if' and 'every' but so, he says, can it to every other term. The example he considers in detail is 'later than'. Its meaning can be fixed, he claims, by the conventional assignment of truth to all statements in which only 'later than' and the admitted logical primitives occur essentially. From this he infers that the technique can be extended to any term whatever (Quine (5), p. 94).

Now it is true that the statements in which only 'later than' and the usual logical primitives occur essentially can be regarded as logical truths. But they do not suffice to fix the sense of 'later than' and a part of this term, the element 'late', does not occur in them essentially. The relevant statements are that if x is later than y, y is not later than x and that if x is later than y and y than z, then x is later than z. These two statements are instances of general principles of asymmetry and transitivity for the radically topic-neutral term 'more than' or 'more ϕ than': (i) $(x)(y)(\phi)(x > \phi y) \rightarrow \sim (y > \phi x)$ and (ii) $(x)(y)(z)(\phi)((x > \phi y) . (y > \phi z)) \rightarrow (x > \phi z)$. But these wholly topic-neutral necessary truths give only part of the meaning of 'later than'. It must also be correlated with particular pairs of temporally distinct events. Statements reporting these indispensable correlative facts will not serve as implicit definitions. First, though this is not a reason that would weigh with Quine, because they are contingent. Secondly, because they must contain terms other than 'later than' and any logical primitives that may occur essentially in them. These further terms will identify the temporally distinct events involved, as in 'the accession of Richard I is later than the accession of Henry I'.

The necessary asymmetry and transitivity of 'later than' do not, then, refute the principle that all necessity is logical. The statements specifying these properties of the predicate are instances of logical truths, in which only 'not', 'and', 'if', the universal quantifier and the topic-neutral term 'more ϕ than' occur essentially, while the element 'late', with its topical reference to time, occurs vacuously. Strawson has suggested that there is a residual deficiency in this account of the matter. The principles of asymmetry and transitivity do not wholly fix the sense of 'more ϕ than' since they remain necessarily true if 'less ϕ than' is put in its place and yet 'more' and 'less' do not mean the same. The solution of this problem is that every statement of the form 'x is more ϕ than y' is equivalent to some statement of the form 'x is less ϕ than y'. If x is more F than y then x is less non-F than y. Possible values of 'ϕ' occur in complementary pairs: old and young, hot and cold, large and small.

Can other necessary truths that are equally resistant to reduction to ordinary logical laws be treated in the same way? Consider the familiar counter-example to the Fregean form of the analytic principle 'nothing can be red and green all over'. The only definition of 'red' that would make 'this is red and green' reducible to an explicit contradiction defines 'red' as 'not green and not blue and . . .'. This is objectionable, first, because it is open-ended and, secondly, because it can be applied only to one colour term if circularity is to be avoided and in that case 'nothing can be blue and white all over' and the rest would still resist reduction.

It could be said that 'nothing can be red and green all over' is an instance of the highly abstract law: 'nothing can be a member of two species of a genus'. Like the transitivity of 'more ϕ than' it fixes only a part of the sense of the terms involved but it is as topic-neutral as could be wished. This is too informal a step to settle the question of whether all necessity is logical. But it does formulate the problem in a way that allows it to be settled by decision. If the principle is interpreted narrowly, as saying that all necessary truths can be reduced with the help of definitions to necessary truths in which only terms whose meaning is *wholly* given by implicit definitions occur essentially, then 'nothing can be red and green all over' is a falsifying exception to it. If, on the other hand, it is interpreted broadly, as saying that all necessary truths rest on the implicit definitions of their terms, or are reducible to those that do, then the principle is correct.

In this chapter I have considered three main lines of argument for the attribution of independent existence to essences or abstract entities, arguments that derive it from abstract reference, from the characteristic reapplicability of general, predicative terms to new instances and from the fact of necessary knowledge. I maintained that abstract reference can be eliminated, that it is an idiom of abbreviation without ontological significance. But abstract reference is too pervasive a feature of discourse for it to be possible to do more than illustrate the manner of its reduction. The reducibility of ordinary statements with abstract subjects (politeness, tuberculosis, the dog etc.) is perhaps not likely to be disputed. But I confronted a more contentious case, that of mathematical truths, often interpreted as making an ineliminable reference to classes. I rejected the platonistic view that our capacities of predication imply the independent existence of universals but conceded that theories of universals make a substantive point, one that could be less troublesomely expressed by asserting the existence of natural classes, as against extreme nominalism. Finally, I argued against the theory that necessary truths must be understood as descriptions of the relations between intellectually inspectable abstract entities. Starting from the uncontentious position that necessary truths are, in some sense, true in virtue of their meaning, I argued that the relevant facts about meaning were the outcome of conventions, were either identities of meaning, established by explicit definitions or ostensive definitions by means of the same natural class, or else logical laws, these being conceived as implicit definitions of purely syntactical, topic-neutral terms.

10

Theory

The nature of science

It is often supposed that the main feature that distinguishes science from ordinary factual knowledge is generality. This is doubly incorrect: much common knowledge is general and not all science is. These points are almost too obvious on a moment's reflection to deserve any very elaborate support. That water puts out fires, that people die if their heads are cut off, that they get angry when they are struck are not scientific truths, in the first instance at any rate, even if the regularities they state come to be absorbed into science by being explained in terms of scientific laws. Empirical discourse with the word 'because' in it is not on that account scientific. But the use of that word, and, as I shall argue, of its close correlate 'if', presupposes the acceptance of some general proposition. The kind of factual inference that the employment of these words indicate is, as Jonathan Bennett has shown in *Rationality*, indispensable to anything that could count as a rational use of language. But science does not monopolise rationality; it is, rather, a particularly dogged and determined way of being rational.

On the other hand a great many propositions of science are singular. Explanation and prediction are at least characteristic scientific activities. On some views they, and not the theoretical understanding of the world, are the essence of scientific activity. Yet explanations are often and predictions are usually singular in form. A particular chemical reaction occurred because that particular substance was introduced into the solution. The sun's light will be eclipsed by the moon at a particular time on a particular day.

I shall indeed argue that general statements, or theories in a wide sense of the term, are the principal aim of scientific inquiry in a way that they are not the aim of everyday, casual observation. But this is very much a matter of degrees of emphasis. Science has to contain and yield singular statements if it is to be confirmed and to carry out its explanatory and predictive functions. Common knowledge has to embody some general statements if it is to be knowledge at all, if the immediate beliefs we are prompted to form by and about our environment are to be criticisable in the way that is essential to their justification.

Three things that do distinguish science from common factual knowledge are its method, its system and, in a somewhat special sense, its theoretical nature. What makes a method of acquiring knowledge scientific is not something that can be defined in a formal way. Inductive reasoning, whether this be conceived with Bacon and Mill as the extraction of laws from singular items of knowledge or with Whewell, Peirce and Popper as critical selection between competing antecedent general conjectures by the verification of their singular consequences, is not peculiar to science. Scientific method is adverbial, an attitude of deliberate explicitness towards the business of empirical investigation; it is not a unique, substantive procedure. What this method imparts to scientific findings is a higher degree of reliability than that possessed by common knowledge, to the extent that those findings are carefully and explicitly set out together with a precise record of the evidence on which they are based. By contrast most common knowledge is loosely formulated and the evidence on which it is based is largely forgotten.

One aspect of scientific discourse that contributes so largely to its precision that it is tempting to regard it as definitive of science is quantification. The singular items of evidence for scientific assertions characteristically take the form, not of qualitative descriptions, but of numerical measurements, commonly and preferably of extensive magnitudes, amenable to the operations of cardinal arithmetic. As was argued earlier the concentration of scientists on the primary qualities of things, which as well as being definitive of material objecthood are also extensively measurable, can be accounted for by the advantages it yields in the way of precision.

This kind of methodical scrupulousness about the formulation of evidence is associated in science with a comparable scrupulousness of an epistemic kind, about the precise weight of support which the evidence confers on the conclusions derived from it. Our expressions of common knowledge or belief tend to be presumptuously categorical. In everyday conversation we are not speaking on oath and we often say that something *is* the case which we are justified only in saying that there is reason to think *may* be the case. And just as 'is' supplants 'may be' so 'all' replaces 'most'. In science precision is sought both in specifying the degree of certainty with which findings are affirmed and in delimiting the scope of their reference.

The second distinguishing feature of science is its systematic character. This is pursued first of all at the level of classification through which the everyday vocabulary of observation with its concentration on obvious but often superficial differences is replaced by a more articulate and organized apparatus of description. This both prepares for and is further influenced by the establishment of empirical laws. These are then systematised by further generalisation, as, for example, laws about the species of a genus are brought together as special cases of a wider law applying to the genus as a whole. Thus the regularities of motion of particular planets in the solar system are unified in Kepler's laws. Then, by a further application of the same procedure, the behaviour of the constituents of the solar system and of bodies freely falling near the surface of the earth are brought together in Newton's gravitational theory. At this level of explanation the laws relating to one kind of familiar and straightforwardly observable thing are subsumed under those relating to a wider and in a way more abstract but still straightforwardly observable class of things. Such systematising laws and explanations are variously called abstractive, phenomenological or macroscopic.

But there is, thirdly, the business of devising scientific theories in the narrow sense, where the existence of altogether new and unfamiliar kinds of entity is supposed in order to explain the properties and behaviour of what can be straightforwardly observed. The theorist in this sense adds to our knowledge of the world, not by discerning hitherto hidden patterns in the relationships and activities of known things, but by the discovery of altogether new kinds of thing which constitute the fine structure of the familiar and straightforwardly observable. Thus molecules, atoms and electrons are invoked to explain the thermal, chemical and electrical properties of ordinarily accessible material objects, micro-organisms to explain the diseases of living creatures already well known, cells to explain the characteristic properties of the material of which living bodies are composed. Such theories about the fine structure and unobservable constituents of familiar things are variously called hypothetical, transcendental or microscopic (not too happily, perhaps, since many of the theoretical entities in question are beyond the reach of any known microscope).

The essential difference between systematisation and theorising can be expressed as that between bringing ordinary things under ever wider and more abstract concepts (planet to heavenly body to body pure and simple, salmon to fish to animal to organism) and analysing the great variety of ordinary things into an ever-decreasing number of kinds of unordinary things that are inaccessible to observation. Both types of scientific advance involve the discovery of what is hidden. But systematisation discovers what is hidden on the observable surface of the world, theorisation what is hidden behind that surface. There is, therefore, nothing particularly primitive or trivial about systematisation as contrasted with theorising in the narrow sense. The massive and profoundly unobvious unification of apparently quite different kinds of motion accomplished by Newton's mechanics is, after all the most celebrated achievement of the scientific imagination, yet it provides an explanation of the systematic rather than of the theoretical kind.

The main ontological problem posed by science concerns the unobservable entities whose existence seems to be asserted by theories about the fine structure of the world. On the most natural interpretation scientific theories affirm or imply that, besides the material objects whose existence is established by ordinary perception, there are material things that cannot be perceived and yet which wholly compose the objects of common experience. But it is a requirement of the kind of empiricism that I have defended in chapter 5 and developed in the introduction to book III that concrete or basic existence, as contrasted with dependent or derived existence, can be ascribed only to those things which can in principle be observed, that is to say whose existence can in principle be asserted in an ostensive statement of the form 'here is an X' which does not depend wholly on its linguistic relations to other, independently introduced, statements for its meaning and on inference from established statements of the related kind for its justification. This implies that only observable entities are substances in the Cartesian sense of presupposing the existence of no other kind of entities. I have argued in book II that common, observable material objects, and not simply sense-impressions, satisfy this requirement. Scientific theory asserts that there are many unobservable things the evidence for whose existence is wholly and inescapably provided by observations made of common objects, notably measuring instruments. But if all possible evidence for the existence of theoretical entities is provided by common observables it follows from the doctrine of chapter 5 that the logically indispensable evidence, and thus the sense, of assertions about theoretical entities must be capable of being expressed in terms of those common observables and thus that theoretical entities can have only a derived and dependent existence. Theoretical entities, that is to say, are not part of the ultimate substantial furniture of the world. The practice of referring to them can at most be a conveniently compact way of referring to ordinary observable things that stand in some complex system of relations to one another.

In chapter 5 I argued that material objects, and not sense-impressions, are the proper objects of perception and, what is more, that they are its *direct* objects in any reasonable sense of the term which is distinct from that in which directness is misleadingly and perhaps inapplicably identified with incorrigible knowability. I argued, furthermore, that assertions about the existence of material objects, even when they are not based on perception directly but derive their justification from inference, still derive their sense from the correlation between the material-object terms they contain and observable states of affairs. To the extent, then, that theoretical entities are taken to be material objects in a straightforwardly literal sense the possibility in principle of establishing that their use in theories conforms with such rules of correlation must remain open. In chapter 2 I defended the thesis that occupancy of space, with its implications of shape, size and position, is the essential characteristic of a material object. The literal sense of these implied concepts involves their perceptual application. If the theoretical entities of science are at once material objects and radically unobservable an inconsistency results.

My main procedure in what follows will be to argue that the type of unobservability characteristic of theoretical entities is not of the sort which implies that they cannot be material objects in the ordinary, literal sense in which chairs and trees and mountains are. But one preliminary qualification needs to be made. While many theoretical entities are ordinarily spoken of and taken to be material objects—microbes and viruses, molecules and atoms, for example—others are not. The gravitational force with which the moon's mass influences the tides does not invite interpretation as a material thing any more than the force with which a footballer propels a ball into a goal. That is not to say that the two kinds of force are not real. Both are mentioned in true and literally interpretable statements. But they no more need to be taken as material objects than the size or velocity of some commonly observable thing needs to be. The fact that the size of a thing can be referred to with a substantival phrase does not in ordinary cases lead us to attribute to it the same sort of substantiality as the thing whose size it is and there is no reason why the defender of a realistic account of theoretical entities should feel constrained to make out that the relational characteristics of those entities are material substances. The question at issue, in other words, is that of the status of theoretical material objects and not of theoretical entities in general. (But, for convenience, I shall generally use the shorter phrase to refer to the narrower, and alone strictly relevant, class.)

There is another preliminary issue to be considered. Could it not be argued that the basic empirical meaning of the concept of a material object and of the other concepts it implies are established by their correlation with common observables and that their application to what is not observable is simply a matter of analogical extrapolation? Unless this possibility is ruled out there is just no problem about the existence of theoretical entities. Many of the material things in whose existence we believe never have been observed and most probably never will be; indeed, if located in the past, never can be. Our ground for believing that there are such things is analogical. Why, therefore, should not analogy suffice in the case of theoretical entities?

The natural inclination here is to answer that there is a difference between analogical *reasonings* in which the terms appearing in both sides of the analogy have the same sense and the analogical *introduction of concepts* in which the new concept has only some of the properties of the original one that served as the basis for the analogy. Thus, when we infer that there are probably large rocks a few feet under the lawn just like those revealed to observation when the neighbouring patch of ground was excavated, the word 'rock' occurs in the same sense in both premises and conclusion. Analogy of a quite different kind is present when by speaking of the emotional disturbance of a frightened man we make an implicit comparison with the physical disturbance of the surface of a stormy sea. That the cases given are entirely different none will deny. The question is, with which type of analogy should theoretical hypotheses of unobservable material objects be assimilated?

The existence of unobservable particles might be held to be simply an instance of analogical reasoning of the unproblematic, inductive type on the following grounds. Ordinary material things are commonly found to be divisible into equally material parts. If this is generalised unrestrictedly and conjoined with the reasonable assumption that there is a lower limit to the size of observable objects the broadly atomistic conclusion follows that every material thing is composed of unobservable material things. I do not think that this short way with non-realistic interpretations of theoretical entities is acceptable. For, as things stand, there is good reason to think that the unrestricted generalisation is false. Beyond a certain point of division, as far as observational evidence is concerned, the generalisation about material things being composed of material parts has no support, indeed observation pure and simple seems to falsify it. This is in effect to say that the perceptual element in the meaning of the expression 'material object' and its associates ('shape', 'size' and so forth) is an essential element and that observability in principle must be attributed to theoretical entities if they are to be literally interpreted as material things. So if a realistic interpretation of theoretical entities is to be sustained it must be shown that they are not unobservable in principle or, more usefully, in a way that would make them material objects only in an extended and figurative sense.

Positivism and realism

There are two main non-realistic accounts of the theoretical entities of science which may be described as positivist in virtue of their agreement that scientific statements must refer to positive, observable things. One, instrumentalism, holds that since sentences containing the names of theoretical entities do not so refer they are not really statements at all but are linguistic devices of calculation or prediction, or, in one version, material rules of inference with the aid of which some experiences or matters of observable fact can be inferred from others. The other, which goes by various names but which I shall call reductionism, holds that the scientific sentences that contain references to theoretical entities are statements all right but really refer to observables and not, as their verbal appearance suggests, to unobservable theoretical entities.

In a good deal of the literature the difference between these two views is either not very explicitly noticed or, if it is noticed, is then not very closely attended to. But the two are very different at first glance. Instrumentalism denies that theoretical sentences can be used to make statements at all; reductionism denies only that they really refer to what they appear to refer to. But they agree, at any rate, that theoretical sentences are not what they seem to be. And certainly, if they are considered in rather remote and general terms, they do tend to coalesce. According to instrumentalism an accepted theory t is a device for inferring some observational consequences o' from observational premises o. Now to accept such a theory amounts to no more and no less than the acceptance of the conditional *if o then o'* or *whenever o then o'*, which is a genuine statement, true or false, which entails, in conjunction with o, the conclusion o' and which is equivalent in meaning, therefore, in the reductionist manner, to the theory t.

I am inclined to think that this simple assimilation of the two interpretations is, in the end, correct but its identification of the acceptance of a theory as an observation-inferring device with acceptance of a corresponding observational conditional may be challenged and should be defended. In practice, of course, theories are a good deal more complicated than this argument assumes; they do not connect just one simply specifiable set of observations with another. In the first place a theory will be associated with a number of distinct connections of this kind. The theory that a body of gas is a vast collection of molecules in random motion is not just a device for inferring from the pressure to the temperature of a given volume of gas but also one for inferring pressure from volume at a given temperature. One of the convenient services of theories, after all, is systematisation. Furthermore the starting-point of the inference, the initial conditions, will ordinarily be more complex than the symbol '*o*' suggests and will mention somewhat heterogeneous observational states of affairs. But these considerations explain rather than justify the thesis that the two positivist interpretations are really quite distinct. The first complication requires only that the conditional corresponding to a theory should be a conjunction of conditionals; the second that it should have a conjunctive antecedent.

There is a point about reductionism that needs to be emphasised. If the view of Carnap and Schlick that I considered in the introduction to book III is adopted, according to which the reducibility of a kind of entities to another more elementary or directly observable kind of entities is without ontological significance, then the reducibility of theoretical entities to common objects should no more impugn the literal, empirical reality of the former, than the reducibility of common objects to sense-impressions asserted by phenomenalism is allowed to impugn the literal, empirical reality of common objects. Unless the existence of derived or constructed entities is taken to be somehow less solid and absolute than that of the basic entities from which they are constructed the logical fact of the reducibility of a kind of entities has no bearing on their ontological status. But most philosophers who have been induced by their empiricism towards positivist interpretations of scientific theory have assumed without question that, since theoretical entities must be reducible if assertions about them are to be empirically significant, their reality must be something less than complete. Logical constructions are, in this field at any rate, taken almost without question to be logical fictions.

The thesis of realism is that the theoretical entities of science are physically real in just the same way and to just the same extent as the common objects whose observation provides the basis for asserting the existence of theoretical entities. In the previous section I have mentioned one way in which this thesis may, and in my view should, be qualified. Not every substantival expression occurring in a theoretical statement which is not susceptible of straightforwardly direct observational confirmation needs to be taken at its referential face value. Relational entities like forces, which require things to exert them and other things to be exerted on, can be paraphrased out in an uncontroversial way. Apparent references to them can be eliminated by translation of the statements in which they occur into statements about the relations between objects exerting force and having forces exerted on them. Then there are pure dispositions, dispositions, that is to say, which are not taken to involve any occurrent basis in the fine structure of the objects possessing them. Apparent references to these can also be eliminated and the information be conveyed by statements of conditional form in which reference is made only to their possessors.

Nothing has done more to encourage positivism about theoretical entities than the development of quantum physics. On the one hand there is the theoretical assertion that electrons cannot be said to have both position and momentum. If this is taken, not as stating a factual limit to what we can find out, but as a logical limit to what we can meaningfully say, and the stronger interpretation is the more usual one, then the status of electrons as material objects is jeopardised. On the other there is the anomalous implication of the two-slit experiment which requires that in one set of circumstances light must be conceived as waves in another as a stream of particles. In the days of the Rutherford-Bohr atom an acceptable account of the ultimate constituents of matter as themselves material particles was available. This is no longer the case. It may well be that the substantival vocabulary of contemporary quantum physics is not capable of being interpreted realistically, in other words that positivism is true of that particular historical piece of scientific theory. From this it does not follow that attempts to turn quantum physics into a realistically interpretable theory are necessarily misguided or, on the other hand, that any such attempts must succeed. Nor again does it follow that, if a positivistic interpretation is the only currently acceptable one for this part of science, then a positivist account of microbes and molecules is correct. What can be said is that there is good inductive ground for supposing that here as elsewhere what is at one time the unknown and only dimly conceived cause of certain more or less accessible phenomena will eventually come to be understood in less promissory terms. The recent history of the concept of the gene, originally conceived as a more or less indeterminate, though presumably very small, something-or-other, conveying inheritable characteristics from parents to children, is instructive. But this at most would justify the search for a realistically interpretable theory. It does not show that any such theory must in fact be discoverable. The point that needs emphasis is that quantum physics seems to ascribe to its fundamental elements properties that are simply inconsistent with their being material objects in the literal sense. But this is true only of the most up-to-date and sophisticated of theoretical unobservables.

Realism about theoretical entities does not, then, have to take the very naive form of supposing that whatever is explicitly referred to in any theoretical assertion that there is good empirical ground for

290

thinking true is on that account a real material existent. Forces and dispositions are real in the sense that real things exert or possess them. Quantum physics, despite the substantival style of its references to electrons and other fundamental particles, may have to be understood in an instrumentalist way as a prediction-device. But these limits to realism do not count against the literal material reality of such things as genes and molecules, which are treated as material things in the theories that contain them and whose only relevant difference from common objects is some defect of direct observability.

There is a variant of realism about theoretical entities, one that is persistent enough to deserve a name of its own though it has no established one, which not only asserts the reality of theoretical entities but also denies full, physical reality to anything else. This position is colloquially expressed in such statements as that common material objects are *really*, or *nothing but*, loose constellations of rapidly-moving atoms, devoid of secondary qualities. Following Ayer, who has some sympathy for it, I shall call it 'scientific realism' (Ayer (7), pp. 333–6). ('Physicalism' and 'scientism' are too closely appropriated to other uses, 'theoreticism' is altogether too barbarous.)

It would be superficial to diagnose this as the result of a simple mistake, namely that of identifying the fact that common objects can be theoretically explained in terms of unobservable physical things with the fact, or non-fact, that they are logically reducible to them. In so far as reducibility is taken to imply the epistemological priority of the basis of the reduction to the entities that are reduced to it, common objects are not reducible to atoms. It might be said that this may well be true of *human* epistemology, which confined itself to the justification of the beliefs of the only holders of rational beliefs that we know of, but that there could have been creatures who perceived the world as an array of atoms or whatever and then, from this immediately perceived basis, went on to construct theoretical concepts of macroscopic objects and to infer theoretical beliefs about them. There are obvious difficulties about this conjecture. If the non-human believers in question are like us in size but with very much finer senses they could become aware of their membership of a society only as the result of a rational achievement of theorisation for which they could not be equipped without conscious recognition of their membership in a society of communicating thinkers. If, on the other hand, they were of the same order of magnitude as what we call atoms, it is hard to conceive how they could have the requisite complexity of organisation to perceive anything unless they and the atomic world they perceived had a theoretical fine structure as well, an order of micro-micro-entities, as it were, which, in accordance with the original line of reasoning would have to be accorded a superior reality to that of the atoms, in our sense, that they perceived. The force of these arguments is to generalise for all possible thinkers a principle that is at any rate true of men: the ultimate elements of explanatory scientific theory cannot be identical with the basic elements of a rational reconstruction of knowledge. In any situation the basic epistemological elements have to be obvious. But the fineness of the distinctions that perceivers have to make between them requires a physically complex perceptual apparatus. There are good reasons why epistemology should be, to this extent, anthropomorphic. If the generalised principle I have stated is correct this anthropomorphism involves no unrepresentative distortion.

In any case the only philosopher who has held that atoms could be the basis of a rational reconstruction of knowledge, as far as I know, is Carnap and he is quite explicit that such a reconstruction would not arrange its ingredients in an epistemological order (Carnap (1), pp. 99–100). It would at most be a formal possibility. In general those I am calling physical realists do not suggest that common objects are strictly reducible to theoretical entities. (It is, after all, a contingent matter what theoretical explanation is true of a range of observable facts. It would not be if those observables were reducible to theoretical entities.) What induces them to accord a superior reality to atoms than to common objects is principally the fact that microphysics is more systematic than macrophysics. Their comparative ontological evaluation of the two orders of things is not entailed by the inconsistencies they claim to discern between such beliefs as that common objects are coloured and that the atomic constituents of those objects are not. I have argued that there is in fact no inconsistency between such pairs of beliefs (cf. chapter 7, pp. 202–7). But if there were, it would not dictate which member of each pair would have to be discarded in order to preserve consistency.

Against the systematic character of microphysics certain countervailing considerations can be set. There is, first of all, the fact that physical theories of the appropriate kind are far less well-confirmed, or, which may come to much the same thing, are less determinate in respect of their precise significance (many apparent modifications of theory can be reinterpreted as revisions in or additions to the sense of theoretical terms), than our beliefs, singular and general, about common objects. Secondly, and relatedly, there is the fact that physical theory changes in a radical kind of way in which common beliefs do not. On the level of common belief we get to know more of the same sort of thing: on the level of theory we come to believe in altogether new kinds of thing. Finally, and arising from the second point, there is the fact that physical theory is open-ended. At any one time there will be, within a reasonably homogeneous scientific community, a type of theoretical explanation that is, at that time, ultimate. But new theories, about yet finer structures, tend to arise to wrest ultimacy from the currently ultimate type. There is no *a priori* objection to Bohm's conjecture that micro-explanation can in principle proceed from level to level indefinitely.

For reasons that I have given in chapter 7 I do not believe that there is any important inconsistency between the common picture of the physical world and the account of the physical world given by science. It is only certain perhaps natural but nevertheless speculative inferences from the common picture of the world, such as that all the parts of a coloured thing must be coloured, that science collides with. These scientific corrections can be accepted without abandoning any of the essential content of the common picture of the world. Now, if this is so the more systematic character of scientific theory, as compared with common belief, has no ontological significance. It is simply the reflection of the distinguishing characteristics of science that were described at the beginning of this chapter: the greater precision it owes to its method and the deliberately articulated and organised way in which its findings are presented.

Realism, then, need not be indiscriminate in according material status to all the substantives of theoretical discourse and it need not accord a reality to theoretical entities that is higher than or exclusive of that of common objects. There are two other extreme forms which realism does not have to take. The first of these is the transcendentalism which asserts the reality of theoretical entities that are in the strongest possible sense unobservable. To the extent that the entities to which reality is ascribed are conceived as material objects they must possess primary qualities, must have in some specification the properties that are involved in the occupancy of space. But those properties are basic empirical properties. The terms for them derive an indispensable part of their sense from ostensive definition. So if theoretical entities are to be conceived as material objects in a more than figurative way, observation of them must be conceivable even if it is not actually achieved for one reason or another.

The final excessive form of realism that I want to consider is what Popper calls 'essentialism' (Popper (3), ch. 3). This is the view that the aim of science is the provision of *ultimate explanations*, that is to say explanations in terms of things and properties that are not susceptible in principle of any further explanation. In giving this position the name 'essentialism' Popper may have had in mind Locke's doctrine of real essences: 'the real internal, but generally in substances unknown, constitution of things, whereon their discoverable properties depend' (Locke, III. 3.15). This ultimate, internal constitution of things, is, according to Locke, known to God and angels and might be discoverable by us if we had 'microscopical eyes', but we do not need to know it in this way and if we did we should be seriously, perhaps disastrously, inconvenienced, for we should have laboriously to work out all sorts of useful things which we can now find out about at a glance.

This conception of a terminal level of theoretical explanation is associated with the idea of a demonstrative natural science, one in which theory not only allows the deduction from it of observable matters of fact, for this is common to all accounts of *natural* science at any rate, but is also composed of certainly true propositions, along the lines of Aristotle's self-evident first principles of science. If the propositions of ultimate theory were necessarily true it would follow that since observational laws are deducible from them they would have to be necessarily true as well. If laws about observables are, as they are universally taken to be, contingent, theories cannot be certain in this way. It is, of course, possible to accept as merely a well-confirmed contingency what is in fact a necessary truth. I may believe that the sum of the numbers from 0 up to n is half n times $n + 1$ on the basis of trying it out on the first few numbers as values of n and generalising. But it is hard to conceive that there is an unnoticed contradiction in the suppositions that the value of g is other than 32 ft/sec^2 or that hydrogen is not combustible. And if the certainty of the ultimate theoretical propositions is not to be the outcome of their proved necessity, and thus intrinsic to them, it can come only from the evidence on which they rest, none of which is certain. Although a conjecture can be certified by an array of independent pieces of evidence each of which is itself less than certain and each of which thus becomes subsequently certain by reason of their consilience, this kind of happy outcome must remain a bare possibility as far as science is concerned. At best it is not demonstrably impossible. It is a possible benefit of systematisation that may serve as some kind of regulative ideal.

The idea, more central to essentialism, that there is a logically final level of theoretical explanation is equally dubious. Up to the present moment, at least, all the evidence points in the opposite direction. Scientific theorising, ever since it became consistently methodical, has continued to penetrate deeper and deeper into the fine structure of nature. It has sometimes been suggested in recent years that with modern physical theory we have in fact reached as far as we can go. It is possible that for the foreseeable future there will be no scientific progress at the deeper theoretical level. But no level of theory declares its own finality. At most continued failure to penetrate further could justify a practical decision to give up the search.

Critique of positivism

If theoretical entities are unobservable in an absolute or logical sense, it follows that the only evidence there could be for their existence must be provided by the objects that we can observe, whatever precisely they may be. Furthermore it is within that body of possible evidence that the empirical content of theoretical statements must be sought. This is the argument on which a reductionist interpretation of scientific theory rests. Certain very general arguments which have been brought against the parallel phenomenalist doctrine about ordinary observable material things are sometimes invoked to undermine reductionism about theoretical entities.

One of these is that categorical statements cannot be reduced to hypotheticals. But asserted without restriction that statement would appear to be false. To say that a given rubber ball is elastic is to say no more and no less than that it will bounce if it is dropped on a moderately hard surface. Although we have good reason to suppose that an explanation in terms of the inner structure of the ball can be found for its elastic disposition, its having an elasticity-explaining structure is not entailed by its elasticity. The defects of phenomenalist translations are more specific than the formal property of identifying the meaning of a categorical statement with a set of hypothetical ones.

Another is that the language into which the reduction is made either does not exist or is logically parasitic on the language from which it is being made. Either impressions cannot be described at all or if they are to be described it must be in terms of the physical properties which they appear to have and the understanding of 'appears to be F' requires the antecedent understanding of 'is F'. This has some force against a phenomenalist account of material objects but none against a reductionist account of theoretical entities, since the language into which the reduction is made, the language of straightforwardly observable material objects, plainly exists and is plainly prior to the language of scientific theory, which is developed by some sort of analogy with it.

Can it be said about scientific reductionism, as it often is about phenomenalism, that the alleged reductions are not in fact forthcoming? Even this seems questionable. A physicist with a fairly encyclopedic grasp of his subject could presumably list all the hypothetical statements about the connections between the observable properties of ordinary material things with whose truth the theory that gas has a molecular structure stands or falls. There would, however, be something arbitrary about this. The molecular theory of gases was introduced to account for certain empirical laws about the relations of pressure, temperature and volume. But the laws it was introduced to explain do not exhaust its content. A literal interpretation of the theory suggested a whole array of new topics of investigation. As Nagel says 'The model for the (kinetic) theory (of gases) suggested questions about the ratios of molecular diameters to the distances between the molecules, about various kinds of forces between the molecules, about the elastic properties of molecules, about the distribution of the velocities of the molecules and so on' (Nagel, p. 113). The essential point is that it is only if molecules are taken to be material objects in a literal sense, things about which the sort of questions listed by Nagel naturally arise and things to which the macroscopically supported laws of mechanics apply, that the observational laws which the molecular theory systematises can be brought into any intelligible, non-arbitrary relation to one another. Until they are connected by the theoretical idea of an increase in the velocity of the molecules of a given volume of gas there is no reason why the correlation between increasing temperature and increasing pressure should be taken to be anything but a brute fact. A body of gas might have been taken to be continuous, not particulate, and just to swell when heated in the way bread-dough does in a hot oven. Such a theory would be simply a more or less graphic restatement of the observable facts. What differentiates it from the molecular theory is that, literally interpreted and conjoined with conceptual truths, about material objects in general and the mechanical laws which generally cover the behaviour of such objects, it implies a whole lot of further and independently testable statements about bodies of gas.

Ramsey's proposal that the unappetisingly transcendental flavour of theories about unobservables should be neutralised by replacing theoretical terms with existentially quantified class-variables is vitiated by this fact of the transcendence by theories of the observable facts that they are originally introduced to explain (Ramsey, ch. 9, A). Instead of saying that the pressure of a gas rises when the temperature does because the velocity of the constituent molecules increases, Ramsey would say, in effect, that this observable effect is found because something happens in the gas which is caused by the rise in temperature and causes the rise in pressure. But this is to say no more than that changes of temperature and pressure are regularly associated. The unspecified whatnot which is caused by one and causes the other is a kind of dotted line, an empty space into which a theory could be fitted, a more or less respectful gesture towards an account of fine structure from which no further consequences follow. As is generally agreed, theories are heuristically indispensable for scientific progress. We have to take them in a literal, non-Ramsey-like way while they are being developed. Ramsey's proposal is really a cosmetic device for concealing after the event the embarrassingly realistic source of the wealth of systematised information about observables which theory enables us to acquire, a *nouveau riche* stratagem. Reductionists, as Grover Maxwell points out, admit that theories prove fertile for the growth of science. But by denying that they really explain, that they really do anything more than link empirical laws in a handily systematic way, reductionists fail to explain why it is that theory, taken literally, manages to have this productive effect (Maxwell).

Most objections to phenomenalism about ordinary material objects amount to claims that the translation required by the doctrine cannot be carried out. This type of objection does not apply directly to reductionism about scientific theory. At any given stage of scientific progress it seems possible, in something like Ramsey's way, to interpret the existing body of theory exclusively in terms of the empirical laws so far associated with it. But the body of such laws associated with a theory will change through time, so that as it enlarges it will be necessary on this view to say that the meaning of the theory itself has changed. But this renders the enlargement unintelligible. It is only because the theory is interpreted literally, and thus as having more content than the set of its current empirical associates, that it raises the questions whose investigation leads to the augmentation of the set. It might be objected that it does not follow from the fact that a theory has more content than its current empirical associates that what it really means is what it can be literally interpreted as saying about unobserved material objects. But it is this literal interpretation that underlies the further empirical exploitation of the theory and is essential if, as is largely the case, the new laws the theory suggests result from the application to its entities of such empirically supported laws about material objects in general as the laws of mechanics.

I conclude that reductionism is mistaken, then, not merely because theories mean more than the empirical laws associated with them at one time but because, in a centrally important group of cases at any rate, they do not undergo the kind of radical changes in meaning as their field of empirical application enlarges that reductionism implies, because it is only if they are literally interpreted that the thought of their wider application can be accounted for and because they must be interpreted as referring to material objects if the general laws about such objects are to apply to their elements so as to make possible the deduction of the new empirical laws.

Now, if reductionism about scientific theory is mistaken, instrumentalism must be mistaken too, if, as I shall now argue, it is simply a disguised form of reductionism. The argument for this identification of the two main types of positivist account of scientific theory is simple. Instrumentalism holds that a theory is a verbal device for calculation or prediction, a rule of inference enjoining the derivation of an observable consequence y from an observable premise x: from x infer y. But what makes a rule of inference acceptable? If it is a deductive inference it is made acceptable by the meaning of its constituent terms alone. If it is not then it can only be the synthetic, empirical truth of the corresponding hypothetical statement: if x then y. In general, rules can apply to all sorts of activity and can be appraised in very various dimensions of success. But rules of prediction or calculation are rules of inference and are acceptable only to the extent that conformity with them leads from truth to truth. A rule itself is not a true or false statement. Some would argue that the sentence 'this rule is acceptable', being an evaluation, is not a statement either, but a general injunction to accept the rule in question. However there can be no doubt that the only relevant criterion of acceptability as far as rules of inference are concerned is yielding truth and to say that the rule 'from x infer y' is truth-yielding is strictly equivalent to the undoubted statement 'it is true that if x then y' or, more compactly, 'if x then y'.

Some philosophers, notably Schlick and Ramsey, have attempted to circumvent the inductiveness of synthetic general statements of all kinds, their lack of conclusive verifiability, by the contention that they are all really rules of inference. It is certainly true that in setting out a body of reasoning it is a matter of choice whether the intellectual connections involved are explicitly included as general statements or are implicitly used as rules of inference. But which choice is made is primarily a question of style or rhetoric. It is tiresome to spell out what the audience can be presumed to know perfectly well already. But any statement whatever can be dissolved into the implicit background of exposition in this way. In saying 'all men are mortal so Socrates is', the deductively essential but stylistically superfluous premise that Socrates is a man is elided. In its place the rule of inference 'from *all men are x* infer *Socrates is x*' is invoked. That does not show that the statement that Socrates is a man is really a rule of inference (cf. Alexander).

What underlies the supposition that rules of inference are somehow prior to or more basic than the statements that correspond to them is the fact that the endeavour to replace all rules of inference by statements is inevitably and viciously regressive, a fact memorably demonstrated by Lewis Carroll's story of Achilles and the tortoise. What Achilles should, of course, have said to the tortoise was that, in professing to agree that it is true that if p and p only if q then q, while not seeing that q follows from p and p only if q, the tortoise was misusing words, probably insincerely. In claiming to believe the conditional statement he was in effect claiming to understand the words expressing it, in particular the word 'if'. But a condition of understanding the word 'if' is readiness to infer q from p and p only if q, that is to say acceptance of the rule of inference corresponding to the statement. Some of the more elementary of the necessary truths that contain a word are indeed logically posterior to the operative acceptance, though not the explicit formulation, of rules of inference covering other forms of statement in which the word occurs. But this does not extend to contingent statements whose truth is prior to the corresponding rules of inference as a condition of their acceptability. In this case the rules do not underlie the statement by setting the convention which the statement represents in the form of an implicit definition.

It is not enough to argue against instrumentalism that it is a matter of free, stylistic choice whether to present a connection in the form of a statement or a rule. For if that were all there is to it then instrumentalism would be, if not exactly a true account of theories, at least a device for avoiding embarrassing questions about their implications of existence. It needs further to be shown, if instrumentalism is to be refuted, that contingent statements are logically prior to material rules of inference. If I have succeeded in doing this, instrumentalism is revealed as no more than reductionism in disguise and falls with it.

I believe this to be a more satisfactory way of dealing with instrumentalism than to object, with Popper, that it cannot explain why scientists should be interested in testing the remoter implications of theories. The virtue of an instrument, he says, is to work effectively in the region for which it was designed. If it does not work outside that region it does not have to be abandoned. Its users must just recognise the limits of its application. The immediate counter that this invites is that one is very naturally going to see if an instrumene that has worked well for some initial purpose is going to be mort widely employable with the same degree of success. The stone axe that cuts firewood so effectively will soon be tried out on the heads of one's enemies. But this objection fails to get to the root of the problem. It too slavishly follows the concretely technical character of Popper's metaphor. The real weakness of instrumentalism is that it fails to explain how it is that theories come to be thought of as having any further, alternative fields of employment than those for which they were designed.

I want to conclude this criticism of positivist accounts of scientific theory by mentioning a style of approaching the problem of its interpretation which contributes an undeserved attractiveness to those accounts. For good and obvious reasons of logical control and explicitness many efforts are made, at one level of precision by scientists themselves, at another, more exquisite one by logicians, to give an axiomatic form to scientific theories. Much of the more mathematically sophisticated reasoning of scientists takes place wholly at the theoretical level. This leads to the idea that a theory can be understood as an uninterpreted axiomatic system which gets related to the empirical world by way of correspondence rules connecting its terms, or some of them, to observable matters of fact.

This approach, much favoured by Carnap, is adopted by analogy with the desirable and illuminating distinction between pure and physical geometry. In pure geometry the basic terms are wholly defined, implicitly, by the axioms of the system. In physical geometry some of the basic terms are ostensively correlated with physical things: light-rays, taut wires, crossed hairs in a telescope. When this is done some at least of the axioms become contingent statements about the properties and relations of the physical things in question.

Carnap recognises that if the correspondence rules are taken as completely specifying the meaning of theoretical terms the result is unqualified reductionism (Carnap (4), ch. 24). To avoid this he claims that correspondence rules only partly determine the meaning of the theoretical terms in question. But in fact they do not even do this. A molecule is defined as a material object of a very small size. In virtue of this, mechanical laws apply to molecules and allow us to infer from the premise that the molecules composing a given volume of gas have been heated, and have thus acquired a greater mean velocity, that the pressure they exert on their container will increase. The correspondence rule connecting a theoretical state of affairs to its observable manifestation is not itself what defines the theoretical terms but is a consequence of the definition of those terms together with the laws that apply to the theoretical objects in virtue of that definition. Since those laws are synthetic, the correspondence laws which cannot be deduced without them are synthetic too. A theoretical entity is not just an indeterminate something which is defined as having certain effects: increases of pressure, onsets of disease, transmission of hereditary characteristics. It is, rather, a perhaps not very precisely specified material object or even micro-organism which, as a matter of fact, has these effects.

Observability

In view of the strong reasons there are for taking at any rate some of the more substantial-looking entities of scientific theory, that is to say the non-relational and non-dispositional ones, as genuine material objects, it might well seem more inviting to adopt the transcendentalist position and admit, in view of the alleged unobservability of such theoretical entities, that material objects can be conceived by an analogy with ordinarily perceivable material things which does not extend to their perceivability. Before making this admission it is proper to inquire whether such entities really are unobservable in a way that requires it.

It is plain that many of the entities whose existence has been asserted on the basis of theoretical reasoning are not unobservable in the relevant way. It is generally believed that Britain was connected to the continent of Europe by a land-bridge at some time in the fairly remote past. Until comparatively recently no one had perceived the other side of the moon. The obstacles to the observation of these things are of a harmlessly contingent nature. If ordinary human perceivers had been at times or places where in fact they were not the things in question would have been observed. Unobservability arises here, not from the intrinsic qualities of the things involved, but from the temporal and spatial relations of observers to them. They are in all intrinsic respects things very much of the sort that can be observed.

The most obvious intrinsic feature of theoretical entities which makes them unobservable is their very small size. But there are some common objects which are only marginally observable. An example is air which is perhaps only directly perceived, in the sense I have elaborated in book II, when it is in motion, in the form of wind. We do, indeed speak of feeling the air in a tyre and of hearing it escape from a tyre but in such cases what we directly perceive is the effects the air produces, the felt hardness of the tyre and the sound that is emitted from it. That the sound is, itself, a disturbance of the air is a piece of theory, very familiar theory, no doubt, but theory none the less.

Many things of whose existence science speaks are not so much unobservable as not commonly observed. All sorts of detail in plants, insects and other neutral objects can be directly observed, if they are attentively examined, which does not ordinarily secure our perceptual attention. These things are at most unobservable in a weakly practical sense. An issue of principle only arises with the objects apparently revealed to our perception when our senses are assisted by various sorts of instrument. The detailed structure of a snow crystal that we see under a magnifying glass is something we should ordinarily regard as having been observed. Is this a legitimate step? What counts in its favour is the fact that all the features of things that are observable without this modest kind of instrumental assistance are still observed with it, along with some other features as well. But once we admit that a thing can be literally observed with a magnifying glass there seems no point at which we can reasonably say that we are observing, not the thing itself, but its effects as we move along the series of ever more refined and sophisticated observational aids: from magnifying glasses to microscopes and from ordinary microscopes to electron microscopes with vast powers of magnification. The argument from continuity applies even to the latter. The properties and constituents of the specimen that are visible without assistance are all seen through the electron microscope at the lower levels of magnification, although greatly enlarged. As the magnification increases some of the detail that was observed at the preceding stage is still there to be seen.

It is, of course, true that the proximate physical cause of our seeing is not the microbe or whatever that we should naturally say we see, it is certain rays of light coming from the lens of the instrument to our eyes. But then that is true of any visual perception whatever. If this line is followed we have to say that nothing is ever really observed but the proximate physical cause of our perceptual beliefs, the stimulus as it reaches the sense-organs. And once this step is taken it may well seem that there is no reason to stop there but that it is correct to proceed, with Russell, to the ultimate physical cause of the perceptual belief in the brain or to its alleged mental correlate, the phenomenological sense-impression. And, this, I have argued, involves a fundamental distortion of the concept of perception.

Another line of objection to recognising instrumentally assisted observation as genuine observation is that the introduction of an unusual causal intermediary between the purported object of perception and the perceputal belief makes this type of perception quite as indirect as what I have contended to be the indirect perception of a car by way of the noise it makes as it goes by, of a man by the shadow he casts or of a hidden cheese by its powerful smell. In such cases, I have argued, we directly perceive a sound, a darkened surface and a smell and infer from them a car, a man and a cheese. Now admittedly we should say in such cases that we had heard a car, seen a man and smelt a cheese. But there is, nevertheless, a fundamental difference of principle between the two types of case. In perceiving the sound or smell of something, or, as we might say, perceiving something by its sound or smell, I do not perceive any of the essential, definitive, primary qualities of the thing in question. At best, sound and smell inform the perceiver about the position of the thing he hears or smells and this position is the position of the sound or smell itself, and only by some kind of inference, can it, or any related position, be ascribed to the material thing which makes the sound or smell. There is certainly no direct awareness of the shape or size of the audible or smelly object.

This line of objection assimilates the *unusualness* of the intermediary instrument in assisted observation to the *indirectness* of observation of things by their auditory or olfactory effects. But what assisted observation should more properly be compared to is the observation of common objects at unusually great distances. In both of these types of case there is a confirming continuity between what is observed in both usual and unusual conditions and in both there is perception of the essential and definitive qualities of the object involved. The only difference is that in one case, that of assisted observation, the unusual conditions yield more information while in the other, that of distant observation, it is the usual conditions that are the more informative.

A central feature of my argument against the traditional view that the only direct objects of perception are private sense-impressions in book II was that incorrigibility is not part of the epistemologically relevant concept of directness. A perception or observation is direct to the extent that it does not wholly depend on inference for its justification. Here, once again, the indirectness which the objection imputes to the type of perception being considered is not of the epistemologically relevant kind. Assisted observation may depend on the employment of unusual intermediaries between observer and object but this does not show it to be fundamentally inferential in nature.

But if assisted observation is literal observation, the physical reality of a great many of the theoretical entities constituting the fine structure of the world according to physical science is vindicated, in particular that of molecules (for large protein molecules can be seen with the aid of an electron microscope) and that of many varieties of micro-organisms. These things are indeed unobservable in a way. Ordinary observers, relying on their unassisted senses, cannot perceive them. But this unobservability is merely practical or technical. It is not the kind of unobservability in principle that is required to substantiate the reduction of these entities to their observable manifestations.

Furthermore the class of things that are in principle observable is radically opened up, as it were, by recognising the authentic and literal nature of assisted observation. Psychological investigation can set fairly definite bounds to the capacities of the unaided senses. But no such limit can be set to the capacities of the senses when instrumentally assisted. No bound can be established *a priori* to the possible technical improvement and refinement of microscopy. It is sometimes argued that scientific theory itself establishes such a bound. We are able to see things, according to theory, because of the light-particles which are transmitted from those things to our eyes. It seems to follow that we could not possibly see the light-particles themselves. To see them we should have to be causally influenced in our optical apparatus by something yet more refined and elusive emanating from them.

This argument appears to be perfectly correct as far as it goes. It seems inescapable that the perception of any kind of object involves a causal mechanism between object and perceiver whose constituents are more refined than the object itself. Thus for any kind of object to be observed it seems to follow that there must be another, more refined kind of object whose operations render the first kind of object observable. But although this is a regress it is not necessarily a vicious one. At any stage the constituents of the machinery of perception of those things that are at the margin of observation so far achieved will not themselves be observable. When they do become perceivable, theory requires that there should be more refined entities that cause perceivers to become aware of them. But there is no necessary terminus to this process of refinement. At each stage theory will invoke unobservables, but further refinements of observation can in principle catch up with them. The process can then be repeated when and if these further refinements are made.

This type of regress, although logically innocuous, may seem unattractive. But the only alternative is even more so, namely to allow that at some stage the perception of things, conceived as a causal interaction between object and perceiver, takes place in some more or less non-physical or, at any rate, non-mechanical way.

In the discussion so far I have been taking it for granted that some material things are literally perceived. I have, indeed, been relying on the recognised observability of middle-sized material things as setting the standard against which to measure the alleged defects in respect of physical reality of the entities of scientific theory. But I have not taken the colloquial propriety of the form of words 'I see x' as a sufficient reason for the attribution of observability, and thus literal material reality, to x. Instead I have required that to be literally observable a thing must be a possible object of direct perception in the sense elaborated in book II. If the weaker condition of observability were admitted there would be no serious problem about the substantial materiality of theoretical entities. A familiar example of this kind of weak observability is provided by the tracks seen in Wilson cloud-chambers. It would be natural for someone who saw the formation of such a track to report his perception by saying that he saw the particle moving. But here, as much as in the case of sounds and smells, it is rather the effects or manifestations of the object in question that are perceived than the object itself. Our general beliefs about mechanical causation make it hard to suppose that such a phenomenon could occur without the passage of a literally material thing along the track. But the existence of such a thing is still an inference.

Feyerabend has suggested that electric currents are observable on the ground that an observer might report his perception of the movement of the needle of an ammeter by saying that he saw that there was an electric current in the wire to which the ammeter was attached. It is certainly true that the observer in such a case sees something which leads him to believe that there is an electric current in the wire. But there would be no artificiality in saying that what he really saw was the movement of the needle. If asked how he arrived at the belief he expressed he would unhesitatingly say that it was because of the movement of the needle. Feyerabend's conclusion is that there is only a most precarious and relative distinction between observation and theory and he proposes a definition of an observation-statement, appropriate to the nebulous character of the distinction, as a statement that is 'quickly decidable' (Feyerabend, p. 145). But the rapidity with which a belief is formed is no conclusive indication of its underived or non-inferential status. Mastery of a broad mass of relevant background knowledge may enable us to present inferential beliefs as if they were direct reports of observation. In communicating with those who possess the same background knowledge we shall not be called upon to substantiate these inferences but when talking to those who are not so equipped we may be called upon to justify such statements and will find no difficulty in doing so. The informed observer does not have consciously to pass from the observation of the needle to an inference about the current but, unless he means no more by his statement about the current than that the needle has moved, he must be able to support what he says about the current by a description of the needle's movement.

However, many discussions of the reality of theoretical entities do not proceed from the assumption I have made that common, middle-sized material objects are literally observable. Until comparatively recent times the most usual view among philosophers has been that the only things that are literally and directly perceivable are private sense-impressions. A reductionist view of theoretical entities is very often associated with a phenomenalist account of ordinary material things. This is natural enough since the former view is the result of applying the same pattern of argument to theoretical entities that phenomenalism applies to ordinary material objects.

The question arises as to whether there really is a special problem about the reality of theoretical entities on this very stringent definition of observability any more than there is on the very loose kind of definition I have been considering. To say with the latter that, in effect, anything is observable which it is colloquially significant to say that one has perceived withholds observability from very little. It certainly fails to distinguish common objects from theoretical entities as these are ordinarily understood. But the same would seem to be true of the more stringent definition. Common objects and theoretical entities are both, on this view, unobservable. In that case one must either, with Carnap, say that provided statements about such unobservables are somehow reducible to statements about sense-experience, and are thus brought under empirical control which allows them to be at least indirectly verified or falsified, the unobservables in question are real just to the extent that statements asserting or implying their existence are well-founded, or one must say that both are equally defective in point of literal reality and possess only derived or constructed existence.

However the holders of subjectivist theories of observation seldom draw this inference. One of the few who does is Pap who says (Pap (4), p. 356), 'theoretical entities are verified through their observable effects, just as the table is verified through the sense-impressions to which it gives rise'. What supports this view that common objects and theoretical entities are in the same ontological boat is the fact that reducibility is defined in terms of logical equivalence and that logical equivalence is transitive. If theoretical entities are reducible to common objects and common objects to sense-impressions it follows that any statement about theoretical entities is logically equivalent to some statement, no doubt exceedingly complicated, about sense-impressions.

On the other hand it might be said that the problem could be formulated under the assumption that only sense-impressions are literally or directly perceived if consideration is given to the relative complexity of the sensory analyses of statements about common objects and theoretical entities. A material object statement p is analysable into a hypothetical statement about sense-impressions of the form 'if a then b'. (In fact, to be at all plausible such an analysis would have to be into a conjunction of disjunctions of such hypotheticals: '(if a then b and if c then d and. . .) or (if e then f and . . .) or (. . .).')

Now a theoretical statement z would itself reduce to a hypothetical about ordinary material objects: if p then q (and here again I shall ignore the complications necessary for plausibility which do not affect the argument). So the final analysis of z in sensory terms will be of the form: if (if a then b) then (if c then d). It will be doubly hypothetical. On this basis it could be argued that while both material things and theoretical entities are unobservable and reducible to sense-impressions the reducibility and unobservability of theoretical entities is, as it were, of the second degree, while that of common objects is only of the first, and thus that their reality is defective in comparison with that of common objects even if that of both kinds of thing is also defective in comparison to that of sense-impressions.

I should argue that there is no need to try to resolve this dilemma, not merely because the reducibilities it presupposes, of theoretical entities to common objects and of common objects to sense-impressions, do not obtain, but, more immediately, because the problem of theoretical entities really concerns the material reality, the existence as literal material things, of theoretical entities. Thus even if phenomenalism were true and common objects were reducible to sense-impressions the central problem would still arise in very much the way it now does as to whether theoretical entities are reducible to common objects or not. It would be possible to be realistic about theoretical entities, and regard them as susceptible of singly hypothetical analysis in sensory terms, while being a phenomenalist about common objects. If a reductionist view is taken about both sorts of objects all that consistency requires is that the same ontological implications should be derived from the fact of reducibility in both cases.

The phenomenalist, then, can raise the problem of the existence of theoretical entities, which, for him as for the perceptual realist, is that of the material reality of those entities. But when he doubts whether such entities are observable he must mean 'observable in the way that common objects are' and this observability is for him indirect, though the indirectness is only of the first degree.

I have argued for a view of observability which falls between the two extremes that I have just been considering. The direct or immediate perception which I have held to be possible of material objects is not the same as the very inclusive concept of the perceivable which allows anything to be observable which can be the object of a verb of perception used in a colloquially significant way nor as the very exclusive concept which holds that only what is incorrigibly known in perception is really observable. But I do not think it can be argued that this view alone permits a definite problem about theoretical entities to be raised. Feyerabend's account of observability relativises the problem in a way that prohibits its conclusive solution. But the problem can be formulated within the framework of a phenomenalist account of material objects.

Causal connections

If theoretical entities are neither strictly transcendental nor, for the most part, mere constructions, there is still one kind of puzzling entity, whose existence is sometimes held to be implied by our scientific beliefs in particular, but, more broadly, by all our general and conditional beliefs, which remains to be considered. These entities are real or causal connections and they are puzzling because on the one hand they are not in principle observable and on the other they are not merely relations of conceptual identity, total or partial, of the sort that account for necessary truth.

There are two different, but closely related, ways in which the irreducibility of such connections can be argued for. In the first place they are invoked to explain the difference between those general statements that express laws and those whose generality is merely accidental in character. General statements of law can be used to explain and predict; accidental generalisations merely summarise a closed set of analogous singular statements but support no inferences to other cases, actual or possible. Secondly, there is a difference between hypothetical statements as we ordinarily use and understand them and the truth-functional or material conditional of formal logic. On the truth-functional interpretation every conditional with a false antecedent or a true consequent is true. This implies the truth of a host of conditionals between whose clauses there is, as we should say, no connection whatever. It further implies the truth of every counterfactual conditional that is, as one could put it, applicable in that the presumption it embodies of the falsity of its antecedent is correct. Finally it implies that every because-statement, which is applicable in virtue of the truth of its components, is true, provided that such statements are, as I should claim, pro-factual conditionals.

What relates these two arguments for the irreducibility of connections is that while the standard criterion for the law-like nature of a general statement is the derivability from it of a corresponding counterfactual the counterfactual is the type of conditional that is most refractory to analysis in the formal logician's truth-functional terms. A reductive account of conditionals which avoids the positing of unobservable connections, and yet which is not exposed to the difficulties that attend the material conditional, takes them to imply, or at least to rest on the essential support of, general statements of law. Thus a vicious circle of explanation is generated. General statements of law require to be explained in terms of conditionals; conditionals in terms of general statements of law. There seems to be more to general statements of law than Humean regularity or constancy of conjunction and to conditionals than the denial of the conjunction of their antecedents with the negation of their consequents. The most compact account of the difference is that the properties in a law or the states of affairs delineated by the clauses of a conditional are related by a real or causal connection. The circle is broken by recourse to something in the world outside the logical relations of general statements and conditionals to each other.

A more direct way to the conclusion that there are real connections is through a naive correspondence theory of conditional statements. Categorical statements, it might be said, correspond to and are verified by straightforwardly observable categorical facts; similarly, hypothetical statements correspond to hypothetical facts, which are, more explicitly, connections between states of affairs, or possible categorical facts. There is something very like this theory in Bradley's

Principles of Logic, although it is heavily encumbered with evasive affectation. He says that 'what is affirmed [in a hypothetical judgement] is the mere ground of the connection; not the actual existing behaviour of the real, but a latent quality of its disposition'. On such a view the categorical fact (the 'actual existing behaviour of the real') is one thing, the hypothetical fact (a 'latent quality' of the real) is another (Bradley (1), p. 87).

The crucial objection to this doctrine is that conditional statements are logically related to categorical ones. 'p and not-q' refutes, and its negation is thus entailed by, 'if p then q'. Furthermore all reasoning in support of conditionals will arrive sooner or later, by way of general statements, at the categorical confirming evidence for those general statements. The task of discovering some reductive interpretation of conditionals in categorical terms is thus doubly attractive. The idea of a realm of connections or dispositions or possibilities to be apprehended only in a non-observational way is repugnantly speculative; the idea of their logical independence of the observable and categorical is plainly false as regards their falsification and highly questionable as regards their confirmation or support.

The truth-functional analysis of the conditional 'if p then q' as the same in meaning as 'not both p and not-q' is the most economical possible rendering of it in categorical terms. Apart from the categorical components the analysis makes use only of the logical notions of negation and conjunction. These are, in the first place, the most primitive logical notions, for negation is essential to any language, to any rule-governed practice of utterance whatever, and conjunction is required to hold together in a single assertion what can in practice only be uttered in sequence. A second virtue is that the analysis is at least partly unquestionable. It undoubtedly constitutes a necessary condition of the truth of the conditional; 'if p then q' certainly entails 'not both p and not-q'. The analysis simply adds that it is a sufficient condition as well.

There are obvious formal advantages in a simple truth-functional analysis of this kind. If conditionals are interpreted in this way arguments and logical laws in which they figure are easy to test for validity or necessary truth, as the case may be. All the arguments and laws involving conditionals that we find intuitively acceptable are ratified by truth-functional logic and a host of valid arguments and true laws are ratified which are beyond the scope of our logical intuition. Unfortunately two very simple laws are demonstrated within truth-functional logic which radically conflict with logical intuition: the 'paradoxes of implication' that the truth of 'if p then q' follows from 'q' and also from 'not-p'. As a consequence of that every counterfactual conditional is true, since every such statement presupposes the falsity of its antecedent. Since every statement of the form 'if p had been the case then q would have been the case' is true, whatever 'p' and 'q' may be, so is every statement of the form 'if p had been the case q would not have been the case'. Thus every pair of opposed counterfactuals, which have the same antecedents but in which the consequent of one is the negation of the consequent of the other, consists of two truths. Yet to logical intuition such pairs are contrary, one member at least must be false. Finally, on this interpretation, it follows that no because-statement is false. Such a statement is either inapplicable, where the presumption that both clauses are true is incorrect, or it is true. For a because-statement 'q because p', as Ryle has argued, is really a profactual conditional in which the truth of p and q is presumed and 'if p then q' is asserted (Ryle (3), vol. 2, ch. 17).

C. I. Lewis developed his system of strict implication in order to overcome the deficiencies of the material conditional. In its place he interpreted the conditional 'if p then q' as meaning 'it is not possible that p and not-q'. An immediate support for this interpretation is that the conversationally natural denial of 'if p then q' is 'it could still have been the case that p although not that q', in other words, 'p and not-q is possible'. It very soon became clear that there are some surprising laws of strict implication, exactly analogous in form to the 'paradoxes of material implication'. 'If p then q' is true, on Lewis's interpretation, if p is contradictory or q is necessary. But it can be argued that these surprising laws are not really paradoxical. That a contradiction entails every statement shows why contradictions should be avoided: to assert everything is to assert nothing. If a necessary statement follows from any statement this simply reflects the emptiness of content which makes a necessary premise logically superfluous in any inference in which it occurs, which is not to say that it may not be psychologically valuable to have it there.

The real weakness of Lewis's interpretation is that it introduces the modal term 'possible', and thus the rest of the modal vocabulary which is definable in terms of it, without explaining it. If the possibility is taken to be logical it follows that all conditionals are necessarily true (or false). To allow for conditionals which, whether true or false, are neither necessary nor self-contradictory some non-logical interpretation of possibility is required.

The readiest to hand is the view which takes factual or empirical possibility to be consistency with the laws of nature. It is (factually) impossible that this F is G if no F are G, or all F are not-G. This account of the matter, then, takes 'if p then q' to mean the same as 'there is a law of nature with which "p and not-q" is inconsistent'. It is in conformity with the point mentioned earlier that the ordinary way in which conditionals are supported is by reference to corresponding general statements. Indeed it makes the corresponding general statement part of the meaning of the conditional.

Now any law of nature that is capable of being logically incompatible with 'p and not-q' must overlap it in content. The terms in 'p' and 'q' must be identical or synonymous with the terms in the corresponding law. To bring this out the form of the conditional must be represented so as to reveal something of its internal structure. Instead of 'if p then q' let us consider the rather less comprehensive 'if Fa then Ga'. The simplest corresponding law to this is 'all F are G'. This is clearly incompatible with 'Fa and not-Ga' and to that extent fills the bill.

But, nevertheless, it is not acceptable. If I say to someone when it is pouring with rain outside 'if you go out you will get wet' it would be generally agreed that what I have said is true. But the immediately corresponding general statement, 'everyone who goes out gets wet' is plainly false. The required amendment is not, however, far to seek. For it is reasonable to hold that the general statement that everyone who goes out *in these circumstances*, namely when it is pouring with rain outside, gets wet. On this view the conditional 'if Fa then Ga' is elliptical. The predicates it contains are not themselves enough, in general, to specify the corresponding general statement, though, of course, they may be, as in 'if his head is cut off he will die'. It asserts that there is a property, or set of properties ϕ, which a possesses and which define the circumstances of a at the time to which the antecedent of the conditional refers, such that everything which is both ϕ and F is also G.

This elliptically referred-to generality is the connection which is missing from the truth-functional account of the conditional. It is what is common to the various different forms of the conditional. It is the whole content of the non-committal conditional 'if a is F then a is G', which assumes nothing about the truth-value of its components. Combined with the assumption that the antecedent is false it yields the counterfactual: 'if a had been F a would have been G.' (The falsity of the consequent is not assumed here: 'if Hitler had invaded England in 1940 he would not have won the war' is acceptable, whether or not it is true, though it might be more natural to insert the word 'still' before 'not'.) Combined with the assumption that both antecedent and consequent are true it yields the profactual or because-statement 'a is (or was) G because a is (or was) F'.

A particular class of because-statements is strictly causal, though by no means all: 'Ga because Fa' does not always translate into 'the cause of a's being G is its being F', its being a square does not cause a plane figure to be four-sided. The elliptical character I have attributed to conditionals in general is a familiar feature of strictly causal statements. To say that x's being F is the cause of its being G is to say that F is an element in one of the plurality of complex sets which are always conjoined with G, where the properties constituting the rest of the complex in question are also properties of x.

On this account of the conditional it follows that general statements are logically prior to conditionals. But, if every conditional presupposes, and indeed embodies as part of its content, some, not necessarily directly corresponding, general statement, the converse is not true. Not every general statement corresponds to, which is to say licenses, together with appropriate assumptions (about the ϕ-hood of a or the truth-value of the component clauses), the derivation of conditionals. This difficulty is a generalised form of an objection to Hume's account of causation as constant conjunction. Although causation implies regularity, regularity does not always imply causation, as with Russell's hooters in Manchester the sounding of which is regularly followed by the stopping of work in London.

A way has been found to account for the connectedness, which is an aspect of conditional statements of all forms but is not provided for in the logicians' truth-functional interpretation, without having to suppose that there are transcendent connections, which would have to be apprehended in some non-observational way. It would be unfortunate if they had to be relied on after all, to distinguish those general statements which support conditionals from those which do not. Is it possible to find an immanent criterion of law-likeness, in terms of the relations of general statements to one another, to distinguish laws from merely accidental generalities?

I believe that it is. Why are we so sure that the hooters in Manchester cannot cause the workers to leave in London? For two, not unrelated, reasons: first, the Manchester hooters are *superfluous* since there is, almost certainly, a better-confirmed causal explanation of the departure of the London workers (a bell in their own factory, the cry of a punctual foreman or something of that sort); secondly, the most natural account of the intervening mechanism between purported cause and effect is inconsistent with other well-confirmed causal beliefs, men cannot hear hooters nearly two hundred miles away from them. Of course, if a highly integrated firm were to connect its branches with its headquarters in Manchester so that the sound of the hooter at headquarters were relayed to the branch factories we should have no hesitation in describing the regular conjunction in question as causal. But the abnormality of this arrangement allows us to take the fact that it is not mentioned in the description of the situation as ruling it out.

What relates the two features of superfluity and inconsistency is that the same mass of supporting background knowledge which underlies the stronger confirmation of the regularity taken to be law-like is also the source of the other laws with which the attribution of law-like status to the original general statement is inconsistent. In the light of this we may conclude that any regularity that is supported by favourable instances, but is not violated by any negative instance, is *prima facie* a law. But its status as a law is defeasible by way of its relation to other general truths that have been established. Suppose it were discovered that all the Church of Scotland clergymen on the island of Mull had the first name Ian. Why should we refuse to conclude that a minister called Hamish stood no chance of being sent there unless he changed his name, that the current uniformity was merely coincidental? We should do so because the implied suggestion that the appointing agency in question would take the first names of candidates into account in selecting them is inconsistent with their known freedom from such aesthetic frivolity.

There is one difficulty which this account of general statements does not have to confront. Logicians have interpreted general statements of the form 'all F and G', first as meaning 'if anything is F it is G', and then, in view of their notion of 'if', as 'there is nothing that is F and not G'. The final version is true if there are no F, but, since the two are not in fact equivalent, the negative existential does not vacuously verify the corresponding general conditional, although it is entailed by it. The same asymmetry holds, in general, between it and the corresponding categorical general statement.

11

Mind

Dualism

Throughout the modern period, and particularly since the writings of Descartes, the idea that minds and mental events constitute a logically distinct category from that of material things and physical events has never failed to occupy a central place in philosophical discussion. Idealists, or mentalists, have in various ways construed material things as logically derivative from mental ones but until the last few decades the attempt to carry out a reduction in the opposite direction, to interpret ideas as a kind or construct of material things, has been taken as a clear sign of philosophical crudity and unsophistication.

In the philosophy of Descartes the dualism of mind and matter was expounded in a manner that has been complicated in numerous ways by his successors but with a clarity and definiteness that has never been improved on. In his presentation each of the two categories has an essential attribute, a determinable characteristic, possessed by all the members of the category and only by them. The essential attribute of the material is extension, by which is meant spatiality, the occupancy of space; that of the mental is consciousness.

The view that matter, and matter alone, is in space is the clearer of the two parts of this doctrine. Imagery and bodily sensations are the most obvious of apparent counter-examples to it. Their power to refute it can be nullified in two ways: by detailed objections in each case and by a general argument which for other reasons, deriving from the concept of consciousness, the dualist is unable to use. Images, even after-images, in a way the most material-seeming of them, are not in real, public space even if they have spatial properties. No doubt there is a literally physically located condition of the eye associated with an after-image, but it could be conceived to exist without its usual associate and its associate could be conceived to exist without it. They are logically distinct existences. A variant of the same manoeuvre, the distinction between a mental event and its customary physical associate, can be used to dispose of the literally spatial character of bodily sensations. What are distinguished here are the feeling and the associated bodily injury or other bodily abnormality. To say that I have a pain in my foot, the dualist contends, is to say either that I have a pain which is introspectively indistinguishable from previous pains caused by injuries to my foot or that I have a pain which I believe to be caused by an injury to my foot. In either case the pain itself is only located in physical space by courtesy, by reason of its causal association directly with a present state or indirectly with a past state of my foot.

The general argument distinguishes between the image or bodily sensation on the one hand and the experience of having it on the other. Those who are willing to draw this distinction would say that it is the latter, the experience, which is really mental and they would contend that the spatial properties of the content of such an experience cannot be significantly attributed to the experience itself. In general, however, dualists reject the possibility of drawing such a distinction. They tend to arrive at a conception of the consciousness that is the essential attribute of the mental which takes the primary mental events at any rate, and these would include images and bodily sensations, to be things which are logically indistinguishable from their owners' awareness of them. At one point Descartes defines the mental as 'all that which so takes place in us that we ourselves are immediately conscious of it'. In the terminology of chapter 6, pp. 146–8, things like pains are incorrigibly known and are self-intimating. I logically cannot believe myself to be in pain unless I am and I logically cannot be in pain without realising that I am. To be in pain and to be aware that I am are one and the same.

The principle that the mental and the mental alone is conscious is less straightforward. The reason for this is the ambiguity of 'conscious', which can be taken in an active sense, as saying of something that it is conscious of something else, is a subject of consciousness, and also in a passive sense, as saying of something that something else is conscious of it, that it is an object of consciousness. We use the word in its active sense when we say of a species of animal or of a man who has recently been knocked out that they are or he is conscious. We use it passively when we speak of a man's dishonesty or envy as conscious.

Certainly minds are consciousnesses *of*, or subjects of consciousness. To say of anything that it has a mind is clearly to say that it is capable of being conscious of things. But does this show that no physical thing is conscious? The minds we really know of are all the minds of physically embodied things. The dualist answer is that we can conceive disembodied minds and that the embodiment of the minds we know is contingent and inessential. A conscious being of this sort is a physical body that happens to be associated, by causation or some other correlation, with a mind, a categorical hybrid.

It is also true that most mental states can, without any unnatural straining, be understood as consciousnesses *of*. Beliefs, desires and emotions necessarily have objects. It is not so clear, however, that moods, like elation and depression do, though it is often clear enough what their causes are, what it is that we are elated or depressed *by*. And, on the received view of images and sensations, where consciousness and its object are one and the same, it is difficult to accommodate the phenomena, thus understood, to the principle.

Brentano held that the defining characteristic of the mental was intentionality, by which he meant that every mental state is of a relational form such that the second term or object of the relation need not exist (or, if propositional, rather than substantival, need not be true). I can believe what is not the case and fear, imagine or hope for what does not exist. This is really no more than a rather formal and articulate version of the principle that the mental, and the mental alone, is actively conscious. One objection to it has already been mentioned: there are mental states which cannot be naturally described in terms of an intellectual relation between a subject and a possibly non-existent object. There is also a difficulty about the converse claim that everything intentional is mental. 'Putting in traffic lights prevented many accidents' is clearly intentional in form, for the 'many accidents' mentioned are asserted not to have occurred, yet it does not describe a mental fact. A defender of Brentano could argue that merely physical instances of intentionality are always reducible, that intentional idioms in such cases can always be eliminated. We could have said instead 'because traffic lights were put in there were fewer accidents than there would otherwise have been.' At most, then, irreducible intentionality could be the defining characteristic of the mental and, in view of the earlier objection, it would be hard to make it out to be more than a sufficient condition of mentality.

The much more usual practice of dualists has been to take consciousness in the passive sense to be the defining characteristic of the mental. At its simplest this position is taken in the Lockean doctrine of sensation and reflection. It is not that the mental is the only possible kind of object of consciousness but that the mental and the physical are objects of distinguishable kinds of consciousness, perceptual in one case, introspective in the other. The weakness of this is its concealed circularity. What leads me to say that my awareness of the actual position of my leg is perceptual while my awareness of the discomfort caused by its being in the position is introspective is my antecedent conviction that its position is a physical state and the resulting discomfort a mental one.

Much the same objection can be made to most versions of the view that mental events are private objects of consciousness. My awareness that there is something stuck in my throat is in an ordinary sense just as private as my awareness that I am in pain. Admittedly no one else could have the sort of evidence I have for the fact that I am in pain; but, equally, no one could have the sort of evidence I have for the fact that there is something stuck in my throat. But, the dualist will reply, there are sorts and sorts. Other people could have just as good evidence as I have for the fact that there is something stuck in my throat, if not better evidence, but no one could have reasons as good as mine for saying that I am in pain.

With this we reach the classical form of the principle that the mental, and only the mental, is conscious, the one intimated by the quotation from Descartes. It distinguishes the mental from the physical as that of which a man is infallibly conscious from that about which his beliefs may always in principle be mistaken. Ignoring for the time being the arguments of chapter 6 against the notion that there can be infallible awareness of contingent, empirical facts, it is clear that by no means all the things and facts we are intuitively disposed to regard as mental are objects of anything like infallible awareness. There is much to be said for taking pains, images and sense-impressions in this way. But it is certainly not a *universal* characteristic of beliefs, desires and emotions for I can honestly *believe* that I believe, want or like something that I do not. And it is not a characteristic at all of personality-traits like generosity or intelligence and yet these must be accommodated by any comprehensive criterion of the mental.

What the dualist must say is that the objects of infallible consciousness are all mental and that they constitute a primary class of mental events or states. Other mental events, unconscious ones in this sense, must be defined in terms of the primary class, in virtue of the analogies between the causes and, more crucially, the behavioural effects of the two.

For the dualist, then, the contents of the world, or its temporal contents at least, if abstract entities are to be taken into account, can be divided into physical things, states and events which are in space and fallibly known and mental things, states and events which are not in space and are either infallibly known or are only identifiable by their analogy to things that are. The two categories are exclusive and exhaustive.

The temporal world is depicted as an array of material bodies, some especially complicated instances of them, human and animal bodies, being associated with minds. Each mind is a world of its own in that it alone is directly aware of itself or its experiences. Other minds can know it only indirectly, by way of an inference, an analogical inference, from the bodily phenomena with which it is associated. In the classical, Cartesian form of dualism the members of the two categories are logically distinct, neither can be reduced to the other. In the terminology of part 2 things of both categories are basic. Mind's independence of body is secured by the infallibility of self-knowledge. What I honestly believe about my mind could not be false but anything I believe about my body, including the belief that I have a body at all, could be false. Therefore, Descartes concludes, I am essentially a conscious, mental thing, a 'thinking substance'.

The body's independence of the mind is less firmly based. It is presented as the conclusion of a causal argument which starts from the fact that some introspectible elements of my mental history are passively received and fall into a systematic order. Because this argument is causal rather than epistemological, offering a possible sufficient condition of the character of our perceptual experience rather than an inescapable necessary condition of it, dualism of this kind has a tendency to collapse into mentalism. For a more economical account of the fact to be explained is at hand in phenomenalism, the theory that material things can be defined in terms of sense-impressions.

Some phenomenalists, unwilling for various reasons to appear to exhibit a partiality between categories, have described their position as neutral monist rather than mentalist. Impressions are the basic stuff of the world, the ultimate substances that require nothing but themselves in order to exist, and they are neither mental nor physical but neutral. Minds and bodies are both complexes of impressions, distinguished by the different principles on which impressions are arranged within them. There are two conclusive reasons for rejecting this interpretation. In the first place, impressions are not the only basic entities that have to be admitted, there are, for example, emotions as well. Now every such basic, infallibly known entity is part of the content of some mind or other and is to that extent mental. But there are many basic entities which do not form part of the content of any material thing, including some impressions, the wild and incoherent ones of hallucinations and dreams. This is the first failure of neutrality. The second is that minds, for the neutral monist, are literally composed of impressions and comparable, directly known things, whereas impressions are not literally parts of material objects. They stand in the more remote and complex relation of being the elements in terms of which statements about material things must be endowed with meaning (cf. Quinton (3)).

Descartes's distinction was drawn for a system in which mental and physical things were logically independent existences, on a level, so to speak, with one another. But the distinction survives even when the physical order has been logically subordinated to the mental. It comes to mark off, not one kind of basic entity from another, but basic, mental things, non-spatial and conscious, from the most important kind of dependent thing defined in terms of them.

Problems of dualism

Dualism has had to face three main kinds of objection: logical, causal and epistemological. The logical difficulty is that of accounting for the unity of the mind. It is a universal conviction that every mental thing or event that is not itself a mind must belong to or form part of the history of a mind. Yet the infallibly known experiences of dualism are represented as wholly distinct logically from one another. Is it just a brute fact that all mental events and states fall unequivocally and without remainder into the groups that constitute or belong to minds? Secondly, given that this is, anyway, a fact, what is the principle that unites the mental states and events uniquely associated with a mind, that compose it or belong to it? Is the mind a distinct thing from its states, which unites them by the relationship to it that is common and peculiar to them, or is it the whole of which they are parts, held together by a relation that they have to each other but that none of them has to anything else?

The causal difficulty is that of giving a coherent account of the apparent causal influence of mental events on bodily ones, in the exercise of the will where desires and decisions lead to bodily movements, and of bodily events on mental ones, in perception where physical stimulation of the sense-organs leads to the formation of beliefs about the external world. This difficulty does not arise from the nebulous idea that mental and bodily events are too dissimilar to be causally related. Hume's requirement that cause and effect must be contiguous in space, which rules non-spatial mental events out of the field of possible causal relationships altogether, could be discarded as the mistaken product of a myopically partial viewpoint, concentrated on the physical world. The real difficulty is that mental events appear to be causally idle. The events they are called in to explain can, it seems, be accounted for in principle in wholly physical terms, as the effects of physical events in the brain and central nervous system.

The epistemological difficulty arises from doubts of the validity of the analogical inferences by which, according to dualism, one mind must justify its belief in the existence of any experiences other than its own. The analogies involved, it is argued, are logically openended in an unacceptable way. Since I can never be directly aware of the experiences of another I can never test the validity of the principles of inference from behaviour to experience on which I rely in any case but my own.

Dualists are radically divided about the solution to the logical problem about the unity of the mind. Some follow Descartes in explaining the unity of the collection or series of mental states associated with a given mind as conferred on them by a mental substance to which they all belong, an analogy with ownership in the literal sense. But Descartes and Berkeley, who held this view, were not comfortable with it and did not press the analogy. A man may be a pauper with no literal property at all, but they maintained that a mental substance must always be active, must always be having some experience or other at any moment at which it exists. Locke, of course, held that this idea was refuted by 'every drowsy nod'. But the hesitation of his opponents had a serious basis. A man, even if he is a property-owner, is also more than that. He can be identified by characteristics that are more intrinsic to him than the property he owns. But a mental substance is describable and identifiable only through the mental states that belong to it. To put the point in general terms, a thing cannot be wholly identified through its relations to other things, it must have some qualities of its own (cf. Anderson, pp. 27–9). It is for this reason that the notion of mental substance is unable to provide a solution to the problem of how particular minds are to be identified. To say that two experiences are part of the history of one and the same mind because they belong to one and the same mental substance is an empty verbal gesture.

The alternative theory of Hume, that a mind is simply the whole composed of a related collection of mental states, presents the problem of the unity of the mind in a manageable form, although Hume's own account of the unifying relations as resemblance and causation is, as he admitted himself, defective. Suppose two men, A and B, take turns looking through a keyhole at moments 1 and 2. Then experiences A1 and B2 will probably be more alike than A1 and A2 or B1 and B2. As for causation: a man's past experiences influence his present ones, but they are very seldom the dominating factor, perhaps only in states of reverie or free association. The usually dominant causes are events in the physical world, including, of course, his own body. However a case has been made out, in chapter 4, for continuity of memory and character as unifying relations which both cover our existing practice and, unlike bodily continuity, cover what it would be natural for our practice to be if exchanges of character and memories between bodies were to occur, perhaps as the result of a transfer of brains.

The problem of ownership, of the apparent fact that every mental state finds a place in one and only one mind remains and is, if anything, exacerbated by the theory of a unifying relation.

Cause and effect are commonly, following Hume, held to be temporally as well as spatially contiguous. This requirement comes into conflict with an apparent feature of the causal relations between mental events and each other, rather than those between mental and bodily events. The feature in question is what Russell called the *mnemic* character of many mental events. My current recollection of a person I met last year, and whom I have not thought about since, is by definition causally dependent on the comparatively remote mental event of perceiving him a year ago. The intervening links in the causal chain between past perception and present recollection could, in principle, be located in any of three places: in the brain, in the mental substance or in the sequence of mental events that makes up the 'stream of consciousness'. The last will serve only if it is held to be uninterrupted, a speculation repudiated by Locke and common sense, and even then it would imply, given our powers of recollection, a detail of character in our mental states which is impossible to reconcile with the dualist conception of them as self-intimating. To locate the links in mental substance is no less empty a manoeuvre than the hypothesis of mental substance itself. But to locate them in the brain is to make the possession of mnemic characteristics dependent on what is, for the dualist, the contingent fact of literal embodiment. Yet all mental life above the level of the most mollusc-like sensitivity involves memory in some form or other, most obviously any kind of recognition. Mnemicness, as Russell pointed out, is a pervasive feature of mentality. If cause and effect must be temporally contiguous and if mind is logically distinct from body it follows that this logical possibility could never be exploited without reducing minds to an almost unrecognisably primordial level (Russell (4), pp. 293–5).

In recent philosophy of mind it is the third of these problems, that of our knowledge of other minds, which has been most influential in undermining dualism. Under the influence of Wittgenstein and Ryle a behaviouristic view of the logical relations of mind and body has been widely accepted, one that sees the mental as logically dependent on the body's behaviour by identifying the fact that a mind is in a certain state with the fact that it is behaving or disposed to behave in a certain way. Such a theory serves its immediate purpose of disposing of scepticism about other minds very effectively. Indeed it does it almost too well since it does not very satisfactorily explain the amount of doubt we do feel about the mental states of others (in Ryle's bluff formula 'other people are relatively tractable and relatively easy to understand') and, by representing our knowledge of our own mental states as a matter of hypothesis, makes this much more conjectural than it actually seems to be. But these are not the only problems with which it has to contend.

Behaviourism

Behaviourism, as a philosophy of mind rather than as a method- ological self-denying ordinance of psychologists, in its primitive form, identified mental states with actual behaviour: emotions with the muscular preliminaries of appropriate bodily movement, thoughts with subvocal motions in the larynx. But in the more sophisticated presentation of Carnap, Hempel, Ryle and, perhaps, Wittgenstein it identifies mental states not with actual behaviour but with dis- positions to behave. This convenient formula is in fact more than a little misleading. In colloquial speech to say of someone that he is disposed to go to bed is to say that he mildly wants to do so, in other words it is to refer directly to a mental state, a desire or inclination. The behaviourist view that anger is a disposition to shout, hit out and go red in the face does not identify it with a desire to do these things but asserts the identity of meaning between the statement that a man is angry and a set of hypothetical statements to the effect that he will or is likely to shout, hit out and go red in the face if such- and-such publicly observable circumstances come to prevail, if, for example, he is subjected to a loud noise or a request to do some- thing tiresome.

This view is better armoured against an obvious line of objection than many of its critics realise. It is rightly observed that a man can be furiously angry without giving the slightest indication of the fact to those around him by his behaviour. But this does not in the least refute behaviourism in its dispositional or hypothetical form. Though he remains outwardly calm the relevant hypothetical statements may perfectly well be true of him, just as a piece of material may be highly inflammable even though no smoke or flames whatever are emerging from it. All the same it is not easy to state just what the antecedents of the hypothetical statements in question are if they are to be expressed wholly in terms of what is publicly observable. It is, after all, not enough for there to *be* a loud noise or a tiresome request; the man to whom anger is attributed must *hear* it and *find* the request tiresome. This difficulty is the exact analogue of a difficulty that confronts phenomenalism as a theory of perception. To say that there is a chair in the next room is to say that I should have impressions of a chair if I were actually and physically to be there and not just if I were to have the impression of being there.

The usual partner of the objection that behaviour can be controlled is that it can be simulated. But here again dispositional behaviourism can overcome the difficulty. If a man behaves in a characteristically angry way it may suggest that the relevant hypotheticals are true, or rather, in these *ex post facto* circumstances, that the relevant because-statements are true. It may suggest that he is shouting and shaking his fist because someone has made a loud noise, when in fact he is behaving in this way for quite different reasons, because he is in a play, perhaps, or because he wants to divert people's attention from the embarrassing subject that has hitherto been under discussion. Of course the corresponding material conditional is true: it is indeed not the case that there is a loud noise and he is not shouting etc. But I have already shown that the material conditional is not an adequate account of what is meant by a hypothetical statement.

As I mentioned earlier it is often questioned whether in fact any philosopher, or at any rate any post-positivist philosopher, really holds this opinion about the nature of mental discourse. For a number of reasons it is unrewarding to make such a claim about the Wittgenstein of the *Philosophical Investigations*. The book is emphatically stated by its author to be an album of philosophical remarks and not a conventional treatise in which settled conclusions are to be looked for. The inviolate character of its theoretical virginity is fiercely protested by Wittgenstein's partisans, who regard his work as a mystery only to be understood by those who have undergone a complex ritual of initiation. One can say only that it contains obviously behaviouristic tendencies. If the formula that an 'inner process' stands in need of outward criteria is taken together with the idea that a criterion is a logically necessary condition and the proscription of a private language is impossible a behaviourist conclusion seems inevitable.

Ryle's *Concept of Mind* is less elusive in expression and is not the beneficiary of a protective cult. At the outset and recurrently throughout the book Ryle attributes the dualism of Descartes to a single, fundamental mistake, the 'category-mistake' of interpreting what are really hypothetical statements about behaviour as if they were, what at first glance they appear to be, categorical statements about inner, private objects and events. Or, as he sometimes puts it, there are not two worlds, one of public physical happenings and another of private mental happenings, but one world of public things, all of which can be described in the idiom of material objects and their straightforwardly perceptible qualities and relations and some of which can be described in hypothetical or dispositional statements about behaviour.

The subject-matter can conveniently be divided into three main kinds. These are fairly natural divisions and behaviourism applies to them to distinguishably different extents. I shall call them traits, states and events. By traits I mean long-run qualities of character or personality, persisting interests and tendencies, capacities and habits. Examples of traits in this sense would be generosity, socialist convictions, a colloquial knowledge of French, irascibility. By states I mean much that would ordinarily be meant by the term: beliefs, emotions and desires, which, while they can have quite a considerable temporal duration, do not last long enough to be regarded as part of the settled personality of their bearer. By events, finally, I mean bodily sensations, sense-impressions and images.

Now behaviourism is at its strongest in application to traits. I find out the unquestionably mental facts that I am generous or know French in very much the same way as others do, by considering my public performance on the occasions appropriate to their manifestation. In this field, notoriously, self-knowledge is less reliable than the knowledge of others. It is a special achievement to have as accurate a knowledge of one's own character as one's closest friends possess. There is good reason for this. One does not need it as much as they do and, if unflattering, it is going to be much more unpleasant for oneself than it is for them. The behaviourist account of traits is clearly altogether superior to the view that a careless dualist might take of them, that they are directly introspectible inner conditions. A more careful dualist might well admit that traits are inferred or constructed entities but claim that the elements of the construction are introspectible feelings. He might argue that a man might consistently perform formally generous actions by reason of a fortuitous coincidence of crassly self-regarding motives, that what makes an act really generous is its being prompted by a generous impulse. But the behaviourist could reply that the identification of an impulse as generous is not as simple a matter as the dualist implies. It does not bear its generosity on its introspectible face, but can be known as generous only by its actual, behavioural fruits.

The honours are perhaps more evenly divided in the case of mental states, narrowly so called. We do accept correction from others at times about our beliefs, emotions and desires and we admit that such states can be unconscious. Both of these facts undermine the logical authority of introspection in this area and suggest that the behavioural criteria are something more than contingent indications. Unconscious mental states could perhaps be explained away as introduced by the analogy between the behaviour that is definitive of them and the behaviour that is regularly contingently associated with the primary, conscious, introspected instances of the same kinds of state. But our rejection of our own, introspectively-based, beliefs about our mental states in favour of the behaviourally evidenced statements of others cannot be circumvented in this way in the interests of dualism.

A distinction of Hampshire's is illuminating here. In a discussion of the *Concept of Mind*, he draws a distinction between two ways in which such a statement as 'I was angry with him' may be taken. If it could be paraphrased as 'I was *really* angry with him' it is assimilated to some extent to the class of traits. In such a case a fairly persisting state of anger is involved. On the other hand, it may claim no more than that I felt angry with him, perhaps just for a moment and until I saw that my anger was unreasonable or until my attention was distracted and I forgot all about him and his supposed offence. In this case the assimilation is in the opposite direction, to the class of what I have called mental events (Hampshire (2), p. 251).

It is to these that behaviourism is least credibly applicable. Certainly in the case of some kinds of mental event, notably pains, there is a characteristic associated pattern of behaviour. But in many cases there is not. As things stand we have no way of telling what imagery a man is having unless he describes it to us and this is true, *a fortiori*, of dreams, which cannot be literally reported in the present tense but only retrospectively. (But there could be quasi-reports of dreams in the present tense. If a sleeper mumbles 'Mary, stop throwing ink at the Mona Lisa' and we know who Mary is, we shall have a fair idea of his current imagery.) But even where there is an associated behaviour-pattern we generally admit the privileged position of the subject of the experience. The plain fact is that we know about our own current sensations and images in a quite different way from that in which others know of them. In so far as the occurrence of mental events has behavioural implications, and many mental events do not, these are no part of what I rely upon or intend to convey when I report a mental event.

In the face of such irresistibly introspective-looking mental events behaviourists have followed rescue-strategies of varying degrees of heroism. Ryle tries to externalise the having of imagery by saying that to have a visual image of something is to fancy that one sees it. If to fancy that one sees something is to suppose, falsely, that one sees it this is an obviously incorrect interpretation. What Ryle means, however, is that one is pretending to see it, in the way that a child in a laundry-basket is pretending to be at sea in an open boat. At least the two activities could be broadly described as imaginative. But on the one hand it would be at any rate natural for imagery of towering waves and so forth to be an ingredient of the child's pretence, in which case literal imaging has not been eliminated, or, on the other, if there is not, the parallel breaks down. The bodily and especially linguistic behaviour of the pretending child, and this is now what his pretence comes to, has no reflection in the man having a visual image (Ryle (1), pp. 264–72).

Malcolm's theory of dreams is the philosophical equivalent of the Charge of the Light Brigade. Dreams, he says, are not experiences had during sleep. We do not dream though it is the case that we have dreamt when, on waking, we are inclined to tell stories as if of experiences undergone during sleep. The crucial argument is that experience implies judgment and judgment implies consciousness. But in sleep we are unconscious. Therefore there can be no experiences in sleep. Certainly we are not conscious of our actual physical environment during sleep but that is not sufficient to sustain Malcolm's case, which also falls foul of the fact that speech, bodily movements and brain-activity occur during sleep (Malcolm (1)).

Before coming on to the theory of avowals with which be-haviourists have qualified the full rigour of their doctrine, to cope with its obvious inapplicability to mental events like sensations and images, we may consider how well the doctrine in its unqualified form avoids the difficulties in which dualism is involved. It certainly deals effectively with the logical problems of unity and ownership. Mentality is disposition to behaviour and a disposition must have a living body as its bearer, thus settling the matter of ownership, a body which can be identified in the same way as any other material object, thus settling the matter of unity.

It might seem that the causal problem of interaction between mind and body is also readily solved by it. Material objects can be caused to acquire dispositions by physical happenings. Continuous pressure on metal can render it fatigued, leaving a slice of bread out for a good length of time renders it hard and frangible. So there is no objection of principle to the idea that physical occurrences can cause dispositions to arise in physical things. But if body–mind causation is thus legitimised the case is different with causation in the other direction, from mind to body. It is not the fragility of a glass that causes it to break when it is dropped, though 'because it is fragile' could possibly be given as an answer to the question 'why did it break', just as 'hedgehogs always do' could be given as an answer to the question 'why did that hedgehog curl up when you touched it'. It is rather the physical basis of the fragile disposition of the glass, the way in which its molecules are combined, a con-tinuing, occurrent and, in principle, observable, state of the fine structure of the glass that would be the cause here. Now the dis-positions of the behaviourist have no fine structure, or, at any rate, it is no part of behaviourism to claim that they do. It was perhaps a perception of this difficulty that led Ryle to adopt a curiously occasionalist view about the causal relations of mind and body in the *Concept of Mind*. He says there that to say that a person's body and mind interact upon each other is a logically improper cause-effect proposition (Ryle (1), p. 168) and that it is absurd to say that corporeal movements have both mechanical and mental causes (Ryle (1), p. 22).

It is not surprising that behaviourism should have solved the particular epistemological problem that provoked it in the first place. But, as we have seen, it solves it too well. It cannot, in its unqualified form, account for the peculiarly direct and intimate knowledge we have of our sensations and images, a knowledge that is not based on the kind of evidence others have for ascribing such things to us and which is apparently impervious to criticism that derives from such behavioural evidence. The qualification with which behaviourists have attempted to meet this difficulty is the theory of avowals and this we must now examine.

An avowal is a statement made by a person about his current state of mind. Or rather that is what it appears to be. It is really, according to the theory, a sentence in the first person singular with a psychological predicate which someone else, speaking in the second or third person, could use to ascribe a state of mind to the subject in question. Examples would be 'I am in pain', 'I want to go home', 'I wish you would stop doing that', 'I am very annoyed'. Wittgenstein says that in saying that I am in pain I do not describe a sensation that I am having but that my utterance is an extension, a conventionalised form, of the natural expression of pain, such as crying out or groaning. Ryle says that 'in its primary employment "I want . . ."' is not used to convey information, but to make a request or demand' (Ryle (1), p. 183). Elsewhere he says: 'The bored man finds out that he is bored, if he does find this out, by finding out that among other things he glumly says to others and to himself "I feel bored" or "how bored I feel". Such a blurted avowal is not merely one fairly reliable index among others. It is the first and best index, since being worded and voluntarily uttered, it is meant to be heard and it is meant to be understood' (Ryle (1), p. 103).

These three quotations make three different points. The first holds that an avowal is not a statement that reports or describes a mental event but an expression of it, in much the same way that a curse expresses annoyance or raised eyebrows express surprise. The second also holds avowals not to be statements but likens them to more or less imperative utterances: 'I am in pain' amounts to 'help me, comfort me'. The third claims that just as others find out that I am bored from my saying so, so do I.

The obvious objection to the view that avowals are not statements is that there is a sense in which they say exactly the same thing as the corresponding utterances in the second or third person and these are plainly statements. 'I am in pain' is incompatible with 'you are (or he is) not in pain' said about me at the same time. It is equivalent to 'he is in pain'. But what is incompatible with or equivalent to a statement must itself be a statement. The supposed virtue of interpreting avowals as something other than statements is that it accounts for their incorrigibility. But does it? Even if avowals were incorrigible they would still be capable of falsehood, if, namely, they were made dishonestly or insincerely. But if they are not statements they cannot be true or false. Is a curse incorrigible? It can, of course, be insincere. 'Oh hell' I might say, out of politeness, when told that some social event that I was dreading had had to be called off. My utterance purports to express an annoyance that I do not in fact feel. I might have served the same social purpose by saying 'oh I am upset'. In saying this my overriding aim is to please rather than to convey information but I convey information, misleading information as it happens, nevertheless. If a hearer doubts my sincerity he will simply contradict me if I say I am upset, but he cannot contradict an expletive, he will have to say something like 'come off it, don't try to make me believe that you are upset', in other words he will have to counter my utterance indirectly by contradicting the statement that it presupposes.

A further objection to the view that avowals are not assertive but expressive is that although some avowable conditions have natural expressions, pain, fear and anger, for example, others, like many wishes and all impressions and images, do not. There is no natural expression of having an image of Salisbury cathedral for 'I am having an image of Salisbury cathedral' to be a conventionalised extension of. The same objection applies to Ryle's view of avowals as requests or demands. There is also a further objection. If somebody rushes into the room shouting that the house is on fire he is not primarily concerned to communicate a piece of interesting information that he has at his disposal. He is enjoining his hearers to get out of the place. But he does so by stating a fact which is a very good reason for following that course of action. A woman says to her husband 'George, my handbag is on the chest of drawers in our bedroom'. This serves her just as well as 'George, please get my handbag from the chest of drawers' but that does not make it any the less a statement of fact. The same is true of 'George, I want you to get my handbag from the chest of drawers'. If George starts wondering whether this remark is true or false he has missed its point, but it is true or false all the same.

The view advanced in the second quotation from Ryle is exceedingly unplausible as a general account of this kind of utterance. It is indeed conceivable that once in a while I may notice myself saying something inattentively and, on that basis, deliberately reassert it. But it is not true that remarks like 'I am bored' are normally or generally uttered in this way. To start with, how else but with such a remark am I to state the fact about myself which noticing myself saying it leads me to find out? Secondly, how did I acquire the capacity to say such things in the first place? Since 'I am bored' is conventionally associated with boredom my early uses of it will be deliberate. Once I have mastered the practice I may indulge in it unreflectively, with my mind on other things. But my unreflective remarks can be evidence for me of their own truth only if I have first learnt to make similar remarks with conscious intent. Automatism is a feature of the maturity not the infancy of a rule-governed practice.

Ryle's view that we find out about our current mental states in the same way that others do, through 'disclosure by unstudied talk', really adapts the doctrine of avowals so as to reinstate unqualified behaviourism. It does so incoherently by first taking avowals, in the usual way, not to be statements and then regarding their occurrence as the speaker's crucial ground for making statements about himself in the very same words. It logically could not be the case that 'I am bored' is always used as an unstudied avowal if it is through such avowals that I find out that I am bored, for in what other way am I to state what it is that I have found out. Nor is it true that the unstudied use of such first-person sentences is prior to their studied use. It is, rather, a common after-effect of study. The attraction of unstudied talk for him is that it is publicly accessible and that it is less likely than studied talk to be dishonest. It is thus available and reliable evidence for others as to my state of mind (provided they are right in thinking that it is unstudied) and when available it can be reliable evidence for me. But it could not conceivably be the only evidence or even the main evidence I have for beliefs about my current mental states.

The standard theory of avowals would agree that they are, as expressions of my mental states, among the criteria which other people have for their beliefs about my state of mind. But it does not regard them as criteria for my corresponding beliefs. They cannot be since the theory implies that a person really has no beliefs about his sensations and images. It makes no sense, according, to Wittgenstein, to say that I know, or that I believe, that I am in pain. But since what I say when I say I am in pain is logically equivalent to various remarks of other people which unquestionably are statements it must be a statement itself. It is a trivial verbal truth that to say that I am in pain is not to *describe* my pain. But nor, when I say 'that is a table', do I describe the table. And I know perfectly well how to describe my pain if I am called upon to do so. I might say 'it is as if a lot of red-hot needles were being pushed through my shoulder'. In most circumstances we do not need or bother to describe our pains; the fact of pain is of much more importance than its precise character. But even here I still report it.

What provoked the theory of avowals was the supposed incorrigibility of what we say about our sensations, images and current feelings generally. It does not really explain this fact since what is neither true nor false is neither corrigible nor incorrigible. But the essential point is, as was argued in chapter 6, that there is really no such fact to be explained.

Materialism

That behaviourism is as plausible as it is, that it can give such a persuasive account of at any rate a very wide range of mental phenomena, shows that there is a close connection between behaviour and mind. But the introspective awareness we have of some of our mental states, an awareness that cannot be disposed of, in the manner of unqualified behaviourism, as ordinary, perceptually based, belief about behavioural dispositions, or, in accordance with the doctrine of avowals, as not really belief at all but as expressive or imperative behaviour, entails that the mental states it reveals to us are logically distinct from behaviour. It is natural to conclude, with the Cartesian and interactionist variety of dualism that introspectible mental states are the causes of behaviour.

Is there any way in which this defensible aspect of dualism, the general conception of mental states as, in some sense, inner causes of behaviour, can be preserved which is not exposed to the logical, causal and epistemological difficulties listed in the second section of this chapter? For it could be argued that it is not the logical distinctness of mental states from the behaviour from which their existence is inferred by other people than their owners that lies at the root of these difficulties. It is rather the *categorial* distinctness of mental states, conceived by the dualist as non-spatial and as ineluctably private, that causes the trouble.

Behaviourism shows that the logical problems of unity and ownership can be solved by establishing a connection between mental states and the body. The main causal problem is that mental states seem redundant as causes of behaviour since there is good reason to suppose that a sufficient causal explanation of behaviour can be discovered in terms of the activities of the brain and the central nervous system, an explanation, furthermore, which abides by the usual principles of the spatial and temporal contiguity of cause and effect. The epistemological problem is generated by the dualist view that the analogy underlying inferences about the mental states of others is vicious since the maker of the inference is logically precluded from any direct access to the fourth term of the analogy, the inferred mental state which is seen as strictly private to its owner.

These three objections to the general idea of mental states as the logically distinct causes of behaviour are overcome by the identification of mental states with states or processes in the brain, an identification which has some warrant from common speech and which is a working assumption of much scientific psychology. On such a view the mental state which a conscious being introspects is the same as the condition of the central nervous system which the scientific psychologist regards as the cause of the behaviour that ordinary belief connects with the mental state.

If mental states are identified with brain states the problem of the mind's unity is solved, for this unity is traced to that of an ordinarily identifiable material thing, the brain. It then becomes clear why in practice the identification of persons, or their minds, is most naturally carried out by way of their bodies, since in fact every brain that we know of has been effectively operative as a part of one and only one living body. But it remains conceivable that the living brain of one body should be transferred to another in such a way that it came to animate that other body and to function as the cause of that other body's actions and utterances. In that case the speculations of chapter 4 about the possibility of a transfer of personality from one body to another would be realised. The problem of ownership is solved by the consideration that there could not be a single, momentary, isolated brain state. This is not indeed a logical impossibility. Some Dr Frankenstein might construct a brain and succeed in bringing it to life for a moment. But in practice brains take a long time to develop and only come to be in the rather complex states which, on this view, are identical to the objects of introspection, as a result of a long process of conditioning and modification. Brains, like other material things, persist and endure and their characteristic properties are tied up with the fact of their persistence.

The causal difficulty is obviously dispelled by the identification of mind and brain. A piece of behaviour does not on this theory have two competing causes, one physical and one non-physical, a condition of the brain and an introspectible mental state, for these are one and the same thing, described in the different ways appropriate to the two different modes of access to them: brain-observation and introspection. Furthermore the spatial and temporal contiguity of cause and effect are preserved by this theory. The anger that makes me shake my fist is located in the brain and a continuous spatial path can be conceived of neural connections between the brain, in its angry condition, and the shaking fist. Equally the past perception that I now remember is temporally linked to the present recollection of it though the persisting modification in the matter of the central nervous system set up in the first instance by the perception and continuing in existence until the present moment.

The theory that mental states just are brain states renders the fourth term of analogical inference from behaviour to mind publicly accessible in principle. In practice we do not know very much about the cerebral or neural features of our mental states but we do already rely on them to inform us about mental states whose owners are not introspectively aware of them, for example dreams and cases of unconscious perception. And as knowledge of what, on this identity theory, would be called the neural properties of mental (or cerebral) states of various introspectible kinds increases we shall no doubt come to rely on them more.

Until very recent times the materialist theory of the mind was generally regarded by conventional philosophical opinion as the most irrevocably exploded of all philosophical doctrines (with the possible exception of ethical naturalism, which will be reinstated in chapter 12). And indeed the version of materialism which the received criticisms were directed against is indefensible. Materialism was taken to be a *logical analysis* of statements about the mind and not a very general *contingent* or *empirical theory* about the nature of mental entities. Typical materialist theses such as 'this emotion is a pattern of excitation in the brain' were taken to be advanced as logically necessary truths and this they are obviously not. Nothing whatever is directly and logically entailed about the state of a man's brain by the fact that he is in a given mental state or by the fact that he is introspectively aware of that mental state. There is no contradiction between the statements that a man is angry or that he knows he is angry, on the one hand, and the statement that his brain is not in the usual state angry men's brains are in or even that he has no brain at all, on the other. As the critics put it, we can learn to speak about our emotions and put this learning into successful use without having any beliefs at all about our brains or having any idea that they are related to our emotions or, indeed, knowing that there are any such things as brains at all. It follows, therefore, that statements about minds cannot be correctly analysed or translated into statements about brains. But the theory that mental states are identical with brain states is not committed to the view that they can be.

As Smart has pointed out, all the traditional arguments invoked to prove the logical distinctness of mind and brain can equally well be brought against the idea that there is a logical connection between lightning and electrical discharge (Smart (1)). A child can learn how to identify a flash of lightning as a public, physical event without ever having heard of electricity. But this does not in the least undermine the truth of the statement that a flash of lightning is an electrical discharge.

His point can be enforced by considering a more deep-seated contingent identity than the one he examines, namely the identity between a material object conceived as the possessor of a set of visual properties and the same object conceived as the possessor of a set of tactual properties. Whitehead emphasised the contingent nature of the relation between the two sets of properties by talking, disconcertingly, of two objects, one visual and one tactual. We are naturally disposed to resist this locution but the fact remains that the object could be conceived to exist with its visual but without its tactual properties or without its visual but with its tactual properties. Indeed for a congenitally blind man the second possibility is realised. What for the sighted are its visual properties are for him complex causal properties of the object to evoke characteristic behaviour and utterances from the sighted and, perhaps, to affect colour-meters calibrated in Braille in certain ways. A visuo-tactual object has two logically distinct kinds of property to which we have access in two logically distinct ways, by sight and touch. But the correlation is so pervasive and deep-seated between properties of the two kinds that we have many words, the words for primary qualities, which straddle the distinction. For a thing to be spherical is, generally, for it to be visibly and tangibly spherical.

One line of objection to the theory that brain and mind are, as a matter of contingent fact, identical is that it collides with the requirement of Leibniz that if a and b are identical then whatever is true of a must be true of b. Some of the particular objections raised under this head rest on a misunderstanding. The theory does not require that if I have an oval after-image there should be an oval pattern of brain-activity or that if I have a throbbing pain my brain must be throbbing. For it is not the pain and the image that are identified by the theory with a state of the brain but the event of *having* the image or the pain. Others rest on applying Leibniz's principle, beyond its field of valid application, to intensional contexts. I can know I have a pain without knowing my brain is in a certain state, but that no more proves that having the pain is different from being in the brain state than my not knowing that someone I know is married to a particular woman makes the man I know distinct from her huband. This by no means exhausts the difficulties that can be raised against the theory from considerations of the logic of identity. But the logic of identity is at once so complex and controversial that it is impossible to forestall them directly. All that can be done is to say that mental states and brain states are held by the theory to be identical in the sense, whatever precisely that may turn out to be, in which a flash of lightning is an electrical discharge or an apple is a system of molecules or, to use an example of Armstrong's, the carrier of inheritable characteristics is a DNA molecule.

Two more clearly delineated objections of principle remain, both derived from Descartes' definition of the mental. The mental, in his view, is not in space, not in the way that the sky is not, but in the radical sense that the attribution of spatial properties to mental entities is senseless. Yet if the identity theory is correct mental states do have a definite position in space, in the brain. In the next section I shall offer an argument to show that the possession of spatial properties by mental events is necessary for their individuation, quite independently of the theory. In the final section of the chapter I shall examine the other Cartesian objection, or rather family of confusingly overlapping objections, arising from the defining consciousness of the mental. I shall resolve this objection into two main forms: (i) that mental states are the private objects of infallible introspection, whereas nothing physical is private, introspected or infallibly known and (ii) that the mental is intentional, or generally so, and that nothing physical is, at any rate, irreducibly intentional.

If these objections can be overcome the existence of a class of mental entities irreducibly distinct from everything physical is refuted, for on this theory mental entities just are a particular, highly complex, kind of physical events, states or processes occurring in a particular kind of physical object. Dualism of body and mind remains a logically conceivable hypothesis just to the extent that the identification involved is contingent. But the traditional problems of dualism remain as objections to it. It might seem that because the rejection of dualism rests on a contingent assumption it is less forceful than the rejections of phenomenalism and platonism that have preceded it. But this is not really so. For even if the causal objections to dualism are dismissed as resting on a controversial concept of causation the logical objections about unity and ownership and the epistemological objection remain. What is strictly contingent in the identity theory is that mental states are *brain* states. But it is not, if the arguments of the next sections are valid, a merely contingent matter that mental entities are physical to the extent of being in space or that there could be other access to them than introspection.

The mind and space

Hume's question 'can anyone conceive of a passion of a yard in length, a foot in breadth or an inch in thickness?' gives emphatic expression to the view that the mind is logically non-spatial, that it is absurd to ascribe spatial qualities to the mental. As was argued earlier, this can be reconciled with the spatial things we say about sensations, impressions and images. Sensations derive their positions by courtesy from the part of the body that causes them, while impressions and images are not literally in space.

Hume goes on to deny that the taste and smell of material things are anywhere in space, in the confused belief that taste and smell are not public and physical, failing to distinguish them from the awareness someone might have of them. But with smell, at any rate, the position is quite clear. We can perfectly well say that there is a smell in a particular place when we are quite convinced that no one is smelling it. Indeed we commonly say such things with the kindly intention of ensuring that no one does smell it. Now a smell, or for that matter a noise, is hardly a material object but it is, nevertheless a public, physical state of affairs. In common speech we can roughly distinguish places where a smell or noise definitely is from places where it definitely is not, but we do not conceive it as having a definite boundary. Scientific inquiry further clarifies the nature of noises and smells. A noise is a disturbance in the air, a smell an array of odoriferous particles, usually with a definite focus, the sounding or smelly object, and steadily diminishing in intensity with distance from the focal object. These identifications are of the same character as that between lightning and an electrical discharge and the one recommended in this chapter between mental events and states of the brain. I shall now argue that Hume's contention that mental entities cannot be intelligibly located can be undermined in much the same way as his contention that it is absurd to regard smells and tastes as being in space.

If the question about the physical location of a mental event or state is put there are two possible answers: the dualist answer of Descartes and Hume (viz., nowhere) or the equally natural answer that they are where the people who are their owners or bearers are, that is, where their owners' bodies are or where the behaviour that manifests them or their proximate physical causes are to be found. In favour of the former choice is the fact that introspection does not appear to yield any spatial information whatever about its objects. Introspection can reveal the mode, intensity and temporal duration of mental states but it seems to convey nothing about position, let alone shape and size.

But if the position of Descartes and Hume is adopted a curious, and indeed artificial-looking, difficulty arises which is that of how mental states are to be individuated. Suppose that two people, A and B, undergo qualitatively indistinguishable sensations that are strictly temporally coincident, beginning and leaving off at the very same moment. How are we to justify the belief, which we should certainly hold in these circumstances, that there are two sensations going on here and not just one? It is part of the hypothesis that the sensations of A and B are not distinguishable from one another in respect of their temporal and other introspectible characteristics. If these do not distinguish them we might turn to the respective causal relationships of the two and individuate them as the sensation caused by the physical stimulus to A and the sensation caused by the physical stimulus to B. We might infer here that the sensations are distinct from the fact that there is no question that the stimulating condition in A's body is distinct from the, no doubt qualitatively closely similar, stimulating condition in B's body. But the inference is not valid. A single effect can arise from two distinct causes, a window can be broken by two bricks that hit it simultaneously. It is no better to distinguish the two sensations as that causing A's report and behaviour and that causing B's report and behaviour and for the same reason. A single event can have distinct and simultaneous effects, two different bricks can be hurled out in different directions by one and the same explosion.

It will, of course, be of no avail here to invoke the principle that cause and effect must be spatially contiguous for this principle is an inevitable casualty of the dualist doctrine. If mental events are non-spatial and yet stand as either term in causal relations to physical occurrences then the requirement of spatial contiguity must be abandoned. The bearing of the alleged privacy of mental events on the issue is harder to evaluate. It is clearly incompatible with any reading of the situation that identifies the sensation felt by A with the sensation felt by B. But which of the two assumptions must give way: that of the privacy of sensations or that of the indistinctness of the indistinguishable? It might be urged that A's sensation must be distinct from B's since he can know for certain that he has it without knowing that B has it or anything like it at the same time. But this would prove the distinctness of the sensations only if it followed from the fact that a sensation had properties of which A was not infallibly aware that it was not a sensation of A's. That principle has only to be stated to be seen to be obviously false. For no one would seriously deny that each of A's sensations has causal properties of which A is not infallibly aware, whether its causes are physical (as interactionists and epiphenomenalists could admit) or only mental.

The difficulty can be more strikingly brought out by the supposition, which the dualist must at least regard as conceivable, that A and B are disembodied, with emotions perhaps substituted for sensations in the example to avoid irrelevant disquiet. What sense can the dualist attach to the idea that the emotions of two disembodied persons, when strictly contemporaneous and identical in introspective content, are distinct? In conceiving the situation he will have to attach the emotions in question to some ghostly but physically located surrogate, a shade or spectral voice, to carry out the indispensable positioning work ordinarily done by the body.

Nor will the dualist derive any support for his claim that there are two distinct mental events in such a situation from the concept of mental substance. Even if we ignore the difficulty of seeing what more is conveyed by the assertion that an experience is owned by a mental substance than that it is a member of a particular related series of experiences there remains the problem of showing why it is that a single experience cannot be owned by two such mental substances.

These arguments are intended to show that we must at least admit that mental events are spatial in the comparatively weak sense of being where the bodies of the people to whom they occur and by whom they are manifested are, the second possibility mentioned in the third paragraph of this section. I would suggest that we implicitly take this for granted, whatever dualistic professions we may make, for, confronted with the situation of two simultaneous, introspectively indistinguishable sensations, the one possibility that does not seriously occur to us is that what is going on here is a single, shared sensation. The weak spatiality of mental events is comparable to that of physical conditions or states of affairs like smells, noises and heat. Common sense gives such things a rough, indeterminate location in space. Scientific inquiry then makes the results of un-assisted observation more precise. It shows that the roughly located olfactory, auditory and thermal entities of common observation are in fact rather complex physical conditions whose constituents have a definite position in space at any one moment.

We could treat mental events in the same way. Common sense can be seen as ascribing a rough position to them that is sufficient to distinguish them from qualitatively identical mental events in other minds that are contemporaneous with them, by locating them in the bodies of their owners. This is a natural consequence of the fact that their proximate causes and effects are in these bodies and is testified to by the universal practice of speaking of mental states as *inner* states. It is up to neurophysiology to discover the precise position of these events and states within the region roughly marked out for them by common observation. Perhaps it does not follow from the fact that mental events are weakly spatial that they have any definite position, they might be where their owners' bodies are and no more. But one could perversely say the same of noises and smells and hold them to be distinct from the air-disturbances and odoriferous particles with which they are at any rate intimately associated. This would be merely token resistance by dualism, a kind of symbolic defiance after the main point, the logically non-spatial character of the mental, had been lost. In the other cases of things commonly located in space in the weak sense scientific inquiry has gone on to establish their location precisely. There is no conceptual reason for supposing that scientific inquiry has not started to do the same for mental events.

Consciousness

I turn, finally, to the problem of whether the consciousness, that has been traditionally held to be definitive of the mental, is an obstacle to the identification of mental states and events with states of and events in the brain and nervous system associated with them. As was mentioned earlier, a complication arises here from the ambiguity of the term 'conscious'. On the one hand it applies, in what may be called an active sense, to persons or subjects of consciousness; on the other, in a passive sense, to the objects of consciousness. When a sleeper awakes the consciousness to which he returns is of the active kind; the consciousness which is thus acquired by his habitual hopes and fears is of the passive kind.

It is obvious that all minds are subjects of consciousness. It seems clear, too, that strictly speaking minds are the only subjects of consciousness. The mental events which compose their history, and are, in one familiar view, as a totality identical with them, are not themselves subjects of consciousness. But they are, at least commonly, consciousnesses *of* something. To derive a general criterion of the mental from the active form of consciousness, it is the acts of consciousness in which subjects of consciousness primarily manifest themselves that must be invoked, rather than the property of actually being a subject of consciousness. Such a criterion would define the mental as that which is an act of consciousness, a consciousness of something, and would derive the mentality of minds themselves from the fact that they are composed of or primarily manifested in such acts.

Brentano's thesis that intentionality is the essential characteristic of the mental is a criterion of this kind. All mental phenomena, for him, are acts of consciousness with an intentional structure, in that they are relations between a subject and an object, the latter of which need not exist, if the object is substantival or need not be true, if the object is propositional.

It is also clear that mental phenomena are objects of consciousness. But stated with that degree of baldness it is hardly a distinguishing feature of the mental. In some sense or other anything can be an object of consciousness: physical objects and abstract entities as much as mental events. The type of consciousness whose objects are, on that account, mental requires some kind of qualification. It is provided in general terms by Descartes, when he says, 'by the word *thought*, I understand all that which so takes place in us that we of ourselves are immediately conscious of it'. The mental, that is to say, is the object, not of consciousness in general, but of immediate consciousness.

In the case of each of these defining characterisations of the mental I shall adopt the same procedure. I shall argue, first, that neither intentionality nor being the object of immediate consciousness is either common or peculiar to mental phenomena. I shall go on to suggest that if these notions are more stringently defined so as to seem plausibly applicable to all and only mental phenomena they are, nevertheless, not so applicable since they do not obviously apply to anything at all. Finally I shall seek to show that even if all and only mental phenomena were intentional or immediately known, in the more stringent senses of these terms, it would not follow that they were therefore logically distinct from physical phenomena.

(i) *Neither common nor peculiar* Is intentionality common to all the events or states of affairs that we should naturally regard as mental? There are two kinds of apparent exception. The first is mental events strictly so called, by which I mean pains, sensations and images. It could be held that *having* a pain or an image is intentional in nature but that the pain or image itself is not. To have a pain or an image is to be conscious of a disagreeable sensation or a mental picture, but the sensation or the picture is not itself a consciousness of anything. Against this it might be objected that a pain involves a belief, or at last an inclination to believe, that the sufferer's body is injured or affected in some way. But this associated belief is rather part of the experience of having the pain than of the pain itself. And that raises the more substantial objection that it is improper to conceive the pain itself as anything more than an aspect of the pain-experience. All pains are pains that are felt or had. The pain itself is no more a mental object than the shape of a table, as contrasted with the table itself, is a physical object. The argument could then proceed on the other side with the objection that, if the pain itself is not a mental object, how can the experience of having a pain be of the required intentional, subject-object, structure?

It is fortunately unnecessary to pursue this somewhat inconcludable-looking debate further since the point at issue is more unequivocally made by the second kind of exception to the thesis that all mental phenomena are intentional. Although emotions, such as anger or embarrassment, typically have objects, which need not be identical with their causes, moods, like elation and depression, typically do not. There will ordinarily be something that explains my elation or depression. If it is the state of my digestion I will probably be unaware of it. If I am aware of the cause of my mood, perhaps receiving the news of some success or failure, I may say that it is what I am elated or depressed *by*. But the good or bad news is not the *object* of my mood.

There are two possible ways of contorting this sort of case to fit the intentional mould. The less inviting is that employed by existentialists in describing the type of apparently objectless anxiety which they regard as metaphysically significant. A pseudo-object, Everything or Nothing, is invoked to fill the gap produced by the insistence that every mental state is intentional in form. A better procedure would be to regard a mood as dispositional in nature, as a propensity to feel emotions of a particular kind towards objects that would not ordinarily evoke such emotions. If I am elated I am delighted by, if depressed repelled by, things that are in the ordinary way emotionally neutral. But although this procedure is preferable to that of manufacturing pseudo-objects it is still a contortion. The thesis that all mental phenomena are intentional can be established only by main force.

Its converse, that all intentional states of affairs are mental, is plainly more important for the case in hand. For if some physical things are intentional then the somewhat dubious intentionality of everything mental cannot be a ground for ruling out the identification of mental events with a certain kind of physical event. Now there plainly are true relational statements concerned wholly with physical things whose object-terms need not refer to anything that exists. 'The change in the river's course prevented a lot of crop-destruction this year' is an example in which the explicit force of the remark is to exclude the existence of a lot of crop-destruction. 'The burning-down of the forest makes possible the erosion of the soil beneath it' leaves the actual occurrence of erosion open, neither affirming nor denying it. To take a propositional, rather than substantival, example: 'it is probable that Mars is uninhabited by living organisms'. Most apparent examples of physical intentionality embody, as do these examples, causal or modal notions. But there are other possible candidates; for instance, 'this table approximates to a perfect circle'. However, even if it is admitted that these forms of words do exhibit intentionality it can be argued that in such cases it is of a readily eliminable kind.

Are all mental phenomena objects of consciousness? We are all thoroughly habituated to the view that there are unconscious beliefs, desires and emotions. One primordial type of resistance to the view that there are mental states whose owners are not conscious of them trades on the active-passive ambiguity of 'conscious'. Mind, it used to be said, is by definition conscious; therefore unconscious mentality is a contradiction in terms. But this is, of course, just a muddle. There is no contradiction involved in supposing that a man both dislikes his brother and is unaware of the fact. We are led to say that he unconsciously dislikes his brother when all the evidence, apart from his own, sincere, report, implies that he does. To the extent that we admit that people can be honestly mistaken about their own mental states we are pretty well constrained to admit that their owners are unconscious of them. If Smith mistakenly believes that he likes his brother, it follows that he really does not like him. If all such mental attitudes were self-intimating he would also have to believe truly that he does not. Now it is not impossible to believe that p and that not-p, but in the case of beliefs with such intimate and accessible subject-matter it would seem at least unusual or unlikely to do so. Once it is recognised that the domain of the mental must include what I have distinguished as traits and states, as well as the more obtrusively self-intimating mental events like pains, it can hardly be denied that there are mental phenomena whose owners are not conscious of them.

Is every object of consciousness mental? For the purpose in hand, again, this is the crucial issue. Plainly not, unless the type of consciousness involved is qualified in some way, as by Descartes' adverb 'immediately'. In the most general way, after all, I am conscious of anything that I can think about, anything to which in thought or overt speech I can successfully refer. But what is it to be 'immediately conscious' of something? On the most natural interpretation it is to become aware of the existence of the thing without inferring it from anything else. But, as I hope has been established by the arguments of part II, one can be non-inferentially aware of the existence of many things besides the existence of one's own current mental states, most notably physical objects, and, in particular, states of one's own body, exemplifying what has been not too happily called 'knowledge without observation'. To rule out ordinary physical things and the state and position of one's own body from the domain of the objects of immediate consciousness a more restricted conception of immediacy is required.

If the mental is to be defined either as the intentional or as the object of immediate consciousness, then, these defining expressions must be limited in their application. If there are mental things which are not intentional, like moods, or not objects of immediate consciousness, such as unconscious desires, it does not matter very much. The mental status of such exceptions could be ratified by their analogy with mental things that do have the properties in question. But if there are physical things which have these properties it follows that the possession of them by what is mental does not entail the logical distinctness between the two categories on which dualism insists.

(ii) *More stringent concepts* Can concepts of intentionality and immediate consciousness be found which can reasonably be held to apply to nothing but the mental? In the former case it has been maintained that the mental alone is *irreducibly* intentional. It is not denied that we can and do use intentional idioms to talk about non-mental states of affairs, but, it is said, these idioms are no more than a stylistic convenience, the facts in question can be stated in a non-intentional way. On the other hand no such translation-out of the intentional mode of description is possible or adequate when the facts in question are mental (Chisholm (1), p. 173).

Consider the four examples given in the preceding sub-section of intentional descriptions of non-mental states of affairs. To say, in the intentional mode, that the change in the river's course prevented a lot of crop-destruction is to say simply that if the river's course had not been changed a lot of the crops would have been destroyed. 'The burning-down of the forest makes possible the erosion of the soil beneath it' translates into 'the soil will not be eroded unless the forest is burnt down' or, in other words 'the soil will be eroded only if the forest is burnt down'. The technique in each case is to replace the intentional description by some hypothetical statement in which only actually existing things (river, crops, forest and soil) are explicitly referred to. In fact the second translation is defective. It does not imply, as the corresponding intentional remark does, that the forest has been burnt down. A more accurate translation would be: 'because the forest has burnt down it is possible that the soil should be eroded'. It could be argued that the second clause in this more accurate translation is itself intentional, since the state of affairs mentioned in its that-clause does not need actually to occur for the because-statement, and thus its two main constituents, to be true.

The modal statement, 'it is possible that the soil should be eroded', is similar to the third example given earlier: 'it is probable that Mars is uninhabited by living organisms'. A rough translation of this, along lines suggested by Chisholm, would be: 'most Mars-like environments are uninhabited'. The roughness is due to the fact that many quite different sets of environments could be properly described as Mars-like while exhibiting very different frequencies of uninhabitedness.

Analogously 'it is possible that the soil should be eroded' could be roughly translated into 'not all tracts of soil like this are un-eroded'. The last example, 'this table approximates to a perfect circle', offers no problem, for it plainly means that this table is almost perfectly circular in shape.

Allowing for a certain roughness, then, which could, I believe, be removed at the cost of a good deal of long-windedness, it appears that the intentional mode of description of non-mental states of affairs can be eliminated. Is a similar elimination impossible in mental examples? Much attention has been given to belief-statements in this connection; reasonably enough if Russell is right when he says that belief is 'the most "mental" thing we do' (Russell (4), p. 231). Can 'A believes that it is raining', which is intentional in implying nothing about the truth or falsity of 'it is raining', be translated into a non-intentional sentence?

One way of doing this, proposed by Carnap (Carnap (2), pp. 247–9), is to interpret belief-sentences linguistically, as concerning the sentences which the believer would utter or to which he would give his assent. Let us say that A accepts a given sentence if and only if A is disposed to utter it or to assent to it if it is uttered by someone else. Then 'A believes that it is raining' could be translated into 'A accepts the sentence "it is raining"'. The conventional objection to this is that A may not understand English. To accommodate the effects of the tower of Babel we must, it seems, say instead, 'A accepts some sentence that means the same as "it is raining" '. But, it is then objected, intentionality has not been avoided, since the proposed translation, through its reference to meaning, is itself intentional. In saying 'the language of semantics is irreducibly intentional' Ayer is representative of many who have investigated this problem (Ayer (8), p. 42).

Now this objection would indeed hold if the translation had been proposed in a different form, as 'A accepts some sentence which means that it is raining'. But this is, I should maintain, an intentionally idiomatic rendering of the explicitly linguistic translation I offered first. Furthermore this type of statement about the meaning of expressions in which the expression, as grammatical object, is said to mean some, presumably abstract, thing, rather than to be the same in meaning as some other expression is intrinsically objectionable. '(The proposition) that p' is an acceptable grammatical complement to 'x means . . .' where 'x' is the name of a *sentence*. But where 'x' is a word or phrase trouble sets in.

Consider two cases where 'x' is a predicate. ' "Procrastinate" means put things off' and ' "Inurbane" means impolitely'. The first of these is simply ill-formed. Certainly 'procrastinate' *means the same as* 'put things off', but 'put things off' is not a grammatically possible complement to the verb 'means' which requires to be followed by a substantival expression. A subliminal recognition of this impropriety is shown by the way some who use this type of formula put the purported grammatical object of the sentence in italics, without explanation of the notational point of doing so, but clearly not for purposes of emphasis (Alston, p. 21).

As for the second example it is simply false: there is nothing impolite about the way in which the Latin word 'inurbane' means what it does. The point can be enforced with an example involving a singular term: ' "Le Néant" means nothing'. This, too, is simply false; 'Le Néant' certainly means something. The truth it is fumblingly trying to express is intelligibly stated by the sentence ' "Le Néant" means the same as "nothing" '. Chisholm makes this mistake when he says that 'in German "Einhorn" designates unicorns', taking 'designate' to mean the same as 'refer'. For it clearly does nothing of the sort: it does not designate or refer to anything since there are no unicorns and it does mean the same as 'unicorn' (Chisholm (1), p. 174).

We can, of course, make ourselves understood by saying such things as ' "daystar" means the sun'. But it would be better expressed either as ' "daystar" means the same as "the sun" ' or as ' "daystar" refers to the sun'. Both are true. The latter follows from the former together with the assumptions (both correct) that 'daystar' is a singular term and that it refers to something. But the linguistic form of the remark about the reference of 'daystar' is superfluous. What it means is simply that the sun is the very same thing as daystar, if I may lapse, innocuously, into the convenient intentional idiom for talking about the meanings of sentences. The linguistic form is superfluous in this example just as it is in saying '"red" is true of the Russian flag' instead of 'the Russian flag is red'.

I conclude that statements about the meaning of words and sentences are not irreducibly intentional, that the favoured and often grammatically improper or merely false intentional forms in which they are stated are more or less undesirable, and certainly dispensable, substitutes for the statements about identity of meaning which are altogether more faithful to the intentions of their users.

This last observation draws attention to an implication of what I have said about meaning; that it is not to be defined, in anything like Grice's way, in terms of the intentions of speakers. Grice defines the meaning of an expression in terms of the intentions of most of those who habitually use it and the meaning with which a particular speaker uses it is defined in terms of the effect, typically a belief, he intends his use of it to bring about in the person to whom he is speaking. On such a view statements about meaning are doubly intentional: first, because statements about what people intend to do are, not surprisingly, intentional, and, secondly, because it defines meaning in terms of belief and thus rules out the kind of analysis of belief in terms of meaning which is needed to show that belief-statements are not intentional.

However I am convinced that Grice's project is misconceived. The reason is that for someone to intend, by doing A, to bring about B he must believe that doing A is likely to bring about B. I cannot say that I am intending to make the bus go faster while it is stuck at the traffic lights by tapping my kneecap unless I believe that doing so is calculated to have that effect. Now how can I intend to bring about the belief in you that it is raining by uttering to you the sentence 'it is raining'? Only if I believe or take 'it is raining' to mean what it does. Meaning cannot be defined in terms of Gricean intentions since the possession of meaning by the verbal instruments involved is necessarily presupposed by making use of them for the carrying out of the intentions in question.

Belief, then, can be purged of intentionality by being defined in terms of meaning and meaning is neither irreducibly nor desirably intentional. '"Es regnet" means the same as "it is raining"' asserts an ordinary, extensional relationship between two actually existing things, two sentences of different languages. However, such statements about the identity of meaning of sentences are abstract and theoretical; they refer to sentence-types, after all. There are various ways in which what they state can be more concretely expressed. One is to interpret the sentence '"s" and "s'"' are the same in meaning' as 'most circumstances in which habitual users of tokens of "s" and "s'" utter them are closely similar'.

In fact this formula could apply only to what Quine calls 'occasion sentences' (Quine (4), pp. 35ff.), what others have called 'observation sentences' and what I have discussed as 'ostensive sentences' in chapter 5, pp. 126–30 above. For what may be called 'introduced' sentences, that is to say sentences whose meaning is specified by correlation with a defining set of ostensive sentences, we must say that they are the same in meaning if and only if the ostensive sentences with which they are respectively correlated are themselves identical in meaning. Unless this were so there would be no difference between the synonymy that relates 'this is a man' and 'this is a rational animal' and the mere coextensiveness that relates 'this is a man' and 'this is a featherless biped'. And if that distinction evaporates, so, as Quine, of course, is happy to agree, does that between analytic and synthetic (Quine (3), p. 31).

But once a reference to the method of learning has been made to explain the identity of meaning between introduced sentences it might seem reasonable to bring it into the definition of synonymy between ostensive sentences. Thus, where p and q are ostensive, p means the same as q if and only if the circumstances in which p and q are taught are closely similar. Assuming the general inductiveness of ostensive learning it will follow from this that any circumstance which disposes a user of p to utter it will be one that disposes a user of q, who happens to be present, to utter it. Quine says that 'just what it means to affirm synonymy . . . is far from clear; but, whatever these interconnections may be, they are grounded in usage' (Quine (3), pp. 24–5). But it is rather that usage exhibits meaning while teaching, which determines usage, actually fixes it.

A further virtue of relating meaning to teaching rather than the usage which teaching determines is that there are misuses. Among the circumstances in which speakers are disposed to utter the sentence 'this is a cow' are some in which there is no cow but only a bull present. Hence the original formula which defined meaning in terms of usage had to restrict itself to the close similarity of *most* circumstances in which habitual users of the sentence utter them. Insincere utterance provides another reason for this restriction. The restriction is certainly to be preferred to the alternative of saying that the circumstances in which two synonymous sentences are uttered are closely similar in respect of what their utterers *believe* in them.

One consequence of this account of meaning is that on most

occasions on which an ostensive sentence is uttered it is true. But this is not a ground of objection. Unless most of the ostensive statements that actually get made were true we should not be able to attach any meaning to the utterances of others at all. This fact supplies us with a reason for the very large reliance on testimony which is characteristic of our acquisition of beliefs. The reliance is vindicated by the logical, and, so to speak, Kantian, limits to the opportunity others have to deceive us (cf. Quinton (3)).

At any rate an account of identity of meaning in terms of the circumstances in which ostensive sentences are learnt largely avoids the problem posed by misuse and insincerity. The proportion of defective or non-standard circumstances in teaching is bound to be much smaller than the proportion of such circumstances in actual usage. No doubt even here there can still be some deviant circumstances. Conceivably I might learn how to recognise horses from a course of instruction in which the only horse available is one which, unknown to my teacher and to me, is made of wood. But the number of such cases is hardly going to be statistically significant.

A final consequence of a linguistic or Carnapian account of belief should be briefly mentioned. It follows from it, as Chisholm has observed (Chisholm (2), pp. 140-1), that animals, and other non-speakers, cannot be said to have beliefs, at least in a primary and literal sense. Chisholm is unclear as to whether this is an advantage or a disadvantage. What is indubitable is that animals behave in ways closely analogous to those in which language-users behave when they accept sentences in the belief-constituting sense I have elaborated. Now in view of the general, causal account of mental states I have defended in section 4 of this chapter I should not in fact wish to *identify* the mental state of belief with a disposition to verbal behaviour, to the assertion and assent covered by the notion of acceptance. Rather I should hold it to be a state of a person which *causes* such acceptance-behaviour. In some, but not all cases, it causes other behaviour as well, in particular where the sentence whose acceptance constitutes the belief is ostensive. But it is just these beliefs which, in virtue of their non-verbal behaviour, we are in the habit of ascribing to animals. From this point of view the ascription of ostensive beliefs to animals, then, is barely analogical and certainly not figurative.

I conclude, then, that mental states of affairs are not irreducibly intentional and thus that a concept of the intentional stringent enough not to apply to physical instances establishes no ultimate logical distinction between the physical and the mental since it does not apply to the mental either.

There are two more stringent conceptions of immediate consciousness which can be disposed of much more rapidly. What is peculiar to the mental, it could be held, is that it alone is the object of *introspective* awareness. This suggestion, is, I think, inadequate, or rather is too good to be true. The concept of introspection pre-supposes the concept of the mental. To become introspectively aware of something is simply to acquire a belief about a current mental state of one's own, without inference or reliance on testi-mony. There seems to be no distinguishing mark by which intro-spective awareness could be picked out from other kinds apart from the mental nature of its objects. In what other way can the view of Stout and more recent believers in 'knowledge without observation' that we are introspectively, because immediately and non-infer-entially, aware of states of our own bodies be ruled out?

The only alternative is to define immediate awareness, and thus the mental nature which is held to be peculiar to its objects, in terms of incorrigibility. Any object whose existence logically follows from the fact that it is believed to exist is, on this view, mental. It is now generally agreed that some mental states are not the objects of incorrigible knowledge. But these more elusively mental entities could earn the title by way of their analogy with those that are mental in the primary, incorrigibly knowable, sense (Pap (4), p. 382). Since it is uncontroversial that there is no incorrigible awareness of physical things and events it would seem that if what is mental is, at least in the primary cases, incorrigibly knowable a logically distin-guishing peculiarity of the mental does after all exist.

I have argued against the idea that any statements of fact are incorrigible in chapter 6 at some length and I shall not rehearse the arguments here. In the light of the conclusions reached in that chapter it is enough to show that the only concept of immediate conscious-ness which could be peculiar to mental objects is that which identifies the immediate with the incorrigible. For in that case, since no matter of fact is incorrigibly known, mental objects have no logically distinguishing peculiarity.

To say this is not to say there is no distinction between the mental and what may be called the *merely* physical. Dualism is not gratui-tous. Our operative conception of the mental embraces those things and events which involve people and with respect to whose existence or occurrence the people in question have a *contingent* authority or privilege: the inner causes of their behaviour. As a matter of fact people do have a non-inferential awareness, in the ordinary, non-logical sense, of facts about themselves which, in practice, other people discover only by inference from the way they behave and in particular what they say. But in all cases this awareness is, in principle, corrigible (in the case of mental states and traits, as contrasted with mental events, it is corrigible in practice) and the inner causes in question, conceived as conditions of the brain and nervous system, are in principle accessible to direct observation by others. The mental, indeed, is not very sharply marked off from the merely physical. It comprises those states of affairs of which we can, and often do, have a direct awareness of a non-logical, corrigible, kind, if we reflect or direct our attention appropriately, and which are private to the extent that there is no well-established way in which others, or I myself using other methods than attentive reflection or introspection, can discover them, except by inference. If a direct check on the findings of introspection becomes available in the form of observation of what is going on in the brain it will be possible to take the cerebral and the criterion of the mental. But this conclusion will be guided and controlled by the operative criterion of the mental that we already have.

(iii) *The distinguishing force of incorrigibility and intentionality* I have argued so far that, in the only forms in which consciousness, in either of its senses, could be a distinguishing peculiarity of the mental, those of incorrigibility and irreducible intentionality, it is not in fact such a peculiarity since nothing at all has these characteristics. But in case the arguments for this conclusion are defective it is important to consider whether, if some mental events were either incorrigibly known or irreducibly intentional, that would entail their non-identity with physical events in the brain and nervous system.

If mental events are incorrigibly knowable and physical events are not then, it is held, they must be distinct. By the diversity of discernibles it follows from the fact that a has a property which b lacks that a is not identical to b. From Leibniz's law: $(x)(y)(\phi)$ $(x = y) \equiv (\phi x \to \phi y)$ it plainly follows that $(E\phi(\phi a \ \& - \phi b) \to (a \neq b)$.

The weakness of this argument is that the property in question, that of being incorrigibly knowable, is not the kind of extensional property to which the application of the predicate-variable 'ϕ' must be restricted if Leibniz's law is to be true. If anything is incorrigibly knowable it is the identity of a thing with itself. John Smith, therefore, has the property of being incorrigibly knowable as identical with John Smith. But although this property is not possessed by the husband of Mary Smith, that is who John Smith may be. In general it may be said that no property whose verbal expression contains an intentional word, such as 'know' or 'believe' is a possible value of the predicate-variable in Leibniz's law. This simple consideration disposes of the argument that, since pains are logically private and the corresponding brain-states are not, a pain cannot be the very same thing as the brain-state corresponding to it, although known to exist in a different way. The intentional properties of things are relative to the ways in which they are described, but the identity of the things themselves is unaffected by the variety of their descriptions.

It might seem that if any property were indubitably intentional it would be that of being intentional and thus that the same argument could be invoked to undermine the distinguishing power claimed for intentionality. What makes this questionable is the fact that the possessors of intentionality are not straightforward things but rather events or states of affairs. It is Smith's believing that p or the fact that Smith believes that p to which intentionality is ascribed. But the criteria for the identity of events and of facts or states of affairs are far from clear.

A favoured criterion for the identity of events is having the same causes and effects and, if that is so, it seems conceivable that an intentional event of believing could have the same causes and effects as a non-intentional event corresponding to it in the brain of the believer. On the other hand, if this is not so, the brain-event corresponding to an event of believing might be, although physical, as irreducibly intentional as the corresponding mental event is alleged to be. The argument is inconclusive at best. It is also rather artificial. What, after all, is an 'event of believing'? Coming to believe something, the acquiring of a belief, seems naturally describable as an event but not the resultant believing itself. But perhaps a state should be conceived simply as a dull kind of event. At any rate the best available criterion for the identity of temporal entities of this kind does not imply that mental events are logically distinct from the corresponding events in the brain. Jones's breaking his arm and Jones's doing something likely to prevent his victory at Wimbledon would by any criterion be held to be same event. 'Jones has done something likely to prevent his winning at Wimbledon.' 'Oh, what?' 'Jones has broken his arm.' The third remark is clearly a further, more specific or intrinsic description of the event reported in the first. But the intentionality of the first description, even if it were irreducible, would not be a sufficient reason for taking it to describe a distinct event from the second.

It is perhaps more natural, however, to ascribe intentionality to facts, by way of the statements that state them, than to events. I suggest that the facts (or statements) that S is P and that S' is P' are identical if and only if S is identical to S' and 'P' means the same as 'P''. The subjects of mental predicates and of the cerebral or neural predicates that correspond to them are uncontroversially identical, namely the people who have the experiences or the brains in question. But no mental predicate means the same as any corresponding cerebral or neural predicate. This has nothing to do with the allegedly irreducible intentionality of mental facts but is a consequence of the contingent nature of the identity which is all that is claimed for mental states and the brain-states that correspond to them. Mental facts (and statements), whether irreducibly intentional or not, are logically distinct from facts (and statements) about the brain and nervous system. Statements (and facts) of the one kind are always logically independent of statements (and facts) of the other kind. The theory of contingent identity between mind and brain cannot therefore be a theory of the identity of facts or statements about mind and brain. But if it is facts or statements that are the real possessors of intentionality its peculiarity to mental facts would be no obstacle to the existence of the identity that is being claimed.

But even if irreducible intentionality does not constitute a conclusive objection to the identification which is actually being asserted, that of mental and cerebral events or states, there is still a further point to the rather protracted attempt in the second subsection to show that the mental is not irreducibly intentional. If the mental, whether carved up into states or facts, is irreducibly intentional it follows that the irreducible, basic existence of abstract entities (concepts, propositions, meanings generally) has to be admitted. My attempt to defend a reductive analysis of intentional idioms, then, is as much directed to supporting the thesis of chapter 9, on essence, as it is to supporting the identification of mind and brain that has been the leading theme of this chapter.

12

Value

Fact, value and antinaturalism

The ethical theory of this century has been dominated by the idea of a philosophically fundamental cleavage between natural fact and value, the idea, as Wittgenstein expresses it, that value is transcendental, that it is not 'in the world' (Wittgenstein (1), 6.4). The conviction that value is not in the natural, material, spatio-temporal world can bear at least two possible interpretations. It may mean that value is in some other world than this, a transcendent world of independently existing values, and it may, on the other hand, mean that values do not exist in any world at all, in other words that the utterances which appear to imply their existence are not really statements, true or false, but have some other function than the assertion of facts of any kind whatever.

What is commonly called antinaturalist ethics, has, indeed, taken both these forms, in temporal succession. Moore's influential critique of naturalism was developed in the interests of a theory of intrinsic values, conceived as non-natural properties of things, inaccessible to the ordinary sources of empirical knowledge and thus requiring for their apprehension a special intuitive faculty. Moore's successors, first Carnap and Ayer, then, more substantially, Stevenson and Hare, have taken over his antinaturalist conclusion but, by basing it on solider foundations than his, they have expounded it in a form which is incompatible with his positive theory. They have derived the indefinability of good and other evaluative terms which he was so anxious to establish from a logical dualism of statements and evaluations which undermines Moore's uncritical assumption that judgments of value were at any rate factual statements about something, even if not matters of natural fact. Persuaded that value-judgments, although they have some sort of significance, are not statements, they have run through the repertory of grammatical kinds to find some non-statemental function of language with which to interpret evaluation. An early suggestion was that value-judg-ments are expressions of emotion, that value-terms are most closely comparable to expletives and have some analogy to the emotionally charged, prejudicial words of national and racial insult. A less influential comparison was Russell's with optatives which took 'this is good' to mean something like 'would that there were more of this' (Russell (6), pp. 235–6). The most successful and persuasive of these noncognitive theories of evaluation has been that which takes evaluative discourse to be essentially imperative in nature.

The origin of this ethical preoccupation is Moore's purported demonstration that naturalism is a 'fallacy' (Moore (1), ch.1). The extraordinary thinness of Moore's arguments poses something of a problem, for seldom can such an uncomplex array of sophisms have exercised such intellectual authority. Moore's refutation of natura-lism consists of two arguments. The first, which I shall call the inspection argument, asks us, when confronted with any naturalistic ethical theory, in other words with any claim that 'good' or any other value-term can be wholly defined or analysed in terms of purely 'natural' or non-evaluative expressions, to concentrate closely on what is actually meant by the terms on either side of the definition, to see whether it is the same in each case. Moore is con-fident that it will not be.

The initial difficulty about the intellectual experiment that Moore invites us to undertake is that it is not quite clear what it is that we are supposed to do. How are we to set about testing by inspection such a definition as 'good' means the same as 'generally satisfying'? Is there any such activity as concentrating on the meaning of the word 'good', as mentally scrutinising the concept of goodness? In the case of more concrete and specific terms there is indeed a fairly straightforwardly inspective activity which more or less fills the bill. Faced with such a definition as '"wife" means the same as "female spouse"' I can form a standard or representative image of each of the kinds of thing to which the purportedly synonymous terms apply. Here at least there is something to go on. But it will not take one in the right direction. The usual imagery associated with a word is not a reliable guide to its meaning. In general, identity of the imagery associated with two words is neither a necessary nor a sufficient condition of the identity of their meaning. I may associate the same image, that of an individual dressed in the working outfit of Fred Astaire, carrying a champagne glass and covered with paper streamers, both with 'bachelor' and 'man of pleasure' which are not synonyms and a pair of quite distinct images with 'bachelor' and 'unmarried man' which are. The point is enforced by the fact that two people who attach the same meaning to a term may associate it with different imagery.

What is available, then, for the type of inspection to which Moore invites us is not relevant to the purpose of the undertaking; it does not provide the requisite information about conceptual relationships. Furthermore, as far as the kind of case in which Moore is interested is concerned nothing much in the way of imagery is even available. It seems clear that Moore implicitly accepted an account of the nature of meaning which makes the repeated rejections of it by his successors by no means otiose. His argument from inspection inevitably presupposes a reification of concepts.

This is also the fundamental weakness of his second and more usually stressed argument, which I shall call the argument from the significance of questions. In order to appraise the claim of any naturalistic definition of 'good', he says, all we have to do is to consider the question: is a thing with the supposed defining property good? If the supposed defining formula were really synonymous with 'good' then that question would be trivial and insignificant, it would be to ask no more than 'is this good thing good?' But, he continues, we shall find that whatever naturalistic definition we consider the corresponding question is clearly significant. It follows that no such definition is correct.

At a certain level there is something to be said for this argument. Moore himself distinguishes between bare synonymies, obvious and uninteresting definitions, on the one hand, and what he calls analyses, unobvious and interesting definitions, on the other. An example of a bare synonymy is the old standby ' "bachelor" means the same as "unmarried man" '. What makes it so bare and obvious is the fact that anyone who knows the meaning of 'bachelor' has learnt it by means of this rule. Thus someone who asks 'is this bachelor an unmarried man?' betrays the fact that he does not know the meaning of the word 'bachelor'. He is not asking for information in the way that is someone who asks 'is this bachelor fond of travel'. If he were to have asked 'is *a* bachelor an unmarried man?' he would be taken to be seeking a piece of linguistic information.

But it is clear that not all definitional equivalences are bare synonymies in this sense. If they were, the making of dictionaries would be a very much easier task than it is. No doubt there must be some bare synonymies if there are to be any analyses, just as there must be intuitively analytic truths if there are to be demonstratively analytic truths. But the general property of questions of the form 'is this A thing B', where 'A' and 'B' are identical in meaning, is that the affirmative answer, 'this A thing is B', is analytic. Only in this highly extended sense are Moorean questions insignificant. Some antinaturalists prefer to establish their principle in this way. Ayer, for example, says that a naturalistic definition, ' "good" means the same as "N" ' is correct only if 'this is good but not N' is contradictory. He goes on to assume, in the spirit of Moore's theory of meaning, that the contradictoriness of a statement is an intuitively obvious property (Ayer (1), pp. 153–4).

It is easy to show that this assumption is incorrect. It is perfectly possible to wonder whether there may not be a largest prime number, in other words meaningfully to consider the possibility that a statement, which is in fact a self-contradiction, is true. In general the analytic or contradictory status of statements, and thus the significance of Moorean questions, is not something that is intuitively obvious. Moore's test for the correctness of definitions is, then, inadequate. It might work in cases where the defining formula is very short. To take a case which he actually considers, if 'good' did mean the same as 'pleasant' it could hardly have escaped our notice. If 'this is good but not pleasant' were a self-contradiction we should know it. But serious naturalistic definitions are not of this pocket-dictionary kind.

In this second argument the same assumption of the obviousness of facts about meaning, and behind it of the simple object-like nature of concepts, is made. As well as being mistaken it is in conflict, as I have mentioned, with Moore's general account of the nature of definition, and, indeed, with the generally painful difficulty with which he worked towards the analyses of philosophically interesting terms.

Even if his test were adequate to the task in hand there would remain other weaknesses in his position. The first is that both his specific antinaturalist arguments can deal with only one naturalistic definition at a time. Any general conclusion about the incorrectness of all such definitions must therefore remain inductive and conjectural. Furthermore if it is to be inductively well-founded it must be supported by a large and varied range of particular examples. But Moore's procedure in this respect is perfunctory. Finally an inductive conclusion is only as good as the positive analogy between its instances. But Moore gives no clear explanation of what it is that makes a definition naturalistic. We get the general idea well enough of course; a natural property is one whose presence or absence is established by the senses, or by empirical means. But while this shows clearly enough that redness and coldness are natural properties, it by no means conclusively establishes that being conducive to the general happiness is.

I conclude that Moore's arguments against naturalism are quite insufficient to demonstrate its mistakenness in principle. The logical facts they require him to prove about identity of meaning, the significance of questions, the analytic or contradictory character of statements, are simply not in general as obvious, intuitive and available to direct inspection as he supposes. Nevertheless to show that antinaturalism is not established by Moore's arguments is not to show that it is in fact mistaken. There is, to start with, a very general persuasion, extending far beyond the ranks of the philosophically-minded, that statements of fact and judgments of value are different in some important and fundamental way and this the naturalist must both account for and either show to be mistaken or else to be really compatible, as it appears not to be, with his position. If, as the naturalist must hold, there is at least a logical connection between natural fact and value, he must demonstrate it by argument, for it is no more intuitively obvious than the disconnection upon which Moore and other antinaturalists insist. Before attempting any such argument I shall consider the very much firmer foundations on which antinaturalism has been based by Moore's successors. They have, I shall argue, discerned a real and important logical difference between judgments of value and some statements of fact but have misrepresented their findings by taking them to justify the antinaturalist principle. Rather their distinction can be used to help establish its opposite.

The practicality of value

The idea that lies behind recent arguments against naturalism is that there is a special relationship or connection between judgments of value and conduct that does not obtain in the case of statements of fact. In very general terms, to address a statement of fact to someone is to provide him with a reason for belief, but to address a judgment of value to him is to provide him with a reason for action.

Some difficulty has been experienced in arriving at a precise and satisfactory formulation of this connection between value-judgments and conduct. The crudest version of it is Stevenson's, which ascribes 'emotive meaning' to an utterance if it has a tendency to cause emotion, and consequently action, in those to whom it is addressed (Stevenson, ch. 3). It is hard to think of an utterance that could not in some circumstances cause emotion in its hearers, or again of an utterance that could not in some circumstances leave its hearers wholly cold and inert. It does not help much to define the connection in terms of a predominating tendency to cause emotion and action. In the first place utterances would be ranged by such a criterion on a continuous scale of practical influence which does not square with the presumption that there are two kinds of utterance that are basically distinct in principle. More important is the fact that such a criterion would inevitably rate the indubitably factual remark 'your hair is on fire' much higher on the scale of practicality than the indubitably evaluative 'you ought not to have done that'.

It is in general objectionable to interpret aspects of the meaning of an utterance in terms of its causal consequences. The meaning of an utterance is determined by the rules for its employment and for it to be an effective instrument of communication it must be in the power of the maker of the utterance in question to ensure that the conditions specified by the rules are satisfied before he makes it. It is impossible that the actual effects of an utterance, rendered comparatively unpredictable by the variety of human feelings and circumstances, should be amongst such establishable preconditions. An alternative account of the connection, then, is to define an utterance as practical if it is *intended* to cause (emotion or) action in its hearers. But this, though less objectionable in principle than a purely causal account like Stevenson's, has many of the same faults. Most conspicuously it entails that many unquestionably factual statements are practical; for example, 'I have leprosy', said by a girl invited to dance, and that many value-judgments are not, for example, 'Himmler was an atrociously wicked man'.

A better way of drawing the distinction can be found by considering the basis on which intentions to influence conduct by speech are formed. To have such an intention I must believe that the utterance I make in fulfilment of it is likely or calculated to bring about the effect at which it is aimed. If I intend to embarrass someone by saying to him that his dinner-jacket is worn out I must suppose him to attach importance to being smartly dressed. In some cases the relevant presumption about the desires, tastes or values of the hearer is so obvious and universally applicable that it is for ordinary purposes superfluous to render it explicit. Since nobody wants their hair burnt off, the remark 'your hair is on fire' is always appropriate for the intention to worry or distress.

But some utterances make no such presumption, however obvious, about the state of mind of the hearer, beyond the fact that he understands the language in which he is being spoken to. The imperative 'shut up' is made relevant to the aim of getting someone to be quiet simply by the established rules for its employment and not by any facts about the hearer's current mental state. It may, of course, be practically wise to take his mental state into account. If he is pugnacious but considerate in character he will be made quiet more reliably by the polite request 'could you please be a little quieter' than by the abrupt imperative.

The most satisfactory account of the distinction between practical or conduct-related and theoretical or merely belief-related discourse confines itself to cases where there is this kind of logical relation, in terms of rules of meaning, between utterance and action, and leaves out cases where the relation depends, contingently and circumstantially, on special facts about the mental state of the hearer. This is the procedure Hare follows in his account of the prescriptive use of language. An utterance is prescriptive, or, in my terminology, practical, if its acceptance by someone to whom it is addressed commits him to acting in a certain way. It is descriptive, or theoretical, if its acceptance commits him only to the adoption or holding of a certain belief (Hare, ch. 8).

Unlike the other two criteria of practicality, in terms of causation and intention, this does distinguish what would on the whole be intuitively recognised as judgments of value from utterances that are recognised, with comparable obviousness, to be statements of fact. If I agree that today is Friday the only conduct to which I am strictly committed is verbal. But if I agree, without qualification, that I ought not to do something I was about to do, I am committed to abstaining from it. Yet 'today is Friday' may cause and be intended to cause the most strenuous non-verbal conduct, while 'you ought not to do that' may neither cause nor be intended to cause its subject to desist, if he does not acknowledge the moral authority or good sense of the speaker and is known by the speaker not to do so.

As against Hare it must be admitted that the commitment undertaken by one who sincerely accepts a value-judgment made to and about him is not absolute. This excessively rigid position has the consequence that no sense can be attached to such things as yielding to temptation or remorse. The implied commitment can be overridden by other, more highly valued commitments; the action involved may turn out to be impossible; where there is a lapse of time between the taking on of the commitment and the action there may have been a change of mind. But there remains a *prima facie* implication of appropriate conduct by the sincere acceptance of a value-judgment or other practical utterance. If the action is not forthcoming, its absence has to be explained in one of a limited number of ways if the sincerity of the acceptance is not to be called in question.

A more fundamental difficulty emerges if belief is defined in terms of dispositions to conduct, as by Bain and modern philosophical behaviourists. For then, it appears, the commitment merely to belief that is the characteristic feature of theoretical utterances, turns out to be a commitment to acting in a certain way. And however the relation of behaviour to mental states is construed there is an uncomfortably indeterminate complexity about the relationship between the conduct of other people, on the one hand, and the beliefs and attitudes we impute to them on the other. I can tell what another man's beliefs are from the way he acts only with the help of assumptions about his practical attitudes, his desires, tastes and values: equally I can tell what his attitudes are from the way he behaves only if I make certain assumptions about what he believes. There is an air of taking in each other's washing about the whole operation.

One possible way out of this difficulty is to say that the sincere acceptance of a theoretical utterance commits one only to hypothetical behaviour, in a double sense. The theoretical belief that the house is on fire implies that I will run for my life only if, first, I believe myself to be inside the house in question and, secondly, and even less substantially, if I desire to avoid being burnt. But the implication for conduct of a practical utterance is more direct and categorical. If I agree to the request to shut up or sincerely accept the judgment that I ought not to do what I am doing I am committed to action without the satisfaction of any further conditions. The practical utterance directly specifies the relevant conduct, while the theoretical utterance at best implies it under certain additional assumptions. Not all practical utterances are direct or categorical in both respects as were the last two examples. A girl who is ordered or recommended not to accept invitations from strange men is told to refuse such invitations *if* she gets any, and she may not. But there is no further condition to be satisfied about her desires or preferences for her to be committed to rejecting such advances if any are made as there would be if she had been brought to accept the merely theoretical statement that if one accepts invitations from strange men one is likely to lose one's reputation for virtue.

I conclude, then, that, provided this last difficulty can be overcome, there is a fundamental distinction between theoretical utterances, whose sincere acceptance implies only belief, and practical utterances, whose sincere acceptance has direct, though defeasible, implications for conduct. It is evident, furthermore, that judgments of value are in this sense practical. The acceptance of a value-judgment amounts, unless it is overridden or otherwise defeated, to a decision to act in the relevant way. But value judgments are not the only kind of practical utterance. Imperatives, in particular, are practical; indeed they are the most obviously practical kind of utterance. I shall argue that it is of the greatest importance to realise that there are other kinds of practical utterance as well.

In order to use this distinction to refute naturalism one further assumption needs to be made; that all statements of fact, true or false, are theoretical. That many, if not most, are there can be no reasonable doubt. If all are, however, we have an *a priori* demonstration of the incorrectness of naturalism, which is, in effect, 'theoreticism', the attempt to analyse utterances which have one sort of meaning, the practical sort, in terms of utterances which have another sort altogether.

This procedure has none of the three methodological defects of Moore's refutation of naturalism. It is not inductive but demonstrative or at least conceptual. It purports to show that practicality is part of the concept of a judgment of value. The two phrases, theoretical and practical, are defined so as to distinguish utterances in terms of the kind of meaning they possess, from which it immediately follows that the whole meaning of an utterance of the latter kind cannot be specified wholly in terms of utterances of the former kind. As for the other two defects of Moore's way of proceeding: since the doctrine of practicality is not inductive there is no need for a wide and varied range of instances. The corresponding problem from this point of view is one of application, of deciding which specific definitions of value-terms are theoretical. Secondly, the problem corresponding to the lack of a clear positive analogy between the specific naturalist theories Moore considers is solved by the provision of an explicit principle for distinguishing between theoretical and practical utterances.

It should also be observed that the principle of the practicality of value-judgments is a complete refutation of the positive theory that Moore advances. For Moore never for a moment questioned the assumption that judgments of value were statements of fact; what he rejected was the none too precise contention that they were statements of natural, empirical fact. He still held them to be descriptive and informative, not about the empirical properties of their subjects but about their transcendental, non-natural characteristics. Indeed, as will be seen, there is no ethical theory that is more conclusively refuted by the principle of the practicality of value than an intuitionism like Moore's.

The assumption that remains to be vindicated, if the practicality of value is to disprove naturalism, is that no statements of fact are practical. It is certainly true that *some* non-statements, some non-cognitive utterances, namely imperatives, are practical. But it would seem that some are not. Simple expressive utterances, expletives and ejaculations, are not theoretical. A man's saying 'damn' or 'hooray' can be judged for appropriateness or inappropriateness, for sincerity or insincerity, but not for truth or falsehood. But they are not really practical either, except in a rather indirect way in the first, rejected, causal sense of the term. Someone's exclamation may infect me with the feeling he expresses and lead to conduct that would not have occurred without it. But there is really no sense to the notion of sincerely accepting an expletive or ejaculation and this notion *is* essential to a definition of practicality adequate to the task of effectively distinguishing judgments of value from neutral statements of fact. And, of course, even if all noncognitive utterances were practical it would not follow that no statements were.

It would appear that unless it is a conceptual truth that all statements of fact are theoretical the modern, post-Moorean antinaturalist must be arguing by analogy. Imperatives are noncognitive, neither true nor false: imperatives and value-judgments are both practical: therefore value-judgments are noncognitive. The usual conclusion is that a value-judgment is some kind of disguised imperative.

What renders this analogical argument questionable from the start is that it flies in the face of the grammatical appearances. From a grammatical point of view value-judgments are indicative in mood, or statement-like. Now indicative statements can be given a non-statement-making use, as, for example, in military orders: 'the battalion will parade at 0900 hours'. But this is a secondary use; the standard employment of sentences of this form is to make statements of a predictive kind. What the antinaturalist invites us to believe is that the standard employment of indicative sentences with such words as 'good', 'right' and 'ought' in them is to do something other than make statements.

There is more to the grammatical analogy between value-judgments and unquestionably factual statements than the fact that both are ordinarily made by sentences in the indicative. Both can be properly, significantly and quite unsurprisingly associated with what I shall call 'epistemic auxiliaries', phrases like 'I know that', 'I believe that', 'I wonder whether', 'is it true that', 'is it false that', 'certainly', 'probably' and so on. 'I ought to go' can be combined with any of these just as well as 'it is raining'. But this is quite obviously not the case with imperatives: 'it is true that clear off' and 'probably shut up' are without sense or use.

These considerations at least put the onus of proof on the non-cognitivist. What he has to show is that if an utterance is a statement of fact it must be theoretical and cannot be practical. There is no better way of showing that he cannot achieve this than by producing a kind of utterance which is at once unquestionably factual and yet at the same time practical. I believe that this can easily be done.

The type of utterance I have in mind for this purpose is what I shall call an appetitive utterance, an utterance about what someone likes or dislikes, enjoys or suffers from, is pleased or satisfied by, is displeased or repelled by. Suppose someone asks me what hotel he should stay at in a town which I know well but he has never visited. There are various ways in which I can give an appropriate answer to his question: 'you ought to stay at the Crown', 'the Crown is the best hotel there' (both value-judgments), 'stay at the Crown' (imperative), 'you will like the Crown best' (appetitive), 'the Crown is the cheapest/quietest/largest/oldest hotel there' (purely theoretical descriptive statements).

As against the noncognitivist I contend that the appetitive reply should be classified with value-judgments and imperatives as practical and not with the descriptive observations about the Crown Hotel. For it, like a value-judgment or imperative, is a direct answer to the request for guidance, an unconditionally relevant reply to the question 'what shall I do'. The descriptive observations are relevant only under the assumption that the questioner likes or values hotels with the qualities in question, which he may well not do. But in the appetitive case there is no substantial assumption that he likes or values what he likes. If a man stays away from the hotel which he has accepted as the smartest or oldest this casts no doubt on the sincerity of his agreement. But if he stays away from the hotel he agrees he would like most then the sincerity of his agreement is brought in question in default of some explanation, such as that it is too expensive.

The point can be brought out by considering Hare's argument against naturalism from the evaluation of strawberries (op. cit., pp. 111–12). Asked why I think a strawberry good I may say that it is because it is red, juicy and sweet. But I cannot *define* 'good' as 'red, juicy and sweet'. To start with, of course, because this would lead to absurd judgments about the goodness of olives and violinists, but, more to the point, because this would deprive the word 'good' of its power, as he puts it, to commend the things to which it is ascribed, in other words, would deprive it of its practicality. But what of the clearly true or false statement 'this is the kind of strawberry people in general most enjoy'. This criterion of goodness does not have the same confinement of application to a particular subject-matter and it is also practical. It is, indeed, pretty obviously the principle by the use of which the specific characteristics which make strawberries or any comparable kind of thing good are collected.

It is necessary to distinguish two points here. All I aim to establish at this point is that appetitive statements (for these utterances clearly are statements) are, like judgments of value, practical. It is another, and much more conjectural point, to suppose that judgments of value actually are, or are analysable in terms of, appetitive statements, though I shall argue for this later. This second point becomes even more questionable if it is judgments of moral value that are under consideration. It could, indeed, be objected that in response to a request for *moral* guidance, to the question 'what, morally, ought I to do', the reply 'what you will most enjoy doing is X' is absolutely irrelevant. In this case it is in the same boat as the reply that doing X will cause the most favourable impression, for neither is even conditionally relevant in the way that information about the smartness or quietness of the Crown was in the hotel-choosing case. But this objection does not matter here since the antinaturalist argument does not confine practicality to judgments of moral value; it is intended to apply to judgments of value of all kinds, including hedonic and prudential ones.

I do not, then, claim to have shown that value-judgments are appetitive statements; only that appetitive statements are, like value-judgments, practical and, therefore, that an utterance can be at once practical and a statement of fact. If this conclusion is conjoined with the grammatical facts about the indicative form and epistemic associability of value-judgments at least a presumption is created that value-judgments are, though practical, nevertheless statements, true or false. What is certainly proved is that it does not follow from the practicality of value-judgments that they are noncognitive, and, in particular, disguised imperatives.

Before going on to argue that value-judgments are conceptually connected, as well as functionally analogous, to appetitive statements I shall pause, first, to consider the bearing of another more informal and atmospheric foundation for noncognitivism about judgments of value and, secondly, to derive some unwelcome consequences from the noncognitivist position. But in what follows I shall accept the principle of the practicality of value while denying that it entails noncognitivism.

Refutation of noncognitivism

A more diffused support for the noncognitivist doctrine than the argument from practicality (or prescriptiveness or commendation) has been the existence of widespread and seemingly irresoluble disagreement about questions of value. The short way with this argument is to say that people make mistakes and are often irrational; the world contains flat-earthers and people who believe in fairies. But this is unsatisfactory. The marked lack of convergence to agreement that there is ought to be explained and not just dismissed as unsurprising evidence of human frailty.

But, to start with, the extent of disagreement about questions of value should not be exaggerated. In the first place disagreement is much more evident in some fields than in others. It is most abundant, perhaps, in the aesthetic realm. There is much of it in the domain of morality though less than an uncritical attention to some of the more peculiar findings of anthropology would suggest. But it is hardly present at all in some spheres. Consider the rather basic evaluative concepts of health and efficiency, systematised in the normative disciplines of pathology and technology. To say that some state or activity of the human body is unhealthy, 'bad for you', is unquestionably practical. But utterances of this kind form the commonsensical basis of the science of pathology about whose scientific status there is no question. No rational person would advance a noncognitive theory of judgments of health. In general pathologists try to obscure the evaluative nature of their discipline by defining an unhealthy condition of the body in terms of statistical abnormality. But it is only a contingent fact, even if one rather deeply rooted in the concept of an animal species, that the bodily states in which people feel best and live longest are much the same for everyone.

A second point is that there are large and persistent disagreements in the theoretical sphere. The most obvious case, that of religion, is no doubt not purely theoretical enough to carry conviction. But the theoretical status of large-scale explanation in history is secure enough and here there is as little convergence to agreement as there is in morals at any rate. The same is true of the developing fringe of physical science. What these examples of seemingly irresoluble disagreement have in common is that they are theoretical in a special sense, the propositions they concern are highly inferential and very remote from primary observation.

This leads to a final consideration of this topic. The argument from disagreement will impinge much less forcefully on a theory of value which represents the value-judgments about which men disagree most persistently as having the same kind of theoretical complexity and remoteness from the obvious as have the more general and speculative parts of history and natural science. A theory of a naively intuitionist kind like Moore's, which takes value-judgments to report the direct apprehension of the presence in things of non-natural properties, is much more exposed to this argument than such a theory as utilitarianism which sees the evaluation of particular things as involving complex inferences about consequences for human satisfaction in the long run and complex estimations of the comparative weight of these consequences. Utilitarianism, which is an appetitive kind of naturalism, can account for a good deal of disagreement by referring to the different circumstances in which men and societies are placed, which ensure that their acts will actually have relevantly different consequences, and to the different beliefs they hold about the world, which ensure that it will be rational for them to have different beliefs about the consequences of their acts. There is much less disagreement about such ultimate principles as that the maximising of satisfaction or the minimising of suffering are good than there is about the specific rights and duties of husbands, fathers and neighbours. Even the type of religious ethics that appears to reject human satisfaction as an ultimate end of conduct, in practice rejects only *earthly* satisfaction; asceticism in the end derives its value from the fact that it is thought to be a means to the incomparable rewards of eternal blessedness.

If it is agreed that practicality is a logical feature of value-judgments, imperatives are the only noncognitive utterances in terms of which they can be interpreted, for neither merely expressive nor optative utterances are practical in the only useful and relevant sense. Ejaculations and the expressions of wishes may invite sympathy but there is really no such activity as accepting them. The notion of sincere acceptance is, however, an essential element in the definition of practicality. So if, despite the grammatical appearances, it is insisted that judgments of value are noncognitive the only type of non-statement available for their interpretation is the imperative.

The imperative theory is not unplausible, indeed, if judgments of value are considered singly. Very often 'you ought not to do that' and 'don't do that' function, are intended to function, in much the same way. They are both generally appropriate answers to the question 'shall I do that'; they are both direct verbal instruments for preventing a particular kind of action. Admittedly they do not 'feel' quite the same to a kind of Moorean inspection but the imperativist will account for this by saying that 'you ought not to do that' is actually a *general* imperative: 'let no one do that (so don't you do it)'.

What this identification fails to do is to explain how it is that imperatives are able to perform the function it assigns to them. Treating them as a given, almost self-explanatory kind of linguistic device, it ignores the problem of accounting for their rational effectiveness. As things are the giving of orders is a broadly effective way of getting things done, or not done. But why should this be so? Why should one man's utterance of an imperative formula have any tendency to modify the conduct of those to whom he speaks? We are not, after all, innately disposed to respond in an appropriate way to utterances in the imperative mood. If imperatives are to have their characteristic practical, action-guiding sense they must frequently be obeyed. If they were not they would be hard to distinguish in function from optatives or even expletives.

To put the point concretely, why should the orders issued to me by others, and their value-judgments too if orders are what they really are, have any influence at all upon my conduct? If a man says to me 'do X' I can reasonably infer that he wants me to do X, but unless his desires are somehow infectious or unless I am generally disposed to please him why should his order be thought to provide me with any reason for acting as he requests?

In fact I think that orders owe their rational effectiveness to any one of three kinds of circumstance. The first kind of order rests on crude power. A muscular-looking man of ferocious aspect approaches me on a narrow footpath. I obey his order to get out of the way because I predict that he will make it very unpleasant for me if I do not. The second kind rests on special knowledge. In a theatre a terrified-looking man runs past me for the exit, shouting 'run for your life'. Here again I infer unpleasant consequences from non-compliance (being burnt to death, mown down by a lunatic with a machine-gun or something of the sort) but this time these consequences are not seen as the outcome of the deliberate action of the order-giver. Finally there is the kind of order that rests on authority. 'Move along there' says the policeman, 'raise your right hand' says the court official, 'about turn' says the sergeant. In this case the primary reason for compliance is the recognition that I ought to obey, though there will usually be the added inducement of unpleasant predictable consequences if I do not do what I am told.

Now if value-judgments are themselves really imperatives it is very hard to see how any sense can be made of the rational effectiveness of this third, authoritative kind of command, of its establishment and persistence as an institution. At any rate it would seem that value-judgments are logically prior to commands of this authoritative kind. They are not, however, logically prior to commands in general. But appetitive statements are and this implies that the practicality of imperatives depends on the prior practicality of appetitive statements. For unless such statements were practical in force the giving of orders could not be a rationally effective institution. Now since the practicality of appetitive statements is prior to that of imperatives (considered as an institution) it is at any rate unnecessary to account for the admitted practicality of judgments of value by construing them as somehow imperative in nature. And imperatives of authority presuppose independently-based judgments of value. It is, therefore, both more economical and more intelligible to interpret value judgments in appetitive rather than imperative terms.

There is an analogy between this argument and that used by Hume to refute the contract theory of political obligation. The contractarian in answer to the question 'why should I obey the state' replies 'because you have promised to do so'. The question then arises: 'why should I keep promises?' The answer to this, which is that doing so is generally advantageous, could just as well have been given to the original question. Similarly here, it is in Hume's phrase an 'unnecessary circuit' to justify the undertaking of a commitment to action involved in accepting an evaluative prescription by taking that prescription to be an order. For the question at once arises: 'why should I do what I'm told?' The answer 'because I ought to', which is in fact a perfectly good one in some cases of this kind, is not available here, for it regressively reinstates the original problem. What is available is the answer that there will be unpleasant consequences if I do not and this could have been given directly to the original question.

The view that appetitive statements are logically prior both to imperatives and value-judgments might be met with the objection that in the development of language expressive and imperative discourse precedes descriptive or fact-stating utterance (cf. Popper (3), pp. 134–5, 295). The primitive speaker, according to this plausible view, begins his linguistic career with ejaculations of glee, fear and rage. He goes on to incite his fellows to act in accordance with his desires. It is only after this that he starts to communicate information. It is too short an answer to reply that temporal precedence is one thing, logical priority another. It is reasonable to suppose that the primitive speaker's predescriptive commands are of the crude power variety and do not rest on either special knowledge or authority. Now it is quite possible for his hearers to have the relevant appetitive beliefs which endow his commands with effectiveness without having the linguistic means to express them. In general, unless they are afraid of what he will do it is hard to see why his remarks should have any influence on them. But the belief that unpleasant results will follow from disobedience is an essential element in such a fear. So the logical priority of appetitive considerations to the giving of commands as an effective institution is preserved even in these unpromising circumstances.

Action, value and desire

So far I have argued that the practicality, which ethical theorists since Moore have held to exclude a naturalistic interpretation of judgments of value, is indeed a property that they possess, but that it is wholly congruous with such an interpretation where the logical connection is held to obtain between value-judgments and appetitive statements, for such statements are practical too. The propriety of such an interpretation has been further defended on the grounds that the usual alternative account that recognises the practicality of value-judgments, that in terms of imperatives, is, first, in conflict with rather far-reaching grammatical appearances and, second, fails to give any explanation of imperative discourse as a rationally effective institution. But these considerations still do not establish that an appetitive naturalism which bases judgments of value on statements about what men like, enjoy or derive satisfaction from is correct. For that some more positive arguments are needed than the elimination of alternatives and a demonstration of formal propriety. I shall offer two.

The first of them is of a broad and essentially empirical nature and on at least two counts can be no more than suggestive. It is, simply, that most of the judgments of value about which there is some sort of general consensus of opinion are just what they would be if to ascribe value to something were to assert that it is such as to give satisfaction to people in general in the long run. On this view a value-judgment is a generalised or impersonal appetitive statement; it says what men in general would wish to be the case, if they were rational, which is not, of course always the same as what they actually wish were the case.

This is most obviously true of valuations with regard to health and efficiency which are at once non-ethical and almost wholly non-controversial. A condition of the body is healthier than another if (i) people in general like being in the former more than they like being in the latter and (ii) if the subsequent bodily conditions to which the condition in question is causally connected are similarly related. Comparably it would seem to be a conclusive demonstration that technique A is more efficient than technique B if it takes less time to carry out (in bringing about one and the same result) and uses less costly material.

A critic might agree that A's using less time and material than B might be very good reason for thinking that A is the more efficient of the two techniques while denying that the connection between reason and conclusion is strictly logical. Is it a contradiction, he might ask, to say that, although A takes less time and material than B, B is nevertheless the more efficient? It must be admitted that perhaps it is not a contradiction. But that is because there is a certain indeterminacy about the criteria of efficiency. Should they include the distress caused to the operator of the technique? If so then the critic's noncontradictory case might be realised, when A was much more burdensome to the technician than B. But something is quite clear about any such marginal criteria; the features or consequences of techniques that they mention must be such that people like or dislike them.

The crucially controversial case, of course, is that of morality. I have argued that if value is interpreted in terms of general satisfation in the long run much of the apparently irresoluble disagreement that exists about moral issues can be seen to be disagreement about something else, indeed about the factual consequences of action, attributable to differing circumstances or differing factual beliefs. Under such relatively superficial variations moral codes generally have three constituents: a set of rules of inhibition, which prohibit or discourage conduct likely to cause suffering to others (killing, bodily assault, theft, destruction of reputation), a set of rules of charity, which enjoin or encourage conduct likely to diminish the suffering of others, whether brought about by natural events or human action, and, finally, a set of rather more conventional rules of obligation of which the most general is the rule of promise-keeping and which more particularly specify the rights and duties attaching to various human situations (father, husband, friend and so forth). Rules of the first two kinds are all that they would be if the ultimate moral end were the diminution of suffering, whether about to be caused by one's own action or already caused in some other way. The same is indirectly true of the third class of rules of obligation. Action in contravention of them is not in itself likely to cause suffering; it will do so only in the light of expectations conventionally established.

The fact that these considerations are rather platitudinous should not be allowed to obscure their importance. For to an imperativist the empirical coincidence involved must be a bare and accidental contingency. For him a moral position is defined by a set of ultimate values which are simply chosen. Many people seem to have chosen as their ultimate prescription: diminish suffering. But this is just their choice. They could just as well have chosen the contrary or something utterly different such as 'increase the population' or 'please God' or 'advance knowledge'.

I said earlier that this type of argument could be no more than suggestive on two counts. The first, and perhaps less significant, is that it lays some weight on the prevailing measure of consensus about values such as it is. But it does not treat the unreflective valuations of all and sundry as imprescriptibly authoritative. And unless at least this much validity is accorded to ordinary convictions it is difficult to see how an inquiry of this kind is to get started.

The second and more serious weakness is that the argument is thoroughly hypothetical. It says that broadly agreed values are as they would be *if* general satisfaction in the long run *were* what value essentially consisted in. But this could be coincidence in principle, though its scale at least suggests that it is not. To show that there is a real connection between actually agreed values and general satisfaction requires something more. One possibility would be to show that in fundamental disputes about questions of value people are in the end driven back to invoking the long-run satisfaction of men in general. But although they often are this is not always the case. Moral controversialists quite commonly take their stand on the intrinsic and unchallengeable authority of a god or an organisation or a principle. I shall have to return to the implications of this fact later.

For the moment I am in need of a conceptual argument to connect value with the satisfaction and suffering of sentient beings. The principle of practicality maintains that there is an essential connection between value and action. What is required in addition to this is some way of establishing a connection between action and satisfaction. Naturalistic theories have traditionally found a link between them in the concept of desire. If all action is prompted or motivated by desire and if the general object of desire is satisfaction then all action is directed towards satisfaction. But if, as the principle of practicality contends, to ascribe value to something is to assert that it is a proper or rational end of action, is to provide a reason for action calculated to bring it about, it follows that to evaluate something is to say something about its capacity for giving satisfaction.

All the steps of this argument are highly controversial (some of them in the slightly depressing sense that the consensus of philosophical opinion is so strongly hostile that it may seem merely contumacious to attempt to reanimate them) and so all will need defence.

I shall begin with what I shall call proposition A: *all desire is for satisfaction*. This is, of course, only a somewhat terminologically cautious variant of Mill's thesis that pleasure alone is the object of desire. There are two obstructively critical ways of interpreting Mill's statement in which it is plainly unacceptable. The first takes the word 'pleasure' in its most straightforwardly vernacular sense, as it occurs in the remarks 'X is a man of pleasure', 'Y is wholly given over to the pursuit of pleasure', 'Z cares about nothing but pleasure' where it refers to a particular class of human satisfactions that are at once bodily, comparatively intense, almost universally enjoyed and innate or instinctive in the sense that no process of conditioning or training is required in order to be gratified by them, such as the satisfactions of food, drink and sexual activity. In this interpretation Mill's thesis is obviously false. To the extent that universal attraction is part of the concept of a pleasure of this kind it is necessarily true that everyone does desire these pleasures but it is not true of anyone that he desires nothing else whatever. For everyone desires health which is not a pleasure of this sort and most people desire to be liked and thought well of. My proposition A excludes this misreading by talking of satisfaction rather than pleasure. The second misinterpretation fastens on the formulation 'pleasure alone is the object of desire' and maintains, quite correctly, of course, that there is no such thing as the enjoyment of 'pleasure alone', pleasure by itself, that is not the pleasure of doing or undergoing something else. Pleasure is a relational concept and so nothing can be a pleasure without being something else, without having some qualities besides. But naturalism does not maintain that it is, unless by a kind of verbal accident. What it claims is that pleasure (or, preferably, satisfaction) is the general or universal object of desire, not that it is the unique object of desire. It is comparable to the concept of wealth in economics which is the general but not the unique object of economic activity and can exist only in some independently characterisable bearer: land, shares, cash, Picassos and so forth.

Proposition A is, in fact, a tautology, for to desire something is, at least in part, to think of it as capable of yielding satisfaction. In some cases, indeed, it would seem to be little more than such a belief, in the cases, that is, where what is desired is very remote and such that there is nothing that the desirer can do to bring the desired end about, for example the desire to win a lottery or that there should be little rain next summer. There are two other propositions about the relations between desire and satisfaction that need to be distinguished from A. One is the undoubted truth that satisfaction is a principal, though not the only, cause of desire. This proposition follows from A together with the uncontentious assumption that we reason inductively. What is better calculated to make me believe that something will give me satisfaction than the fact that it has already done so? But not all desires are in this way the fruit of past experiences of satisfaction. Some desires, and aversions, are strictly instinctive.

The other proposition about desire and satisfaction that needs to be distinguished from A is the falsehood that satisfaction is always obtained from the achievement of the object of a desire, from what, in another sense of the word, is quite properly called its satisfaction. To desire something is to believe that it will yield satisfaction; but the belief may be false, the expected satisfaction may not accrue. There are ill-founded desires, those, namely, that are or involve false beliefs about the power of their objects to satisfy, and it is just for this reason that factual information can have a direct influence on our desires. A desire, it should be pointed out, is not necessarily irrational because it is ill-founded, though many ill-founded desires are irrational. If I have enjoyed every oyster I have eaten hitherto it is rational for me to desire the oyster that is now on the plate in front of me; but it may be bad. But if an object I have been led to desire by an advertisement turns out not to give satisfaction I should blame my failure to use my knowledge of the broadly fictional nature of commercial advertising and not the unanticipatable complexity and variety of the world.

All desire, then, is for satisfaction but not all achieved objects of desire produce it. If, as proposition B asserts, *all action is motivated by desire*, it follows that all action is directed towards satisfaction. This supposition is even more widely rejected than proposition A. It is not denied that a great deal of action is motivated by desire. Probably the commonest and most straightforward way of explaining what led someone to act in a certain fashion is to state what want or desire he was seeking to satisfy by acting thus. The chicken crossed the road because it wanted to get to the other side. But it seems quite obvious that we often do things that we do not want to do. It would not matter if these were all cases of literal external compulsion, producing bodily movements that are not properly actions at all. But they are not. I spend the morning writing about ethics although I should much prefer to be out in the sun. I pay a long-standing debt although I should much prefer to spend the money on taking somebody out for the evening. I take the dry-looking biscuit although I should much prefer the chocolate éclair. In such cases I say that I spent the morning writing, paid the debt, took the dry biscuit although I didn't want to.

The short and simple answer to this objection is, of course, that one very often has to do something that one does not want to do for the sake of something else that one wants very much. I write instead of sitting in the sun in order to preserve my self-respect or to advance my reputation or to earn my living. Proposition B does not assert that one desires to do everything one does, only that everything one does is motivated by some desire or other. To follow a fashionable way of speaking, one does not desire to do what one does under every possible description of the action, in particular under what is, in the circumstances the natural or normal description of what one is up to. But, proposition B maintains, there is some description, perhaps unnatural, elaborate and causal, under which one does desire to do it. Even if I don't want to write more than to sit in the sun, I do want to make myself financially secure more than I want to intensify my suntan.

It could also be said that the phrase 'I don't want' operates in colloquial speech in the same way as 'I don't believe' in that its sense would be more strictly conveyed by the phrase 'I want not' (in the parallel case 'I disbelieve'). Now 'I want not to do X' is compatible with 'I want to do X' while it is not strictly compatible with 'I don't want to do X'. I can, that is to say, both want to do X and want not to do it at the same time. I want to do it, considered as something that will please my children, and I want not to do it, considered as something that will cost a lot of money. Thus it does not follow from the fact that I can truly say 'I don't want to do X' that it is false that I want to do it.

Much stress has been laid in connection with this problem on the special status of morally motivated activity. Kant put forward a sharply dualistic theory of action in which the moral motive (sense of duty or reverence for the law) was radically distinguished from inclination, which he held to cover everything from the farthest-seeing prudence to the most momentary impulse. The sense of duty, according to Kant, is purely rational and thus distinct from all 'pathological' (i.e. emotional) sources of action. This dichotomy is hard to credit. Moral motivation varies from one person to another, just as do prudence or fondness for travel or the appetite for food. Like these other springs of action it can be modified by education and training and its fulfilment and frustration have comparable emotional accompaniments. The strength of a man's conscience is a natural fact about him, like his carefulness as a driver, and is susceptible of the same general sort of explanation, in both cases rather restricted as things stand. There is a well-known kind of satisfaction that attends the carrying out of virtuous or conscientious action, a sense of well-being that is independent of the non-moral satisfaction of having acted so as to stand well in the eyes of others which is also effective in producing morally correct conduct. On the other hand there is the experience of guilt which attends failure to do what is morally required, much as embarrassment accompanies clumsiness, whether manipulative or social, and regret accompanies the failure, whether through laziness, inattention or the operation of an overriding desire, to achieve some straightforwardly desired object. Bishop Butler was quite right to classify conscience together with benevolence, prudence and more specific desires. Although there are differences between them, basically in respect of the remoteness and complexity of their objects, and consequently in respect of the amount of thought and deliberation that goes into the pursuit of these objects, they are all springs of action or desires. As Kant came near to seeing, in his account of the 'holy will', a being without desires would not literally *act* at all. It could move, of course, but it would not be a genuine agent, it would not perform actions.

A really more puzzling case for proposition B to accommodate is that of habitual action. If I have the habit of putting on my trousers before I put on my shirt when dressing the only desire it seems reasonable to advance in explanation of my reaching for my trousers before I have my shirt on, when I do it for the ten thousandth time, is the desire to do the usual thing. Certainly I shall be mildly annoyed or discomposed if some officious bystander offers me my shirt before I have got my trousers on. I may once have had a reason for establishing this routine; perhaps that I should be in a seemly state to move about the house sooner if I dress in this order than in the reverse, but if I have totally forgotten this reason it is absurdly artificial to say that the desire behind the order of my actions now is to get respectably dressed as soon as possible. It seems most reasonable to say that the habit is itself a desire to do things in a certain way. Once a real or supposed consequence of this mode of action was the thing desired. With the passage of time this desire has faded or become disconnected from the routine of action but its attractive force has been transferred, in the mechanism of habit-formation, to the routine itself. Unless a habit has become an addiction the desire for the familiar it embraces can, of course, be overridden by another desire.

If A and B are both correct it follows that all action is for the sake of, or directed towards, some satisfaction of the agent. The principle of practicality, as applied to judgments of value, says that to accept such a judgment is to commit oneself, subject to some possible qualifications, to acting in a certain way. Now if, as I have argued, judgments of value, are, as they grammatically appear to be and quite compatibly with their being practical, statements of fact, it follows that they must be statements about the capacity of actions, possible to me, to produce satisfying states of affairs. The only beliefs that can move me to action are those beliefs about the conditions of satisfaction which are, at least partly, constitutive of desires. In short, judgments of value move to action, action is motivated by desire, desire is for satisfaction; therefore, value-judgments state the conditions of satisfaction, not, as appetitive statements do, with reference to particular people or a particular situation, but with reference to people in general and over the long run. And their validity is determined by whether the claims they make about long-run general satisfaction are true or false.

A consequence of this naturalistic account of value is that there can be no value without sentience, without emotion and desire. This conflicts with the findings of Moore's thought-experiment about the two worlds, one beautiful, one ugly and filthy, neither of which is ever the object of any consciousness (Moore (1), pp. 83–5). Moore maintained that it was evident to him that it was intrinsically better that if one of the two worlds had to exist it should be the beautiful one. It is hard not to suspect that he has ignored the stated conditions of the experiment. Once one of these worlds exists can its sequestration really be guaranteed? Might not a sentient being somehow blunder into it, or evolve within it? If the guarantee were firm would it not be rational to prefer that the ugly world should exist? It would be a secure dumping-ground for a lot of potentially distressing stuff and one could not but regret the waste involved in the existence of the beautiful world. In a Berkeleyan way, of course, the conditions of the experiment are impossible to satisfy, for even if Moore and his readers do not perceive either world they have to conceive them. In the end, however, Moore rejects the findings of his experiment by implication when he maintains, in his final chapter, that the only things that possess intrinsic value are human states of mind.

There is an affinity between the main argument of this section and Mill's celebrated justification of the utilitarian principle. Having said that ultimate ends do not admit of proof and that the best he can do to show that the general happiness is the *summum bonum* is to set out some considerations capable of inclining the intellect to give or withhold its assent, he proceeds to come up with a set of assertions that would be a proof if only the reasoning behind the assertions had been cogent. All desire is for pleasure or happiness. Since each man desires his own happiness everyone desires the general happiness. What is desired (by everyone?) is desirable. Therefore the general happiness is desirable. I have defended the first of these propositions and, in a way, the third. It is not so much that what men do desire is good, for many desires are, as their possessors come to admit, ill-founded; it is what they would desire if they were fully rational and informed, namely what would yield the greatest satisfaction.

Bentham's procedure is even more economical. Nature has placed mankind under the sovereign mastery of pleasure and pain. Since pleasure is all that men can seek, he seems to suggest, it is all they should seek. Critics have argued that psychological and ethical hedonism are incongruous, that if all men can seek is pleasure then there can be no point in telling them that they ought to seek it. This objection cannot be sustained since it ignores the fact that 'pleasure' has different meanings in the two hedonistic principles: it refers to expected pleasure in the first, to actual pleasure in the second. If it is, in the end, only expected satisfaction that moves men to act, it is only by influencing men's beliefs about their prospects of satisfaction that judgments of value can have any bearing on their conduct.

There is a view about the concept of happiness whose correctness would undermine much of the argument of this chapter. This is that happiness is itself an evaluative notion and not a straightforwardly factual or descriptive one. If this were true it would follow that an analysis of value in terms of happiness would not be naturalistic; it would be a logically innocuous manoeuvre like pronouncing that murder (i.e. wrongful killing) and theft (i.e. wrongful taking) are wrong. No doubt the concept of happiness can take this form. There is a drawing by James Thurber in which a severe cleric looks disapprovingly down on a dilapidated woman, her hat and clothes awry, who is gleefully waving a glass about and singing. 'Unhappy woman', the caption reports him as saying. For the cleric she would be happy only if her satisfaction were of a morally praiseworthy kind. The ludicrousness of the situation shows the marginal character of this use of the concept. Even if it were general we should need some word like 'satisfaction' to pick out the cases to be distinguished as really and only apparently happy.

The nature of morality

Up to this point in the chapter value has been treated in very general terms. This is contrary to the ordinary procedure in this field. Few modern philosophers appear to think of themselves as theorists of value, but rather as ethical theorists, in a strict sense of 'ethical'. Some regard moral value as unique and special in nature. By them other forms of valuation are briefly dismissed either as merely subjective or else as uncontroversially factual. They take 'this is good', in its non-moral applications, to mean either simply 'I like this' or else 'this conduces to such-and-such an empirically discoverable end'. Such a position is the natural correlate of a Kantian account of motivation which singles out moral conduct as the outcome of a very special kind of motive and lumps all other activity together as the result of inclination. But it does not cohere very well with the thesis that value-judgments are practical, with its assertion that all kinds of valuation are bound together by a very fundamental community of character.

So ethical theorists who act on this implication of the principle of practicality take moral valuation to be representative of all other kinds rather than as unique. This point of view is certainly preferable to that which treats the ethical in complete isolation. The community of character of different kinds of valuation has more obvious grounds than the principle of practicality. The most important is that all forms of value-judgment share a basic vocabulary: 'good', 'bad', 'right', 'wrong', 'ought' and 'ought not' occur in counsels of prudence, technical prescriptions and critical judgments as ineliminably as they do in moral injunctions. Morality can very naturally seem to be the most important and most interesting type of valuation. But this does not justify the ascription of a theoretically unique status to it. The result of such a narrowing of attention is that the light thrown by the non-moral kinds of valuation on the nature of value in general is not profited from.

All the same there is a distinction within the domain of practical or evaluative discourse between the moral and non-moral. There are some evaluative terms, for example 'virtuous', 'vicious', 'obligatory', 'sin' and 'conscience', which are exclusively moral, in their literal employment at any rate. The force of that last statement depends on the firmness of the distinction between literal and figurative uses of such words. More generally the concept of a moral species of valuation requires a criterion for distinguishing between it and the other species of that genus. Now there is a reasonable degree of intuitive agreement as to which kinds of action are morally right or wrong and which actions are right or wrong in other ways; there is a fair coincidence in the allocations reflective people would make of particular varieties of conduct to the two categories. But considerable difficulty has been experienced in arriving at a general criterion for the distinction.

In general recent ethical theorists have concentrated their endeavours on the search for a *formal* criterion for the moral character of a judgment of value. By this I mean a criterion which mentions only rather abstract and logical properties of judgments, and the reasoning that supports them, and says nothing about the nature of the ends whose pursuit they enjoin. I shall briefly consider four of these proposed formal criteria. All stem ultimately from Kant.

The first and most discussed of these is the criterion of universalisability. By this a prescription of the form 'X ought to do Y' is moral if and only if the prescription is asserted not with particular reference to X but is based on or expresses a universal principle to the effect that anyone in X's position should do Y. A moral judgment, on this view, is one from which all proper names or other singular terms can in principle be eliminated. The moral judgment 'you ought to return that book to John' implies or presupposes the universal principle 'everyone should return prized objects to those from whom they have borrowed them'. I do not wish to question the claim that all moral prescriptions are universalisable in this way. What I reject is the conjoined claim that all universalisable prescriptions are moral. Universalisability is not a sufficient condition of the moral character of a prescription, though it is, in a way, a necessary condition since, I shall contend, all value-judgments, whether moral or not, are universalisable. It is what distinguishes judgments of value from appetitive statements with a particular reference. Consider the intuitively prudential judgment 'you ought to put some money aside for your old age' or the intuitively technical judgment 'you ought to hammer that nail into the wall with small strokes to start with'. If there is to be any reason for you to do either of these things then it will also be an equally good reason for anyone else, situated broadly as you are, and not, say, under sentence of death or animated by a preponderating desire to do an injury to the owner of the wall, to act likewise. There is, as I shall try to show, a special kind of generality about moral judgments, but it is not brought out by the requirement of universalisability.

A second formal criterion of moral character is that moral prescriptions are somehow absolute, categorical or unconditional, other prescriptions being merely hypothetical imperatives. Non-moral injunctions, like that about putting money aside for old age, carry implicitly, it is said, an associated if-clause with them, about the desires or interests of the particular person to whom they are addressed. Moral injunctions, on the other hand, do not; they are asserted with no such conditional qualification. Now there is a point behind this suggestion. If I address a moral injunction to someone I have a kind of interest in his acting in accordance with it which I do not have in the case of prudential or technical injunctions addressed to others. It may not matter much to me one way or the other if he suffers the miseries of destitution in old age or makes a mess of his wall. But I am necessarily concerned if he acts in a way that is prejudicial to the general welfare for I have a share in that end, I am a part of the generality.

But what really underlies this criterion is the idea that the moral rightness of conduct is not derivative from the end to which it conduces, whereas the prudential or technical rightness of conduct is. A non-moral prescription, it is implied, always leaves room for the question 'why should I?'; a moral prescription does not. Or again, the moral rightness of an act is intrinsic to it, whereas the non-moral rightness of an act is dependent on its consequences. The view that categoricalness is the criterion of the morality of a prescription is bound up with the formalist or deontological theory that the moral rightness or wrongness of action is independent of its consequences.

There are three main arguments for this position. The first is Kant's, that the moral rightness of an act is not undermined by the fact that it, perhaps because of 'the niggardliness of a stepmotherly nature', has bad after-effects. But the moral irrelevance of a particular act's actual consequences does not entail the moral irrelevance of consequences in general. The relevant consequences are those which it would be rational to predict and they, inductive rationality being what it is, are those which acts of this precise kind have usually been found to have. Now if these consequences are bad the claim that an act is morally right is undermined, as is shown by the way in which moral convictions about the rightness of acts have altered over time with the change of rationally predictable consequences or with an improved awareness of what they are.

Secondly, there is the view that some principles of conduct, some rules specifying what we morally ought to do, are self-evident and axiomatic. There is at least one plausible example of this: the principle that one ought to keep promises. What makes this look self-evident is the fact that it is very nearly analytic. A promise is a verbal formula by which one conventionally puts oneself under an obligation to do something. Thus 'one ought to keep promises' means much the same as 'one ought, or one is under an obligation, to do what one has put oneself under an obligation to do'. This is generally, but not universally, and so not analytically, true, just as 'one is under an umbrella under which one has put oneself' is generally but not universally true. In the umbrella case one may have moved away; in the promising case a more stringent obligation may have arisen to cancel the obligation to keep the promise. Kant generalised this case to cover all moral obligations in his first formulation of the categorical imperative. Notoriously his attempt to show that rejection of the ordinarily recognised principles of duty leads to self-contradiction is defective both in taking the rejection of a principle to be equivalent to the acceptance of its extreme contrary opposite and in its illicit importation of consequences.

The final argument is essentially Prichard's (Prichard (1), ch.1). For him the moral irrelevance of consequences is proved by the fact that even if we are quite sure that acting in accordance with some recognised principle of duty will have bad consequences in this particular case we still admit that we ought to act in the way the principle requires. The direct answer to this is that it is just false. If I have made a promise whose breach will cause only minor annoyance and then, on the way to carry it out, find myself in circumstances where only by breaking it can I prevent some large disaster, not only am I not obliged to keep my promise, I am obliged not to.

A third criterion of the moral character of a prescription is that it possesses overriding authority as compared with other, competing prescriptions. This is not very satisfactory in its own formal terms. In the first place it seems that sometimes one moral prescription comes into conflict with another. I ought to tell him the truth but also I ought not to cause him pain. Secondly, unless there is something that I morally ought to do in every situation of choice and action in which I find myself, there will be situations in which the competing practical claims, including that which does or should override the others, will be non-moral. Thus moral prescriptions can be overridden and non-moral claims can override.

A more fundamental objection, however, is that it is impossible to give this criterion an effective formulation. What does it mean to say that moral prescriptions are characterised by the possession of overriding authority? Does it mean that moral prescriptions always do override others? This is pretty obviously false unless Hare's account of sincere acceptance of a moral affirmation as complete conformity of action to it is adopted. (It should be noted that he cannot both define the acceptance involved in practicality in this totalistic way and maintain that morality is overridingly authoritative in this sense unless he equates the moral and the practical.) The more plausible interpretation of the thesis that moral prescriptions have overriding authority is that they ought to be complied with. But what sort of 'ought' can this be? If it is the moral 'ought' then the thesis is rendered vacuous: it states that what one morally ought to do is what one morally ought to do. If it is not the moral 'ought' an incoherence ensues: the distinction between the moral and the non-moral is obliterated. If, for example, it is a prudential 'ought' then in a situation where there are conflicting prescriptions about what one ought to do, that which has a moral claim on one is that which it is most prudent to comply with: morality becomes identified with prudence.

There is nevertheless a serious point behind this third criterion in terms of overriding authority. There are two ways in which moral considerations have a kind of priority over others. The first is that everyone has an interest in conformity with them. Secondly, and more important, is the fact that moral claims have a special kind of urgency. It is not so much that unless morality is broadly sustained society will disintegrate and life become intolerable. Life is intolerable, for as long as it lasts, for those who never heed the counsels of prudence. It is rather that morality, of all the schemes and styles of conduct, is that which has the least reliable and immediate natural motivation. Instinctive sympathy with the welfare of others is fitful; the socialising effect of early moral conditioning and education has powerful primordial forces to contend with; the prudential justification of broadly altruistic or other-regarding conduct involves a comparatively long and so forgettable train of reasoning. In consequence the claims of morality need special emphasis.

The fourth and last formal criterion of the moral picks it out from other forms of evaluation as autonomous or self-legislated. Rules of conduct are moral, on this view, if they are chosen by the agent for himself. It is not easy to see what this requirement is meant to be contrasted with. Does it mean that a principle is moral if and only if someone who guides his actions by it has not come to adopt it on the authority or under the influence of someone else? If so autonomy is neither necessary nor sufficient to the morality of a rule. Many people absorb rules of conduct uncritically from their social environment, never feeling impelled to challenge the guidance of parents and other authorities. It is unreasonable to say that rules thus acquired are not really moral if they cover the correct subject-matter (action as bearing on the satisfaction and suffering of others) and, if the characteristically moral emotions are provoked by breach of the rules (guilt if the agent deviates, indignation if others do).

Some people gradually hammer out a morality of their own; others are content to make do with the socially accepted article. Just the same is true of prudence or technique. Some people have their own way of opening a tin; others get along well enough with the manufacturer's instructions. If no one ever criticises and modifies accepted rules, in morality or elsewhere, practice ossifies. If everyone makes up their own rules of conduct there will be muddle and chaos, particularly dangerous chaos in the case of moral rules. This criterion of autonomy appears to dress up a particular moral taste as neutral analysis. No doubt there is something supine and feeble, especially in a rapidly changing world, in the uncritical absorption of conventional moral opinions. But by and large virtue consists in adherence to the rules one actually has, not in having rules arrived at in a particularly critical and enterprising way. (In the extreme case, that of the Nazi fanatic, the rules themselves are morally intolerable, but because of their content rather than their mode of acceptance.)

A comparison can be drawn between morality and science. Unless some people arrived at new theories or reinforced old ones by the methods of science there would be no science, only an inheritance of perhaps practically useful myths about the world. But scientific theories can be understood and used by those who have not discovered them for themselves and who do not know the evidence on which they are based. Most people, and this includes most scientists, take most of science on authority. Similarly with morals. Unless there were morally critical and reflective individuals morality would degenerate into taboo. But all moral agents are largely consumers, beneficiaries of the moral innovations, made piecemeal by others. Neither the moral agent nor the moral critic, any more than the technician or the scientist, operates in complete isolation. Any such person who imagines that he does is the victim of a megalomaniac illusion. Science and morality are both, quite literally, social products.

The failure of these attempts to provide a formal criterion of the moral reinforces the suggestion, arising from the survey of the general moral consensus in the fifth paragraph of section four, that there is a common character to the subject-matter of moral prescriptions. A material criterion of morality would be that a value-judgment is moral if it evaluates actions in the light of their bearing on the satisfaction and suffering of everyone affected by them. It is prudential, by contrast, if it evaluates actions in the light of their bearing on the long-run satisfaction of the agent; technical if the evaluating factor is the minimisation of time and cost; aesthetic if it is the reward of satisfaction available in the long run to a contemplative spectator; and so on. My claim for this criterion is simply that it does cover reasonably well, and certainly much more closely than the formal proposals I have discussed, those rules of conduct which most people would intuitively classify as moral. It has the further merit of implying a sensible account of the nature of morality as a social institution. A society is a regularly interacting group of people. Interaction can take a negative form, as conflict, or a positive form, as co-operation. What I have called rules of inhibition are designed to minimise conflict, with its consequences of violence and social disintegration. Rules of charity have a broadly co-operative character. Their purpose is to better man's condition by a combining of human powers. The co-operative interaction of men requires a higher degree of predictability than the instinctive regularities of human nature provide. What I have called rules of obligation are the artifice by means of which such a reliability of expectation is established.

Bibliography

The books listed here are those that are mentioned in the text, where they are cited by the author's *surname* and, in the case of authors more than one of whose books are mentioned, *number*.

Alexander, H. G., 'General Statements as Rules of Inference', in *Minnesota Studies in the Philosophy of Science*, vol. 2, 1958, 309–29.

Alston, W. P., *The Philosophy of Language*, Prentice-Hall, Englewood Cliffs, 1964.

Anderson, John, *Studies in Empirical Philosophy*, Angus & Robertson, Sydney, 1962.

Anscombe, G. E. M., 'The Principle of Individuation', in *Aristotelian Society*, supplementary volume 27, 1953, 83–96.

Aristotle, *De Anima*, in *The Basic Works of Aristotle*, ed. R. McKeon, Random House, New York, 1941, 535–603.

Armstrong, D. M. (1) *Perception and the Physical World*, Routledge & Kegan Paul, London, 1961.

(2) 'Is Introspective Knowledge Incorrigible?', in *Philosophical Review*, vol. 72, 1963, 417–32.

(3) *A Materialist Theory of the Mind*, Routledge & Kegan Paul, London, 1968.

Aune, Bruce, *Knowledge, Mind and Nature*, Random House, New York, 1967.

Austin, J. L. (1) *Philosophical Papers*, Oxford, 1961.

(2) *Sense and Sensibilia*, Oxford, 1962.

Ayer, A. J. (1) *Language, Truth and Logic*, Gollancz, London, 1936.

(2) *The Foundations of Empirical Knowledge*, Macmillan, London, 1940.

(3) 'Individuals', in *Philosophical Essays*, Macmillan, London, 1954, 1–25.

(4) 'Basic Propositions', in *Philosophical Essays*, Macmillan, London, 1954, 105–24.

(5) *The Problem of Knowledge*, Macmillan, London, 1956.

(6) 'Names and Descriptions', in *The Concept of a Person*, Macmillan, London, 1963, 129–61.

(7) *The Origins of Pragmatism*, Macmillan, London, 1968.

(8) *Metaphysics and Common Sense*, Macmillan, London, 1969.

Barker, S. F., *Induction and Hypothesis*, Cornell, Ithaca, 1957.

Benacerraf, Paul, 'What Numbers Could Not Be', in *Philosophical Review*, no. 74, 1965, 47–73.

Berlin, Isaiah, 'Empirical Propositions and Hypothetical Statements', in *Mind*, vol. 59, 1950, 289–312.

Blanshard, Brand, *The Nature of Thought*, Allen & Unwin, London, 1939.

Bradley, F. H. (1) *The Principles of Logic*, Oxford, 1922 (1st ed. 1883).

(2) *Appearance and Reality*, Oxford, 1930 (1st ed. 1893).

Broad, C. D., 'Are there synthetic *a priori* truths?', in *Aristotelian Society*, supplementary volume 15, 1936, 102–17.

Carnap, Rudolf (1) *The Logical Structure of the World*, Routledge & Kegan Paul, London, 1967 (German 1st ed. 1928).

(2) *The Logical Syntax of Language*, Routledge, London, 1937 (German 1st ed. 1934).

(3) *The Logical Foundations of Probability*, Chicago, 1950.

(4) *Philosophical Foundations of Physics*, Basic Books, New York, 1966.

Case, Thomas, *Physical Realism*, Longmans, London, 1888.

Chisholm, R. M. (1) *Perceiving*, Cornell, Ithaca, 1957.

(2) 'Fallibilism and Belief', in *Studies in the Philosophy of C. S. Peirce*, ed. P. P. Wiener and F. H. Young, Harvard, Cambridge, 1952, 93–110.

(3) 'Sentences about Believing', in *Aristotelian Society*, vol. 56, 1955–6, 125–48.

Collingwood, R. G., 'Sensation and Thought', in *Aristotelian Society*, vol. 24, 1923–4, 55–76.

Ewing, A. C., 'The Linguistic theory of *a priori* propositions', in *Aristotelian Society*, vol. 40, 1939–40, 207–44.

Feyerabend, P. K., 'An attempt at a realistic interpretation of experience', in *Aristotelian Society*, vol. 58, 1957–8, 143–70.

Firth, Roderick, 'Coherence, certainty and epistemic priority', in *Journal of Philosophy*, vol. 61, 1964, 545–57.

Frege, Gottlob, *The Foundations of Arithmetic*, Blackwell, Oxford, 1950 (German 1st ed. 1884).

Gasking, D. A. T., 'The Philosophy of John Wisdom', in *Australasian Journal of Philosophy*, vol. 32, 1954, 136–56 and 185–212.

Geach, Peter (1) *Mental Acts*, Routledge & Kegan Paul, London, 1957.

(2) *Reference and Generality*, Cornell, Ithaca, 1962.

Goodman, Nelson (1) *The Structure of Appearance*, Harvard, Cambridge, 1951.

(2) 'Sense and Certainty', in *Philosophical Review*, vol. 61, 1952, 160–7.

Grice, H. P., 'Meaning', in *Philosophical Review*, vol. 66, 1957, 377–88.

Hampshire, Stuart (1) 'Scepticism and Meaning', in *Philosophy*, vol. 25, 1950, 235–46.

(2) 'Critical Notice of *The Concept of Mind*', in *Mind*, vol. 59, 1950, 237–55.

(3) 'Self-knowledge and the Will', in *Revue Internationale de Philosophie*, vol. 7, 1953, 230–45.

(4) *Thought and Action*, Chatto, London, 1959.

Hare, R. M., *The Language of Morals*, Oxford, 1952.

Hume, David, *Treatise of Human Nature*, ed. L. A. Selby-Bigge, Oxford, 1888.

Kant, Immanuel, 'Fundamental Principles of the Metaphysic of Morals', in *Critique of Practical Reason and other works*, translated by T. K. Abbott, Longmans, London, 1873.

Kneale, W. C. and M., *The Development of Logic*, Oxford, 1962.

Kotarbinski, Tadeusz, *Gnosiology*, Pergamon, Oxford, 1966 (Polish 1st ed. 1929).

Leibniz, G. W., *Selections*, ed. P. P. Wiener, Scribners, New York, 1951.

Lewis, C. I. (1) *Mind and the World-Order*, Scribners, New York, 1929.

(2) *Analysis of Knowledge and Valuation*, Open Court, La Salle, 1946.

(3) *Collected Papers*, Stanford, 1970.

Locke, John, *An Essay concerning Human Understanding*, ed. A. C. Fraser, Oxford, 1894.

Mabbott, J. D., 'Substance', in *Philosophy*, vol. 10, 1935, 186–99.

Mackie, J. L., 'Are there any incorrigible empirical statements?', in *Australasian Journal of Philosophy*, vol. 41, 1963, 12–28.

McTaggart, J. M. E. (1) *The Nature of Existence*, Cambridge, 1921 (vol. 1), 1927 (vol. 2).

(2) 'Personality', in *Philosophical Studies*, Arnold, London, 1934, 69–96.

Malcolm, Norman (1) *Dreaming*, Routledge & Kegan Paul, London, 1959.

(2) *Knowledge and Certainty*, Prentice-Hall, Englewood Cliffs, 1963.

Martin, C. B. and Deutscher, Max, 'Remembering', in *Philosophical Review*, vol. 75, 1966, 161–96.

Maxwell, Grover, 'The Ontological Status of Theoretical Entities', in *Minnesota Studies in the Philosophy of Science*, vol. 3, 1962, 3–27.

Mill, J. S., *An Examination of Sir William Hamilton's Philosophy*, Longmans, London, 1872 (1st ed. 1865).

Moore, G. E. (1) *Principia Ethica*, Cambridge, 1903.

(2) *Philosophical Papers*, Allen & Unwin, London, 1959.

Nagel, Ernest, *The Structure of Science*, Routledge & Kegan Paul, London, 1961.

Pap, Arthur (1) *Elements of Analytic Philosophy*, Macmillan, New York, 1949.

(2) *Semantics and Necessary Truth*, Yale, New Haven, 1958.

(3) 'Nominalism, empiricism and universals', in *Philosophical Quarterly*, vol. 9, 1959, 330–40 and vol. 10, 1960, 44–60.

(4) *Introduction to the Philosophy of Science*, Free Press, New York, 1962.

Passmore, John, *Philosophical Reasoning*, Duckworth, London, 1961.

Pears, D. F., 'Universals', in *Philosophical Quarterly*, vol. 1, 1950–1, 218–27.

Pearson, Karl, *The Grammar of Science*, Everyman edition, London, 1937.

Peirce, C. S. (1) 'Question concerning certain faculties claimed for man', in *Collected Papers*, Harvard, Cambridge, vol. 5, 135–55.

(2) 'Some consequences of four incapacities', in *Collected Papers*, Harvard, Cambridge, vol. 5, 156–89.

Popper, K. R. (1) *The Logic of Scientific Discovery*, Hutchinson, London, 1959 (German 1st ed. 1934–5).

(2) *The Open Society and its enemies*, Routledge, London, 1945.

(3) *Conjectures and Refutations*, Routledge & Kegan Paul, London, 1963.

(4) 'The Propensity Interpretation of Probability', in *British Journal for the Philosophy of Science*, vol. 10, 1959, 25–42.

Price, H. H. (1) *Perception*, Methuen, London, 1932.

(2) *Truth and Corrigibility*, Oxford, 1935.

Prichard, H. A. (1) 'Does Moral Philosophy Rest on a Mistake?', in *Moral Obligation*, Oxford, 1949, 1–17.

(2) 'The Sense-Datum Fallacy', in *Knowledge and Perception*, Oxford, 1950, 200–14.

Quine, W. V. (1) *Mathematical Logic*, Harvard, Cambridge, 1947.

(2) *Methods of Logic*, Holt, New York, 1950.

(3) *From A Logical Point Of View*, Harvard, Cambridge, 1953.

(4) *Word And Object*, M.I.T. and Wiley, Boston and New York, 1960.

(5) *The Ways of Paradox*, Random House, New York, 1966.

Quinton, A. M. (1) 'Properties and Classes', in *Aristotelian Society*, vol. 58, 1957–8, 33–58.

(2) 'Spaces and Times', in *Philosophy*, vol. 37, 1962, 130–47.

(3) 'Authority and autonomy in knowledge', in *Proceedings of the Philosophy of Education Society of Great Britain*, supplementary issue, vol. 5, 1971, 201–15.

(4) 'Russell's philosophy of mind', in *Bertrand Russell*, ed. D. F. Pears, Doubleday, Garden City, 1972, 80–109.

Ramsey, F. P., *The Foundations of Mathematics*, Kegan Paul, London, 1931.

Reichenbach, Hans, *Experience and Prediction*, Chicago, 1938.

Reid, Thomas, *Philosophical Works*, ed. Sir W. Hamilton, Thin, Edinburgh, 1895.

Russell, Bertrand (1) *The Problems of Philosophy*, Oxford, 1946 (1st ed. 1912).

(2) 'The Philosophy of Logical Atomism', in *Russell's Logical Atomism*, ed. D. F. Pears, Fontana, London, 1972 (1st ed. 1918).

(3) *Introduction to Mathematical Philosophy*, Allen & Unwin, London, 1918.

(4) *The Analysis of Mind*, Allen & Unwin, London, 1921.

(5) *An Outline of Philosophy*, Allen & Unwin, London, 1927.

(6) *Religion and Science*, Thornton Butterworth, London, 1935.

(7) *An Inquiry into Meaning and Truth*, Allen & Unwin, London, 1940.

(8) *Human Knowledge*, Allen & Unwin, London, 1948.

Ryle, Gilbert (1) *The Concept of Mind*, Hutchinson, London, 1949.

(2) *Dilemmas*, Cambridge, 1956.

(3) *Collected Papers*, Hutchinson, London, 1971.

Schlick, Moritz, 'The Foundation of Knowledge', in *Logical Positivism*, ed. A. J. Ayer, Free Press, Chicago, 1959, 209–27.

Sellars, Wilfrid, *Science, Perception and Reality*, Routledge & Kegan Paul, London, 1964.

Shoemaker, Sydney (1) 'Personal Identity and Memory', in *Journal of Philosophy*, vol. 56, 1959, 868–82.

(2) *Self-knowledge and Self-identity*, Cornell, Ithaca, 1963.

Smart, J. J. C. (1) 'Sensations and Brain Processes', in *Philosophical Review*, vol. 68, 1959, 141–56.

(2) *Philosophy and Scientific Realism*, Routledge & Kegan Paul, London, 1963.

Spencer, Herbert, *The Principles of Psychology*, London, 1872.

Stace, W. T. (1) 'The Problem of Unreasoned Beliefs', in *Mind*, vol. 54, 1945, 27–49 and 122–47.

(2) 'The Parmenidean Dogma', in *Philosophy*, vol. 24, 1949, 195–204.

Stebbing, L. S., *Philosophy and the Physicists*, Methuen, London, 1937.

Stevenson, C. L., *Ethics and Language*, Yale, New Haven, 1944.

Strawson, P. F. (1) 'Truth', in *Analysis*, vol. 9, 1949, 83–97.

(2) 'Truth', in *Aristotelian Society*, supplementary volume 24, 1950, 129–56 (and in *Strawson* (7)).

(3) 'On Referring', in *Mind*, vol. 54, 1950, 320–44 (and in *Strawson* (7)).

(4) 'Singular terms, ontology and identity', in *Mind*, vol. 60, 1956, 433–54.

(5) *Individuals*, Methuen, London, 1959.

(6) 'Identifying reference and truth-value', in *Theoria*, vol. 30, 1964. 96–118 (and in *Strawson* (7)).

(7) *Logico-Linguistic Papers*, Methuen, London, 1971.

Waismann, Friedrich, 'Language Strata', in *Logic and Language, Second Series*, ed. A. Flew, Blackwell, Oxford, 1953, 11–31.

Walsh, W. H., *Metaphysics*, Hutchinson, London, 1963.

Watkins, J. W. N. (1) 'Between analytic and empirical', in *Philosophy*, vol. 32, 1957, 112–31.

(2) 'Confirmable and influential metaphysics', in *Mind*, vol. 67, 1958, 344–65.

Wiggins, David (1) 'Individuation of things and places', in *Aristotelian Society*, supplementary volume 38, 1963, 177–202.

(2) *Identity and Spatio-Temporal Continuity*, Blackwell, Oxford, 1970.

Williams, B. A. O., 'Personal Identity and Individuation', in *Aristotelian Society*, vol. 57, 1956–7, 229–52.

Wittgenstein, L. (1) *Tractatus Logico-Philosophicus*, Routledge & Kegan Paul, 1961.

(2) *Philosophical Investigations*, Blackwell, Oxford, 1953.

Woozley, A. D., *Theory of Knowledge*, Hutchinson, London, 1949.

Index

Names

Aenesidemus, 150
Agrippa, 150
Alexander, H. G., 298
Alexander, S., 238
Alston, W. P., 343
Anaximander, 62–3
Anaximenes, 62
Anderson, John, 6, 245, 320
Anscombe, G. E. M., 61
Aristotle, 103, 104, 109, 247, 249, 250; on form and matter, 3, 4, 8, 9, 27, 29
Armstrong, D. M., 166–8, 194, 201, 206, 333
Aune, Bruce, 83
Ayer, A. J., 91, 97–9, 112–14, 118, 154, 291, 343, 351, 353–4; on corrigibility, 137, 148–9, 159–60, 162–7, 171, 184–5, 188, 230; on phenomenalism, 5, 173, 177; on sense-data, 6, 27–8, 187; on singular terms, 4, 20, 22–4, 35, 38–9

Bacon, Francis, 283
Bain, Alexander, 99, 357
Barker, S. F., 14
Benacerraf, P., 256–7
Bennett, Jonathan, 282
Bentham, Jeremy, 374
Berkeley, George, 7, 27, 97, 99, 174, 237, 239, 240, 247, 320
Berlin, Isaiah, 175–6
Blanshard, Brand, 271
Bohm, D., 293
Boscovitch, R. G., 86–7
Bradley, F. H., 99, 118, 260, 308–9
Brentano, F., 316, 338

Broad, C. D., 194, 267–8, 273–4
Butler, Joseph, 372

Carnap, Rudolf, 6, 111, 112, 117, 237, 292, 300, 322, 342–3, 351; on ontology, 243, 244, 247–8, 289, 305
Carroll, Lewis, 298
Case, Thomas, 198
Chisholm, Roderick, 200, 222; on intentionality, 341–3, 346
Collingwood, R. G., 181
Cook Wilson, J., 148

Democritus, 4, 9, 62, 250
Descartes, R., 173–5, 237, 239, 240, 245, 314–15, 317–19, 335; on scepticism and certainty, 110, 146, 152, 153–5, 219–21, 239, 338, 341; on substance, 5, 8, 10, 46–9, 320
Deutscher, Max, 93
Duhem, Pierre, 197

Eddington, Sir A., 202
Empedocles, 63
Epicurus, 251
Ewing, A. C., 268, 271–2

Feyerabend, P. K., 304–5, 307
Firth, Roderick, 217–18
Frege, G., 57, 110, 112, 115, 127, 130, 267, 276, 277
Freud, Sigmund, 133, 233
Fries, J. F., 227–8

Gassendi, P., 251
Geach, P. T., 57, 131

387

Subjects